Programming
with
POSIX® Threads

Addison-Wesley Professional Computing Series

Brian W. Kernighan, Consulting Editor

Ken Arnold/John Peyton, *A C User's Guide to ANSI C*

David R. Butenhof, *Programming with POSIX® Threads*

Tom Cargill, *C++ Programming Style*

William R. Cheswick/Steven M. Bellovin, *Firewalls and Internet Security: Repelling the Wily Hacker*

David A. Curry, *UNIX® System Security: A Guide for Users and System Administrators*

Erich Gamma/Richard Helm/Ralph Johnson/John Vlissides, *Design Patterns: Elements of Reusable Object-Oriented Software*

David R. Hanson, *C Interfaces and Implementations: Techniques for Creating Reusable Software*

Srinivasan Keshav, *An Engineering Approach to Computer Networking: ATM Networks, The Internet, and the Telephone Network*

John Lakos, *Large-Scale C++ Software Design*

Scott Meyers, *Effective C++: 50 Specific Ways to Improve Your Programs and Designs*

Scott Meyers, *More Effective C++: 35 New Ways to Improve Your Programs and Designs*

Robert B. Murray, *C++ Strategies and Tactics*

David R. Musser/Atul Saini, *STL Tutorial and Reference Guide: C++ Programming with the Standard Template Library*

John K. Ousterhout, *Tcl and the Tk Toolkit*

Craig Partridge, *Gigabit Networking*

J. Stephen Pendergrast Jr., *Desktop KornShell Graphical Programming*

Radia Perlman, *Interconnections: Bridges and Routers*

David M. Piscitello/A. Lyman Chapin, *Open Systems Networking: TCP/IP and OSI*

Stephen A. Rago, *UNIX® System V Network Programming*

Curt Schimmel, *UNIX® Systems for Modern Architectures: Symmetric Multiprocessing and Caching for Kernel Programmers*

W. Richard Stevens, *Advanced Programming in the UNIX® Environment*

W. Richard Stevens, *TCP/IP Illustrated, Volume 1: The Protocols*

W. Richard Stevens, *TCP/IP Illustrated, Volume 3: TCP for Transactions, HTTP, NNTP, and the UNIX Domain Protocols*

Gary R. Wright/W. Richard Stevens, *TCP/IP Illustrated, Volume 2: The Implementation*

Programming
with
POSIX® Threads

David R. Butenhof

ADDISON-WESLEY

An Imprint of Addison Wesley Longman, Inc.

Reading, Massachusetts • Harlow, England • Menlo Park, California
Berkeley, California • Don Mills, Ontario • Sydney
Bonn • Amsterdam • Tokyo • Mexico City

Trademark acknowledgments:

UNIX is a registered trademark in the United States and other countries, licensed exclusively through X/Open Company Ltd. Digital, DEC, Digital UNIX, DECthreads, VMS, and OpenVMS are trademarks of Digital Equipment Corporation. Solaris, SPARC, SunOS, and Sun are trademarks of Sun Microsystems Incorporated. SGI and IRIX are trademarks of Silicon Graphics, Incorporated. HP-UX is a trademark of Hewlett-Packard Company. AIX, IBM, and OS/2 are trademarks or registered trademarks of the IBM Corporation. X/Open is a trademark of X/Open Company Ltd. POSIX is a registered trademark of the Institute of Electrical and Electronics Engineers, Inc.

Many of the designations used by manufacturers and sellers to distinguish their products are claimed as trademarks. Where those designations appear in this book and Addison-Wesley was aware of a trademark claim, the designations have been printed in initial caps or all caps.

The authors and publishers have taken care in the preparation of this book, but make no expressed or implied warranty of any kind and assume no responsibility for errors or omissions. No liability is assumed for incidental or consequential damages in connection with or arising out of the use of the information or programs contained herein.

The publisher offers discounts on this book when ordered in quantity for special sales.

For more information, please contact:

Corporate & Professional Publishing Group
Addison-Wesley Publishing Company
One Jacob Way
Reading, Massachusetts 01867

Library of Congress Cataloging-in-Publication Data
Butenhof, David R., 1956-
    Programming with POSIX threads / David R. Butenhof.
        p.   cm. -- (Addison-Wesley professional computing series)
    Includes bibliographical references and index.
    ISBN 0-201-63392-2 (pbk.)
    1. Threads (Computer programs)   2. POSIX (Computer software
standard)   3. Electronic digital computers--Programming.   I. Title.
II. Series.
QA76.76.T55B88   1997
005.4'32--dc21   97-6635
                                                                                    CIP

ISBN 0-201-63392-2

1 2 3 4 5 6 7 8 9 MA 00999897
First printing, May 1997

To Anne, Amy,
    and
      Alyssa.

Quote acknowledgments:

American Heritage Dictionary of the English Language: page 1.

ISO/IEC 9945-1:1996, © 1996 by IEEE: page 29.

Lewis Carroll, *Alice's Adventures in Wonderland:* pages xv, 47, 70, 88, 97, 98, 106, 131, 142, 161, 189, 197. Reproduced by permission of Macmillan Children's Books.

Lewis Carroll, *Through the Looking-Glass:* pages 1, 4, 8, 20, 25, 29, 35, 45, 172, 214, 241, 283, 290, 302. Reproduced by permission of Macmillan Children's Books.

Lewis Carroll, *The Hunting of the Snark:* pages 3, 13, 28, 39, 120, 131, 134, 289, 367. Reproduced by permission of Macmillan Children's Books.

Contents

Example programs

Preface

This book is about "threads" and how to use them. "Thread" is just a name for a basic software "thing" that can do work on a computer. A thread is smaller, faster, and more maneuverable than a traditional process. In fact, once threads have been added to an operating system, a "process" becomes just data—address space, files, and so forth—plus one or more threads that do something with all that data.

With threads, you can build applications that utilize system resources more efficiently, that are more friendly to users, that run blazingly fast on multiprocessors, and that may even be easier to maintain. To accomplish all this, you need only add some relatively simple function calls to your code, adjust to a new way of thinking about programming, and leap over a few yawning chasms. Reading this book carefully will, I hope, help you to accomplish all that without losing your sense of humor.

The threads model used in this book is commonly called "Pthreads," or "POSIX threads." Or, more formally (since you haven't yet been properly introduced), the POSIX 1003.1c–1995 standard. I'll give you a few other names later—but for now, "Pthreads" is all you need to worry about.

As I write this, Sun's Solaris, Digital's Digital UNIX, and SGI's IRIX already support Pthreads. The other major commercial UNIX operating systems will soon have Pthreads as well, maybe even by the time you read this, including IBM's AIX and Hewlett-Packard's HP-UX. Pthreads implementations are also available for Linux and other UNIX operating systems.

In the personal computer market, Microsoft's Win32 API (the primary programming interface to both Windows NT and Windows 95) supports threaded programming, as does IBM's OS/2. These threaded programming models are quite different from Pthreads, but the important first step toward using them productively is understanding concurrency, synchronization, and scheduling. The rest is (more or less) a matter of syntax and style, and an experienced thread programmer can adapt to any of these models.

The threaded model can be (and has been) applied with great success to a wide range of programming problems. Here are just a few:

- Large scale, computationally intensive programs
- High-performance application programs and library code that can take advantage of multiprocessor systems
- Library code that can be used by threaded application programs
- Realtime application programs and library code
- Application programs and library code that perform I/O to slow external devices (such as networks and human beings).

Intended audience

This book assumes that you are an experienced programmer, familiar with developing code for an operating system in "the UNIX family" using the ANSI C language. I have tried not to assume that you have any experience with threads or other forms of asynchronous programming. The *Introduction* chapter provides a general overview of the terms and concepts you'll need for the rest of the book. If you don't want to read the Introduction first, that's fine, but if you ever feel like you're "missing something" you might try skipping back to get introduced.

Along the way you'll find examples and simple analogies for everything. In the end I hope that you'll be able to continue comfortably threading along on your own. Have fun, and "happy threading."

About the author

I have been involved in the Pthreads standard since it began, although I stayed at home for the first few meetings. I was finally forced to spend a grueling week in the avalanche-proof concrete bunker at the base of Snowbird ski resort in Utah, watching hard-working standards representatives from around the world wax their skis. This was very distracting, because I had expected a standards meeting to be a formal and stuffy environment. As a result of this misunderstanding, I was forced to rent ski equipment instead of using my own.

After the Pthreads standard went into balloting, I worked on additional thread synchronization interfaces and multiprocessor issues with several POSIX working groups. I also helped to define the Aspen threads extensions, which were fast-tracked into X/Open XSH5.

I have worked at Digital Equipment Corporation for (mumble, mumble) years, in various locations throughout Massachusetts and New Hampshire. I was one of the creators of Digital's own threading architecture, and I designed (and implemented much of) the Pthreads interfaces on Digital UNIX 4.0. I have been helping people develop and debug threaded code for more than eight years.

My unofficial motto is "Better Living Through Concurrency." Threads are not sliced bread, but then, we're programmers, not bakers, so we do what we can.

Acknowledgments

This is the part where I write the stuff that I'd like to see printed, and that my friends and coworkers want to see. You probably don't care, and I promise not to be annoyed if you skip over it——but if you're curious, by all means read on.

No project such as this book can truly be accomplished by a single person, despite the fact that only one name appears on the cover. I could have written a book about threads without any help—I know a great deal about threads, and I am at least reasonably competent at written communication. However, the result would not have been *this* book, and *this* book is better than that hypothetical work could possibly have been.

Thanks first and foremost to my manager Jean Fullerton, who gave me the time and encouragement to write this book on the job—and thanks to the rest of the DECthreads team who kept things going while I wrote, including Brian Keane, Webb Scales, Jacqueline Berg, Richard Love, Peter Portante, Brian Silver, Mark Simons, and Steve Johnson.

Thanks to Garret Swart who, while he was with Digital at the Systems Research Center, got us involved with POSIX. Thanks to Nawaf Bitar who worked with Garret to create, literally overnight, the first draft of what became Pthreads, and who became *POSIX thread evangelist* through the difficult period of getting everyone to understand just what the heck this threading thing was all about anyway. Without Garret, and especially Nawaf, Pthreads might not exist, and certainly wouldn't be as good as it is. (The lack of perfection is not their responsibility—that's the way life is.)

Thanks to everyone who contributed to the design of cma, Pthreads, UNIX98, and to the users of DCE threads and DECthreads, for all the help, thought-provoking discourse, and assorted skin-thickening exercises, including Andrew Birrell, Paul Borman, Bob Conti, Bill Cox, Jeff Denham, Peter Gilbert, Rick Greer, Mike Grier, Kevin Harris, Ken Hobday, Mike Jones, Steve Kleiman, Bob Knighten, Leslie Lamport, Doug Locke, Paula Long, Finnbarr P. Murphy, Bill Noyce, Simon Patience, Harold Seigel, Al Simons, Jim Woodward, and John Zolnowsky.

Many thanks to all those who patiently reviewed the drafts of this book (and even to those who didn't seem so patient at times). Brian Kernighan, Rich Stevens, Dave Brownell, Bill Gallmeister, Ilan Ginzburg, Will Morse, Bryan O'Sullivan, Bob Robillard, Dave Ruddock, Bil Lewis, and many others suggested or motivated improvements in structure and detail—and provided additional skin-thickening exercises to keep me in shape. Devang Shah and Bart Smaalders answered some Solaris questions, and Bryan O'Sullivan suggested what became the "bailing programmers" analogy.

Thanks to John Wait and Lana Langlois at Addison Wesley Longman, who waited with great patience as a first-time writer struggled to balance writing a book with engineering and consulting commitments. Thanks to Pamela Yee and Erin Sweeney, who managed the book's production process, and to all the team (many of whose names I'll never know), who helped.

Thanks to my wife, Anne Lederhos, and our daughters Amy and Alyssa, for all the things for which any writers may thank their families, including support, tolerance, and just being there. And thanks to Charles Dodgson (Lewis Carroll), who wrote extensively about threaded programming (and nearly everything else) in his classic works *Alice's Adventures in Wonderland*, *Through the Looking-Glass*, and *The Hunting of the Snark*.

Dave Butenhof
Digital Equipment Corporation
110 Spit Brook Road, ZKO2-3/Q18
Nashua, NH 03062
butenhof@zko.dec.com
December 1996

1 Introduction

"The time has come," the Walrus said,
"To talk of many things;
Of shoes—and ships—and sealing wax—
Of cabbages—and kings—
And why the sea is boiling hot—
And whether pigs have wings."
      —Lewis Carroll, *Through the Looking-Glass*

In a dictionary, you would probably see that one of several definitions for "thread" is along the lines of the third definition in the American Heritage paperback dictionary on my desk: "Anything suggestive of the continuousness and sequence of thread." In computer terms, a thread is the set of properties that suggest "continuousness and sequence" within the machine. A thread comprises the machine state necessary to execute a sequence of machine instructions—the location of the current instruction, the machine's address and data registers, and so forth.

A UNIX process can be thought of as a thread, plus an address space, file descriptors, and an assortment of other data. Some versions of UNIX support "lightweight" or "variable weight" processes that allow you to strip some or all of that data from some of your processes for efficiency. Now, whether you're using a "thread" or a "lightweight process," you still need the address space, file descriptors, and everything else. So, you might ask, what's the point? The point is that you can have many threads sharing an address space, doing different things. On a multiprocessor, the threads in a process can be doing different things simultaneously.

When computers lived in glass caves and were fed carefully prepared punch cards, the real world outside could be kept waiting with no consequences more severe than some grumbling programmers. But the real world doesn't do one thing at a time, and gradually computers began to model that world by adding capabilities such as multiprogramming, time sharing, multiprocessing, and, eventually, threads.

Threads can help you bring your application out of the cave, and Pthreads helps you do it in a way that will be neat, efficient, and portable. This chapter briefly introduces you to what you need to begin understanding and using threads. Don't worry—the rest of the book will follow up on the details left dangling in this chapter.

Section 1.1 presents the framework for a number of analogies that I will use to explain threading as we go. There is nothing all that unusual in the brief story—

but hereafter you will understand when I talk about programmers and buckets, which, otherwise, might seem mildly odd.

Section 1.2 defines some essential concepts and terms used in this book. The most important of these concepts deserves a special introduction, which will also serve to demonstrate the convention with which various particularly important points shall be emphasized throughout this book:

> **Asynchronous:**
> Any two operations are "asynchronous" when they can proceed independently of each other.

Section 1.3 describes how you already use asynchronous programming on a regular basis, both as a UNIX programmer and user, and as a human being in the real world. I wouldn't dare to claim that asynchronous programming is easy, but the basic concepts it tries to model are so easy and natural that you rarely need even to think about them until you try to apply them to software.

Threads are, to some extent, just one more way to make applications asynchronous, but threads have some advantages over other models that have been used to build asynchronous applications. Section 1.5 will show you some of the advantages as we apply various programming methods in several versions of a simple alarm clock. You will get to see "threads in action" right away, with a brief description of the few Pthreads interfaces needed to build this simple application.

Armed, now, with a basic understanding of what threads are all about, you can go on to Section 1.6, where we will explore some of the fundamental advantages of a threaded programming model.

Although there are a lot of excellent reasons to use threads, there is a price to be paid. Section 1.7 provides a counterpoint to the previous section by describing some of the costs. What it boils down to, though, is simply that you need to learn how the model works, and then apply it carefully. It is not as hard as some folks would have you believe.

You have seen some of the fundamental benefits and costs. It may be obvious that you do not want to rush out and put threads into every application or library you write. Section 1.8 asks the question "To thread, or not to thread?" and I will attempt to guide you toward determining the proper answer in various cases.

You will know at that point what threads are, what they do, and when to use them. Aside from brief examples, you haven't yet seen any detailed information about the particular programming interfaces (APIs) that compose Pthreads. Section 1.9 points out some of the basic landmarks of the Pthreads universe to get you oriented before we plunge ahead. The most important part of this section is 1.9.3, which describes the Pthreads model for reporting errors—which is somewhat different than the rest of UNIX and POSIX.

1.1 The "bailing programmers"

This was charming, no doubt: but they shortly found out
That the Captain they trusted so well
Had only one notion for crossing the ocean,
And that was to tingle his bell.
—Lewis Carroll, The Hunting of the Snark

Three programmers sail out to sea one fine day in a small boat. They sail quite some distance from shore, enjoying the sun and sea breeze, allowing the wind to carry them. The sky darkens, and a storm strikes. The small boat is tossed violently about, and when the storm abates the programmers are missing their boat's sail and most of the mast. The boat has sprung a small leak, and there is no land in sight.

The boat is equipped with food, water, oars, and a bailing bucket, and the programmers set to work. One programmer rows, and monitors the accumulating water in the bottom of the boat. The other programmers alternately sleep, watch the water level, or scan the horizon for sight of land or another ship.

An idle programmer may notice rising water in the boat, and begin bailing. When both idle programmers are awake, and become simultaneously concerned regarding their increasing dampness, they may both lunge for the bailing bucket—but one will inevitably reach it first, and the other will have to wait.

If the rower decides that bailing is required while both his companions sleep, a nudge is usually sufficient to awaken a programmer, allowing the other to continue sleeping. But if the rower is in a bad mood, he may resort to a loud yell, awakening both sleeping programmers. While one programmer assumes the necessary duty, the other can try to fall asleep again.

When the rower tires, he can signal one of the other programmers to take over the task, and immediately fall into a deep sleep waiting to be signaled in turn. In this way, they journey on for some time.

So, just what do the Bailing Programmers have to do with threads? I'm glad you asked! The elements of the story represent analogies that apply to the Pthreads programming model. We'll explore some additional analogies in later sections, and even expand the story a little, but for now consider a few basics:

A **programmer** is an entity that is capable of independent activity. Our programmers represent *threads*. A thread is not really much like a programmer, who, as we all know, is a fascinatingly sophisticated mixture of engineer, mathematician, and artist that no computer can match. Still, as a representation of the "active element" in our programming model, it will be sufficient.

The **bailing bucket** and the **oars** are "tokens" that can be held by only one individual at a time. They can be thought of as shared data, or as synchronization objects. The primary Pthreads synchronization object, by the way, is called a *mutex*.

Nudges and **shouts** are communication mechanisms associated with a synchronization object, on which individuals wait for some condition. Pthreads provides *condition variables*, which may be signaled or broadcast to indicate changes in shared data state.

1.2 Definitions and terminology

"When I use a word," Humpty Dumpty said, in rather a scornful tone,
"it means just what I choose it to mean—neither more nor less."
   —Lewis Carroll, Through the Looking-Glass

This book will use several critical terms that may be unfamiliar to you unless you've already had some experience with parallel or asynchronous programming. Even if you are familiar with them, some of the terms have seen assorted and even contradictory uses within research and industry, and that is clearly not going to help communication. We need to begin by coming to a mutual agreement regarding the meaning of these terms, and, since I am writing the book, we will agree to use my definitions. (Thank you.)

1.2.1 Asynchronous

Asynchronous means that things happen independently (concurrently) unless there's some enforced dependency. Life is asynchronous. The dependencies are supplied by nature, and events that are not dependent on one another can occur simultaneously. A programmer cannot row without the oars, or bail effectively without the bucket—but a programmer with oars can row while another programmer with a bucket bails. Traditional computer programming, on the other hand, causes all events to occur in series unless the programmer takes "extraordinary measures" to allow them to happen concurrently.

The greatest complication of "asynchrony" has been that there's little advantage to being asynchronous unless you can have more than one activity going at a time. If you can start an asynchronous operation, but then you can do nothing but wait for it, you're not getting much benefit from the asynchrony.

1.2.2 Concurrency

Concurrency, which an English dictionary will tell you refers to things happening at the same time, is used to refer to things that appear to happen at the same time, but which may occur serially. Concurrency describes the behavior of threads or processes on a uniprocessor system. The definition of concurrent execution in POSIX requires that "functions that suspend the execution of the calling thread shall not cause the execution of other threads to be indefinitely suspended."

Concurrent operations may be arbitrarily interleaved so that they make progress independently (one need not be completed before another begins), but concurrency does not imply that the operations proceed simultaneously. Nevertheless, concurrency allows applications to take advantage of asynchronous capabilities, and "do work" while independent operations are proceeding.

Most programs have asynchronous aspects that may not be immediately obvious. Users, for example, prefer asynchronous interfaces. They expect to be able to issue a command while they're thinking about it, even before the program has finished with the last one. And when a windowing interface provides separate windows, don't you intuitively *expect* those windows to act asynchronously? Nobody likes a "busy" cursor. Pthreads provides you with both concurrency and asynchrony, and the combination is exactly what you need to easily write responsive and efficient programs. Your program can "wait in parallel" for slow I/O devices, and automatically take advantage of multiprocessor systems to compute in parallel.

1.2.3 Uniprocessor and multiprocessor

The terms *uniprocessor* and *multiprocessor* are fairly straightforward, but let's define them just to make sure there's no confusion. By *uniprocessor*, I mean a computer with a single programmer-visible execution unit (processor). A single general-purpose processor with superscalar processing, or vector processors, or other math or I/O coprocessors is still usually considered a uniprocessor.

By *multiprocessor*, I mean a computer with more than one processor sharing a common instruction set and access to the same physical memory. While the processors need not have equal access to all physical memory, it should be possible for any processor to gain access to most memory. A "massively parallel processor" (MPP) may or may not qualify as a multiprocessor for the purposes of this book. Many MPP systems do qualify, because they provide access to all physical memory from every processor, even though the access times may vary widely.

1.2.4 Parallelism

Parallelism describes concurrent sequences that proceed simultaneously. In other words, software "parallelism" is the same as English "concurrency" and different from software "concurrency." Parallelism has a vaguely redeeming analogy to the English definition: It refers to things proceeding in the same direction independently (without intersection).

True parallelism can occur only on a multiprocessor system, but concurrency can occur on both uniprocessor and multiprocessor systems. Concurrency can occur on a uniprocessor because concurrency is, essentially, the illusion of parallelism. While parallelism requires that a program be able to perform two computations at once, concurrency requires only that the programmer be able to pretend that two things can happen at once.

1.2.5 Thread safety and reentrancy

"Thread-safe" means that the code can be called from multiple threads without destructive results. It does not require that the code run *efficiently* in multiple threads, only that it can operate *safely* in multiple threads. Most existing functions can be made thread-safe using tools provided by Pthreads—mutexes, condition variables, and thread-specific data. Functions that don't require persistent context can be made thread-safe by serializing the entire function, for example, by locking a mutex on entry to the function, and unlocking the mutex before returning. Functions made thread-safe by serializing the entire function can be called in multiple threads—but only one thread can truly perform the function at a time.

More usefully, thread-safe functions can be broken down into smaller critical sections. That allows more than one thread to execute within the function, although not within the same part. Even better, the code can be redesigned to protect critical data rather than critical code, which may allow fully parallel execution of the code, when the threads don't need to use the same data at the same time.

The `putchar` function, for example, which writes a character into a standard I/O (*stdio*) buffer, might be made thread-safe by turning `putchar` into a critical section. That is, `putchar` might lock a "`putchar` mutex," write the character, and then unlock the `putchar` mutex. You could call `putchar` from two threads, and no data would be corrupted—it would be thread-safe. However, only one thread could write its character at a time, and the others would wait, even if they were writing to different *stdio* streams.

The correct solution is to associate the mutex with the stream, protecting the data rather than the code. Now your threads, as long as they are writing to different streams, can execute `putchar` in parallel. More importantly, all functions that access a stream can use the same mutex to safely coordinate their access to that stream.

The term "reentrant" is sometimes used to mean "efficiently thread-safe." That is, the code was made thread-safe by some more sophisticated measures than converting the function or library into a single serial region. Although existing code can usually be made thread-safe by adding mutexes and thread-specific data, it is often necessary to change the interface to make a function reentrant. Reentrant code should avoid relying on static data and, ideally, should avoid reliance on any form of synchronization between threads.

Often, a function can avoid internal synchronization by saving state in a "context structure" that is controlled by the caller. The caller is then responsible for any necessary synchronization of the data. The UNIX `readdir` function, for example, returns each directory entry in sequence. To make `readdir` thread-safe, you might add a mutex that `readdir` locked each time it was called, and unlocked before it returned to the caller. Another approach, as Pthreads has taken with `readdir_r`, is to avoid any locking within the function, letting the caller allocate a structure that maintains the context of `readdir_r` as it searches a directory.

At first glance, it may seem that we're just making the caller perform what ought to be the job of `readdir_r`. But remember that only the caller knows how the data will be used. If only one thread uses this particular directory context, for example, then no synchronization is needed. Even when the data is shared between threads, the caller may be able to supply more efficient synchronization, for example, if the context can be protected using a mutex that the application also uses for other data.

1.2.6 Concurrency control functions

Any "concurrent system" must provide a core set of essential functions that you need to create concurrent execution contexts, and control how they operate within your library or application. Here are three essential facilities, or aspects, of any concurrent system:

1. *Execution context* is the state of a concurrent entity. A concurrent system must provide a way to create and delete execution contexts, and maintain their state independently. It must be able to save the state of one context and dispatch to another at various times, for example, when one needs to wait for an external event. It must be able to continue a context from the point where it last executed, with the same register contents, at a later time.
2. *Scheduling* determines which context (or set of contexts) should execute at any given point in time, and switches between contexts when necessary.
3. *Synchronization* provides mechanisms for concurrent execution contexts to coordinate their use of shared resources. We use this term in a way that is nearly the opposite of the standard dictionary meaning. You'll find a definition much like "cause to occur at the same time," whereas we usually mean something that might better be expressed as "prevent from occurring at the same time." In a thesaurus, you may find that "cooperate" is a synonym for "synchronize"—and synchronization is the mechanism by which threads *cooperate* to accomplish a task. This book will use the term "synchronization," though, because that is what you'll see used, almost universally.

There are many ways to provide each of these facilities—but they are always present in some form. The particular choices presented in this book are dictated by the book's subject—Pthreads. Table 1.1 shows a few examples of the three facilities in various systems.

	Execution context	**Scheduling**	**Synchronization**
Real traffic	automobile	traffic lights and signs	turn signals and brake lights
UNIX (before threads)	process	priority (`nice`)	`wait` and pipes
Pthreads	thread	policy, priority	condition variables and mutexes

TABLE 1.1 *Execution contexts, schedulers, and synchronization*

A system's scheduling facility may allow each thread to run until it voluntarily yields the processor to another thread ("run until block"). It may provide time-slicing, where each thread is forced to periodically yield so that other threads may run ("round-robin"). It may provide various scheduling policies that allow the application to control how each thread is scheduled according to that thread's function. It may provide a "class scheduler" where dependencies between threads are described so that, for example, the scheduler can ensure that members of a tightly coupled parallel algorithm are scheduled at the same time.

Synchronization may be provided using a wide variety of mechanisms. Some of the most common forms are mutexes, condition variables, semaphores, and events. You may also use message passing mechanisms, such as UNIX pipes, sockets, POSIX message queues, or other protocols for communicating between asynchronous processes—on the same system or across a network. Any form of communication protocol contains some form of synchronization, because passing data around with no synchronization results in chaos, not *communication.*

The terms *thread*, *mutex*, and *condition variable* are the main topics of this book. For now, it is enough to know that a *thread* represents an "executable thing" on your computer. A *mutex* provides a mechanism to prevent threads from colliding unexpectedly, and a *condition variable* allows a thread, once it has avoided such a collision, to wait until it is safe to proceed. Both mutexes and condition variables are used to synchronize the operation of threads.

1.3 Asynchronous programming is intuitive ...

"In most gardens," the Tiger-lily said,
   "they make the beds too soft—so that the flowers are always asleep."
This sounded a very good reason, and Alice was quite
   pleased to know it.
"I never thought of that before!" she said.
   —Lewis Carroll, Through the Looking-Glass

If you haven't been involved in traditional realtime programming, asynchronous programming may seem new and different. But you've probably been using asynchronous programming techniques all along. You've probably used UNIX, for example, and, even as a user, the common UNIX shells from sh to ksh have been designed for asynchronous programming. You've also been using asynchronous "programming" techniques in real life since you were born.

Most people understand asynchronous behavior much more thoroughly than they expect, once they get past the complications of formal and restricted definitions.

1.3.1 ... because UNIX is asynchronous

In any UNIX system, processes execute asynchronously with respect to each other, even when there is only a single processor. Yes, until recently it was difficult to write individual programs for UNIX that behaved asynchronously—but UNIX has always made it fairly easy for *you* to behave asynchronously. When you type a command to a shell, you are really starting an independent program—if you run the program in the background, it runs asynchronously with the shell. When you pipe the output of one command to another you are starting several independent programs, which synchronize between themselves using the pipe.

   ❙ Time is a synchronization mechanism.

In many cases you provide synchronization between a series of processes yourself, maybe without even thinking about it. For example, you run the compiler *after* you've finished editing the source files. It wouldn't occur to you to compile them first, or even at the same time. That's elementary real-life synchronization.

   ❙ UNIX pipes and files can be synchronization mechanisms.

In other cases you may use more complicated software synchronization mechanisms. When you type "ls|more" to a shell to pass the output of the ls command into the more command, you're describing synchronization by specifying a data dependency. The shell starts both commands right away, but the more command can't generate any output until it receives input from ls through the pipe. Both commands proceed concurrently (or even in parallel on a multiprocessor) with ls supplying data and more processing that data, independently of each other. If the pipe buffer is big enough, ls could complete before more ever started; but more can't ever get ahead of ls.

Some UNIX commands perform synchronization internally. For example, the command "cc -o thread thread.c" might involve a number of separate processes. The cc command might be a "front end" to the C language environment, which runs a filter to expand preprocessor commands (like #include and #if), a compiler to translate the program into an intermediate form, an optimizer to reorder the translation, an assembler to translate the intermediate form into object language, and a loader to translate that into an executable binary file. As with ls|more, all these programs may be running at the same time, with synchronization provided by pipes, or by access to temporary files.

UNIX processes can operate asynchronously because each process includes all the information needed to execute code. The operating system can save the state of one process and switch to another without affecting the operation of either. Any general-purpose asynchronous "entity" needs enough state to enable the operating system to switch between them arbitrarily. But a UNIX process includes additional state that is not directly related to "execution context," such as an address space and file descriptors.

A thread is the part of a process that's necessary to execute code. On most computers that means each thread has a pointer to the thread's current instruction (often called a "PC" or "program counter"), a pointer to the top of the thread's stack (SP), general registers, and floating-point or address registers if they are kept separate. A thread may have other things, such as processor status and coprocessor control registers. A thread does not include most of the rest of the state associated with a process; for example, threads do not have their own file descriptors or address space. All threads within a process share all of the files and memory, including the program text and data segments.

I Threads are "simpler" than processes.

You can think of a thread as a sort of "stripped down" process, lean and mean and ready to go. The system can switch between two threads within a process much faster than it can switch between processes. A large part of this advantage comes from the fact that threads within a process share the address space—code, data, stack, everything.

When a processor switches between two processes, all of the hardware state for that process becomes invalid. Some may need to be changed as part of the context switch procedure—data cache and virtual memory translation entries may be flushed, for example. Even when they do not need to be flushed immediately, however, the data is not useful to the new process. Each process has a separate virtual memory address space, but threads running within the same process share the virtual address space and all other process data.

Threads can make high-bandwidth communication easier between independent parts of your program. You don't have to worry about message passing mechanisms like pipes or about keeping shared memory region address references consistent between several different address spaces. Synchronization is faster, and programming is much more natural. If you create or open a file, all threads can use it. If you allocate a dynamic data structure with malloc, you can pass the address to other threads and they can reference it. Threads make it easy to take advantage of concurrency.

1.3.2 ... because the world is asynchronous

Thinking asynchronously can seem awkward at first, but it'll become natural with a little practice. Start by getting over the unnatural expectation that everything will happen serially unless you do something "unusual." On a one-lane road cars proceed one at a time—but on a two-lane road two cars go at once. You can go out for a cup of coffee, leaving your computer compiling some code and fully expecting that it will proceed without you. Parallelism happens everywhere in the real world, and you expect it.

A row of cashiers in a store serve customers in parallel; the customers in each line generally wait their turn. You can improve throughput by opening more lines, as long as there are registers and cashiers to serve them, and enough customers to be served by them. Creating two lines for the same register may avoid confusion by keeping lines shorter—but nobody will get served faster. Opening three registers to serve two customers may look good, but it is just a waste of resources.

In an assembly line, workers perform various parts of the complete job in parallel, passing work down the line. Adding a station to the line may improve performance if it parallels or subdivides a step in the assembly that was so complicated that the operator at the next station spent a lot of time waiting for each piece. Beware of improving one step so much that it generates more work than the next step on the assembly line can handle.

In an office, each project may be assigned to a "specialist." Common specialties include marketing, management, engineering, typing pool, sales, support, and so forth. Each specialist handles her project independently on behalf of the customer or some other specialist, reporting back in some fashion when done. Assigning a second specialist to some task, or defining narrower specialties (for example, assigning an engineer or manager permanently to one product) may improve performance as long as there's enough work to keep her busy. If not, some specialists play games while others' in-baskets overflow.

Motor vehicles move in parallel on a highway. They can move at different speeds, pass each other, and enter and exit the highway independently. The drivers must agree to certain conventions in order to avoid collisions. Despite speed limits and traffic signs, compliance with the "rules of the road" is mostly voluntary. Similarly, threads must be coded to "agree" to rules that protect the program, or risk ending up undergoing emergency debugging at the thread hospital.

Software can apply parallelism in the same ways you might use it in real life, and for the same reasons. When you have more than one "thing" capable of doing work, you naturally expect them to all do work at the same time. A multiprocessor system can perform multiple computations, and any time-sharing system can perform computations while waiting for an external device to respond. Software parallelism is subject to all of the complications and problems that we have seen in real life—and the solutions may not be as easy to see or to apply. You need enough threads, but not too many; enough communication, but not too much. A key to good threaded programming is learning how to judge the proper balance for each situation.

Each thread can process similar parts of a problem, just like supermarket cashiers handling customers. Each thread can perform a specific operation on each data item in turn, just like the workers on an assembly line. Each thread can specialize in some specific operation and perform that operation repeatedly on behalf of other threads. You can combine these basic models in all sorts of ways; for example, in parallel assembly lines with some steps performed by a pool of servers.

As you read this book you'll be introduced to concepts that may seem unfamiliar: mutexes, condition variables, race conditions, deadlocks, and priority inversions. Threaded programming may feel daunting and unnatural. But I'll explain all those concepts as we move through this book, and once you've been writing multithreaded code for a while you may find yourself noticing real-world analogies to the concepts. Threads and all this other stuff are formalized and restricted representations of things you already understand.

If you find yourself thinking that someone shouldn't interrupt you because you have the conversation mutex locked, you've begun to develop an intuitive understanding of threaded programming.* You can apply that understanding to help you design better threaded code with less effort. If something wouldn't make sense in real life, you probably shouldn't try it in a program either.

1.4 About the examples in this book

This book contains a number of examples. All are presented as complete programs, and they have been built and tested on Digital UNIX 4.0d and Solaris 2.5.

All of these programs do something, but many do not do anything of any particular importance. The purpose of the examples is to demonstrate thread management and synchronization techniques, which are mere overhead in most real programs. They would be less effective at revealing the details if that "overhead" was buried within large programs that "did something."

Within the book, examples are presented in sections, usually one function at a time. The source code is separated from the surrounding text by a header and trailer block which include the file name and, if the example comprises more than one section, a section number and the name of the function. Each line of the source code has a line number at the left margin. Major functional blocks of each section are described in specially formatted paragraphs preceding the source code. These paragraphs are marked by line numbers outside the left margin of

---

* It may also be a good time to take a break and read some healthy escapist fiction for a while.

the paragraph, denoting the line numbers in the source listing to which the paragraph refers. Here's an example:

1-2   These lines show the header files included in most of the examples. The `<pthread.h>` header file declares constants and prototypes for the Pthreads functions, and the `errors.h` header file includes various other headers and some error-checking functions.

■ sample.c   part 1   sampleinfo

```
1  #include <pthread.h>
2  #include "errors.h"
```

■ sample.c   part 1   sampleinfo

I have written these examples to use error checking everywhere. That is, I check for errors on each function call. As long as you code carefully, this isn't necessary, and some experts recommend testing only for errors that can result from insufficient resources or other problems beyond your control. I disagree, unless of course you're the sort of programmer who never makes a mistake. Checking for errors is not that tedious, and may save you a lot of trouble during debugging.

You can build and run all of the examples for yourself—the source code is available online at http://www.aw.com/butenhof/posixcode.html. A Makefile is provided to build all of the examples, though it requires modifications for various platforms. On Digital UNIX, the examples were built with `CFLAGS=-pthread -std1 -w1`. On Solaris, they were built with `CFLAGS=-D_REENTRANT -D_POSIX_C_SOURCE=199506 -lpthread`. Some of the examples require interfaces that may not be in the Pthreads library on your system, for example, `clock_gettime`, which is part of the POSIX.1b realtime standard. The additional realtime library is specified by the `RTFLAGS` variable, which is defined as `RTFLAGS=-lrt` on Digital UNIX, and as `RTFLAGS=-lposix4` on Solaris.

On Solaris 2.5 systems, several of the examples require calls to `thr_setconcurrency` to ensure proper operation. This function causes Solaris to provide the process with additional concurrency. In a few cases, the example will not operate at all without this call, and in other cases, the example would fail to demonstrate some behavior.

1.5 Asynchronous programming, by example

"In one moment I've seen what has hitherto been
Enveloped in absolute mystery,
And without extra charge I will give you at large
A Lesson in Natural History."

   —Lewis Carroll, The Hunting of the Snark

This section demonstrates some basic asynchronous programming, using a simple program that does something vaguely useful, by pretending to be an alarm clock with a command interface for which you would not consider paying a dime in a store. But then, this book is about threads, not user interfaces, and the code that I need to show takes up quite enough space already.

The program prompts for input lines in a loop until it receives an error or end of file on stdin. On each line, the first nonblank token is interpreted as the number of seconds to wait, and the rest of the line (up to 64 characters) is a message that will be printed when the wait completes. I will offer two additional versions—one using multiple processes, and one using multiple threads. We'll use the three examples to compare the approaches.

1.5.1 The baseline, synchronous version

1   Include the header file errors.h, which includes standard headers like <unistd.h> and <stdio.h> and defines error reporting macros that are used throughout the examples in this book. We don't use the error reporting macros in this particular example, but consistency is nice, sometimes.

9-26   The "baseline" version, alarm.c, is a synchronous alarm program with a single routine, main. Most of main is a loop, which processes simple commands until fgets returns a NULL (error or end of file). Each line is "parsed" with sscanf to separate the number of seconds to wait (%d, the first sequence of digits) from the message string to print (%64[^\n], the rest of the line, up to 64 characters excluding newline).

■ alarm.c

```
1   #include "errors.h"
2
3   int main (int argc, char *argv[])
4   {
5       int seconds;
6       char line[128];
7       char message[64];
8
9       while (1) {
10          printf ("Alarm> ");
11          if (fgets (line, sizeof (line), stdin) == NULL) exit (0);
12          if (strlen (line) <= 1) continue;
13
14          /*
15           * Parse input line into seconds (%d) and a message
16           * (%64[^\n]), consisting of up to 64 characters
17           * separated from the seconds by whitespace.
18           */
```

```
19          if (sscanf (line, "%d %64[^\n]",
20              &seconds, message) < 2) {
21              fprintf (stderr, "Bad command\n");
22          } else {
23              sleep (seconds);
24              printf ("(%d) %s\n", seconds, message);
25          }
26      }
27  }
```

■ `alarm.c`

The problem with the program `alarm.c` is that only one alarm request can be active at a time. If you set an alarm to remind you to do something in 10 minutes (600 seconds), you can't decide to have it remind you of something else in 5 minutes. The program is doing something synchronously that you would probably like to be asynchronous.

1.5.2 A version using multiple processes

There are lots of ways to make this program asynchronous; for example, you could run more than one copy of the program. One way to run multiple copies is to `fork` a child process for each command, as shown in `alarm_fork.c`. The new version is asynchronous—you can enter commands at any time, and they will be carried out independently. It isn't much more complicated than the original, which is nice.

27-37   The main difference between `alarm.c` and `alarm_fork.c` is that instead of calling `sleep` directly, it uses `fork` to create a new child process, which then calls `sleep` (and, eventually, `printf`) *asynchronously*, while the parent process continues.

42-46   The primary complication in this version is the need to "reap" any child processes that have terminated. If the program fails to do this, the system will save them all until the program terminates. The normal way to reap terminated child processes is to call one of the `wait` functions. In this case, we call `waitpid`, which allows the caller to specify the WNOHANG flag. The function will immediately reap one child process if any have terminated, or will immediately return with a process ID (`pid`) of 0. The parent process continues to reap terminated child processes until there are no more to reap. When the loop terminates, `main` loops back to line 13 to read a new command.

■ `alarm_fork.c`

```
1  #include <sys/types.h>
2  #include <wait.h>
3  #include "errors.h"
4
```

```
 5  int main (int argc, char *argv[])
 6  {
 7      int status;
 8      char line[128];
 9      int seconds;
10      pid_t pid;
11      char message[64];
12
13      while (1) {
14          printf ("Alarm> ");
15          if (fgets (line, sizeof (line), stdin) == NULL) exit (0);
16          if (strlen (line) <= 1) continue;
17
18          /*
19           * Parse input line into seconds (%d) and a message
20           * (%64[^\n]), consisting of up to 64 characters
21           * separated from the seconds by whitespace.
22           */
23          if (sscanf (line, "%d %64[^\n]",
24              &seconds, message) < 2) {
25              fprintf (stderr, "Bad command\n");
26          } else {
27              pid = fork ();
28              if (pid == (pid_t)-1)
29                  errno_abort ("Fork");
30              if (pid == (pid_t)0) {
31                  /*
32                   * In the child, wait and then print a message
33                   */
34                  sleep (seconds);
35                  printf ("(%d) %s\n", seconds, message);
36                  exit (0);
37              } else {
38                  /*
39                   * In the parent, call waitpid() to collect children
40                   * that have already terminated.
41                   */
42                  do {
43                      pid = waitpid ((pid_t)-1, NULL, WNOHANG);
44                      if (pid == (pid_t)-1)
45                          errno_abort ("Wait for child");
46                  } while (pid != (pid_t)0);
47              }
48          }
49      }
50  }
```

■ alarm_fork.c

1.5.3 A version using multiple threads

Now, let us try another alarm program, `alarm_thread.c`. It is much like the fork version in `alarm_fork.c`, except that it uses threads instead of child processes to create asynchronous alarms. Four Pthreads calls are used in this program:

- `pthread_create` creates a thread running the routine specified in the third argument (`alarm_thread`), returning an identifier for the new thread to the variable referenced by `thread`.
- `pthread_detach` allows Pthreads to reclaim the thread's resources as soon as it terminates.
- `pthread_exit` terminates the calling thread.
- `pthread_self` returns the calling thread's identifier.

4-7   The `alarm_t` structure defines the information stored for each alarm command, the number of `seconds` until the alarm is due, and the `message` string that will be printed by the thread.

■ `alarm_thread.c`   part 1   definitions

```
1  #include <pthread.h>
2  #include "errors.h"
3
4  typedef struct alarm_tag {
5      int         seconds;
6      char        message[64];
7  } alarm_t;
```

■ `alarm_thread.c`   part 1   definitions

1-8   The `alarm_thread` function is the "alarm thread." That is, each alarm thread is created running this function, and when the function returns the thread terminates. The function's argument (`void *arg`) is the fourth argument that was passed to `pthread_create`, in this case, a pointer to the control packet (`alarm_t`) created for the alarm request that the thread is to satisfy. The thread starts by "mapping" the `void *` argument as a pointer to a control packet. The thread *detaches* itself by calling `pthread_detach`, which informs Pthreads that the application does not need to know when the thread terminates or its termination status.

9-12   The thread sleeps for the number of seconds specified in its control packet, and then prints the message string. Finally, the thread frees the control packet and returns. When a thread returns from its initial routine, as it does here, the thread terminates. Normally, Pthreads would hold the thread's resources so that another thread could later determine that it had exited and retrieve a final result. Because the thread detached itself, none of that is necessary.

■ alarm_thread.c   part 2   alarm_thread

```
1  void *alarm_thread (void *arg)
2  {
3      alarm_t *alarm = (alarm_t*)arg;
4      int status;
5
6      status = pthread_detach (pthread_self ());
7      if (status != 0)
8          err_abort (status, "Detach thread");
9      sleep (alarm->seconds);
10     printf ("(%d) %s\n", alarm->seconds, alarm->message);
11     free (alarm);
12     return NULL;
13 }
```

■ alarm_thread.c   part 2   alarm_thread

The `main` program of `alarm_thread.c` is much the same as the other two variants. It loops, reading and interpreting command lines as long as it can read from `stdin`.

12–25   In this variation, `main` allocates heap storage (`alarm_t`) for each alarm command. The alarm time and message are stored in this structure, so each thread can be given the appropriate information. If the `sscanf` call fails to "parse" a correct command, the heap storage is freed.

26–29   An alarm thread is created, running function `alarm_thread`, with the alarm data (`alarm_t`) as the thread's argument.

■ alarm_thread.c   part 3   main

```
1  int main (int argc, char *argv[])
2  {
3      int status;
4      char line[128];
5      alarm_t *alarm;
6      pthread_t thread;
7
8      while (1) {
9          printf ("Alarm> ");
10         if (fgets (line, sizeof (line), stdin) == NULL) exit (0);
11         if (strlen (line) <= 1) continue;
12         alarm = (alarm_t*)malloc (sizeof (alarm_t));
13         if (alarm == NULL)
14             errno_abort ("Allocate alarm");
15
16         /*
17          * Parse input line into seconds (%d) and a message
18          * (%64[^\n]), consisting of up to 64 characters
19          * separated from the seconds by whitespace.
20          */
```

```
21          if (sscanf (line, "%d %64[^\n]",
22              &alarm->seconds, alarm->message) < 2) {
23              fprintf (stderr, "Bad command\n");
24              free (alarm);
25          } else {
26              status = pthread_create (
27                  &thread, NULL, alarm_thread, alarm);
28              if (status != 0)
29                  err_abort (status, "Create alarm thread");
30          }
31      }
32  }
```

■ `alarm_thread.c`   part 3   main

1.5.4 Summary

A good way to start thinking about threads is to compare the two asynchronous versions of the alarm program. First, in the fork version, each alarm has an independent address space, copied from the main program. That means we can put the seconds and message values into local variables—once the child has been created (when `fork` returns), the parent can change the values without affecting the alarm. In the threaded version, on the other hand, all threads share the same address space—so we call `malloc` to create a new structure for each alarm, which is passed to the new thread. The extra bookkeeping required introduces a little complexity into the threaded version.

In the version using `fork`, the main program needs to tell the kernel to free resources used by each child process it creates, by calling `waitpid` or some other member of the `wait` "family." The `alarm_fork.c` program, for example, calls `waitpid` in a loop after each command, to collect all child processes that have completed. You do not need to wait for a thread unless you need the thread's return value—in `alarm_thread.c`, for example, each alarm thread *detaches* itself (at line 6, part 2) so that the resources held by the thread will be returned immediately when it terminates.

In the threaded version, the "primary activities" (sleeping and printing the message) must be coded in a separate routine. In `alarm.c` and `alarm_fork.c`, those activities were performed without a call. In simple cases such as our alarm program, it is often easier to understand the program with all code in one place, so that might seem like an advantage for `alarm_fork.c`. In more complicated programs, though, it is rare that a program's "primary activities" are so simple that they can be performed in a single routine without resulting in total confusion.

In a real alarm program, you wouldn't want to create a process for each alarm. You might easily have hundreds of alarms active, and the system probably wouldn't let you create that many processes. On the other hand, you probably can create hundreds of threads within a process. While there is no real need to maintain a stack and thread context for each alarm request, it is a perfectly viable design.

A more sophisticated version of `alarm_thread.c` might use only two threads: one to read input from the user, and another to wait for expiration of the next alarm—I'll show that version later, after we've worked through some more basic concepts. You could do the same thing with two processes, of course, but it would be more cumbersome. Passing information between two threads is easy and fast—no shared memory to map, no pipes to read or write, no concerns about whether you are passing addresses that may not mean the same thing in both processes. Threads share everything in their address space—any address that's valid in one thread is valid in all threads.

1.6 Benefits of threading

"'O Looking-Glass creatures,' quoth Alice, 'draw near!
'Tis an honour to see me, a favour to hear:
'Tis a privilege high to have dinner and tea
Along with the Red Queen, the White Queen, and me!'"
  —Lewis Carroll, Through the Looking-Glass

Some advantages of the multithreaded programming model follow:

1. Exploitation of program parallelism on multiprocessor hardware. Parallelism is the only benefit that requires special hardware. The others can help most programs without special hardware.
2. More efficient exploitation of a program's natural concurrency, by allowing the program to perform computations while waiting for slow I/O operations to complete.
3. A modular programming model that clearly expresses relationships between independent "events" within the program.

These advantages are detailed in the following sections.

1.6.1 Parallelism

On a multiprocessor system, threading allows a process to perform more than one independent computation at the same time. A computation-intensive threaded application running on two processors may achieve nearly twice the performance of a traditional single-threaded version. "Nearly twice" takes into account the fact that you'll always have some overhead due to creating the extra thread(s) and performing synchronization. This effect is often referred to as "scaling." A two-processor system may perform 1.95 times as fast as a single processor, a three-processor system 2.9 times as fast, a four-processor system 3.8 times as fast, and so forth. Scaling almost always falls off as the number of processors increases because there's more chance of lock and memory collisions, which cost time.

$$Speedup = \frac{1}{(1 - p) + \dfrac{p}{n}}$$

FIGURE 1.1 *Amdahl's law*

Scaling can be predicted by "Amdahl's law," which is shown in Figure 1.1. In the equation, p represents the ratio of "parallelizable code" over "total execution time," and n represents the number of processors the code can use. The total elapsed time for a parallel job is the sum of the elapsed time for the nonparallelizable work $(1 - p)$ and the elapsed time for each processor executing the parallelizable work (p/n).

Amdahl's law is a simple relationship showing how parallelism is limited by the amount of serialization needed. When the program has no parallelizable code (p is 0), the speedup is 1. That is, it is not a parallel program. If the program requires no synchronization or other serial code (p is 1), then the speedup is n (the number of processors). As more synchronization is required, parallelism provides less benefit. To put it another way, you'll get better scaling with activities that are completely independent than with activities that are highly dependent: The independent activities need less synchronization.

The diagram in Figure 1.2 shows the effect of Amdahl's law. "Clock time" progresses from left to right across the page, and the diagram shows the number of processors working in parallel at any moment. Areas where the diagram has only a single horizontal line show that the process is serialized. Areas that have several horizontal lines in parallel show where the process benefits from multiple processors. If you can apply multiple processors for only 10% of your program's execution time, and you have four processors, then Amdahl's law predicts a speedup of `1/(0.9+(0.1/4))`, or about 8%.

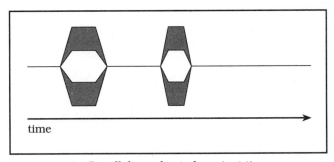

time

FIGURE 1.2 *Parallelism charted against time*

Operations on large matrices can often be "parallelized" by splitting the matrix into pieces. For example, each thread may be able to operate on a set of rows or columns without requiring any data written by threads operating on other slices. You still generally need to synchronize threads at the beginning and end of processing the matrix, frequently using a *barrier*.* Amdahl's law shows that you'll get better performance by giving each thread a large and relatively independent "chunk" of work, requiring infrequent synchronization, than by giving them smaller chunks.

Amdahl's law is an excellent thought exercise to help you understand scaling. It is not, however, a practical tool, because it is nearly impossible to accurately compute *p* for any program. To be accurate, you need to consider not only all serialized regions within your code, but also within the operating system kernel and even in hardware. Multiprocessor hardware must have some mechanism to synchronize access to the contents of memory. When each processor has a private data cache, the contents of those caches must be kept consistent with each other and with the data in memory. All of this serialization must be included in any accurate calculation.

1.6.2 Concurrency

The threaded programming model allows the program to make computational progress while waiting for blocking operations like I/O. This is useful for network servers and clients, and it is the main reason that client/server systems (such as OSF DCE) use threads. While one thread waits for a long network read or write operation, that thread is blocked and other threads in your application can execute independently. Some systems support asynchronous I/O operations, which can give similar advantages; but most UNIX-based systems do not have asynchronous I/O.† Furthermore, asynchronous I/O is generally a lot more complicated to use than threads.

For example, you need to either handle asynchronous notification when the I/O completes, or poll for completion. If you issued an asynchronous I/O and then entered a polling loop, you would lose the advantage of asynchronous I/O— your application would just wait. If you poll elsewhere, or handle asynchronous notification, then *issuing* the I/O and *processing* the resulting data occur in different locations within your program. That makes the code more difficult to

---

*A barrier is a simple synchronization mechanism that blocks each thread until a certain number has reached the barrier; then all threads are unblocked. Barriers can be used, for example, to keep any thread from executing a parallel region of code until all threads are ready to execute the region. Section 7.1.1 describes barriers in more detail, and demonstrates the construction of a simple barrier package.

† UNIX systems support "nonblocking I/O," but this is not the same thing as asynchronous I/O. Nonblocking I/O allows the program to defer issuing an I/O operation until it can complete without blocking, but asynchronous I/O can proceed while the program does something else.

analyze and maintain. When you use synchronous I/O you just perform the I/O and then do whatever comes next. Synchronous I/O within multiple threads gives nearly all the advantages of asynchronous I/O. In most cases you will find it much easier to write complex asynchronous code using threads than using traditional asychronous programming techniques.

You could write an *alarm* program, like those shown in Section 1.5, as an asynchronous program without using processes or threads, with timer signals for the alarms and asynchronous reads for input. Using timer signals is more complicated in many ways, since you are severely limited in what you can do within a signal handler. Asynchronous I/O does not allow you to take advantage of the convenience of *stdio* functions. The basic program function will be scattered through a series of signal handlers and functions, and will probably be harder to understand.

Asynchronous I/O does have one advantage over threaded concurrency, though. Just as a thread is usually "cheaper" (in execution time and storage space) than a process, the context required for an asynchronous I/O operation is almost always cheaper than a thread. If you plan to have a lot of asynchronous I/O operations active at the same time, that might be important enough to justify using the more complicated programming model. But watch out—some "asynchronous I/O" packages just distribute your I/O requests across a pool of threads! Most of the time you will be better off using threads.

Another method of coding an asynchronous application is for each action to be treated as an "event." Events are queued by some "hidden" process, and dispatched serially to be handled by the application, usually through "callback" routines registered with the dispatcher. Event dispatchers have been popularized by windowing interface systems such as the Apple Macintosh toolbox, Microsoft Windows, and X Windows on UNIX (used by Motif and CDE).

The event mechanism alleviates much of the complication of using signals and asynchronous I/O, as long as the events are supported directly by the event dispatcher. All, for example, handle input from the keyboard or pointer device, and generally one can request a timer event to be inserted automatically at a desired time. Thus, the alarm program, written to an event interface, need only initialize the event dispatcher and enter a loop to process events. Input events would be dispatched to the parser, resulting in a request for a new timer event; and timer events would be dispatched to a function that would format and print the alarm message.

For very simple applications (and the alarm program here is certainly one example), an event-based implementation may be simpler than the multiprocess or multithread variations I've shown—at least when the (often substantial) overhead of initializing the event dispatcher is removed. The limitations of events become more obvious when you build larger and more sophisticated applications—the problem is that the events are sequential.

Events are not concurrent, and the program can do only one thing at a time. Your application receives an event, processes it, and then receives the next event. If processing an event takes a long time, for example, sorting a large database, the user interface may remain unresponsive for quite a while. If an event involves a long wait, for example, reading data over a slow network connection, then, again, the user must wait.

The response problems can be minimized by liberally sprinkling extended operations with calls to the event dispatcher—but getting them in the right place, without substantially impacting the performance of the operation, can be difficult. Furthermore, you may not have that option, if the database sort is taking place in a shared library you bought from somebody else.

On the other hand, one might code the application to create a new thread that runs the database sort, or reads from the slow network, leaving the "user interface" thread to immediately request another event. The application becomes responsive, while the slow operation continues to run. You can do this even if a database package, for example, cannot tolerate being run in multiple threads, by queuing a "sort" command to a server thread that runs database operations serially—while still retaining interface responsiveness.

1.6.3 Programming model

It may be surprising that programming with threads is a good idea even if you know your code will never run on a multiprocessor. But it is true. Writing with threads forces you to think about and plan for the synchronization requirements of your program. You've always had to think about program dependencies, but threads help to move the requirements from comments into the executable structure of the program.

Assembly language programs can use all the same sequential control structures (loops, conditional code) as programs written in a high-level language. However, it can be difficult to determine whether a branch instruction represents the top or bottom of a loop, a simple conditional, a "conditional goto," or something more exotic. Switching to a higher-level language that supports these sequential controls directly in source, for example, the C language do, while, for, if, and switch statements, makes these sequential programming constructs explicit in the source language. Making control structures explicit in the program source code means that more of your program's design is explicit in the source, and that makes it easier for someone else to understand.

Similarly, a C language program (or even an assembler program) may use data encapsulation and polymorphism by adhering to programming conventions, and with luck those conventions may be carefully documented and the documentation kept updated. But if that same code is written in an object-oriented language, the encapsulation and polymorphism become explicit in the source language.

In a sequential program, synchronization requirements are implicit in the ordering of operations. The true synchronization requirements, for example, that "a file must be opened before data can be read from the file," may be documented only by source comments, if at all. When you program using threads, sequential assumptions are (or at least should be) limited to small segments of contiguous code—for example, within a single function. More global assumptions, to be at all safe, must be protected by explicit synchronization constructs.

In traditional serial programming you call function A to do one thing, then call another function B to do something else, even when those two functions don't require serialization. If a developer is trying to determine what the program is doing, perhaps to trace a bug, it often isn't obvious that there may be no need to follow both calls. Furthermore, the strictly serial model makes it easy for someone to inadvertently make function B dependent on some side effect of function A. If a later modification reverses the order of the calls, the program may break in ways that aren't obvious. Program dependencies may be documented using source code comment blocks, but comments are often ambiguous and may not be properly updated when code is changed.

The threaded programming model isolates independent or loosely coupled functional execution streams (threads) in a clear way that's made explicit in the program's source code. If activities are designed as threads, each function must include explicit synchronization to enforce its dependencies. Because synchronization is executable code, it can't be ignored when dependencies are changed. The presence of synchronization constructs allows anyone reading the code to follow temporal dependencies within the code, which can make maintenance substantially easier, especially for large programs with a lot of independent code.

An assembly language programmer can write better, more maintainable assembly code by understanding high-level language programming; a C language programmer can write better, more maintainable C code by understanding object-oriented programming. Even if you never write a threaded program, you may benefit from understanding the threaded programming model of independent functions with explicit dependencies. These are "mental models" (or that dreadfully overused word, "paradigms") that are more or less independent of the specific code sequences you write. Cleanly isolating functionally independent code may even make sequential programs easier to understand and maintain.

1.7 Costs of threading

All this time the Guard was looking at her, first through a telescope, then through a microscope, and then through an opera-glass.
At last he said, "You're traveling the wrong way,"
and shut up the window, and went away.
    —Lewis Carroll, Through the Looking-Glass

Of course there's always "the flip side." As I showed in the previous section, threads provide definite and powerful advantages, even on uniprocessor systems. They provide even more advantages on a multiprocessor.

So why *wouldn't* you want to use threads? Everything has a cost, and threaded programming is no exception. In many cases the advantage exceeds the cost; in others it doesn't. To be fair, the following subsections discuss the cost of threaded programming.

1.7.1 Computing overhead

Overhead costs in threaded code include direct effects such as the time it takes to synchronize your threads. Many clever algorithms are available for avoiding synchronization in some cases, but none of them is portable. You'll have to use some synchronization in just about any threaded code. It is easy to lose performance by using too much synchronization; for example, by separately protecting two variables that are always used together. Protecting each variable separately means you spend a lot more time on synchronization without gaining parallelism, since any thread that needs one variable will need the other as well.

The overhead of threaded programming can also include more subtle effects. For example, threads that constantly write the same memory locations may spend a lot of time synchronizing the memory system on processors that support "read/write ordering." Other processors may spend that time synchronizing only when you use special instructions such as a memory barrier, or a "multiprocessor atomic" operation like test-and-set. Section 3.4 says a lot more about these effects.

Removing a bottleneck in your code, for example, by adding threads to perform multiple concurrent I/O operations, may end up revealing another bottleneck at a lower level—in the ANSI C library, the operating system, the file system, the device driver, the memory or I/O architecture, or the device controller. These effects are often difficult to predict, or measure, and are usually not well documented.

A compute-bound thread, which rarely blocks for any external event, cannot effectively share a processor with other compute-bound threads. An I/O thread might interrupt it once in a while, but the I/O thread would block for another external event and the compute-bound thread would run again. When you create more compute-bound threads than there are available processors, you may gain better code structuring over a single-threaded implementation, but you will have worse performance. The performance suffers because the multithreaded implementation adds thread synchronization and scheduling overhead to the work you wanted to accomplish—and does it all using the same compute resources.

1.7.2 Programming discipline

Despite the basic simplicity of the threaded programming model, writing real-world code is never trivial. Writing code that works well in multiple threads takes careful thought and planning. You have to keep track of synchronization protocols and program invariants. You have to avoid deadlocks, races, and priority inversions. I'll describe all of these things in later sections, show how to design code to avoid the problems, and how to find and repair them after the fact.

You will almost certainly use library code that you did not write. Some will be supplied with the operating system you use, and most of the more common libraries will likely be safe to use within multiple threads. POSIX guarantees that most functions specified by ANSI C and POSIX must be safe for use by multithreaded applications. However, a lot of "interesting" functions you will probably need are not included in that list. You will often need to call libraries that are not supplied with the operating system, for example, database software. Some of that code will not be thread-safe. I will discuss techniques to allow you to use most unsafe code, but they will not always work, and they can be ugly.

All threads within a process share the same address space, and there's no protection boundary between the threads. If a thread writes to memory through an uninitialized pointer, it can wipe out another thread's stack, or heap memory being used by some other thread. The eventual failure will most likely occur in the innocent victim, possibly long after the perpetrator has gone on to other things. This can be especially important if arbitrary code is run within a thread. For example, in a library that supports callbacks to functions supplied by its caller, be sure that the callback, as well as the library, is thread-safe.

The important points are that good sequential code is not necessarily good threaded code, and bad threaded code will break in ways that are more difficult to locate and repair. Thinking about real-life parallelism can help a lot, but programming requires a lot more detailed work than most things in real life.

1.7.3 Harder to debug

You will learn more about debugging threaded code, and, more importantly, *not* debugging threaded code, in Chapter 8. You will see some of the tools you may encounter as well as some techniques you can use on your own. By then you will know all about mutexes and memory visibility, and you will be ready to deal with deadlocks and races. Don't worry about the details now—the point of this brief section is to demonstrate that you *will* have to learn about threaded debugging, and it is not as easy yet as anyone would like it to be. (So when was debugging *ever* easy?)

Systems that support threads generally extend traditional sequential debugging tools to provide basic debugging support. The system may provide a debugger that allows you to see the call tree for all of your program's threads, for example, and set breakpoints that activate only in particular threads. The system may provide some form of performance analyzer that lets you measure the processor time accumulated within each function for a specific thread or across all threads.

Unfortunately that's only the beginning of the problems when you're debugging asynchronous code. Debugging inevitably changes the timing of events. That doesn't matter much when you're debugging sequential code, but it is critical when you're debugging asynchronous code. If one thread runs even slightly slower than another because it had to process a debugger trap, the problem you're trying to track down may not happen. Every programmer has run into problems that won't reproduce under the debugger. You'll run into a lot more of them when you use threads.

It is difficult to track down a memory corruptor, for example, a function that writes through an uninitialized pointer, in a sequential program. It is even harder in a threaded program. Did some other thread write to memory without using a mutex? Did it use the wrong mutex? Did it count on another thread setting up a pointer without explicit synchronization? Was it just an old fashioned sequential memory corruptor?

Various additional tools are provided by some systems to help you. None of these is standard or widely available. Tools may check source code for obvious violations of locking protocol, given a definition of which variables are shared and how they should be locked. They may record thread interactions while the program runs, and allow you to analyze or even replay the interactions to determine what happened. They may record and measure synchronization contention and overhead. They may detect complicated deadlock conditions between a set of mutexes.

Your most powerful and portable thread debugging tool is your mind, applied through the old fashioned manual human-powered code review. You'll probably spend a lot of time setting up a few breakpoints and examining lots of states to try to narrow the problem down a little and then carefully reading the code to find problems. It is best if you have someone available who didn't write the code, because a lot of the worst errors are embarrassingly obvious to someone who's not burdened with detailed knowledge of what the code was *supposed* to do.

1.8 To thread or not to thread?

"My poor client's fate now depends on your votes."
Here the speaker sat down in his place,
And directed the Judge to refer to his notes
And briefly to sum up the case.

   —Lewis Carroll, The Hunting of the Snark

Threads don't necessarily provide the best solution to every programming problem. They're not always easier to use, and they don't always result in better performance.

A few problems are really "inherently nonconcurrent," and adding threads will only slow the program down and complicate it. If every step in your program depends directly on the result of the previous step, then using threads probably won't help. Each thread would have to wait for another thread to complete.

The most obvious candidates for threaded coding are new applications that accomplish the following:

1. Perform extensive computation that can be parallelized (or "decomposed") into multiple threads, and which is intended to run on multiprocessor hardware, *or*
2. Perform substantial I/O which can be overlapped to improve throughput—many threads can wait for different I/O requests at the same time. Distributed server applications are good candidates, since they may have work to do in response to multiple clients, and they must also be prepared for unsolicited I/O over relatively slow network connections.

Most programs have some natural concurrency, even if it is only reading a command from the input device while processing the previous command. Threaded applications are often faster, and usually more responsive, than sequential programs that do the same job. They are generally much easier to develop and maintain than nonthreaded asynchronous applications that do the same job.

So should you use threads? You probably won't find them appropriate for every programming job you approach. But threaded programming is a technique that all software developers should understand.

1.9 POSIX thread concepts

"You seem very clever at explaining words, Sir," said Alice.
"Would you kindly tell me the meaning of the poem
called 'Jabberwocky'?"
"Let's hear it," said Humpty Dumpty. "I can explain all
the poems that ever were invented—and a good many
that haven't been invented just yet."
—Lewis Carroll, Through the Looking-Glass

First of all, this book focuses on "POSIX threads." Technically, that means the thread "application programming interfaces" (API) specified by the international formal standard POSIX 1003.1c–1995. This standard was approved by the IEEE in June 1995. A new edition of POSIX 1003.1, called *ISO/IEC 9945-1:1996 (ANSI/ IEEE Std 1003.1, 1996 Edition)* is available from the IEEE.[*] This new document includes 1003.1b–1993 (realtime), 1003.1c–1995 (threads), and 1003.1i–1995 (corrections to 1003.1b–1993). Unless you are writing an implementation of the standard, or are extremely curious, you probably don't want to bother buying the

---

[*] Contact the IEEE at 1-800-678-IEEE. *9945–1:1996 Information Technology—Portable Operating System Interface (POSIX)—Part 1: System Application: Program Interface (API) [C Language]*, ISBN 1-55937-573-6, order number SH94352.

POSIX standard. For writing threaded code, you'll find books like this one much more useful, supplemented by the programming documentation for the operating system you're using.

As I explained in the preface, I will use the informal term "Pthreads" to refer to "POSIX 1003.1c–1995." I will use the slightly more formal term "POSIX.1b" to refer to "POSIX 1003.1b–1993" in the text, "POSIX.14" to refer to the POSIX 1003.14 "Multiprocessor Profile," and similar abbreviated notation for other POSIX standards. I'll use the full names where precision is important, for example, to compare POSIX 1003.1–1990 and POSIX 1003.1–1996, and also in section titles and captions that appear in the table of contents.

1.9.1 Architectural overview

You may remember from Section 1.2 that the three essential aspects of a thread system are execution context, scheduling, and synchronization. When you evaluate any thread system, or compare any two thread systems, start by categorizing the features into capabilities that support execution contexts, scheduling, and synchronization.

With Pthreads, you create an execution context (thread) by calling `pthread_create`. Creating a thread also schedules the thread for execution, and it will begin by calling a "thread start function" that you specified. Pthreads allows you to specify scheduling parameters either at the time you create the thread, or later on while the thread is running. A thread normally terminates when it calls `pthread_exit`, or returns from the thread start function, although we will encounter a few other possibilities later.

The primary Pthreads synchronization model uses *mutexes* for protection and *condition variables* for communication. You can also use other synchronization mechanisms such as semaphores, pipes, and message queues. A mutex allows one thread to *lock* shared data while using it so that other threads cannot accidentally interfere. A condition variable allows a thread to wait for shared data to reach some desired state (such as "queue not empty" or "resource available").

1.9.2 Types and interfaces

This section briefly outlines the Pthreads data types, and some of the rules for interpreting them. For a full description of the "object" represented by each type and how to create and use those objects in a program, see the appropriate sections later in this book, as shown in Table 1.2.

Type	Section	Description
pthread_t	2	thread identifier
pthread_mutex_t	3.2	mutex
pthread_cond_t	3.3	condition variable
pthread_key_t	5.4	"access key" for thread-specific data
pthread_attr_t	5.2.3	thread attributes object
pthread_mutexattr_t	5.2.1	mutex attributes object
pthread_condattr_t	5.2.2	condition variable attributes object
pthread_once_t	5.1	"one time initialization" control context

TABLE 1.2   *POSIX threads types*

> All Pthreads types are "opaque."
> Portable code cannot make assumptions regarding the representation
> of these types.

All of the "pthread" types listed in Table 1.2 are considered *opaque*. There is no public definition of these types' representation, and programmers should never assume anything about the representation. You should use them only in the manner specifically described by the standard. A thread identifier, for example, may be an integer, or a pointer, or a structure, and any code that uses a thread identifier in a way that is not compatible with all of those definitions is incorrect.

1.9.3 Checking for errors

> Pthreads introduces a new way to report errors, without using the
> errno variable.

The Pthreads amendment is the first part of POSIX to depart from the ancient UNIX and C language conventions regarding error status. Traditionally, functions that succeed returned a useful value if appropriate, or otherwise indicated success by returning the value 0. On failure, they returned the special value –1, and set the global value errno to a code specifying the type of error.

The old mechanism has a number of problems, including the fact that it is difficult to create a function that can both report an error *and* return a useful value of –1. There are even worse problems when you add multiple threads to a process. In traditional UNIX systems, and in the original POSIX.1–1990 standard, errno was an extern int variable. Since such a variable can have only one value at a time, it can support only a single stream of execution within the process.

| Pthreads functions don't set `errno` on errors!
| (But most other POSIX functions do.)

New functions in the Pthreads standard reserve the return value for error status, and errno is not used. Pthreads functions return the value 0 on success, and include an extra output parameter to specify an address where "useful results" are stored. When a function cannot complete successfully, an error code from the <errno.h> header file is returned instead of 0 as the function value.

Pthreads also provides a per-thread errno, which supports other code that uses errno. This means that when one thread calls some function that reports an error using errno, the value cannot be overwritten, or read, by any other thread—you may go on using errno just as you always have. But if you're designing new interfaces you should consider following the new Pthreads convention for reporting errors. Setting or reading the per-thread errno involves more overhead than reading or writing a memory location, or returning a value from a function.

To wait for a thread, for example, and check for an error, you might use code like that shown in the following code example, thread_error.c. The pthread_join function, used to wait for a thread to terminate, will report an invalid thread identifier by returning the error code ESRCH. An uninitialized pthread_t is likely to be an invalid thread identifier on most implementations. The result of running this program should be a message such as "error 3: no such process."

In the unlikely event that the uninitialized thread variable has a pthread_t value that is not invalid, it should be the ID of the initial thread (there are no other threads in this process). In this case, pthread_join should either fail with EDEADLK, if your implementation of Pthreads detects self-deadlock, or the thread will hang waiting for itself to exit.

■ thread_error.c

```
1    #include <pthread.h>
2    #include <stdio.h>
3    #include <errno.h>
4
5    int main (int argc, char *argv[])
6    {
7        pthread_t thread;
8        int status;
9
10       /*
11        * Attempt to join with an uninitialized thread ID. On most
12        * implementations, this will return an ESRCH error code. If
13        * the local (and uninitialized) pthread_t happens to be a valid
14        * thread ID, it is almost certainly that of the initial thread,
15        * which is running main(). In that case, your Pthreads
16        * implementation may either return EDEADLK (self-deadlock),
17        * or it may hang. If it hangs, quit and try again.
18        */
```

```
19      status = pthread_join (thread, NULL);
20      if (status != 0)
21          fprintf (stderr, "error %d: %s\n", status, strerror (status));
22      return status;
23  }
```

■ thread_error.c

Note that there is no equivalent to the perror function to format and print an error value returned by the Pthreads interfaces. Instead, use strerror to get a string description of the error number, and print the string to the file stream stderr.

To avoid cluttering each function call in the example programs with a block of code to report each error and call abort, I have built two error macros—err_abort detects a standard Pthreads error, and errno_abort is used when a value of −1 means that errno contains an error code. The following header file, called errors.h, shows these macros. The errors.h header file also includes several system header files, which would otherwise be required by most of the example programs—this helps to reduce the size of the examples.

■ errors.h

```
1   #ifndef __errors_h
2   #define __errors_h
3
4   #include <unistd.h>
5   #include <errno.h>
6   #include <stdio.h>
7   #include <stdlib.h>
8   #include <string.h>
9
10  /*
11   * Define a macro that can be used for diagnostic output from
12   * examples. When compiled -DDEBUG, it results in calling printf
13   * with the specified argument list. When DEBUG is not defined, it
14   * expands to nothing.
15   */
16  #ifdef DEBUG
17  # define DPRINTF(arg) printf arg
18  #else
19  # define DPRINTF(arg)
20  #endif
21
22  /*
23   * NOTE: the "do {" ... "} while (0);" bracketing around the macros
24   * allows the err_abort and errno_abort macros to be used as if they
25   * were function calls, even in contexts where a trailing ";" would
26   * generate a null statement. For example,
```

```
27    *
28    *         if (status != 0)
29    *             err_abort (status, "message");
30    *         else
31    *             return status;
32    *
33    * will not compile if err_abort is a macro ending with "}", because
34    * C does not expect a ";" to follow the "}". Because C does expect
35    * a ";" following the ")" in the do...while construct, err_abort and
36    * errno_abort can be used as if they were function calls.
37    */
38  #define err_abort(code,text) do { \
39        fprintf (stderr, "%s at \"%s\":%d: %s\n", \
40            text, __FILE__, __LINE__, strerror (code)); \
41        abort (); \
42        } while (0)
43  #define errno_abort(text) do { \
44        fprintf (stderr, "%s at \"%s\":%d: %s\n", \
45            text, __FILE__, __LINE__, strerror (errno)); \
46        abort (); \
47        } while (0)
48
49  #endif
```

■ errors.h

The one exception to the Pthreads error rules is `pthread_getspecific`, which returns the thread-specific data value of a shared "key." Section 5.4 describes thread-specific data in detail, but for now we're just concerned with error reporting. The capability of managing thread-specific data is critical to many applications, and the function has to be as fast as possible, so the `pthread_getspecific` function doesn't report errors at all. If the `pthread_key_t` value is illegal, or if no value has been set in the thread, `pthread_getspecific` just returns the value NULL.

2 Threads

Threads are (and perhaps this will come as no surprise) the essential basis of the style of programming that I am advocating. Although this chapter focuses on threads, you will never learn everything you need to know about threads by simply skipping to this chapter and reading it. Threads are a critical part of the landscape, but you can't do much with only threads. Nevertheless, one must start somewhere, and here we are.

Section 2.1 describes the programming aspects of creating and managing threads in your program, that is, how to create threads, how they are represented in your program, and the most basic things you can do to them once you've created them.

Section 2.2 describes the life cycle of a thread, from creation through "recycling," taking you through all the scheduling states threads can assume along the way.

2.1 Creating and using threads

```
pthread_t thread;
int pthread_equal (pthread_t t1, pthread_t t2);
int pthread_create (pthread_t *thread,
    const pthread_attr_t *attr,
    void *(*start)(void *), void *arg);
pthread_t pthread_self (void);
int sched_yield (void);
int pthread_exit (void *value_ptr);
int pthread_detach (pthread_t thread);
int pthread_join (pthread_t thread, void **value_ptr);
```

The introduction covered some of the basics of what a thread is, and what it means to the computer hardware. This section begins where the introduction left off. It explains how a thread is represented in your program, what it means to your program, and some of the operations you can perform on threads. If you haven't read the introduction, this would be a good time to skip back to it. (I'll wait for you here.)

Within your program a thread is represented by a thread identifier, of the opaque type pthread_t. To create a thread, you must declare a variable of type pthread_t somewhere in your program. If the identifier is needed only within a function, or if the function won't return until the thread is done, you could declare the identifier with auto storage class. Most of the time, though, the identifier will be stored in a shared (static or extern) variable, or in a structure allocated from the heap.

A Pthreads thread begins by calling some function that you provide. This "thread function" should expect a single argument of type void *, and should return a value of the same type. You create a thread by passing the thread function's address, and the argument value with which you want the function to be called, to pthread_create.

When you create a thread, pthread_create returns an identifier, in the pthread_t value referred to by the thread argument, by which your code refers to the new thread. A thread can also get its own identifier using the pthread_self function. There is no way to find a thread's identifier unless either the creator or the thread itself stores the identifier somewhere. You need to have a thread's identifier to do anything to the thread. If you'll need to know when a thread completes, for example, you must keep the identifier somewhere.

Pthreads provides the pthread_equal function to compare two thread identifiers. You can only test for equality. It doesn't make any sense to ask whether one thread identifier is "greater than" or "less than" another, because there is no ordering between threads. The pthread_equal function returns a nonzero value if the thread identifiers refer to the same thread, and the value 0 if they do not refer to the same thread.

❚ The initial thread (main) is special.

When a C program runs, it begins in a special function named `main`. In a threaded program, this special stream of execution is called the "initial thread" or sometimes the "main thread." You can do anything within the initial thread that you can do within any other thread. It can determine its own thread identifier by calling `pthread_self`, for example, or terminate itself by calling `pthread_exit`. If the initial thread stores its thread identifier somewhere accessible to another thread, that thread can wait for the initial thread to terminate, or detach the initial thread.

The initial thread is special because Pthreads retains traditional UNIX process behavior when the function `main` returns; that is, the process terminates without allowing other threads to complete. In general, you do not want to do this in a threaded program, but sometimes it can be convenient. In many of the programs in this book, for example, threads are created that have no effect on anything outside the process. It doesn't really matter what those threads are doing, then, if the process goes away. When the process exits, those threads, all their states, and anything they might accomplish, simply "evaporate"—there's no reason to clean up.

> Detaching a thread that is still running doesn't affect the thread in any way—it just informs the system that the thread's resources can be reclaimed when the thread eventually terminates.

Although "thread evaporation" is sometimes useful, most of the time your process will outlive the individual threads you create. To be sure that resources used by terminated threads are available to the process, you should always detach each thread you create when you're finished with it. Threads that have terminated but are not detached may retain virtual memory, including their stacks, as well as other system resources. Detaching a thread tells the system that you no longer need that thread, and allows the system to reclaim the resources it has allocated to the thread.

If you create a thread that you will never need to control, you can use an *attribute* to create the thread so that it is already detached. (We'll get to attributes later, in Section 5.2.3.) If you do not want to wait for a thread that you created, and you know that you will no longer need to control that thread, you can detach it at any time by calling `pthread_detach`. A thread may detach itself, or any other thread that knows its `pthread_t` identifier may detach it at any time. If you need to know a thread's return value, or if you need to know when a thread has completed, call `pthread_join`. The `pthread_join` function will block the caller until the thread you specify has terminated, and then, optionally, store the terminated thread's return value. Calling `pthread_join` *detaches* the specified thread automatically.

As we've seen, threads within a process can execute different instructions, using different stacks, all at the same time. Although the threads execute independently of each other, they always share the same address space and file descriptors. The shared address space provides an important advantage of the threaded programming model by allowing threads to communicate efficiently.

Some programs may create threads that perform unrelated activities, but most often a set of threads works together toward a common goal. For example, one set of threads may form an assembly line in which each performs some specific task on a shared data stream and then passes the data on to the next thread. A set of threads may form a work crew and divide independent parts of a common task. Or one "manager" thread may take control and divide work among a "crew" of worker threads. You can combine these models in a variety of ways; for example, a work crew might perform some complicated step in a pipeline, such as transforming a slice of an array.

The following program, lifecycle.c, creates a thread. We'll refer to this simple example in the following sections about a thread's life cycle.

7-10 The thread function, thread_routine, returns a value to satisfy the standard thread function prototype. In this example the thread returns its argument, and the value is always NULL.

18-25 The program creates a thread by calling pthread_create, and then waits for it by calling pthread_join. You don't need to wait for a thread, but if you don't, you'll need to do something else to make sure the process runs until the thread completes. Returning from main will cause the process to terminate, along with all threads. You could, for example, code the main thread to terminate by calling pthread_exit, which would allow the process to continue until all threads have terminated.

26-29 When the join completes, the program checks the thread's return value, to be sure that the thread returned the value it was given. The program exits with 0 (success) if the value is NULL, or with 1 otherwise.

It is a good idea for all thread functions to return something, even if it is simply NULL. If you omit the return statement, pthread_join will still return some value—whatever happens to be in the place where the thread's start function would have stored a return value (probably a register).

■ lifecycle.c

```
1   #include <pthread.h>
2   #include "errors.h"
3
4   /*
5    * Thread start routine.
6    */
7   void *thread_routine (void *arg)
8   {
9       return arg;
10  }
11
12  main (int argc, char *argv[])
13  {
14      pthread_t thread_id;
15      void *thread_result;
```

```
16      int status;
17
18      status = pthread_create (
19          &thread_id, NULL, thread_routine, NULL);
20      if (status != 0)
21          err_abort (status, "Create thread");
22
23      status = pthread_join (thread_id, &thread_result);
24      if (status != 0)
25          err_abort (status, "Join thread");
26      if (thread_result == NULL)
27          return 0;
28      else
29          return 1;
30  }
```

■ lifecycle.c

If the "joining" thread doesn't care about the return value, or if it knows that the "joinee" (the thread with which it is joining) didn't return a value, then it can pass NULL instead of &retval in the call to pthread_join. The joinee's return value will be ignored.

When the call to pthread_join returns, the joinee has been *detached* and you can't join with it again. In the rare cases where more than one thread might need to know when some particular thread has terminated, the threads should wait on a condition variable instead of calling pthread_join. The terminating thread would store its return value (or any other information) in some known location, and broadcast the condition variable to wake all threads that might be interested.

2.2 The life of a thread

Come, listen, my men, while I tell you again
The five unmistakable marks
By which you may know, wheresoever you go,
The warranted genuine Snarks.
  —Lewis Carroll, The Hunting of the Snark

At any instant, a thread is in one of the four basic states described in Table 2.1. In implementations, you may see additional "states" that distinguish between various reasons for entering the four basic states. Digital UNIX, for example, represents these finer distinctions as "substates," of which each state may have several. Whether they're called "substates" or additional states, "terminated" might be divided into "exited" and "cancelled"; "blocked" might be broken up into "blocked on condition variable," "blocked on mutex," "blocked in read," and so forth.

State	Meaning
Ready	The thread is able to run, but is waiting for a processor. It may have just started, or just been unblocked, or preempted by another thread.
Running	The thread is currently running; on a multiprocessor there may be more than one running thread in the process.
Blocked	The thread is not able to run because it is waiting for something; for example, it may be waiting for a condition variable, or waiting to lock a mutex, or waiting for an I/O operation to complete.
Terminated	The thread has terminated by returning from its start function, calling `pthread_exit`, or having been cancelled and completing all cleanup handlers. It was not detached, and has not yet been joined. Once it is detached or joined, it will be recycled.

TABLE 2.1   *Thread states*

These finer distinctions can be important in debugging and analyzing threaded programs. However, they do not add substantially to the basic understanding of thread scheduling, and we will not deal with them here.

Threads begin in the *ready* state. When the new thread runs it calls your specified thread start function. It may be preempted by other threads, or block itself to wait for external events any number of times. Eventually it completes and either returns from the thread start function or calls the `pthread_exit` function. In either case it *terminates*. If the thread has been *detached*, it is immediately recycled. (Doesn't that sound nicer than "destroyed"—and most systems reuse the resources to make new threads.) Otherwise the thread remains in the *terminated* state until joined or detached. Figure 2.1 shows the relationships between these thread states, and the events that cause threads to move from one state to another.

2.2.1 Creation

The "initial thread" of a process is created when the process is created. In a system that fully supports threaded programming, there's probably no way to execute any code without a thread. A thread is likely to be the only software context that includes the hardware state needed to execute code: registers, program counter, stack pointer, and so forth.

Additional threads are created by explicit calls. The primary way to create threads on a Pthreads system is to call `pthread_create`. Threads may also be created when the process receives a POSIX signal if the process signal notify mechanism is set to `SIGEV_THREAD`. Your system may provide additional nonstandard mechanisms to create a thread.

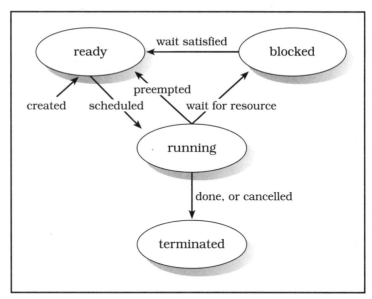

FIGURE 2.1 *Thread state transitions*

When a new thread is created, its state is *ready*. Depending on scheduling constraints, it may remain in that state for a substantial period of time before executing. Section 5.5 contains more information on thread scheduling. Going back to lifecycle.c, the thread running thread_routine becomes *ready* during main's call to pthread_create, at line 18.

The most important thing to remember about thread creation is that there is no synchronization between the creating thread's return from pthread_create and the scheduling of the new thread. That is, the thread may start before the creating thread returns. The thread may even run to completion and terminate before pthread_create returns. Refer to Section 8.1.1 for more information and warnings about what to expect when you create a thread.

2.2.2 Startup

Once a thread has been created, it will eventually begin executing machine instructions. The initial sequence of instructions will lead to the execution of the *thread start function* that you specified to pthread_create. The thread start function is called with the argument value you specified when you created the thread. In lifecycle.c, for example, the thread begins executing user code at function thread_routine, with the formal parameter argument having a value of NULL.

In the initial thread, the thread "start function" (main) is called from outside your program; for example, many UNIX systems link your program with a file called crt0.o, which initializes the process and then calls your main. This is a minor implementation distinction, but it is important to remember because there are a few ways in which the initial thread is different. For one thing, main is called with different arguments than a thread start function: the program's argument array (argc and argv) instead of a single void* argument. For another thing, when a thread start function returns, the thread terminates but other threads continue to run. When the function main returns in the initial thread, the process will be terminated immediately. If you want to terminate the initial thread while allowing other threads in the process to continue running, call pthread_exit instead of returning from main.

Another important difference to remember is that on most systems, the initial thread runs on the default process stack, which can grow to a substantial size. "Thread" stacks may be much more limited on some implementations, and the program will fail with a segmentation fault or bus error if a thread overflows its stack.

2.2.3 Running and blocking

Like us, threads usually can't stay awake their entire life. Most threads occasionally go to sleep. A thread can go to sleep because it needs a resource that is not available (it becomes "blocked") or because the system reassigned the processor on which it was running (it is "preempted"). A thread spends most of its active life in three states: *ready*, *running*, and *blocked*.

A thread is *ready* when it is first created, and whenever it is unblocked so that it is once again eligible to run. *Ready* threads are waiting for a processor. Also, when a *running* thread is preempted, for example, if it is *timesliced* (because it has run too long), the thread immediately becomes *ready*.

A thread becomes *running* when it was *ready* and a processor selects the thread for execution. Usually this means that some other thread has blocked, or has been preempted by a timeslice—the blocking (or preempted) thread saves its context and restores the context of the next ready thread to replace itself. On a multiprocessor, however, a previously unused processor may execute a readied thread without any other thread blocking.

A thread becomes *blocked* when it attempts to lock a mutex that is currently locked, when it waits on a condition variable, when it calls sigwait for a signal that is not currently pending, or when it attempts an I/O operation that cannot be immediately completed. A thread may also become blocked for other system operations, such as a page fault.

When a thread is unblocked after a wait for some event, it is made *ready* again. It may execute immediately, for example, if a processor is available. In lifecycle.c, the main thread blocks at line 23, in pthread_join, to wait for the thread it created to run. If the thread had not already run at this point, it would move from *ready* to *running* when main becomes *blocked*. As the thread runs to completion and returns, the main thread will be unblocked—returning to the *ready* state. When processor resources are available, either immediately or after the thread becomes *terminated*, main will again become *running*, and complete.

2.2.4 Termination

A thread usually terminates by returning from its start function (the one you pass to the `pthread_create` function). The thread shown in `lifecycle.c` terminates by returning the value `NULL`, for example. Threads that call `pthread_exit` or that are cancelled using `pthread_cancel` also terminate after calling each cleanup handler that the thread registered by calling `pthread_cleanup_push` and that hasn't yet been removed by calling `pthread_cleanup_pop`. Cleanup handlers are discussed in Section 5.3.3.

Threads may have private "thread-specific data" values (thread-specific data is discussed in Section 5.4). If the thread has any non-`NULL` thread-specific data values, the associated destructor functions for those keys (if any) are called.

If the thread was already detached it moves immediately to the next section, *recycling*. Otherwise, the thread becomes *terminated*. It will remain available for another thread to join with it using `pthread_join`. This is analogous to a UNIX process that's terminated but hasn't yet been "reaped" by a wait operation. Sometimes it is called a "zombie" because it still exists even though it is "dead." A zombie may retain most or all of the system resources that it used when running, so it is not a good idea to leave threads in this state for longer than necessary. Whenever you create a thread with which you won't need to join, you should use the `detachstate` attribute to create it "detached" (see Section 5.2.3).

At a minimum, a terminated thread retains the identification (`pthread_t` value) and the `void*` return value that was returned from the thread's start function or specified in a call to `pthread_exit`. The only external difference between a thread that terminated "normally" by returning or calling `pthread_exit`, and one that terminated through cancellation, is that a cancelled thread's return value is always `PTHREAD_CANCELLED`. (This is why "cancelled" is not considered a distinct thread state.)

If any other thread is waiting to join with the terminating thread, that thread is awakened. It will return from its call to `pthread_join` with the appropriate return value. Once `pthread_join` has extracted the return value, the terminated thread is detached by `pthread_join`, and may be recycled before the call to `pthread_join` returns. This means that, among other things, the returned value should never be a stack address associated with the terminated thread's stack— the value at that address could be overwritten by the time the caller could use it. In `lifecycle.c`, the main thread will return from the `pthread_join` call at line 23 with the value `NULL`.

❙ `pthread_join` is a convenience, not a rule.

Even when you need a return value from a thread that you create, it is often at least as simple to create the thread detached and devise your own customized return mechanism as it is to use `pthread_join`. For example, if you pass information to a worker thread in some form of structure that another thread can find later, you might have the worker thread simply place the result in that same structure and broadcast a condition variable when done. The Pthreads context for the thread, including the thread identifier, can then be recycled immediately when the thread is done, and you still have the part you really need, the return value, where you can find it easily at any time.

If `pthread_join` does exactly what you want, then by all means use it. But remember that it is nothing more than a convenience for the simplest and most limited model of communicating a thread's results. If it does not do exactly what you need, build your own return mechanism instead of warping your design to fit the limitations of `pthread_join`.

2.2.5 Recycling

If the thread was created with the *detachstate* attribute set to PTHREAD_ CREATE_DETACHED (see Section 5.2.3), or if the thread or some other thread has already called `pthread_detach` for the thread's identifier, then the thread is immediately recycled when it becomes terminated.

If the thread has not been detached when it terminates, it remains in the *terminated* state until the thread's `pthread_t` identifier is passed to `pthread_detach` or `pthread_join`. When either function returns, the thread cannot be accessed again. In `lifecycle.c`, for example, the thread that had run `thread_routine` will be recycled by the time the main thread returns from the `pthread_join` call at line 23.

Recycling releases any system or process resources that weren't released at termination. That includes the storage used for the thread's return value, the stack, memory used to store register state, and so forth. Some of these resources may have been released at termination; it is important to remember that none of it should be accessed from any other thread after termination. For example, if a thread passes a pointer to its stack storage to another thread through shared data, you should treat that information as obsolete from the time the thread that owns the stack terminates.

3 Synchronization

*"That's right!" said the Tiger-lily. "The daisies are worst of all.
When one speaks, they all begin together, and it's
enough to make one wither to hear the way they go on!"*
　　　—Lewis Carroll, Through the Looking-Glass

To write a program of any complexity using threads, you'll need to share data between threads, or cause various actions to be performed in some coherent order across multiple threads. To do this, you need to *synchronize* the activity of your threads.

Section 3.1 describes a few of the basic terms we'll be using to talk about thread synchronization: *critical section* and *invariant*.

Section 3.2 describes the basic Pthreads synchronization mechanism, the mutex.

Section 3.3 describes the *condition variable*, a mechanism that your code can use to communicate changes to the state of *invariants* protected by a mutex.

Section 3.4 completes this chapter on synchronization with some important information about threads and how they view the computer's memory.

3.1 Invariants, critical sections, and predicates

*"I know what you're thinking about,"
said Tweedledum; "but it isn't so, nohow."
"Contrariwise," continued Tweedledee,
"if it was so, it might be; and if it were so, it would be;
but as it isn't, it ain't. That's logic."*
　　　—Lewis Carroll, Through the Looking-Glass

Invariants are assumptions made by a program, especially assumptions about the relationships between sets of variables. When you build a queue package, for example, you need certain data. Each queue has a queue header, which is a pointer to the first queued data element. Each data element includes a pointer to the next data element. But the data isn't all that's important—your queue package relies on relationships between that data. The queue header, for example, must either be NULL or contain a pointer to the first queued data element. Each data element must contain a pointer to the next data element, or NULL if it is the last. Those relationships are the *invariants* of your queue package.

It is hard to write a program that doesn't have invariants, though many of them are subtle. When a program encounters a broken invariant, for example, if it dereferences a queue header containing a pointer to something that is not a valid data element, the program will probably produce incorrect results or fail immediately.

Critical sections (also sometimes called "serial regions") are areas of code that affect a shared state. Since most programmers are trained to think about program *functions* instead of program *data*, you may well find it easier to recognize critical sections than data invariants. However, a critical section can almost always be translated into a data invariant, and vice versa. When you remove an element from a queue, for example, you can see the code performing the removal as a critical section, or you can see the state of the queue as an invariant. Which you see first may depend on how you're thinking about that aspect of your design.

Most invariants can be "broken," and are routinely broken, during isolated areas of code. The trick is to be sure that broken invariants are always repaired before "unsuspecting" code can encounter them. That is a large part of what "synchronization" is all about in an asynchronous program. Synchronization protects your program from broken invariants. If your code locks a mutex whenever it must (temporarily) break an invariant, then other threads that rely on the invariant, and which also lock the mutex, will be delayed until the mutex is unlocked—when the invariant has been restored.

Synchronization is voluntary, and the participants must cooperate for the system to work. The programmers must agree not to fight for (or against) possession of the bailing bucket. The bucket itself does not somehow magically ensure that one and only one programmer bails at any time. Rather, the bucket is a reliable shared token that, if used properly, can allow the programmers to manage their resources effectively.

"Predicates" are logical expressions that describe the state of invariants needed by your code. In English, predicates can be expressed as statements like "the queue is empty" or "the resource is available." A predicate may be a boolean variable with a TRUE or FALSE value, or it may be the result of testing whether a pointer is NULL. A predicate may also be a more complicated expression, such as determining whether a counter is greater than some threshold. A predicate may even be a value returned from some function. For example, you might call select or poll to determine whether a file is ready for input.

3.2 Mutexes

"How are you getting on?" said the Cat,
as soon as there was mouth enough for it to speak with.
Alice waited till the eyes appeared, and then nodded.
"It's no use speaking to it," she thought,
"till its ears have come, or at least one of them."
—Lewis Carroll, *Alice's Adventures in Wonderland*

Most threaded programs need to share some data between threads. There may be trouble if two threads try to access shared data at the same time, because one thread may be in the midst of modifying some data invariant while another acts on the data as if it were consistent. This section is all about protecting the program from that sort of trouble.

The most common and general way to synchronize between threads is to ensure that all memory accesses to the same (or related) data are "mutually exclusive." That means that only one thread is allowed to write at a time—others must wait for their turn. Pthreads provides mutual exclusion using a special form of Edsger Dijkstra's semaphore [*Dijkstra, 1968a*], called a *mutex*. The word *mutex* is a clever combination of "mut" from the word "mutual" and "ex" from the word "exclusion."

Experience has shown that it is easier to use mutexes correctly than it is to use other synchronization models such as a more general semaphore. It is also easy to build any synchronization models using mutexes in combination with condition variables (we'll meet them at the next corner, in Section 3.3). Mutexes are simple, flexible, and can be implemented efficiently.

The programmers' bailing bucket is something like a mutex (Figure 3.1). Both are "tokens" that can be handed around, and used to preserve the integrity of the concurrent system. The bucket can be thought of as protecting the bailing critical section—each programmer accepts the responsibility of bailing while holding the bucket, and of avoiding interference with the current bailer while not holding the bucket. Or, the bucket can be thought of as protecting the invariant that water can be removed by only one programmer at any time.

Synchronization isn't important just when you modify data. You also need synchronization when a thread needs to read data that was written by another thread, if the order in which the data was written matters. As we'll see a little later, in Section 3.4, many hardware systems don't guarantee that one processor will see shared memory accesses in the same order as another processor without a "nudge" from software.

FIGURE 3.1   *Mutex analogy*

Consider, for example, a thread that writes new data to an element in an array, and then updates a max_index variable to indicate that the array element is valid. Now consider another thread, running simultaneously on another processor, that steps through the array performing some computation on each valid element. If the second thread "sees" the new value of max_index before it sees the new value of the array element, the computation would be incorrect. This may seem irrational, but memory systems that work this way can be substantially faster than memory systems that guarantee predictable ordering of memory accesses. A mutex is one general solution to this sort of problem. If each thread locks a mutex around the section of code that's using shared data, only one thread will be able to enter the section at a time.

Figure 3.2 shows a timing diagram of three threads sharing a mutex. Sections of the lines that are above the rounded box labeled "mutex" show where the associated thread does not own the mutex. Sections of the lines that are below the center line of the box show where the associated thread owns the mutex, and sections of the lines hovering above the center line show where the thread is waiting to own the mutex.

Initially, the mutex is unlocked. Thread 1 locks the mutex and, because there is no contention, it succeeds immediately—thread 1's line moves below the center

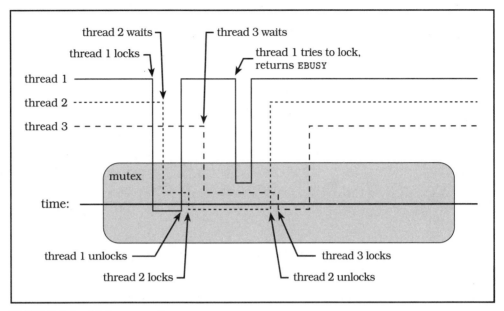

FIGURE 3.2 *Mutex operation*

of the box. Thread 2 then attempts to lock the mutex and, because the mutex is already locked, thread 2 blocks, its line remaining above the center line. Thread 1 unlocks the mutex, unblocking thread 2, which then succeeds in locking the mutex. Slightly later, thread 3 attempts to lock the mutex, and blocks. Thread 1 calls pthread_mutex_trylock to try to lock the mutex and, because the mutex is locked, returns immediately with EBUSY status. Thread 2 unlocks the mutex, which unblocks thread 3 so that it can lock the mutex. Finally, thread 3 unlocks the mutex to complete our example.

3.2.1 Creating and destroying a mutex

```
pthread_mutex_t mutex = PTHREAD_MUTEX_INITIALIZER;
int pthread_mutex_init (
    pthread_mutex_t *mutex, pthread_mutexattr_t *attr);
int pthread_mutex_destroy (pthread_mutex_t *mutex);
```

A mutex is represented in your program by a variable of type pthread_mutex_t. You should never make a copy of a mutex, because the result of using a copied mutex is undefined. You can, however, freely copy a pointer to a mutex so that various functions and threads can use it for synchronization.

Most of the time you'll probably declare mutexes using `extern` or `static` storage class, at "file scope," that is, outside of any function. They should have "normal" (`extern`) storage class if they are used by other files, or `static` storage class if used only within the file that declares the variable. When you declare a static mutex that has default attributes, you should use the `PTHREAD_MUTEX_INITIALIZER` macro, as shown in the `mutex_static.c` program shown next. (You can build and run this program, but don't expect anything interesting to happen, since main is empty.)

■ `mutex_static.c`

```
1  #include <pthread.h>
2  #include "errors.h"
3
4  /*
5   * Declare a structure, with a mutex, statically initialized. This
6   * is the same as using pthread_mutex_init, with the default
7   * attributes.
8   */
9  typedef struct my_struct_tag {
10     pthread_mutex_t    mutex;  /* Protects access to value */
11     int                value;  /* Access protected by mutex */
12  } my_struct_t;
13
14  my_struct_t data = {PTHREAD_MUTEX_INITIALIZER, 0};
15
16  int main (int argc, char *argv[])
17  {
18      return 0;
19  }
```

■ `mutex_static.c`

Often you cannot initialize a mutex statically, for example, when you use `malloc` to create a structure that contains a mutex. Then you will need to call `pthread_mutex_init` to initialize the mutex dynamically, as shown in `mutex_dynamic.c`, the next program. You can also dynamically initialize a mutex that you declare statically—but you must ensure that each mutex is initialized before it is used, and that each is initialized only once. You may initialize it before creating any threads, for example, or by calling `pthread_once` (Section 5.1). Also, if you need to initialize a mutex with nondefault attributes, you must use dynamic initialization (see Section 5.2.1).

■ `mutex_dynamic.c`

```
1  #include <pthread.h>
2  #include "errors.h"
3
```

```
4   /*
5    * Define a structure, with a mutex.
6    */
7   typedef struct my_struct_tag {
8       pthread_mutex_t    mutex;  /* Protects access to value */
9       int                value;  /* Access protected by mutex */
10  } my_struct_t;
11
12  int main (int argc, char *argv[])
13  {
14      my_struct_t *data;
15      int status;
16
17      data = malloc (sizeof (my_struct_t));
18      if (data == NULL)
19          errno_abort ("Allocate structure");
20      status = pthread_mutex_init (&data->mutex, NULL);
21      if (status != 0)
22          err_abort (status, "Init mutex");
23      status = pthread_mutex_destroy (&data->mutex);
24      if (status != 0)
25          err_abort (status, "Destroy mutex");
26      (void)free (data);
27      return status;
28  }
```

■ `mutex_dynamic.c`

It is a good idea to associate a mutex clearly with the data it protects, if possible, by keeping the definition of the mutex and data together. In `mutex_static.c` and `mutex_dynamic.c`, for example, the mutex and the data it protects are defined in the same structure, and line comments document the association.

When you no longer need a mutex that you dynamically initialized by calling `pthread_mutex_init`, you should destroy the mutex by calling `pthread_mutex_destroy`. You do not need to destroy a mutex that was statically initialized using the `PTHREAD_MUTEX_INITIALIZER` macro.

> You can destroy a mutex as soon as you are sure no threads are blocked on the mutex.

It is safe to destroy a mutex when you know that no threads can be blocked on the mutex, and no additional threads will try to lock the mutex. The best way to know this is usually within a thread that has just unlocked the mutex, when program logic ensures that no threads will try to lock the mutex later. When a thread locks a mutex within some heap data structure to remove the structure from a list and free the storage, for example, it is safe (and a good idea) to unlock and destroy the mutex before freeing the storage that the mutex occupies.

3.2.2 Locking and unlocking a mutex

```
int pthread_mutex_lock (pthread_mutex_t *mutex);
int pthread_mutex_trylock (pthread_mutex_t *mutex);
int pthread_mutex_unlock (pthread_mutex_t *mutex);
```

In the simplest case, using a mutex is easy. You lock the mutex by calling either pthread_mutex_lock or pthread_mutex_trylock, do something with the shared data, and then unlock the mutex by calling pthread_mutex_unlock. To make sure that a thread can read consistent values for a series of variables, you need to lock your mutex around any section of code that reads *or* writes those variables.

You cannot lock a mutex when the calling thread already has that mutex locked. The result of attempting to do so may be an error return, or it may be a self-deadlock, with the unfortunate thread waiting forever for itself to unlock the mutex. (If you have access to a system supporting the UNIX98 thread extensions, you can create mutexes of various types, including *recursive* mutexes, which allow a thread to relock a mutex it already owns. The mutex *type* attribute is discussed in Section 10.1.2.)

The following program, alarm_mutex.c, is an improved version of alarm_thread.c (from Chapter 1). It lines up multiple alarm requests in a single "alarm server" thread.

12-17   The alarm_t structure now contains an absolute time, as a standard UNIX time_t, which is the number of seconds from the UNIX Epoch (Jan 1 1970 00:00) to the expiration time. This is necessary so that alarm_t structures can be sorted by "expiration time" instead of merely by the requested number of seconds. In addition, there is a link member to connect the list of alarms.

19-20   The alarm_mutex mutex coordinates access to the list head for alarm requests, called alarm_list. The mutex is statically initialized using default attributes, with the PTHREAD_MUTEX_INITIALIZER macro. The list head is initialized to NULL, or empty.

■ alarm_mutex.c   part 1   definitions

```
1   #include <pthread.h>
2   #include <time.h>
3   #include "errors.h"
4
5   /*
6    * The "alarm" structure now contains the time_t (time since the
7    * Epoch, in seconds) for each alarm, so that they can be
8    * sorted. Storing the requested number of seconds would not be
9    * enough, since the "alarm thread" cannot tell how long it has
10   * been on the list.
11   */
```

```
12  typedef struct alarm_tag {
13      struct alarm_tag    *link;
14      int                 seconds;
15      time_t              time;   /* seconds from EPOCH */
16      char                message[64];
17  } alarm_t;
18
19  pthread_mutex_t alarm_mutex = PTHREAD_MUTEX_INITIALIZER;
20  alarm_t *alarm_list = NULL;
```

■ alarm_mutex.c   part 1   definitions

The code for the alarm_thread function follows. This function is run as a thread, and processes each alarm request in order from the list alarm_list. The thread never terminates—when main returns, the thread simply "evaporates." The only consequence of this is that any remaining alarms will not be delivered—the thread maintains no state that can be seen outside the process.

If you would prefer that the program process all outstanding alarm requests before exiting, you can easily modify the program to accomplish this. The main thread must notify alarm_thread, by some means, that it should terminate when it finds the alarm_list empty. You could, for example, have main set a new global variable alarm_done and then terminate using pthread_exit rather than exit. When alarm_thread finds alarm_list empty and alarm_done set, it would immediately call pthread_exit rather than waiting for a new entry.

29-30   If there are no alarms on the list, alarm_thread needs to block itself, with the mutex unlocked, at least for a short time, so that main will be able to add a new alarm. It does this by setting sleep_time to one second.

31-42   If an alarm is found, it is removed from the list. The current time is retrieved by calling the time function, and it is compared to the requested time for the alarm. If the alarm has already expired, then alarm_thread will set sleep_time to 0. If the alarm has not expired, alarm_thread computes the difference between the current time and the alarm expiration time, and sets sleep_time to that number of seconds.

52-58   The mutex is always unlocked before sleeping or yielding. If the mutex remained locked, then main would be unable to insert a new alarm on the list. That would make the program behave synchronously—the user would have to wait until the alarm expired before doing anything else. (The user would be able to enter a single command, but would not receive another prompt until the next alarm expired.) Calling sleep blocks alarm_thread for the required period of time—it cannot run until the timer expires.

Calling sched_yield instead is slightly different. We'll describe sched_yield in detail later (in Section 5.5.2)—for now, just remember that calling sched_yield will yield the processor to a thread that is ready to run, but will return immediately if there are no *ready* threads. In this case, it means that the main thread will be allowed to process a user command if there's input waiting—but if the user hasn't entered a command, sched_yield will return immediately.

64-67   If the alarm pointer is not NULL, that is, if an alarm was processed from
alarm_list, the function prints a message indicating that the alarm has expired.
After printing the message, it frees the alarm structure. The thread is now ready
to process another alarm.

■ alarm_mutex.c   part 2   alarm_thread

```
1   /*
2    * The alarm thread's start routine.
3    */
4   void *alarm_thread (void *arg)
5   {
6       alarm_t *alarm;
7       int sleep_time;
8       time_t now;
9       int status;
10
11      /*
12       * Loop forever, processing commands. The alarm thread will
13       * be disintegrated when the process exits.
14       */
15      while (1) {
16          status = pthread_mutex_lock (&alarm_mutex);
17          if (status != 0)
18              err_abort (status, "Lock mutex");
19          alarm = alarm_list;
20
21          /*
22           * If the alarm list is empty, wait for one second. This
23           * allows the main thread to run, and read another
24           * command. If the list is not empty, remove the first
25           * item. Compute the number of seconds to wait -- if the
26           * result is less than 0 (the time has passed), then set
27           * the sleep_time to 0.
28           */
29          if (alarm == NULL)
30              sleep_time = 1;
31          else {
32              alarm_list = alarm->link;
33              now = time (NULL);
34              if (alarm->time <= now)
35                  sleep_time = 0;
36              else
37                  sleep_time = alarm->time - now;
38  #ifdef DEBUG
39              printf ("[waiting: %d(%d)\"%s\"]\n", alarm->time,
40                  sleep_time, alarm->message);
41  #endif
42          }
43
```

```
44              /*
45               * Unlock the mutex before waiting, so that the main
46               * thread can lock it to insert a new alarm request. If
47               * the sleep_time is 0, then call sched_yield, giving
48               * the main thread a chance to run if it has been
49               * readied by user input, without delaying the message
50               * if there's no input.
51               */
52              status = pthread_mutex_unlock (&alarm_mutex);
53              if (status != 0)
54                  err_abort (status, "Unlock mutex");
55              if (sleep_time > 0)
56                  sleep (sleep_time);
57              else
58                  sched_yield ();
59
60              /*
61               * If a timer expired, print the message and free the
62               * structure.
63               */
64              if (alarm != NULL) {
65                  printf ("(%d) %s\n", alarm->seconds, alarm->message);
66                  free (alarm);
67              }
68          }
69  }
```

■ alarm_mutex.c   part 2   alarm_thread

And finally, the code for the main program for `alarm_mutex.c`. The basic structure is the same as all of the other versions of the alarm program that we've developed—a loop, reading simple commands from `stdin` and processing each in turn. This time, instead of waiting synchronously as in `alarm.c`, or creating a new asynchronous entity to process each alarm command as in `alarm_fork.c` and `alarm_thread.c`, each request is queued to a server thread, `alarm_thread`. As soon as `main` has queued the request, it is free to read the next command.

8-11   Create the server thread that will process all alarm requests. Although we don't use it, the thread's ID is returned in local variable `thread`.

13-28   Read and process a command, much as in any of the other versions of our alarm program. As in `alarm_thread.c`, the data is stored in a heap structure allocated by `malloc`.

30-32   The program needs to add the alarm request to `alarm_list`, which is shared by both `alarm_thread` and `main`. So we start by locking the mutex that synchronizes access to the shared data, `alarm_mutex`.

33   Because `alarm_thread` processes queued requests, serially, it has no way of knowing how much time has elapsed between reading the command and processing it. Therefore, the alarm structure includes the absolute time of the alarm expiration, which we calculate by adding the alarm interval, in seconds, to the

current number of seconds since the UNIX Epoch, as returned by the time function.

39-49   The alarms are sorted in order of expiration time on the alarm_list queue. The insertion code searches the queue until it finds the first entry with a time greater than or equal to the new alarm's time. The new entry is inserted preceding the located entry. Because alarm_list is a simple linked list, the traversal maintains a current entry pointer (this) and a pointer to the previous entry's link member, or to the alarm_list head pointer (last).

56-59   If no alarm with a time greater than or equal to the new alarm's time is found, then the new alarm is inserted at the end of the list. That is, if the alarm pointer is NULL on exit from the search loop (the last entry on the list always has a link pointer of NULL), the previous entry (or queue head) is made to point to the new entry.

■ alarm_mutex.c   part 3   main

```
1   int main (int argc, char *argv[])
2   {
3       int status;
4       char line[128];
5       alarm_t *alarm, **last, *next;
6       pthread_t thread;
7
8       status = pthread_create (
9           &thread, NULL, alarm_thread, NULL);
10      if (status != 0)
11          err_abort (status, "Create alarm thread");
12      while (1) {
13          printf ("alarm> ");
14          if (fgets (line, sizeof (line), stdin) == NULL) exit (0);
15          if (strlen (line) <= 1) continue;
16          alarm = (alarm_t*)malloc (sizeof (alarm_t));
17          if (alarm == NULL)
18              errno_abort ("Allocate alarm");
19
20          /*
21           * Parse input line into seconds (%d) and a message
22           * (%64[^\n]), consisting of up to 64 characters
23           * separated from the seconds by whitespace.
24           */
25          if (sscanf (line, "%d %64[^\n]",
26              &alarm->seconds, alarm->message) < 2) {
27              fprintf (stderr, "Bad command\n");
28              free (alarm);
29          } else {
30              status = pthread_mutex_lock (&alarm_mutex);
```

```
31                  if (status != 0)
32                      err_abort (status, "Lock mutex");
33              alarm->time = time (NULL) + alarm->seconds;
34
35              /*
36               * Insert the new alarm into the list of alarms,
37               * sorted by expiration time.
38               */
39              last = &alarm_list;
40              next = *last;
41              while (next != NULL) {
42                  if (next->time >= alarm->time) {
43                      alarm->link = next;
44                      *last = alarm;
45                      break;
46                  }
47                  last = &next->link;
48                  next = next->link;
49              }
50              /*
51               * If we reached the end of the list, insert the new
52               * alarm there. ("next" is NULL, and "last" points
53               * to the link field of the last item, or to the
54               * list header).
55               */
56              if (next == NULL) {
57                  *last = alarm;
58                  alarm->link = NULL;
59              }
60  #ifdef DEBUG
61              printf ("[list: ");
62              for (next = alarm_list; next != NULL; next = next->link)
63                  printf ("%d(%d)[\"%s\"] ", next->time,
64                      next->time - time (NULL), next->message);
65              printf ("]\n");
66  #endif
67              status = pthread_mutex_unlock (&alarm_mutex);
68              if (status != 0)
69                  err_abort (status, "Unlock mutex");
70          }
71      }
72  }
```

■ alarm_mutex.c   part 3   main

This simple program has a few severe failings. Although it has the advantage, compared to alarm_fork.c or alarm_thread.c, of using fewer resources, it is less responsive. Once alarm_thread has accepted an alarm request from the queue, it sleeps until that alarm expires. When it fails to find an alarm request on the list, it sleeps for a second anyway, to allow main to accept another alarm command. During all this sleeping, it will fail to notice any alarm requests added to the head of the queue by main, until it returns from sleep.

This problem could be addressed in various ways. The simplest, of course, would be to go back to alarm_thread.c, where a thread was created for each alarm request. That wasn't so bad, since threads are relatively cheap. They're still not as cheap as the alarm_t data structure, however, and we'd like to make efficient programs—not just responsive programs. The best solution is to make use of condition variables for signaling changes in the state of shared data, so it shouldn't be a surprise that you'll be seeing one final version of the alarm program, alarm_cond.c, in Section 3.3.4.

3.2.2.1 Nonblocking mutex locks

When you lock a mutex by calling pthread_mutex_lock, the calling thread will block if the mutex is already locked. Normally, that's what you want. But occasionally you want your code to take some alternate path if the mutex is locked. Your program may be able to do useful work instead of waiting. Pthreads provides the pthread_mutex_trylock function, which will return an error status (EBUSY) instead of blocking if the mutex is already locked.

When you use a nonblocking mutex lock, be careful to *unlock* the mutex only if pthread_mutex_trylock returned with success status. Only the thread that owns a mutex may unlock it. An erroneous call to pthread_mutex_unlock may return an error, or it may unlock the mutex while some other thread relies on having it locked—and that will probably cause your program to break in ways that may be very difficult to debug.

The following program, trylock.c, uses pthread_mutex_trylock to occasionally report the value of a counter—but only when its access does not conflict with the counting thread.

4   This definition controls how long counter_thread holds the mutex while updating the counter. Making this number larger increases the chance that the pthread_mutex_trylock in monitor_thread will occasionally return EBUSY.

14-39   The counter_thread wakes up approximately each second, locks the mutex, and spins for a while, incrementing counter. The counter is therefore increased by SPIN each second.

46-72   The monitor_thread wakes up every three seconds, and tries to lock the mutex. If the attempt fails with EBUSY, monitor_thread counts the failure and waits another three seconds. If the pthread_mutex_trylock succeeds, then monitor_thread prints the current value of counter (scaled by SPIN).

80-88   On Solaris 2.5, call thr_setconcurrency to set the thread concurrency level to 2. This allows the counter_thread and monitor_thread to run concurrently on a uniprocessor. Otherwise, monitor_thread would not run until counter_thread terminated.

■ trylock.c
_____

```
1  #include <pthread.h>
2  #include "errors.h"
3
4  #define SPIN 10000000
5
6  pthread_mutex_t mutex = PTHREAD_MUTEX_INITIALIZER;
7  long counter;
8  time_t end_time;
9
10 /*
11  * Thread start routine that repeatedly locks a mutex and
12  * increments a counter.
13  */
14 void *counter_thread (void *arg)
15 {
16     int status;
17     int spin;
18
19     /*
20      * Until end_time, increment the counter each second. Instead of
21      * just incrementing the counter, it sleeps for another second
22      * with the mutex locked, to give monitor_thread a reasonable
23      * chance of running.
24      */
25     while (time (NULL) < end_time)
26     {
27         status = pthread_mutex_lock (&mutex);
28         if (status != 0)
29             err_abort (status, "Lock mutex");
30         for (spin = 0; spin < SPIN; spin++)
31             counter++;
32         status = pthread_mutex_unlock (&mutex);
33         if (status != 0)
34             err_abort (status, "Unlock mutex");
35         sleep (1);
36     }
37     printf ("Counter is %#lx\n", counter);
38     return NULL;
39 }
40
41 /*
42  * Thread start routine to "monitor" the counter. Every 3
43  * seconds, try to lock the mutex and read the counter. If the
44  * trylock fails, skip this cycle.
45  */
46 void *monitor_thread (void *arg)
```

```
47  {
48      int status;
49      int misses = 0;
50
51
52      /*
53       * Loop until end_time, checking the counter every 3 seconds.
54       */
55      while (time (NULL) < end_time)
56      {
57          sleep (3);
58          status = pthread_mutex_trylock (&mutex);
59          if (status != EBUSY)
60          {
61              if (status != 0)
62                  err_abort (status, "Trylock mutex");
63              printf ("Counter is %ld\n", counter/SPIN);
64              status = pthread_mutex_unlock (&mutex);
65              if (status != 0)
66                  err_abort (status, "Unlock mutex");
67          } else
68              misses++;                /* Count "misses" on the lock */
69      }
70      printf ("Monitor thread missed update %d times.\n", misses);
71      return NULL;
72  }
73
74  int main (int argc, char *argv[])
75  {
76      int status;
77      pthread_t counter_thread_id;
78      pthread_t monitor_thread_id;
79
80  #ifdef sun
81      /*
82       * On Solaris 2.5, threads are not timesliced. To ensure
83       * that our threads can run concurrently, we need to
84       * increase the concurrency level to 2.
85       */
86      DPRINTF (("Setting concurrency level to 2\n"));
87      thr_setconcurrency (2);
88  #endif
89
90      end_time = time (NULL) + 60;        /* Run for 1 minute */
91      status = pthread_create (
92          &counter_thread_id, NULL, counter_thread, NULL);
93      if (status != 0)
94          err_abort (status, "Create counter thread");
```

```
95      status = pthread_create (
96          &monitor_thread_id, NULL, monitor_thread, NULL);
97      if (status != 0)
98          err_abort (status, "Create monitor thread");
99      status = pthread_join (counter_thread_id, NULL);
100     if (status != 0)
101         err_abort (status, "Join counter thread");
102     status = pthread_join (monitor_thread_id, NULL);
103     if (status != 0)
104         err_abort (status, "Join monitor thread");
105     return 0;
106 }
```

■ trylock.c

3.2.3 Using mutexes for atomicity

Invariants, as we saw in Section 3.1, are statements about your program that must always be true. But we also saw that invariants probably aren't always true, and many can't be. To be always true, data composing an invariant must be modified atomically. Yet it is rarely possible to make multiple changes to a program state atomically. It may not even be possible to guarantee that a single change is made atomically, without substantial knowledge of the hardware and architecture and control over the executed instructions.

| "Atomic" means indivisible. But most of the time, we just mean that threads don't see things that would confuse them.

Although some hardware will allow you to set an array element and increment the array index in a single instruction that cannot be interrupted, most won't. Most compilers don't let you control the code to that level of detail even if the hardware can do it, and who wants to write in assembler unless it is *really* important? And, more importantly, most interesting invariants are more complicated than that.

By "atomic," we really mean only that other threads can't accidentally find invariants broken (in intermediate and inconsistent states), even when the threads are running simultaneously on separate processors. There are two basic ways to do that when the hardware doesn't support making the operation indivisible and noninterruptable. One is to detect that you're looking at a broken invariant and try again, or reconstruct the original state. That's hard to do reliably unless you know a lot about the processor architecture and are willing to design nonportable code.

When there is no way to enlist true atomicity in your cause, you need to create your own synchronization. Atomicity is nice, but synchronization will do just as well in most cases. So when you need to update an array element and the index variable atomically, just perform the operation while a mutex is locked.

Whether or not the store and increment operations are performed indivisibly and noninterruptably by the hardware, you know that no cooperating thread can peek until you're done. The transaction is, for all practical purposes, "atomic." The key, of course, is the word "cooperating." Any thread that is sensitive to the invariant must use the same mutex before modifying or examining the state of the invariant.

3.2.4 Sizing a mutex to fit the job

How big is a mutex? No, I don't mean the amount of memory consumed by a `pthread_mutex_t` structure. I'm talking about a colloquial and completely inaccurate meaning that happens to make sense to most people. This colorful usage became common during discussions about modifying existing nonthreaded code to be thread-safe. One relatively simple way to make a library thread-safe is to create a single mutex, lock it on each entry to the library, and unlock it on each exit from the library. The library becomes a single serial region, preventing any conflict between threads. The mutex protecting this big serial region came to be referred to as a "big" mutex, clearly larger in some metaphysical sense than a mutex that protects only a few lines of code.

By irrelevant but inevitable extension, a mutex that protects two variables must be "bigger" than a mutex protecting only a single variable. So we can ask, "How big should a mutex be?" And we can answer only, "As big as necessary, but no bigger."

When you need to protect two shared variables, you have two basic strategies: You can assign a small mutex to each variable, or assign a single larger mutex to both variables. Which is better will depend on a lot of factors. Furthermore, the factors will probably change during development, depending on how many threads need the data and how they use it.

These are the main design factors:

1. Mutexes aren't free. It takes time to lock them, and time to unlock them. Therefore, code that locks fewer mutexes will usually run faster than code that locks more mutexes. So use as few as practical, each protecting as much as makes sense.

2. Mutexes, by their nature, serialize execution. If a lot of threads frequently need to lock a single mutex, the threads will spend most of their time waiting. That's bad for performance. If the pieces of data (or code) protected by the mutex are unrelated, you can often improve performance by splitting the big mutex into several smaller mutexes. Fewer threads will need the smaller mutexes at any time, so they'll spend less time waiting. So use as many as makes sense, each protecting as little as is practical.

3. Items 1 and 2 conflict. But that's nothing new or unique, and you can deal with it once you understand what's going on.

In a complicated program it will usually take some experimentation to get the right balance. Your code will be *simpler* in most cases if you start with large mutexes and then work toward smaller mutexes as experience and performance data show where the heavy contention happens. Simple is good. Don't spend too much time optimizing until you know there's a problem.

On the other hand, in cases where you can tell from the beginning that the algorithms will make heavy contention inevitable, don't oversimplify. Your job will be a lot easier if you start with the necessary mutexes and data structure design rather than adding them later. You will get it wrong sometimes, because, especially when you are working on your first major threaded project, your intuition will not always be correct. Wisdom, as they say, comes from experience, and experience comes from lack of wisdom.

3.2.5 Using more than one mutex

Sometimes one mutex isn't enough. This happens when your code "crosses over" some boundary within the software architecture. For example, when multiple threads will access a queue data structure at the same time, you may need a mutex to protect the queue header and another to protect data within a queue element. When you build a tree structure for threaded programming, you may need a mutex for each node in the tree.

Complications can arise when using more than one mutex at the same time. The worst is deadlock—when each of two threads holds one mutex and needs the other to continue. More subtle problems such as priority inversion can occur when you combine mutexes with priority scheduling. For more information on deadlock, priority inversion, and other synchronization problems, refer to Section 8.1.

3.2.5.1 Lock hierarchy

If you can apply two separate mutexes to completely independent data, do it. You'll almost always win in the end by reducing the time when a thread has to wait for another thread to finish with data that this thread doesn't even need. And if the data is independent you're unlikely to run into many cases where a given function will need to lock both mutexes.

The complications arise when data isn't completely independent. If you have some program invariant—even one that's rarely changed or referenced—that affects data protected by two mutexes, sooner or later you'll need to write code that must lock *both* mutexes at the same time to ensure the integrity of that invariant. If one thread locks `mutex_a` and then locks `mutex_b`, while another thread locks `mutex_b` and then `mutex_a`, you've coded a classic deadlock, as shown in Table 3.1.

First thread	Second thread
`pthread_mutex_lock (&mutex_a);` `pthread_mutex_lock (&mutex_b);`	`pthread_mutex_lock (&mutex_b);` `pthread_mutex_lock (&mutex_a);`

TABLE 3.1   *Mutex deadlock*

Both of the threads shown in Table 3.1 may complete the first step about the same time. Even on a uniprocessor, a thread might complete the first step and then be timesliced (preempted by the system), allowing the second thread to complete its first step. Once this has happened, neither of them can ever complete the second step because each thread needs a mutex that is already locked by the other thread.

Consider these two common solutions to this type of deadlock:

- **Fixed locking hierarchy:** All code that needs both mutex_a and mutex_b must *always* lock mutex_a first and then mutex_b.
- **Try and back off:** After locking the first mutex of some set (which can be allowed to block), use pthread_mutex_trylock to lock additional mutexes in the set. If an attempt fails, release all mutexes in the set and start again.

There are any number of ways to define a fixed locking hierarchy. Sometimes there's an obvious hierarchical order to the mutexes anyway, for example, if one mutex controls a queue header and one controls an element on the queue, you'll probably have to have the queue header locked by the time you need to lock the queue element anyway.

When there's no obvious logical hierarchy, you can create an arbitrary hierarchy; for example, you could create a generic "lock a set of mutexes" function that sorts a list of mutexes in order of their identifier address and locks them in that order. Or you could assign them names and lock them in alphabetical order, or integer sequence numbers and lock them in numerical order.

To some extent, the order doesn't really matter as long as it is always the same. On the other hand, you will rarely need to lock "a set of mutexes" at one time. Function A will need to lock mutex 1, and then call function B, which needs to also lock mutex 2. If the code was designed with a functional locking hierarchy, you will usually find that mutex 1 and mutex 2 are being locked in the proper order, that is, mutex 1 is locked first and then mutex 2. If the code was designed with an arbitrary locking order, especially an order not directly controlled by the code, such as sorting pointers to mutexes initialized in heap structures, you may find that mutex 2 should have been locked before mutex 1.

If the code invariants permit you to unlock mutex 1 safely at this point, you would do better to avoid owning both mutexes at the same time. That is, unlock mutex 1, and then lock mutex 2. If there is a broken invariant that requires mutex 1 to be owned, then mutex 1 cannot be released until the invariant is restored. If this situation is possible, you should consider using a backoff (or "try and back off") algorithm.

"Backoff" means that you lock the first mutex normally, but any additional mutexes in the set that are required by the thread are locked conditionally by calling `pthread_mutex_trylock`. If `pthread_mutex_trylock` returns EBUSY, indicating that the mutex is already locked, you must unlock *all* of the mutexes in the set and start over.

The backoff solution is less efficient than a fixed hierarchy. You may waste a lot of time trying and backing off. On the other hand, you don't need to define and follow strict locking hierarchy conventions, which makes backoff more flexible. You can use the two techniques in combination to minimize the cost of backing off. Follow some fixed hierarchy for well-defined areas of code, but apply a backoff algorithm where a function needs to be more flexible.

The program below, `backoff.c`, demonstrates how to avoid mutex deadlocks by applying a backoff algorithm. The program creates two threads, one running function `lock_forward` and the other running function `lock_backward`. The two threads loop ITERATIONS times, each iteration attempting to lock all of three mutexes in sequence. The `lock_forward` thread locks mutex 0, then mutex 1, then mutex 2, while `lock_backward` locks the three mutexes in the opposite order. Without special precautions, this design will always deadlock quickly (except on a uniprocessor system with a sufficiently long timeslice that either thread can complete before the other has a chance to run).

15   You can see the deadlock by running the program as `backoff 0`. The first argument is used to set the `backoff` variable. If `backoff` is 0, the two threads will use `pthread_mutex_lock` to lock each mutex. Because the two threads are starting from opposite ends, they will crash in the middle, and the program will hang. When `backoff` is nonzero (which it is unless you specify an argument), the threads use `pthread_mutex_trylock`, which enables the backoff algorithm. When the mutex lock fails with EBUSY, the thread will release all mutexes it currently owns, and start over.

16   It is possible that, on some systems, you may not see any mutex collisions, because one thread is always able to lock all mutexes before the other thread has a chance to lock any. You can resolve that problem by setting the `yield_flag` variable, which you do by running the program with a second argument, for example, `backoff 1 1`. When `yield_flag` is 0, which it is unless you specify a second argument, each thread's mutex locking loop may run uninterrupted, preventing a deadlock (at least, on a uniprocessor). When `yield_flag` has a value greater than 0, however, the threads will call `sched_yield` after locking each mutex, ensuring that the other thread has a chance to run. And if you set `yield_flag` to a value less than 0, the threads will `sleep` for one second after locking each mutex, to be *really* sure the other thread has a chance to run.

70–75   After locking all of the three mutexes, each thread reports success, and tells how many times it had to back off before succeeding. On a multiprocessor, or when you've set `yield_flag` to a nonzero value, you'll usually see a lot more nonzero backoff counts. The thread unlocks all three mutexes, in the reverse order of locking, which helps to avoid unnecessary backoffs in other threads. Calling `sched_yield` at the end of each iteration "mixes things up" a little so one thread doesn't always start each iteration first. The `sched_yield` function is described in Section 5.5.2.

■ backoff.c

```
1   #include <pthread.h>
2   #include "errors.h"
3
4   #define ITERATIONS 10
5
6   /*
7    * Initialize a static array of 3 mutexes.
8    */
9   pthread_mutex_t mutex[3] = {
10      PTHREAD_MUTEX_INITIALIZER,
11      PTHREAD_MUTEX_INITIALIZER,
12      PTHREAD_MUTEX_INITIALIZER
13      };
14
15  int backoff = 1;            /* Whether to backoff or deadlock */
16  int yield_flag = 0;             /* 0: no yield, >0: yield, <0: sleep */
17
18  /*
19   * This is a thread start routine that locks all mutexes in
20   * order, to ensure a conflict with lock_reverse, which does the
21   * opposite.
22   */
23  void *lock_forward (void *arg)
24  {
25      int i, iterate, backoffs;
26      int status;
27
28      for (iterate = 0; iterate < ITERATIONS; iterate++) {
29          backoffs = 0;
30          for (i = 0; i < 3; i++) {
31              if (i == 0) {
32                  status = pthread_mutex_lock (&mutex[i]);
33                  if (status != 0)
34                      err_abort (status, "First lock");
35              } else {
36                  if (backoff)
37                      status = pthread_mutex_trylock (&mutex[i]);
38                  else
39                      status = pthread_mutex_lock (&mutex[i]);
40                  if (status == EBUSY) {
41                      backoffs++;
42                      DPRINTF ((
43                          " [forward locker backing off at %d]\n",
44                          i));
45                      for (; i >= 0; i--) {
46                          status = pthread_mutex_unlock (&mutex[i]);
47                          if (status != 0)
```

```
48                             err_abort (status, "Backoff");
49                         }
50                     } else {
51                         if (status != 0)
52                             err_abort (status, "Lock mutex");
53                         DPRINTF ((" forward locker got %d\n", i));
54                     }
55                 }
56                 /*
57                  * Yield processor, if needed to be sure locks get
58                  * interleaved on a uniprocessor.
59                  */
60                 if (yield_flag) {
61                     if (yield_flag > 0)
62                         sched_yield ();
63                     else
64                         sleep (1);
65                 }
66             }
67             /*
68              * Report that we got 'em, and unlock to try again.
69              */
70             printf (
71                 "lock forward got all locks, %d backoffs\n", backoffs);
72             pthread_mutex_unlock (&mutex[2]);
73             pthread_mutex_unlock (&mutex[1]);
74             pthread_mutex_unlock (&mutex[0]);
75             sched_yield ();
76         }
77     return NULL;
78 }
79
80 /*
81  * This is a thread start routine that locks all mutexes in
82  * reverse order, to ensure a conflict with lock_forward, which
83  * does the opposite.
84  */
85 void *lock_backward (void *arg)
86 {
87     int i, iterate, backoffs;
88     int status;
89
90     for (iterate = 0; iterate < ITERATIONS; iterate++) {
91         backoffs = 0;
92         for (i = 2; i >= 0; i--) {
93             if (i == 2) {
94                 status = pthread_mutex_lock (&mutex[i]);
95                 if (status != 0)
96                     err_abort (status, "First lock");
```

```
97                  } else {
98                      if (backoff)
99                          status = pthread_mutex_trylock (&mutex[i]);
100                     else
101                         status = pthread_mutex_lock (&mutex[i]);
102                     if (status == EBUSY) {
103                         backoffs++;
104                         DPRINTF ((
105                             " [backward locker backing off at %d]\n",
106                             i));
107                         for (; i < 3; i++) {
108                             status = pthread_mutex_unlock (&mutex[i]);
109                             if (status != 0)
110                                 err_abort (status, "Backoff");
111                         }
112                     } else {
113                         if (status != 0)
114                             err_abort (status, "Lock mutex");
115                         DPRINTF ((" backward locker got %d\n", i));
116                     }
117                 }
118                 /*
119                  * Yield processor, if needed to be sure locks get
120                  * interleaved on a uniprocessor.
121                  */
122                 if (yield_flag) {
123                     if (yield_flag > 0)
124                         sched_yield ();
125                     else
126                         sleep (1);
127                 }
128             }
129             /*
130              * Report that we got 'em, and unlock to try again.
131              */
132             printf (
133                 "lock backward got all locks, %d backoffs\n", backoffs);
134             pthread_mutex_unlock (&mutex[0]);
135             pthread_mutex_unlock (&mutex[1]);
136             pthread_mutex_unlock (&mutex[2]);
137             sched_yield ();
138         }
139     return NULL;
140 }
141
142 int main (int argc, char *argv[])
143 {
144     pthread_t forward, backward;
```

```
145        int status;
146
147  #ifdef sun
148        /*
149         * On Solaris 2.5, threads are not timesliced. To ensure
150         * that our threads can run concurrently, we need to
151         * increase the concurrency level.
152         */
153        DPRINTF (("Setting concurrency level to 2\n"));
154        thr_setconcurrency (2);
155  #endif
156
157        /*
158         * If the first argument is absent, or nonzero, a backoff
159         * algorithm will be used to avoid deadlock. If the first
160         * argument is zero, the program will deadlock on a lock
161         * "collision."
162         */
163        if (argc > 1)
164            backoff = atoi (argv[1]);
165
166        /*
167         * If the second argument is absent, or zero, the two threads
168         * run "at speed." On some systems, especially uniprocessors,
169         * one thread may complete before the other has a chance to run,
170         * and you won't see a deadlock or backoffs. In that case, try
171         * running with the argument set to a positive number to cause
172         * the threads to call sched_yield() at each lock; or, to make
173         * it even more obvious, set to a negative number to cause the
174         * threads to call sleep(1) instead.
175         */
176        if (argc > 2)
177            yield_flag = atoi (argv[2]);
178        status = pthread_create (
179            &forward, NULL, lock_forward, NULL);
180        if (status != 0)
181            err_abort (status, "Create forward");
182        status = pthread_create (
183            &backward, NULL, lock_backward, NULL);
184        if (status != 0)
185            err_abort (status, "Create backward");
186        pthread_exit (NULL);
187  }
```

■ backoff.c

Whatever type of hierarchy you choose, *document* it, carefully, completely, and
often. Document it in each function that uses any of the mutexes. Document it
where the mutexes are defined. Document it where they are declared in a project

header file. Document it in the project design notes. Write it on your whiteboard. And then tie a string around your finger to be sure that you do not forget.

You are free to unlock the mutexes in whatever order makes the most sense. Unlocking mutexes cannot result in deadlock. In the next section, I will talk about a sort of "overlapping hierarchy" of mutexes, called a "lock chain," where the normal mode of operation is to lock one mutex, lock the next, unlock the first, and so on. If you use a "try and back off" algorithm, however, you should always try to release the mutexes in reverse order. That is, if you lock mutex 1, mutex 2, and then mutex 3, you should unlock mutex 3, then mutex 2, and finally mutex 1. If you unlock mutex 1 and mutex 2 while mutex 3 is still locked, another thread may have to lock both mutex 1 and mutex 2 before finding it cannot lock the entire hierarchy, at which point it will have to unlock mutex 2 and mutex 1, and then retry. Unlocking in reverse order reduces the chance that another thread will need to back off.

3.2.5.2 Lock chaining

"Chaining" is a special case of locking hierarchy, where the scope of two locks overlap. With one mutex locked, the code enters a region where another mutex is required. After successfully locking that second mutex, the first is no longer needed, and can be released. This technique can be very valuable in traversing data structures such as trees or linked lists. Instead of locking the entire data structure with a single mutex, and thereby preventing any parallel access, each node or link has a unique mutex. The traversal code would first lock the queue head, or tree root, find the desired node, lock it, and then release the root or queue head mutex.

Because chaining is a special form of hierarchy, the two techniques are compatible, if you apply them carefully. You might use hierarchical locking when balancing or pruning a tree, for example, and chaining when searching for a specific node.

Apply lock chaining with caution, however. It is exceptionally easy to write code that spends most of its time locking and unlocking mutexes that never exhibit any contention, and that is wasted processor time. Use lock chaining only when multiple threads will almost always be active within different parts of the hierarchy.

3.3 Condition variables

"There's no sort of use in knocking," said the Footman, "and that for two reasons. First, because I'm on the same side of the door as you are: secondly, because they're making such a noise inside, no one could possibly hear you."

—Lewis Carroll, *Alice's Adventures in Wonderland*

FIGURE 3.3 *Condition variable analogy*

A condition variable is used for communicating information about the state of shared data. You would use a condition variable to signal that a queue was no longer empty, or that it had become empty, or that anything else needs to be done or can be done within the shared data manipulated by threads in your program.

Our seafaring programmers use a mechanism much like condition variables to communicate (Figure 3.3). When the rower nudges a sleeping programmer to signal that the sleeping programmer should wake up and start rowing, the original rower "signals a condition." When the exhausted ex-rower sinks into a deep slumber, secure that another programmer will wake him at the appropriate time, he is "waiting on a condition." When the horrified bailer discovers that water is seeping into the boat faster than he can remove it, and he yells for help, he is "broadcasting a condition."

When a thread has mutually exclusive access to some shared state, it may find that there is no more it can do until some other thread changes the state. The state may be correct, and consistent—that is, no invariants are broken—but the current state just doesn't happen to be of interest to the thread. If a thread servicing a queue finds the queue empty, for example, the thread must wait until an entry is added to the queue.

The shared data, for example, the queue, is protected by a mutex. A thread must lock the mutex to determine the current state of the queue, for example, to determine that it is empty. The thread must unlock the mutex before waiting (or no other thread would be able to insert an entry onto the queue), and then it must wait for the state to change. The thread might, for example, by some means block itself so that a thread inserting a new queue entry can find its identifier and awaken it. There is a problem here, though—the thread is running between unlocking and blocking.

If the thread is still running while another thread locks the mutex and inserts an entry onto the queue, that other thread cannot determine that a thread is waiting for the new entry. The waiting thread has already looked at the queue and found it empty, and has unlocked the mutex, so it will now block itself without knowing that the queue is no longer empty. Worse, it may not yet have recorded the fact that it intends to wait, so it may wait forever because the other thread cannot find its identifier. The unlock and wait operations must be atomic, so that no other thread can lock the mutex before the waiter has become blocked, and is in a state where another thread can awaken it.

> ❚ A condition variable wait always returns with the mutex locked.

That's why *condition variables* exist. A condition variable is a "signaling mechanism" associated with a mutex and by extension is also associated with the shared data protected by the mutex. *Waiting* on a condition variable atomically releases the associated mutex and waits until another thread *signals* (to wake one waiter) or *broadcasts* (to wake all waiters) the condition variable. The mutex must always be locked when you wait on a condition variable and, when a thread wakes up from a condition variable wait, it always resumes with the mutex locked.

The shared data associated with a condition variable, for example, the queue "full" and "empty" conditions, are the *predicates* we talked about in Section 3.1. A condition variable is the mechanism your program uses to wait for a predicate to become true, and to communicate to other threads that it might be true. In other words, a condition variable allows threads using the queue to exchange information about the changes to the queue state.

> ❚ Condition variables are for *signaling,* not for mutual exclusion.

Condition variables do not provide mutual exclusion. You need a mutex to synchronize access to the shared data, including the predicate for which you wait. That is why you must specify a mutex when you wait on a condition variable. By making the unlock atomic with the wait, the Pthreads system ensures that no thread can change the predicate after you have unlocked the mutex but before your thread is waiting on the condition variable.

Why isn't the mutex created as part of the condition variable? First, mutexes are used separately from any condition variable as often as they're used with condition variables. Second, it is common for one mutex to have more than one associated condition variable. For example, a queue may be "full" or "empty." Although you may have two condition variables to allow threads to wait for either condition, you must have one and only one mutex to synchronize *all* access to the queue header.

A condition variable should be associated with a single predicate. If you try to share one condition variable between several predicates, or use several condition variables for a single predicate, you're risking deadlock or race problems. There's nothing wrong with doing either, as long as you're careful—but it is easy to confuse your program (computers aren't very smart) and it is usually not worth the risk. I will expound on the details later, but the rules are as follows: First, when you share a condition variable between multiple predicates, you must always *broadcast*, never *signal*; and second, *signal* is more efficient than *broadcast*.

Both the condition variable and the predicate are shared data in your program; they are used by multiple threads, possibly at the same time. Because you're thinking of the condition variable and predicate as being locked together, it is easy to remember that they're always controlled using the same mutex. It is possible (and legal, and often even reasonable) to *signal* or *broadcast* a condition variable without having the mutex locked, but it is safer to have it locked.

Figure 3.4 is a timing diagram showing how three threads, thread 1, thread 2, and thread 3, interact with a condition variable. The rounded box represents the condition variable, and the three lines represent the actions of the three threads.

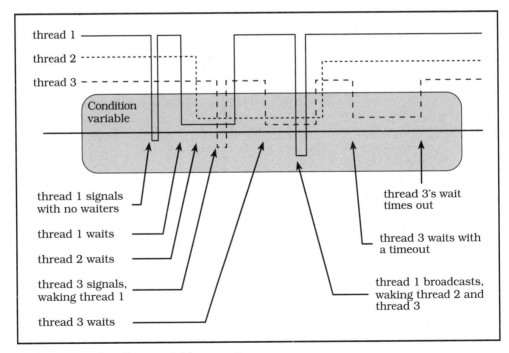

FIGURE 3.4 *Condition variable operation*

When a line goes within the box, it is "doing something" with the condition variable. When a thread's line stops before reaching below the middle line through the box, it is waiting on the condition variable; and when a thread's line reaches below the middle line, it is signaling or broadcasting to awaken waiters.

Thread 1 signals the condition variable, which has no effect since there are no waiters. Thread 1 then waits on the condition variable. Thread 2 also blocks on the condition variable and, shortly thereafter, thread 3 signals the condition variable. Thread 3's signal unblocks thread 1. Thread 3 then waits on the condition variable. Thread 1 broadcasts the condition variable, unblocking both thread 2 and thread 3. Thread 3 waits on the condition variable shortly thereafter, with a timed wait. Some time later, thread 3's wait times out, and the thread awakens.

3.3.1 Creating and destroying a condition variable

```
pthread_cond_t cond = PTHREAD_COND_INITIALIZER;
int pthread_cond_init (pthread_cond_t *cond,
    pthread_condattr_t *condattr);
int pthread_cond_destroy (pthread_cond_t *cond);
```

A condition variable is represented in your program by a variable of type pthread_cond_t. You should never make a copy of a condition variable, because the result of using a copied condition variable is undefined. It would be like telephoning a disconnected number and expecting an answer. One thread could, for example, wait on one copy of the condition variable, while another thread signaled or broadcast the other copy of the condition variable—the waiting thread would not be awakened. You can, however, freely pass pointers to a condition variable so that various functions and threads can use it for synchronization.

Most of the time you'll probably declare condition variables using the extern or static storage class at file scope, that is, outside of any function. They should have normal (extern) storage class if they are used by other files, or static storage class if used only within the file that declares the variable. When you declare a static condition variable that has default attributes, you should use the PTHREAD_COND_INITIALIZER initialization macro, as shown in the following example, cond_static.c.

■   cond_static.c
```
1   #include <pthread.h>
2   #include "errors.h"
3
4   /*
5    * Declare a structure, with a mutex and condition variable,
6    * statically initialized. This is the same as using
```

```
 7      * pthread_mutex_init and pthread_cond_init, with the default
 8      * attributes.
 9      */
10     typedef struct my_struct_tag {
11         pthread_mutex_t    mutex;   /* Protects access to value */
12         pthread_cond_t     cond;    /* Signals change to value */
13         int                value;   /* Access protected by mutex */
14     } my_struct_t;
15
16     my_struct_t data = {
17         PTHREAD_MUTEX_INITIALIZER, PTHREAD_COND_INITIALIZER, 0};
18
19     int main (int argc, char *argv[])
20     {
21         return 0;
22     }
```

■ cond_static.c

| Condition variables and their predicates are "linked"—for best results, treat them that way!

When you declare a condition variable, remember that a condition variable and the associated predicate are "locked together." You may save yourself (or your successor) some confusion by always declaring the condition variable and predicate together, if possible. I recommend that you try to encapsulate a set of invariants and predicates with its mutex and one or more condition variables as members in a structure, and carefully document the association.

Sometimes you cannot initialize a condition variable statically; for example, when you use malloc to create a structure that contains a condition variable. Then you will need to call pthread_cond_init to initialize the condition variable dynamically, as shown in the following example, cond_dynamic.c. You can also dynamically initialize condition variables that you declare statically—but you must ensure that each condition variable is initialized before it is used, and that each is initialized only once. You may initialize it before creating any threads, for example, or by using pthread_once (Section 5.1). If you need to initialize a condition variable with nondefault attributes, you must use dynamic initialization (see Section 5.2.2).

■ cond_dynamic.c

```
1    #include <pthread.h>
2    #include "errors.h"
3
4    /*
5     * Define a structure, with a mutex and condition variable.
6     */
7    typedef struct my_struct_tag {
```

```
 8        pthread_mutex_t      mutex;   /* Protects access to value */
 9        pthread_cond_t       cond;    /* Signals change to value */
10        int                  value;   /* Access protected by mutex */
11    } my_struct_t;
12
13    int main (int argc, char *argv[])
14    {
15        my_struct_t *data;
16        int status;
17
18        data = malloc (sizeof (my_struct_t));
19        if (data == NULL)
20            errno_abort ("Allocate structure");
21        status = pthread_mutex_init (&data->mutex, NULL);
22        if (status != 0)
23            err_abort (status, "Init mutex");
24        status = pthread_cond_init (&data->cond, NULL);
25        if (status != 0)
26            err_abort (status, "Init condition");
27        status = pthread_cond_destroy (&data->cond);
28        if (status != 0)
29            err_abort (status, "Destroy condition");
30        status = pthread_mutex_destroy (&data->mutex);
31        if (status != 0)
32            err_abort (status, "Destroy mutex");
33        (void)free (data);
34        return status;
35    }
```

■ cond_dynamic.c

When you dynamically initialize a condition variable, you should destroy the condition variable when you no longer need it, by calling pthread_cond_destroy. You do not need to destroy a condition variable that was statically initialized using the PTHREAD_COND_INITIALIZER macro.

It is safe to destroy a condition variable when you know that no threads can be blocked on the condition variable, and no additional threads will try to wait on, signal, or broadcast the condition variable. The best way to determine this is usually within a thread that has just successfully broadcast to unblock all waiters, when program logic ensures that no threads will try to use the condition variable later.

When a thread removes a structure containing a condition variable from a list, for example, and then broadcasts to awaken any waiters, it is safe (and also a very good idea) to destroy the condition variable before freeing the storage that the condition variable occupies. The awakened threads should check their wait predicate when they resume, so you must make sure that you don't free resources required for the predicate before they've done so—this may require additional synchronization.

3.3.2 Waiting on a condition variable

```
int pthread_cond_wait (pthread_cond_t *cond,
    pthread_mutex_t *mutex);
int pthread_cond_timedwait (pthread_cond_t *cond,
    pthread_mutex_t *mutex,
    struct timespec *expiration);
```

Each condition variable must be associated with a specific mutex, and with a predicate condition. When a thread waits on a condition variable it must always have the associated mutex locked. Remember that the condition variable wait operation will *unlock* the mutex for you before blocking the thread, and it will *relock* the mutex before returning to your code.

All threads that wait on any one condition variable concurrently (at the same time) must specify the *same* associated mutex. Pthreads does not allow thread 1, for example, to wait on condition variable A specifying mutex A while thread 2 waits on condition variable A specifying mutex B. It is, however, perfectly reasonable for thread 1 to wait on condition variable A specifying mutex A while thread 2 waits on condition variable B specifying mutex A. That is, each condition variable must be associated, at any given time, with only one mutex—but a mutex may have any number of condition variables associated with it.

It is important that you test the predicate after locking the appropriate mutex and before waiting on the condition variable. If a thread signals or broadcasts a condition variable while no threads are waiting, nothing happens. If some other thread calls pthread_cond_wait right after that, it will keep waiting regardless of the fact that the condition variable was just signaled, which means that if a thread waits when it doesn't have to, it may never wake up. Because the mutex remains locked until the thread is blocked on the condition variable, the predicate cannot become set between the predicate test and the wait—the mutex is locked and no other thread can change the shared data, including the predicate.

| Always test your predicate; and then test it again!

It is equally important that you test the predicate again when the thread wakes up. You should always wait for a condition variable in a loop, to protect against program errors, multiprocessor races, and spurious wakeups. The following short program, cond.c, shows how to wait on a condition variable. Proper predicate loops are also shown in all of the examples in this book that use condition variables, for example, alarm_cond.c in Section 3.3.4.

20-37   The wait_thread sleeps for a short time to allow the main thread to reach its condition wait before waking it, sets the shared predicate (data.value), and then signals the condition variable. The amount of time for which wait_thread will sleep is controlled by the hibernation variable, which defaults to one second.

51-52   If the program was run with an argument, interpret the argument as an integer value, which is stored in `hibernation`. This controls the amount of time for
which `wait.thread` will sleep before signaling the condition variable.

68-83   The main thread calls `pthread_cond_timedwait` to wait for up to two seconds
(from the current time). If `hibernation` has been set to a value of greater than two
seconds, the condition wait will time out, returning `ETIMEDOUT`. If `hibernation`
has been set to two, the main thread and `wait_thread` race, and, in principle, the
result could differ each time you run the program. If `hibernation` is set to a value
less than two, the condition wait should not time out.

■ cond.c
───

```
 1  #include <pthread.h>
 2  #include <time.h>
 3  #include "errors.h"
 4
 5  typedef struct my_struct_tag {
 6      pthread_mutex_t    mutex;   /* Protects access to value */
 7      pthread_cond_t     cond;    /* Signals change to value */
 8      int                value;   /* Access protected by mutex */
 9  } my_struct_t;
10
11  my_struct_t data = {
12      PTHREAD_MUTEX_INITIALIZER, PTHREAD_COND_INITIALIZER, 0};
13
14  int hibernation = 1;              /* Default to 1 second */
15
16  /*
17   * Thread start routine. It will set the main thread's predicate
18   * and signal the condition variable.
19   */
20  void *
21  wait_thread (void *arg)
22  {
23      int status;
24
25      sleep (hibernation);
26      status = pthread_mutex_lock (&data.mutex);
27      if (status != 0)
28          err_abort (status, "Lock mutex");
29      data.value = 1;               /* Set predicate */
30      status = pthread_cond_signal (&data.cond);
31      if (status != 0)
32          err_abort (status, "Signal condition");
33      status = pthread_mutex_unlock (&data.mutex);
34      if (status != 0)
35          err_abort (status, "Unlock mutex");
36      return NULL;
37  }
```

```
38
39   int main (int argc, char *argv[])
40   {
41       int status;
42       pthread_t wait_thread_id;
43       struct timespec timeout;
44
45       /*
46        * If an argument is specified, interpret it as the number
47        * of seconds for wait_thread to sleep before signaling the
48        * condition variable.  You can play with this to see the
49        * condition wait below time out or wake normally.
50        */
51       if (argc > 1)
52           hibernation = atoi (argv[1]);
53
54       /*
55        * Create wait_thread.
56        */
57       status = pthread_create (
58           &wait_thread_id, NULL, wait_thread, NULL);
59       if (status != 0)
60           err_abort (status, "Create wait thread");
61
62       /*
63        * Wait on the condition variable for 2 seconds, or until
64        * signaled by the wait_thread. Normally, wait_thread
65        * should signal. If you raise "hibernation" above 2
66        * seconds, it will time out.
67        */
68       timeout.tv_sec = time (NULL) + 2;
69       timeout.tv_nsec = 0;
70       status = pthread_mutex_lock (&data.mutex);
71       if (status != 0)
72           err_abort (status, "Lock mutex");
73
74       while (data.value == 0) {
75           status = pthread_cond_timedwait (
76               &data.cond, &data.mutex, &timeout);
77           if (status == ETIMEDOUT) {
78               printf ("Condition wait timed out.\n");
79               break;
80           }
81           else if (status != 0)
82               err_abort (status, "Wait on condition");
83       }
84
85       if (data.value != 0)
86           printf ("Condition was signaled.\n");
```

```
87        status = pthread_mutex_unlock (&data.mutex);
88        if (status != 0)
89            err_abort (status, "Unlock mutex");
90        return 0;
91  }
```

■ cond.c

There are a lot of reasons why it is a good idea to write code that does not assume the predicate is always true on wakeup, but here are a few of the main reasons:

Intercepted wakeups: Remember that threads are asynchronous. Waking up from a condition variable wait involves locking the associated mutex. But what if some other thread acquires the mutex first? It may, for example, be checking the predicate before waiting itself. It doesn't have to wait, since the predicate is now true. If the predicate is "work available," it will accept the work. When it unlocks the mutex there may be no more work. It would be expensive, and usually counterproductive, to ensure that the latest awakened thread got the work.

Loose predicates: For a lot of reasons it is often easy and convenient to use approximations of actual state. For example, "there may be work" instead of "there is work." It is often much easier to signal or broadcast based on "loose predicates" than on the real "tight predicates." If you always test the tight predicates before and after waiting on a condition variable, you're free to signal based on the loose approximations when that makes sense. And your code will be much more robust when a condition variable is signaled or broadcast accidentally. Use of loose predicates or accidental wakeups may turn out to be a performance issue; but in many cases it won't make a difference.

Spurious wakeups: This means that when you wait on a condition variable, the wait may (occasionally) return when no thread specifically broadcast or signaled that condition variable. Spurious wakeups may sound strange, but on some multiprocessor systems, making condition wakeup completely predictable might substantially slow all condition variable operations. The race conditions that cause spurious wakeups should be considered rare.

It usually takes only a few instructions to retest your predicate, and it is a good programming discipline. Continuing without retesting the predicate could lead to serious application errors that might be difficult to track down later. So don't make assumptions: Always wait for a condition variable in a `while` loop testing the predicate.

You can also use the `pthread_cond_timedwait` function, which causes the wait to end with an ETIMEDOUT status after a certain time is reached. The time is an absolute clock time, using the POSIX.1b `struct timespec` format. The timeout is absolute rather than an interval (or "delta time") so that once you've computed the timeout it remains valid regardless of spurious or intercepted wakeups. Although it might seem easier to use an interval time, you'd have to recompute it every time the thread wakes up, before waiting again—which would require determining how long it had already waited.

When a timed condition wait returns with the ETIMEDOUT error, you should test your predicate before treating the return as an error. If the condition for which you were waiting is true, the fact that it may have taken too long usually isn't important. Remember that a thread always relocks the mutex before returning from a condition wait, even when the wait times out. Waiting for a locked mutex after timeout can cause the timed wait to appear to have taken a lot longer than the time you requested.

3.3.3 Waking condition variable waiters

```
int pthread_cond_signal (pthread_cond_t *cond);
int pthread_cond_broadcast (pthread_cond_t *cond);
```

Once you've got a thread waiting on a condition variable for some predicate, you'll probably want to wake it up. Pthreads provides two ways to wake a condition variable waiter. One is called "signal" and the other is called "broadcast." A signal operation wakes up a single thread waiting on the condition variable, while broadcast wakes up all threads waiting on the condition variable.

The term "signal" is easily confused with the "POSIX signal" mechanisms that allow you to define "signal actions," manipulate "signal masks," and so forth. However, the term "signal," as we use it here, had independently become well established in threading literature, and even in commercial implementations, and the Pthreads working group decided not to change the term. Luckily, there are few situations where we might be tempted to use both terms together—it is a very good idea to avoid using signals in threaded programs when at all possible. If we are careful to say "signal a condition variable" or "POSIX signal" (or "UNIX signal") where there is any ambiguity, we are unlikely to cause anyone severe discomfort.

It is easy to think of "broadcast" as a generalization of "signal," but it is more accurate to think of signal as an optimization of broadcast. Remember that it is never wrong to use broadcast instead of signal since waiters have to account for intercepted and spurious wakes. The only difference, in fact, is efficiency: A broadcast will wake additional threads that will have to test their predicate and resume waiting. But, in general, you can't replace a broadcast with a signal. "When in doubt, broadcast."

Use signal when only one thread needs to wake up to process the changed state, and when *any* waiting thread can do so. If you use one condition variable for several program predicate conditions, you can't use the signal operation; you couldn't tell whether it would awaken a thread waiting for that predicate, or for another predicate. Don't try to get around that by resignaling the condition variable when you find the predicate isn't true. That might not pass on the signal as you expect; a spurious or intercepted wakeup could result in a series of pointless resignals.

If you add a single item to a queue, and only threads waiting for an item to appear are blocked on the condition variable, then you should probably use a signal. That'll wake up a single thread to check the queue and let the others sleep undisturbed, avoiding unnecessary context switches. On the other hand, if you add more than one item to the queue, you will probably need to broadcast. For examples of both broadcast and signal operations on condition variables, check out the "read/write lock" package in Section 7.1.2.

Although you must have the associated mutex locked to wait on a condition variable, you can signal (or broadcast) a condition variable with the associated mutex unlocked if that is more convenient. The advantage of doing so is that, on many systems, this may be more efficient. When a waiting thread awakens, it must first lock the mutex. If the thread awakens while the signaling thread holds the mutex, then the awakened thread must immediately block on the mutex—you've gone through two context switches to get back where you started.*

Weighing on the other side is the fact that, if the mutex is not locked, any thread (not only the one being awakened) can lock the mutex prior to the thread being awakened. This race is one source of intercepted wakeups. A lower-priority thread, for example, might lock the mutex while another thread was about to awaken a very high-priority thread, delaying scheduling of the high-priority thread. If the mutex remains locked while signaling, this cannot happen—the high-priority waiter will be placed before the lower-priority waiter on the mutex, and will be scheduled first.

3.3.4 One final alarm program

It is time for one final version of our simple alarm program. In `alarm_mutex.c`, we reduced resource utilization by eliminating the use of a separate execution context (thread or process) for each alarm. Instead of separate execution contexts, we used a single thread that processed a list of alarms. There was one problem, however, with that approach—it was not responsive to new alarm commands. It had to finish waiting for one alarm before it could detect that another had been entered onto the list with an earlier expiration time, for example, if one entered the commands "10 message 1" followed by "5 message 2."

---

*There is an optimization, which I've called "wait morphing," that moves a thread directly from the condition variable wait queue to the mutex wait queue in this case, without a context switch, when the mutex is locked. This optimization can produce a substantial performance benefit for many applications.

Now that we have added condition variables to our arsenal of threaded programming tools, we will solve that problem. The new version, creatively named `alarm_cond.c`, uses a timed condition wait rather than `sleep` to wait for an alarm expiration time. When `main` inserts a new entry at the head of the list, it signals the condition variable to awaken `alarm_thread` immediately. The `alarm_thread` then requeues the alarm on which it was waiting, to sort it properly with respect to the new entry, and tries again.

20,22 Part 1 shows the declarations for `alarm_cond.c`. There are two additions to this section, compared to `alarm_mutex.c`: a condition variable called `alarm_cond` and the `current_alarm` variable, which allows `main` to determine the expiration time of the alarm on which `alarm_thread` is currently waiting. The `current_alarm` variable is an optimization—`main` does not need to awaken `alarm_thread` unless it is either idle, or waiting for an alarm later than the one `main` has just inserted.

■ `alarm_cond.c`   part 1   declarations

```
 1  #include <pthread.h>
 2  #include <time.h>
 3  #include "errors.h"
 4
 5  /*
 6   * The "alarm" structure now contains the time_t (time since the
 7   * Epoch, in seconds) for each alarm, so that they can be
 8   * sorted. Storing the requested number of seconds would not be
 9   * enough, since the "alarm thread" cannot tell how long it has
10   * been on the list.
11   */
12  typedef struct alarm_tag {
13      struct alarm_tag    *link;
14      int                 seconds;
15      time_t              time;   /* seconds from EPOCH */
16      char                message[64];
17  } alarm_t;
18
19  pthread_mutex_t alarm_mutex = PTHREAD_MUTEX_INITIALIZER;
20  pthread_cond_t alarm_cond = PTHREAD_COND_INITIALIZER;
21  alarm_t *alarm_list = NULL;
22  time_t current_alarm = 0;
```

■ `alarm_cond.c`   part 1   declarations

Part 2 shows the new function `alarm_insert`. This function is nearly the same as the list insertion code from `alarm_mutex.c`, except that it signals the condition variable `alarm_cond` when necessary. I made `alarm_insert` a separate function because now it needs to be called from two places—once by `main` to insert a new alarm, and now also by `alarm_thread` to reinsert an alarm that has been "preempted" by a new earlier alarm.

9-14   I have recommended that mutex locking protocols be documented, and here is
           an example: The `alarm_insert` function points out explicitly that it must be
           called with the `alarm_mutex` locked.

48-53   If `current_alarm` (the time of the next alarm expiration) is 0, then the `alarm_`
           `thread` is not aware of any outstanding alarm requests, and is waiting for new
           work. If `current_alarm` has a time greater than the expiration time of the new
           alarm, then `alarm_thread` is not planning to look for new work soon enough to
           handle the new alarm. In either case, signal the `alarm_cond` condition variable so
           that `alarm_thread` will wake up and process the new alarm.

■ alarm_cond.c   part 2   alarm_insert

```
1  /*
2   * Insert alarm entry on list, in order.
3   */
4  void alarm_insert (alarm_t *alarm)
5  {
6      int status;
7      alarm_t **last, *next;
8
9      /*
10      * LOCKING PROTOCOL:
11      *
12      * This routine requires that the caller have locked the
13      * alarm_mutex!
14      */
15     last = &alarm_list;
16     next = *last;
17     while (next != NULL) {
18         if (next->time >= alarm->time) {
19             alarm->link = next;
20             *last = alarm;
21             break;
22         }
23         last = &next->link;
24         next = next->link;
25     }
26     /*
27      * If we reached the end of the list, insert the new alarm
28      * there.  ("next" is NULL, and "last" points to the link
29      * field of the last item, or to the list header.)
30      */
31     if (next == NULL) {
32         *last = alarm;
33         alarm->link = NULL;
34     }
35 #ifdef DEBUG
36     printf ("[list: ");
```

```
37        for (next = alarm_list; next != NULL; next = next->link)
38            printf ("%d(%d)[\"%s\"] ", next->time,
39                next->time - time (NULL), next->message);
40        printf ("]\n");
41  #endif
42        /*
43         * Wake the alarm thread if it is not busy (that is, if
44         * current_alarm is 0, signifying that it's waiting for
45         * work), or if the new alarm comes before the one on
46         * which the alarm thread is waiting.
47         */
48        if (current_alarm == 0 || alarm->time < current_alarm) {
49            current_alarm = alarm->time;
50            status = pthread_cond_signal (&alarm_cond);
51            if (status != 0)
52                err_abort (status, "Signal cond");
53        }
54  }
```

■ alarm_cond.c   part 2   alarm_insert

Part 3 shows the alarm_thread function, the start function for the "alarm server" thread. The general structure of alarm_thread is very much like the alarm_thread in alarm_mutex.c. The differences are due to the addition of the condition variable.

26-31   If the alarm_list is empty, alarm_mutex.c could do nothing but sleep anyway, so that main would be able to process a new command. The result was that it could not see a new alarm request for at least a full second. Now, alarm_thread instead waits on the alarm_cond condition variable, with no timeout. It will "sleep" until you enter a new alarm command, and then main will be able to awaken it immediately. Setting current_alarm to 0 tells main that alarm_thread is idle. Remember that pthread_cond_wait unlocks the mutex before waiting, and relocks the mutex before returning to the caller.

35   The new variable expired is initialized to 0; it will be set to 1 later if the timed condition wait expires. This makes it a little easier to decide whether to print the current alarm's message at the bottom of the loop.

36-42   If the alarm we've just removed from the list hasn't already expired, then we need to wait for it. Because we're using a timed condition wait, which requires a POSIX.1b struct timespec, rather than the simple integer time required by sleep, we convert the expiration time. This is easy, because a struct timespec has two members—tv_sec is the number of seconds since the Epoch, which is exactly what we already have from the time function, and tv_nsec is an additional count of nanoseconds. We will just set tv_nsec to 0, since we have no need of the greater resolution.

43   Record the expiration time in the current_alarm variable so that main can determine whether to signal alarm_cond when a new alarm is added.

44-53   Wait until either the current alarm has expired, or `main` requests that `alarm_`
          `thread` look for a new, earlier alarm. Notice that the predicate test is split here,
          for convenience. The expression in the while statement is only half the predicate,
          detecting that `main` has changed `current_alarm` by inserting an earlier timer.
          When the timed wait returns `ETIMEDOUT`, indicating that the current alarm has
          expired, we exit the while loop with a `break` statement at line 49.

54-55   If the while loop exited when the current alarm had not expired, `main` must
          have asked `alarm_thread` to process an earlier alarm. Make sure the current
          alarm isn't lost by reinserting it onto the list.

57   If we remove from `alarm_list` an alarm that has already expired, just set the
          expired variable to 1 to ensure that the message is printed.

■ `alarm_cond.c`   part 3   `alarm_routine`

```
1   /*
2    * The alarm thread's start routine.
3    */
4   void *alarm_thread (void *arg)
5   {
6       alarm_t *alarm;
7       struct timespec cond_time;
8       time_t now;
9       int status, expired;
10
11      /*
12       * Loop forever, processing commands. The alarm thread will
13       * be disintegrated when the process exits. Lock the mutex
14       * at the start -- it will be unlocked during condition
15       * waits, so the main thread can insert alarms.
16       */
17      status = pthread_mutex_lock (&alarm_mutex);
18      if (status != 0)
19          err_abort (status, "Lock mutex");
20      while (1) {
21          /*
22           * If the alarm list is empty, wait until an alarm is
23           * added. Setting current_alarm to 0 informs the insert
24           * routine that the thread is not busy.
25           */
26          current_alarm = 0;
27          while (alarm_list == NULL) {
28              status = pthread_cond_wait (&alarm_cond, &alarm_mutex);
29              if (status != 0)
30                  err_abort (status, "Wait on cond");
31          }
32          alarm = alarm_list;
33          alarm_list = alarm->link;
34          now = time (NULL);
```

```
35              expired = 0;
36              if (alarm->time > now) {
37  #ifdef DEBUG
38                  printf ("[waiting: %d(%d)\"%s\"]\n", alarm->time,
39                      alarm->time - time (NULL), alarm->message);
40  #endif
41                  cond_time.tv_sec = alarm->time;
42                  cond_time.tv_nsec = 0;
43                  current_alarm = alarm->time;
44                  while (current_alarm == alarm->time) {
45                      status = pthread_cond_timedwait (
46                          &alarm_cond, &alarm_mutex, &cond_time);
47                      if (status == ETIMEDOUT) {
48                          expired = 1;
49                          break;
50                      }
51                      if (status != 0)
52                          err_abort (status, "Cond timedwait");
53                  }
54                  if (!expired)
55                      alarm_insert (alarm);
56              } else
57                  expired = 1;
58              if (expired) {
59                  printf ("(%d) %s\n", alarm->seconds, alarm->message);
60                  free (alarm);
61              }
62          }
63  }
```

■ alarm_cond.c   part 3   alarm_routine

Part 4 shows the final section of alarm_cond.c, the main program. It is nearly identical to the main function from alarm_mutex.c.

38   Because the condition variable signal operation is built into the new alarm_insert function, we call alarm_insert rather than inserting a new alarm directly.

■ alarm_cond.c   part 4   main

```
1  int main (int argc, char *argv[])
2  {
3      int status;
4      char line[128];
5      alarm_t *alarm;
6      pthread_t thread;
7
8      status = pthread_create (
9          &thread, NULL, alarm_thread, NULL);
```

```
10        if (status != 0)
11            err_abort (status, "Create alarm thread");
12        while (1) {
13            printf ("Alarm> ");
14            if (fgets (line, sizeof (line), stdin) == NULL) exit (0);
15            if (strlen (line) <= 1) continue;
16            alarm = (alarm_t*)malloc (sizeof (alarm_t));
17            if (alarm == NULL)
18                errno_abort ("Allocate alarm");
19
20            /*
21             * Parse input line into seconds (%d) and a message
22             * (%64[^\n]), consisting of up to 64 characters
23             * separated from the seconds by whitespace.
24             */
25            if (sscanf (line, "%d %64[^\n]",
26                &alarm->seconds, alarm->message) < 2) {
27                fprintf (stderr, "Bad command\n");
28                free (alarm);
29            } else {
30                status = pthread_mutex_lock (&alarm_mutex);
31                if (status != 0)
32                    err_abort (status, "Lock mutex");
33                alarm->time = time (NULL) + alarm->seconds;
34                /*
35                 * Insert the new alarm into the list of alarms,
36                 * sorted by expiration time.
37                 */
38                alarm_insert (alarm);
39                status = pthread_mutex_unlock (&alarm_mutex);
40                if (status != 0)
41                    err_abort (status, "Unlock mutex");
42            }
43        }
44  }
```

■ alarm_cond.c   part 4   main

3.4 Memory visibility between threads

The moment Alice appeared, she was appealed to by all three to settle the question, and they repeated their arguments to her, though, as they all spoke at once, she found it very hard to make out exactly what they said.

—Lewis Carroll, Alice's Adventures in Wonderland

In this chapter we have seen how you should use mutexes and condition variables to synchronize (or "coordinate") thread activities. Now we'll journey off on a tangent, for just a few pages, and see what is really meant by "synchronization" in the world of threads. It is more than making sure two threads don't write to the same location at the same time, although that's part of it. As the title of this section implies, it is about how threads see the computer's memory.

Pthreads provides a few basic rules about memory visibility. You can count on all implementations of the standard to follow these rules:

1. Whatever memory values a thread can see when it calls `pthread_create` can also be seen by the new thread when it starts. Any data written to memory after the call to `pthread_create` may not necessarily be seen by the new thread, even if the write occurs before the thread starts.

2. Whatever memory values a thread can see when it unlocks a mutex, either directly or by waiting on a condition variable, can also be seen by any thread that later locks the same mutex. Again, data written after the mutex is unlocked may not necessarily be seen by the thread that locks the mutex, even if the write occurs before the lock.

3. Whatever memory values a thread can see when it terminates, either by cancellation, returning from its start function, or by calling `pthread_exit`, can also be seen by the thread that joins with the terminated thread by calling `pthread_join`. And, of course, data written after the thread terminates may not necessarily be seen by the thread that joins, even if the write occurs before the join.

4. Whatever memory values a thread can see when it signals or broadcasts a condition variable can also be seen by any thread that is awakened by that signal or broadcast. And, one more time, data written after the signal or broadcast may not necessarily be seen by the thread that wakes up, even if the write occurs before it awakens.

Figures 3.5 and 3.6 demonstrate some of the consequences. So what should you, as a programmer, do?

First, where possible make sure that only one thread will ever access a piece of data. A thread's registers can't be modified by another thread. A thread's stack and heap memory a thread allocates is private unless the thread communicates pointers to that memory to other threads. Any data you put in `register` or `auto` variables can therefore be read at a later time with no more complication than in a completely synchronous program. Each thread *is* synchronous with itself. The less data you share between threads, the less work you have to do.

Second, any time two threads need to access the same data, you have to apply one of the Pthreads memory visibility rules, which, in most cases, means using a mutex. This is not only to protect against multiple writes—even when a thread only reads data it must use a mutex to ensure that it sees the most recent value of the data written while the mutex was locked.

This example does everything correctly. The left-hand code (running in thread A) sets the value of several variables while it has a mutex locked. The right-hand code (running in thread B) reads those values, also while holding the mutex.

Thread A	Thread B
```pthread_mutex_lock (&mutex1); variableA = 1; variableB = 2; pthread_mutex_unlock (&mutex1);```	```pthread_mutex_lock (&mutex1); localA = variableA; localB = variableB; pthread_mutex_unlock (&mutex1);```

Rule 2: visibility from `pthread_mutex_unlock` to `pthread_mutex_lock`. When thread B returns from `pthread_mutex_lock`, it will see the same values for `variableA` and `variableB` that thread A had seen at the time it called `pthread_mutex_unlock`. That is, 1 and 2, respectively.

FIGURE 3.5 *Correct memory visibility*

This example shows an error. The left-hand code (running in thread A) sets the value of variables after unlocking the mutex. The right-hand code (running in thread B) reads those values while holding the mutex.

Thread A	Thread B
```pthread_mutex_lock (&mutex1); variableA = 1; pthread_mutex_unlock (&mutex1); variableB = 2;```	```pthread_mutex_lock (&mutex1); localA = variableA; localB = variableB; pthread_mutex_unlock (&mutex1);```

Rule 2: visibility from `pthread_mutex_unlock` to `pthread_mutex_lock`. When thread B returns from `pthread_mutex_lock`, it will see the same values for `variableA` and `variableB` that thread A had seen at the time it called `pthread_mutex_unlock`. That is, it will see the value 1 for `variableA`, but may not see the value 2 for `variableB` since that was written after the mutex was unlocked.

FIGURE 3.6 *Incorrect memory visibility*

As the rules state, there are specific cases where you do not need to use a mutex to ensure visibility. If one thread sets a global variable, and then creates a new thread that reads the same variable, you know that the new thread will not see an old value. But if you create a thread and *then* set some variable that the new thread reads, the thread may not see the new value, even if the creating thread succeeds in writing the new value before the new thread reads it.

> Warning! We are now descending below the Pthreads API into details
> of hardware memory architecture that you may prefer not to know. You
> may want to skip this explanation for now and come back later.

If you are willing to just trust me on all that (or if you've had enough for now), you may now skip past the end of this section. This book is not about multiprocessor memory architecture, so I will just skim the surface—but even so, the details are a little deep, and if you don't care right now, you do not need to worry about them yet. You will probably want to come back later and read the rest, though, when you have some time.

In a single-threaded, fully synchronous program, it is "safe" to read or write any memory at any time. That is, if the program writes a value to some memory address, and later reads from that memory address, it will always receive the last value that it wrote to that address.

When you add asynchronous behavior (which includes multiprocessors) to the program, the assumptions about memory visibility become more complicated. For example, an asynchronous signal could occur at any point in the program's execution. If the program writes a value to memory, a signal handler runs and writes a different value to the same memory address, when the main program resumes and reads the value, it may not receive the value it wrote.

That's not usually a major problem, because you go to a lot of trouble to declare and use signal handlers. They run "specialized" code in a distinctly different environment from the main program. Experienced programmers know that they should write global data only with extreme care, and it is possible to keep track of what they do. If that becomes awkward, you block the signal around areas of code that use the global data.

When you add multiple threads to the program the asynchronous code is no longer special. Each thread runs normal program code, and all in the same unrestricted environment. You can hardly ever be sure you always know what each thread may be doing. It is likely that they will all read and write some of the same data. Your threads may run at unpredictable times or even simultaneously on different processors. And that's when things get interesting.

By the way, although we are talking about programming with multiple threads, none of the problems outlined in this section is specific to threads. Rather, they are artifacts of memory architecture design, and they apply to any situation where two "things" independently access the same memory. The two things may be threads running on separate processors, but they could instead be processes running on separate processors and using shared memory. Or one "thing" might be code running on a uniprocessor, while an independent I/O controller reads or writes the same memory.

> A memory address can hold only one value at a time; don't let threads
> "race" to get there first.

When two threads write different values to the same memory address, one after the other, the final state of memory is the same as if a single thread had written those two values in the same sequence. Either way only one value remains in memory. The problem is that it becomes difficult to know which write occurred last. Measuring some absolute external time base, it may be obvious that "processor B" wrote the value "2" several microseconds after "processor A" wrote the value "1." That doesn't mean the final state of memory will have a "2."

Why? Because we haven't said anything about how the machine's cache and memory bus work. The processors probably have cache memory, which is just fast, local memory used to keep quickly accessible copies of data that were recently read from main memory. In a write–back cache system, data is initially written only to cache, and copied ("flushed") to main memory at some later time. In a machine that doesn't guarantee read/write ordering, each cache block may be written whenever the processor finds it convenient. If two processors write different values to the same memory address, each processor's value will go into its own cache. Eventually both values will be written to main memory, but at essentially random times, not directly related to the order in which the values were written to the respective processor caches.

Even two writes from within a single thread (processor) need not appear in memory in the same order. The memory controller may find it faster, or just more convenient, to write the values in "reverse" order, as shown in Figure 3.7. They may have been cached in different cache blocks, for example, or interleaved to different memory banks. In general, there's no way to make a program aware of these effects. If there was, a program that relied on them might not run correctly on a different model of the same processor family, much less on a different type of computer.

The problems aren't restricted to two threads *writing* memory. Imagine that one thread writes a value to a memory address on one processor, and then another thread reads from that memory address on another processor. It may seem obvious that the thread will see the last value written to that address, and on some hardware that will be true. This is sometimes called "memory coherence" or "read/write ordering." But it is complicated to ensure that sort of synchronization between processors. It slows the memory system and the overhead provides no benefit to most code. Many modern computers (usually among the fastest) don't guarantee any ordering of memory accesses between different processors, unless the program uses special instructions commonly known as *memory barriers*.

Time	Thread 1	Thread 2
t	write "1" to address 1 (cache)	
t+1	write "2" to address 2 (cache)	read "0" from address 1
t+2	cache system flushes address 2	
t+3		read "2" from address 2
t+4	cache system flushes address 1	

FIGURE 3.7 *Memory ordering without synchronization*

Memory accesses in these computers are, at least in principle, queued to the memory controller, and may be processed in whatever order becomes most efficient. A read from an address that is not in the processor's cache may be held waiting for the cache fill, while later reads complete. A write to a "dirty" cache line, which requires that old data be flushed, may be held while later writes complete. A memory barrier ensures that all memory accesses that were initiated by the processor prior to the memory barrier have completed before any memory accesses initiated after the memory barrier can complete.

❚ A "memory barrier" is a moving wall, not a "cache flush" command.

A common misconception about memory barriers is that they "flush" values to main memory, thus ensuring that the values are visible to other processors. That is not the case, however. What memory barriers do is ensure an order between sets of operations. If each memory access is an item in a queue, you can think of a memory barrier as a special queue token. Unlike other memory accesses, however, the memory controller cannot remove the barrier, or look past it, until it has completed all previous accesses.

A mutex lock, for example, begins by locking the mutex, and completes by issuing a memory barrier. The result is that any memory accesses issued while the mutex is locked cannot complete before other threads can see that the mutex was locked. Similarly, a mutex unlock begins by issuing a memory barrier and completes by unlocking the mutex, ensuring that memory accesses issued while the mutex is locked cannot complete after other threads can see that the mutex is unlocked.

This memory barrier model is the logic behind my description of the Pthreads memory rules. For each of the rules, we have a "source" event, such as a thread calling `pthread_mutex_unlock`, and a "destination" event, such as another thread returning from `pthread_mutex_lock`. The passage of "memory view" from the first to the second occurs because of the memory barriers carefully placed in each.

Even without read/write ordering and memory barriers, it may seem that writes to a single memory address must be atomic, meaning that another thread will always see either the intact original value or the intact new value. But that's not always true, either. Most computers have a natural memory granularity, which depends on the organization of memory and the bus architecture. Even if the processor naturally reads and writes 8-bit units, memory transfers may occur in 32- or 64-bit "memory units."

That may mean that 8-bit writes aren't atomic with respect to other memory operations that overlap the same 32- or 64-bit unit. Most computers write the full memory unit (say, 32 bits) that contains the data you're modifying. If two threads write different 8-bit values within the same 32-bit memory unit, the result may be that the last thread to write the memory unit specifies the value of both bytes, overwriting the value supplied by the first writer. Figure 3.8 shows this effect.

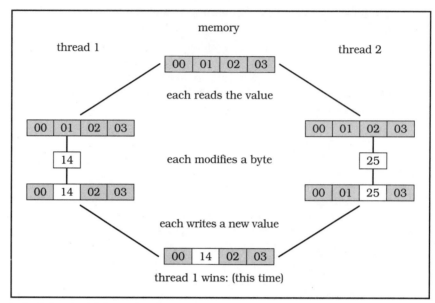

FIGURE 3.8   *Memory conflict*

If a variable crosses the boundary between memory units, which can happen if the machine supports unaligned memory access, the computer may have to send the data in two bus transactions. An unaligned 32-bit value, for example, may be sent by writing the two adjacent 32-bit memory units. If either memory unit involved in the transaction is simultaneously written from another processor, half of the value may be lost. This is called "word tearing," and is shown in Figure 3.9.

We have finally returned to the advice at the beginning of this section: If you want to write portable Pthreads code, you will always guarantee correct memory visibility by using the Pthreads memory visibility rules instead of relying on any assumptions regarding the hardware or compiler behavior. But now, at the bottom of the section, you have some understanding of why this is true. For a substantially more in-depth treatment of multiprocessor memory architecture, refer to *UNIX Systems for Modern Architectures* [Schimmel, 1994].

Figure 3.10 shows the same sequence as Figure 3.7, but it uses a mutex to ensure the desired read/write ordering. Figure 3.10 does not show the cache flush steps that are shown in Figure 3.7, because those steps are no longer relevant. Memory visibility is guaranteed by passing mutex ownership in steps t+3 and t+4, through the associated memory barriers. That is, when thread 2 has

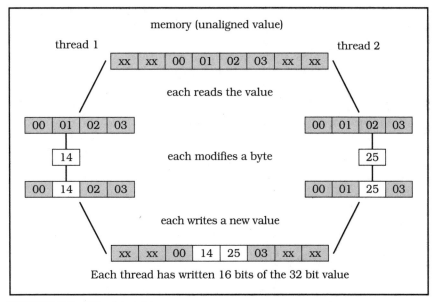

FIGURE 3.9 *Word tearing*

successfully locked the mutex previously unlocked by thread 1, thread 2 is guaranteed to see memory values "at least as recent" as the values visible to thread 1 at the time it unlocked the mutex.

Time	Thread 1	Thread 2
t	lock mutex (memory barrier)	
t+1	write "1" to address 1 (cache)	
t+2	write "2" to address 2 (cache)	
t+3	(memory barrier) unlock mutex	
t+4		lock mutex (memory barrier)
t+5		read "1" from address 1
t+6		read "2" from address 2
t+7		(memory barrier) unlock mutex

FIGURE 3.10 *Memory ordering with synchronization*

4 A few ways to use threads

"They were obliged to have him with them," the Mock Turtle said.
"No wise fish would go anywhere without a porpoise."
"Wouldn't it, really?" said Alice, in a tone of great surprise.
"Of course not," said the Mock Turtle. "Why, if a fish came to me,
and told me he was going on a journey, I should say 'With what porpoise?'"
—Lewis Carroll, *Alice's Adventures in Wonderland*

During the introduction to this book, I mentioned some of the ways you can structure a threaded solution to a problem. There are infinite variations, but the primary models of threaded programming are shown in Table 4.1.

Pipeline	Each thread repeatedly performs the same operation on a sequence of data sets, passing each result to another thread for the next step. This is also known as an "assembly line."
Work crew	Each thread performs an operation on its own data. Threads in a work crew may all perform the same operation, or each a separate operation, but they always proceed independently.
Client/server	A client "contracts" with an independent server for each job. Often the "contract" is anonymous—a request is made through some interface that queues the work item.

TABLE 4.1   *Thread programming models*

All of these models can be combined in arbitrary ways and modified beyond all recognition to fit individual situations. A step in a pipeline could involve requesting a service from a server thread, and the server might use a work crew, and one or more workers in the crew might use a pipeline. Or a parallel search "engine" might initiate several threads, each trying a different search algorithm.

4.1 Pipeline

"I want a clean cup," interrupted the Hatter: "let's all move one place on."
He moved on as he spoke, and the Dormouse followed him: the March Hare
moved into the Dormouse's place, and Alice rather unwillingly took the
place of the March Hare. The Hatter was the only one who got any
advantage from the change; and Alice was a good deal worse off than
before, as the March Hare had just upset the milk-jug into his plate.
—*Lewis Carroll, Alice's Adventures in Wonderland*

In pipelining, a stream of "data items" is processed serially by an ordered set
of threads (Figure 4.1). Each thread performs a specific operation on each item in
sequence, passing the data on to the next thread in the pipeline.

For example, the data might be a scanned image, and thread A might process
an image array, thread B might search the processed data for a specific set of features, and thread C might collect the serial stream of search results from thread B
into a report. Or each thread might perform a single step in some sequence of
modifications on the data.

The following program, called `pipe.c`, shows the pieces of a simple pipeline
program. Each thread in the pipeline increments its input value by 1 and passes
it to the next thread. The main program reads a series of "command lines" from
`stdin`. A command line is either a number, which is fed into the beginning of the
pipeline, or the character "=," which causes the program to read the next result
from the end of the pipeline and print it to `stdout`.

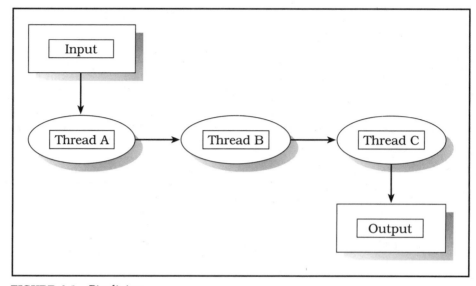

FIGURE 4.1 *Pipelining*

9-17   Each stage of a pipeline is represented by a variable of type `stage_t`. `stage_t` contains a `mutex` to synchronize access to the stage. The `avail` condition variable is used to signal a stage that data is ready for it to process, and each stage signals its own `ready` condition variable when it is ready for new data. The `data` member is the data passed from the previous stage, `thread` is the thread operating this stage, and `next` is a pointer to the following stage.

23-29   The `pipe_t` structure describes a pipeline. It provides pointers to the first and last stage of a pipeline. The first stage, `head`, represents the first thread in the pipeline. The last stage, `tail`, is a special `stage_t` that has no thread—it is a place to store the final result of the pipeline.

■ pipe.c   part 1   definitions

```
1   #include <pthread.h>
2   #include "errors.h"
3
4   /*
5    * Internal structure describing a "stage" in the
6    * pipeline. One for each thread, plus a "result
7    * stage" where the final thread can stash the value.
8    */
9   typedef struct stage_tag {
10      pthread_mutex_t     mutex;          /* Protect data */
11      pthread_cond_t      avail;          /* Data available */
12      pthread_cond_t      ready;          /* Ready for data */
13      int                 data_ready;     /* Data present */
14      long                data;           /* Data to process */
15      pthread_t           thread;         /* Thread for stage */
16      struct stage_tag    *next;          /* Next stage */
17  } stage_t;
18
19  /*
20   * External structure representing the entire
21   * pipeline.
22   */
23  typedef struct pipe_tag {
24      pthread_mutex_t     mutex;          /* Mutex to protect pipe */
25      stage_t             *head;          /* First stage */
26      stage_t             *tail;          /* Final stage */
27      int                 stages;         /* Number of stages */
28      int                 active;         /* Active data elements */
29  } pipe_t;
```

■ pipe.c   part 1   definitions

Part 2 shows `pipe_send`, a utility function used to start data along a pipeline, and also called by each stage to pass data to the next stage.

17-23   It begins by waiting on the specified pipeline stage's `ready` condition variable until it can accept new data.

28-30   Store the new data value, and then tell the stage that data is available.

■ pipe.c   part 2   pipe_send

```
1   /*
2    * Internal function to send a "message" to the
3    * specified pipe stage. Threads use this to pass
4    * along the modified data item.
5    */
6   int pipe_send (stage_t *stage, long data)
7   {
8       int status;
9
10      status = pthread_mutex_lock (&stage->mutex);
11      if (status != 0)
12          return status;
13      /*
14       * If there's data in the pipe stage, wait for it
15       * to be consumed.
16       */
17      while (stage->data_ready) {
18          status = pthread_cond_wait (&stage->ready, &stage->mutex);
19          if (status != 0) {
20              pthread_mutex_unlock (&stage->mutex);
21              return status;
22          }
23      }
24
25      /*
26       * Send the new data
27       */
28      stage->data = data;
29      stage->data_ready = 1;
30      status = pthread_cond_signal (&stage->avail);
31      if (status != 0) {
32          pthread_mutex_unlock (&stage->mutex);
33          return status;
34      }
35      status = pthread_mutex_unlock (&stage->mutex);
36      return status;
37  }
```

■ pipe.c   part 2   pipe_send

Part 3 shows `pipe_stage`, the start function for each thread in the pipeline. The thread's argument is a pointer to its `stage_t` structure.

16-27   The thread loops forever, processing data. Because the mutex is locked outside the loop, the thread appears to have the pipeline stage's `mutex` locked all the time. However, it spends most of its time waiting for new data, on the avail condition variable. Remember that a thread automatically unlocks the mutex associated with a condition variable, while waiting on that condition variable. In reality, therefore, the thread spends most of its time with mutex unlocked.

22-26 When given data, the thread increases its own data value by one, and passes the result to the next stage. The thread then records that the stage no longer has data by clearing the data_ready flag, and signals the ready condition variable to wake any thread that might be waiting for this pipeline stage.

■ pipe.c   part 3   pipe_stage

```
1  /*
2   * The thread start routine for pipe stage threads.
3   * Each will wait for a data item passed from the
4   * caller or the previous stage, modify the data
5   * and pass it along to the next (or final) stage.
6   */
7  void *pipe_stage (void *arg)
8  {
9      stage_t *stage = (stage_t*)arg;
10     stage_t *next_stage = stage->next;
11     int status;
12
13     status = pthread_mutex_lock (&stage->mutex);
14     if (status != 0)
15         err_abort (status, "Lock pipe stage");
16     while (1) {
17         while (stage->data_ready != 1) {
18             status = pthread_cond_wait (&stage->avail, &stage->mutex);
19             if (status != 0)
20                 err_abort (status, "Wait for previous stage");
21         }
22         pipe_send (next_stage, stage->data + 1);
23         stage->data_ready = 0;
24         status = pthread_cond_signal (&stage->ready);
25         if (status != 0)
26             err_abort (status, "Wake next stage");
27     }
28     /*
29      * Notice that the routine never unlocks the stage->mutex.
30      * The call to pthread_cond_wait implicitly unlocks the
31      * mutex while the thread is waiting, allowing other threads
32      * to make progress. Because the loop never terminates, this
33      * function has no need to unlock the mutex explicitly.
34      */
35 }
```

■ pipe.c   part 3   pipe_stage

Part 4 shows `pipe_create`, the function that creates a pipeline. It can create a pipeline of any number of stages, linking them together in a list.

18-34   For each stage, it allocates a new `stage_t` structure and initializes the members. Notice that one additional "stage" is allocated and initialized to hold the final result of the pipeline.

36-37   The `link` member of the final stage is set to NULL to terminate the list, and the pipeline's `tail` is set to point at the final stage. The `tail` pointer allows `pipe_result` to easily find the final product of the pipeline, which is stored into the final stage.

52-59   After all the stage data is initialized, `pipe_create` creates a thread for each stage. The extra "final stage" does not get a thread—the termination condition of the `for` loop is that the current stage's `next` link is not NULL, which means that it will not process the final stage.

■ pipe.c   part 4   pipe_create

```
 1  /*
 2   * External interface to create a pipeline. All the
 3   * data is initialized and the threads created. They'll
 4   * wait for data.
 5   */
 6  int pipe_create (pipe_t *pipe, int stages)
 7  {
 8      int pipe_index;
 9      stage_t **link = &pipe->head, *new_stage, *stage;
10      int status;
11
12      status = pthread_mutex_init (&pipe->mutex, NULL);
13      if (status != 0)
14          err_abort (status, "Init pipe mutex");
15      pipe->stages = stages;
16      pipe->active = 0;
17
18      for (pipe_index = 0; pipe_index <= stages; pipe_index++) {
19          new_stage = (stage_t*)malloc (sizeof (stage_t));
20          if (new_stage == NULL)
21              errno_abort ("Allocate stage");
22          status = pthread_mutex_init (&new_stage->mutex, NULL);
23          if (status != 0)
24              err_abort (status, "Init stage mutex");
25          status = pthread_cond_init (&new_stage->avail, NULL);
26          if (status != 0)
27              err_abort (status, "Init avail condition");
28          status = pthread_cond_init (&new_stage->ready, NULL);
29          if (status != 0)
30              err_abort (status, "Init ready condition");
31          new_stage->data_ready = 0;
32          *link = new_stage;
```

```
33                link = &new_stage->next;
34        }
35
36        *link = (stage_t*)NULL;      /* Terminate list */
37        pipe->tail = new_stage;      /* Record the tail */
38
39        /*
40         * Create the threads for the pipe stages only after all
41         * the data is initialized (including all links). Note
42         * that the last stage doesn't get a thread, it's just
43         * a receptacle for the final pipeline value.
44         *
45         * At this point, proper cleanup on an error would take up
46         * more space than worthwhile in a "simple example," so
47         * instead of cancelling and detaching all the threads
48         * already created, plus the synchronization object and
49         * memory cleanup done for earlier errors, it will simply
50         * abort.
51         */
52        for (    stage = pipe->head;
53                 stage->next != NULL;
54                 stage = stage->next) {
55            status = pthread_create (
56                  &stage->thread, NULL, pipe_stage, (void*)stage);
57            if (status != 0)
58                err_abort (status, "Create pipe stage");
59        }
60        return 0;
61 }
```

───

■ pipe.c   part 4   pipe_create

───

Part 5 shows pipe_start and pipe_result. The pipe_start function pushes an item of data into the beginning of the pipeline and then returns immediately without waiting for a result. The pipe_result function allows the caller to wait for the final result, whenever the result might be needed.

9-22   The pipe_start function sends data to the first stage of the pipeline. The function increments a count of "active" items in the pipeline, which allows pipe_result to detect that there are no more active items to collect, and to return immediately instead of blocking. You would not always want a pipeline to behave this way—it makes sense for this example because a single thread alternately "feeds" and "reads" the pipeline, and the application would hang forever if the user inadvertently reads one more item than had been fed.

28-47   The pipe_result function first checks whether there is an active item in the pipeline. If not, it returns with a status of 0, after unlocking the pipeline mutex.

49-55   If there is another item in the pipeline, pipe_result locks the tail (final) stage, and waits for it to receive data. It copies the data and then resets the stage so it can receive the next item of data. Remember that the final stage does not have a thread, and cannot reset itself.

■ `pipe.c`   part 5   `pipe_start,pipe_result`

```
 1   /*
 2    * External interface to start a pipeline by passing
 3    * data to the first stage. The routine returns while
 4    * the pipeline processes in parallel. Call the
 5    * pipe_result return to collect the final stage values
 6    * (note that the pipe will stall when each stage fills,
 7    * until the result is collected).
 8    */
 9   int pipe_start (pipe_t *pipe, long value)
10   {
11       int status;
12
13       status = pthread_mutex_lock (&pipe->mutex);
14       if (status != 0)
15           err_abort (status, "Lock pipe mutex");
16       pipe->active++;
17       status = pthread_mutex_unlock (&pipe->mutex);
18       if (status != 0)
19           err_abort (status, "Unlock pipe mutex");
20       pipe_send (pipe->head, value);
21       return 0;
22   }
23
24   /*
25    * Collect the result of the pipeline. Wait for a
26    * result if the pipeline hasn't produced one.
27    */
28   int pipe_result (pipe_t *pipe, long *result)
29   {
30       stage_t *tail = pipe->tail;
31       long value;
32       int empty = 0;
33       int status;
34
35       status = pthread_mutex_lock (&pipe->mutex);
36       if (status != 0)
37           err_abort (status, "Lock pipe mutex");
38       if (pipe->active <= 0)
39           empty = 1;
40       else
41           pipe->active--;
42
43       status = pthread_mutex_unlock (&pipe->mutex);
44       if (status != 0)
45           err_abort (status, "Unlock pipe mutex");
46       if (empty)
47           return 0;
48
49       pthread_mutex_lock (&tail->mutex);
```

```
50      while (!tail->data_ready)
51          pthread_cond_wait (&tail->avail, &tail->mutex);
52      *result = tail->data;
53      tail->data_ready = 0;
54      pthread_cond_signal (&tail->ready);
55      pthread_mutex_unlock (&tail->mutex);
56      return 1;
57  }
```

■ pipe.c   part 5   pipe_start,pipe_result

Part 6 shows the main program that drives the pipeline. It creates a pipeline, and then loops reading lines from stdin. If the line is a single "=" character, it pulls a result from the pipeline and prints it. Otherwise, it converts the line to an integer value, which it feeds into the pipeline.

■ pipe.c   part 6   main

```
1   /*
2    * The main program to "drive" the pipeline...
3    */
4   int main (int argc, char *argv[])
5   {
6       pipe_t my_pipe;
7       long value, result;
8       int status;
9       char line[128];
10
11      pipe_create (&my_pipe, 10);
12      printf ("Enter integer values, or \"=\" for next result\n");
13
14      while (1) {
15          printf ("Data> ");
16          if (fgets (line, sizeof (line), stdin) == NULL) exit (0);
17          if (strlen (line) <= 1) continue;
18          if (strlen (line) <= 2 && line[0] == '=') {
19              if (pipe_result (&my_pipe, &result))
20                  printf ("Result is %ld\n", result);
21              else
22                  printf ("Pipe is empty\n");
23          } else {
24              if (sscanf (line, "%ld", &value) < 1)
25                  fprintf (stderr, "Enter an integer value\n");
26              else
27                  pipe_start (&my_pipe, value);
28          }
29      }
30  }
```

■ pipe.c   part 6   main

4.2 Work crew

The twelve jurors were all writing very busily on slates.
"What are they doing?" Alice whispered to the Gryphon.
  "They ca'n't have anything to put down yet, before the trial's begun."
"They're putting down their names," the Gryphon whispered in reply,
  "for fear they should forget them before the end of the trial."
  —Lewis Carroll, Alice's Adventures in Wonderland

In a work crew, data is processed independently by a set of threads
(Figure 4.2). A "parallel decomposition" of a loop generally falls into this category.
A set of threads may be created, for example, each directed to process some set of
rows or columns of an array. A single set of data is split between the threads, and
the result is a single (filtered) set of data. Because all the threads in the work
crew, in this model, are performing the same operation on different data, it is
often known as SIMD parallel processing, for "single instruction, multiple data."
The original use of SIMD was in an entirely different form of parallelism, and
doesn't literally apply to threads—but the concept is similar.

The threads in a work crew don't have to use a SIMD model, though. They
may perform entirely different operations on different data. The members of our
work crew, for example, each remove work requests from a shared queue, and do
whatever is required by that request. Each queued request packet could describe

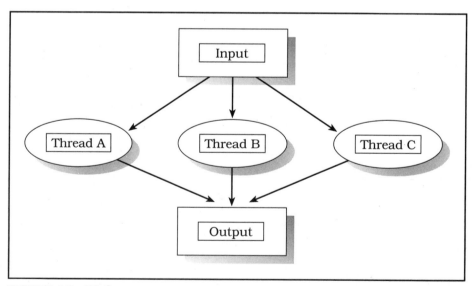

FIGURE 4.2   *Work crew*

a variety of operations—but the common queue and "mission statement" (to process that queue) make them a "crew" rather than independent worker threads. This model can be compared to the original definition of MIMD parallel processing, "multiple instruction, multiple data."

Section 7.2, by the way, shows the development of a more robust and general (and more complicated) "work queue manager" package. A "work crew" and a "work queue" are related in much the same way as "invariants" and "critical sections"—it depends on how you look at what's happening. A work *crew* is the set of threads that independently processes data, whereas a work *queue* is a mechanism by which your code may request that data be processed by anonymous and independent "agents." So in this section, we develop a "work crew," whereas in Section 7.2 we develop a more sophisticated "work queue." The focus differs, but the principle is the same.

The following program, called `crew.c`, shows a simple work crew. Run the program with two arguments, a string, and a file path. The program will queue the file path to the work crew. A crew member will determine whether the file path is a file or a directory—if a file, it will search the file for the string; if a directory, it will use `readdir_r` to find all directories and regular files within the directory, and queue each entry as new work. Each file containing the search string will be reported on `stdout`.

Part 1 shows the header files and definitions used by the program.

7   The symbol `CREW_SIZE` determines how many threads are created for each work crew.

13–17   Each item of work is described by a `work_t` structure. This structure has a pointer to the next work item (set to `NULL` to indicate the end of the list), a pointer to the file path described by the work item, and a pointer to the string for which the program is searching. As currently constructed, all work items point to the same search string.

23–27   Each member of a work crew has a `worker_t` structure. This structure contains the `index` of the crew member in the crew vector, the thread identifier of the crew member (`thread`), and a pointer to the `crew_t` structure (`crew`).

33–41   The `crew_t` structure describes the work crew state. It records the number of members in the work crew (`crew_size`) and an array of `worker_t` structures (`crew`). It also has a counter of how many work items remain to be processed (`work_count`) and a list of outstanding work items (`first` points to the earliest item, and `last` to the latest). Finally, it contains the various Pthreads synchronization objects: a mutex to control access, a condition variable (`done`) to wait for the work crew to finish a task, and a condition variable on which crew members wait to receive new work (`go`).

43–44   The allowed size of a file name and path name may vary depending on the file system to which the path leads. When a crew is started, the program calculates the allowable file name and path length for the specified file path by calling `pathconf`, and stores the values in `path_max` and `name_max`, respectively, for later use.

```
1   #include <sys/types.h>
2   #include <pthread.h>
3   #include <sys/stat.h>
4   #include <dirent.h>
5   #include "errors.h"
6
7   #define CREW_SIZE       4
8
9   /*
10   * Queued items of work for the crew. One is queued by
11   * crew_start, and each worker may queue additional items.
12   */
13  typedef struct work_tag {
14      struct work_tag     *next;          /* Next work item */
15      char                *path;          /* Directory or file */
16      char                *string;        /* Search string */
17  } work_t, *work_p;
18
19  /*
20   * One of these is initialized for each worker thread in the
21   * crew. It contains the "identity" of each worker.
22   */
23  typedef struct worker_tag {
24      int                 index;          /* Thread's index */
25      pthread_t           thread;         /* Thread for stage */
26      struct crew_tag     *crew;          /* Pointer to crew */
27  } worker_t, *worker_p;
28
29  /*
30   * The external "handle" for a work crew. Contains the
31   * crew synchronization state and staging area.
32   */
33  typedef struct crew_tag {
34      int                 crew_size;      /* Size of array */
35      worker_t            crew[CREW_SIZE];/* Crew members */
36      long                work_count;     /* Count of work items */
37      work_t              *first, *last;  /* First & last work item */
38      pthread_mutex_t     mutex;          /* Mutex for crew data */
39      pthread_cond_t      done;           /* Wait for crew done */
40      pthread_cond_t      go;             /* Wait for work */
41  } crew_t, *crew_p;
42
43  size_t  path_max;                       /* Filepath length */
44  size_t  name_max;                       /* Name length */
```

Part 2 shows `worker_routine`, the start function for crew threads. The outer loop repeats processing until the thread is told to terminate.

20-23   POSIX is a little ambiguous about the actual size of the `struct dirent` type. The actual requirement for `readdir_r` is that you pass the address of a buffer large enough to contain a `struct dirent` with a name member of at least `NAME_MAX` bytes. To ensure that we have enough space, allocate a buffer the size of the system's `struct dirent` plus the maximum size necessary for a file name on the file system we're using. This may be bigger than necessary, but it surely won't be too small.

33-37   This condition variable loop blocks each new crew member until work is made available.

61-65   This wait is a little different. While the work list is empty, wait for more work. The crew members never terminate—once they're all done with the current assignment, they're ready for a new assignment. (This example doesn't take advantage of that capability—the process will terminate once the single search command has completed.)

73-76   Remove the first work item from the queue. If the queue becomes empty, also clear the pointer to the last entry, `crew->last`.

81-83   Unlock the work crew mutex, so that the bulk of the crew's work can proceed concurrently.

89   Determine what sort of file we've got in the work item's `path` string. We use `lstat`, which will return information for a symbolic link, rather than `stat`, which would return information for the file to which the link pointed. By not following symbolic links, we reduce the amount of work in this example, and, especially, avoid following links into other file systems where our `name_max` and `path_max` sizes may not be sufficient.

91-95   If the file is a link, report the name, but do nothing else with it. Note that each message includes the thread's work crew index (`mine->index`), so that you can easily see "concurrency at work" within the example.

96-165   If the file is a directory, open it with `opendir`. Find all entries in the directory by repeatedly calling `readdir_r`. Each directory entry is entered as a new work item.

166-206   If the file is a regular file, open it and read all text, looking for the search string. If we find it, write a message and exit the search loop.

207-218   If the file is of any other type, write a message attempting to identify the type.

232-252   Relock the work crew mutex, and report that another work item is done. If the count reaches 0, then the crew has completed the assignment, and we broadcast to awaken any threads waiting to issue a new assignment. Note that the work count is decreased only after the work item is fully processed—the count will never reach 0 if any crew member is still busy (and might queue additional directory entries).

```
 1  /*
 2   * The thread start routine for crew threads. Waits until "go"
 3   * command, processes work items until requested to shut down.
 4   */
 5  void *worker_routine (void *arg)
 6  {
 7      worker_p mine = (worker_t*)arg;
 8      crew_p crew = mine->crew;
 9      work_p work, new_work;
10      struct stat filestat;
11      struct dirent *entry;
12      int status;
13
14      /*
15       * "struct dirent" is funny, because POSIX doesn't require
16       * the definition to be more than a header for a variable
17       * buffer. Thus, allocate a "big chunk" of memory, and use
18       * it as a buffer.
19       */
20      entry = (struct dirent*)malloc (
21          sizeof (struct dirent) + name_max);
22      if (entry == NULL)
23          errno_abort ("Allocating dirent");
24
25      status = pthread_mutex_lock (&crew->mutex);
26      if (status != 0)
27          err_abort (status, "Lock crew mutex");
28
29      /*
30       * There won't be any work when the crew is created, so wait
31       * until something's put on the queue.
32       */
33      while (crew->work_count == 0) {
34          status = pthread_cond_wait (&crew->go, &crew->mutex);
35          if (status != 0)
36              err_abort (status, "Wait for go");
37      }
38
39      status = pthread_mutex_unlock (&crew->mutex);
40      if (status != 0)
41          err_abort (status, "Unlock mutex");
42
43      DPRINTF (("Crew %d starting\n", mine->index));
44
45      /*
46       * Now, as long as there's work, keep doing it.
47       */
```

```
48      while (1) {
49          /*
50           * Wait while there is nothing to do, and
51           * the hope of something coming along later. If
52           * crew->first is NULL, there's no work. But if
53           * crew->work_count goes to zero, we're done.
54           */
55          status = pthread_mutex_lock (&crew->mutex);
56          if (status != 0)
57              err_abort (status, "Lock crew mutex");
58
59          DPRINTF (("Crew %d top: first is %#lx, count is %d\n",
60                  mine->index, crew->first, crew->work_count));
61          while (crew->first == NULL) {
62              status = pthread_cond_wait (&crew->go, &crew->mutex);
63              if (status != 0)
64                  err_abort (status, "Wait for work");
65          }
66
67          DPRINTF (("Crew %d woke: %#lx, %d\n",
68                  mine->index, crew->first, crew->work_count));
69
70          /*
71           * Remove and process a work item.
72           */
73          work = crew->first;
74          crew->first = work->next;
75          if (crew->first == NULL)
76              crew->last = NULL;
77
78          DPRINTF (("Crew %d took %#lx, leaves first %#lx, last %#lx\n",
79                  mine->index, work, crew->first, crew->last));
80
81          status = pthread_mutex_unlock (&crew->mutex);
82          if (status != 0)
83              err_abort (status, "Unlock mutex");
84
85          /*
86           * We have a work item. Process it, which may involve
87           * queuing new work items.
88           */
89          status = lstat (work->path, &filestat);
90
91          if (S_ISLNK (filestat.st_mode))
92              printf (
93                  "Thread %d: %s is a link, skipping.\n",
94                  mine->index,
95                  work->path);
96          else if (S_ISDIR (filestat.st_mode)) {
```

```
97              DIR *directory;
98              struct dirent *result;
99
100             /*
101              * If the file is a directory, search it and place
102              * all files onto the queue as new work items.
103              */
104             directory = opendir (work->path);
105             if (directory == NULL) {
106                 fprintf (
107                     stderr, "Unable to open directory %s: %d (%s)\n",
108                     work->path,
109                     errno, strerror (errno));
110                 continue;
111             }
112
113             while (1) {
114                 status = readdir_r (directory, entry, &result);
115                 if (status != 0) {
116                     fprintf (
117                         stderr,
118                         "Unable to read directory %s: %d (%s)\n",
119                         work->path,
120                         status, strerror (status));
121                     break;
122                 }
123                 if (result == NULL)
124                     break;                   /* End of directory */
125
126                 /*
127                  * Ignore "." and ".." entries.
128                  */
129                 if (strcmp (entry->d_name, ".") == 0)
130                     continue;
131                 if (strcmp (entry->d_name, "..") == 0)
132                     continue;
133                 new_work = (work_p)malloc (sizeof (work_t));
134                 if (new_work == NULL)
135                     errno_abort ("Unable to allocate space");
136                 new_work->path = (char*)malloc (path_max);
137                 if (new_work->path == NULL)
138                     errno_abort ("Unable to allocate path");
139                 strcpy (new_work->path, work->path);
140                 strcat (new_work->path, "/");
141                 strcat (new_work->path, entry->d_name);
142                 new_work->string = work->string;
143                 new_work->next = NULL;
144                 status = pthread_mutex_lock (&crew->mutex);
```

```
145              if (status != 0)
146                  err_abort (status, "Lock mutex");
147              if (crew->first == NULL) {
148                  crew->first = new_work;
149                  crew->last = new_work;
150              } else {
151                  crew->last->next = new_work;
152                  crew->last = new_work;
153              }
154              crew->work_count++;
155              DPRINTF ((
156                  "Crew %d: add %#lx, first %#lx, last %#lx, %d\n",
157                  mine->index, new_work, crew->first,
158                  crew->last, crew->work_count));
159              status = pthread_cond_signal (&crew->go);
160              status = pthread_mutex_unlock (&crew->mutex);
161              if (status != 0)
162                  err_abort (status, "Unlock mutex");
163          }
164
165      closedir (directory);
166  } else if (S_ISREG (filestat.st_mode)) {
167      FILE *search;
168      char buffer[256], *bufptr, *search_ptr;
169
170      /*
171       * If this is a file, not a directory, then search
172       * it for the string.
173       */
174      search = fopen (work->path, "r");
175      if (search == NULL)
176          fprintf (
177              stderr, "Unable to open %s: %d (%s)\n",
178              work->path,
179              errno, strerror (errno));
180      else {
181
182          while (1) {
183              bufptr = fgets (
184                  buffer, sizeof (buffer), search);
185              if (bufptr == NULL) {
186                  if (feof (search))
187                      break;
188                  if (ferror (search)) {
189                      fprintf (
190                          stderr,
191                          "Unable to read %s: %d (%s)\n",
192                          work->path,
```

```
193                              errno, strerror (errno));
194                          break;
195                      }
196                  }
197              search_ptr = strstr (buffer, work->string);
198              if (search_ptr != NULL) {
199                  printf (
200                      "Thread %d found \"%s\" in %s\n",
201                      mine->index, work->string, work->path);
202                  break;
203              }
204          }
205          fclose (search);
206      }
207  } else
208      fprintf (
209          stderr,
210          "Thread %d: %s is type %o (%s))\n",
211          mine->index,
212          work->path,
213          filestat.st_mode & S_IFMT,
214          (S_ISFIFO (filestat.st_mode) ? "FIFO"
215           : (S_ISCHR (filestat.st_mode) ? "CHR"
216              : (S_ISBLK (filestat.st_mode) ? "BLK"
217                 : (S_ISSOCK (filestat.st_mode) ? "SOCK"
218                    : "unknown")))));

220  free (work->path);                   /* Free path buffer */
221  free (work);                         /* We're done with this */

223  /*
224   * Decrement count of outstanding work items, and wake
225   * waiters (trying to collect results or start a new
226   * calculation) if the crew is now idle.
227   *
228   * It's important that the count be decremented AFTER
229   * processing the current work item. That ensures the
230   * count won't go to 0 until we're really done.
231   */
232  status = pthread_mutex_lock (&crew->mutex);
233  if (status != 0)
234      err_abort (status, "Lock crew mutex");

236  crew->work_count--;
237  DPRINTF (("Crew %d decremented work to %d\n", mine->index,
238           crew->work_count));
239  if (crew->work_count <= 0) {
240      DPRINTF (("Crew thread %d done\n", mine->index));
241      status = pthread_cond_broadcast (&crew->done);
```

```
242                if (status != 0)
243                    err_abort (status, "Wake waiters");
244                status = pthread_mutex_unlock (&crew->mutex);
245                if (status != 0)
246                    err_abort (status, "Unlock mutex");
247                break;
248            }
249
250            status = pthread_mutex_unlock (&crew->mutex);
251            if (status != 0)
252                err_abort (status, "Unlock mutex");
253
254        }
255
256    free (entry);
257    return NULL;
258 }
```

■ crew.c   part 2   worker_routine

Part 3 shows `crew_create`, the function used to create a new work crew. This simple example does not provide a way to destroy a work crew, because that is not necessary—the work crew would be destroyed only when the main program was prepared to exit, and process exit will destroy all threads and process data.

12–15　　　The `crew_create` function begins by checking the `crew_size` argument. The size of the crew is not allowed to exceed the size of the crew array in `crew_t`. If the requested size is acceptable, copy it into the structure.

16–31　　　Start with no work and an empty work queue. Initialize the crew's synchronization objects.

36–43　　　Then, for each crew member, initialize the member's `worker_t` data. The index of the member within the crew array is recorded, and a pointer back to the `crew_t`. Then the crew member thread is created, with a pointer to the member's `worker_t` as its argument.

■ crew.c   part 3   crew_create

```
 1 /*
 2  * Create a work crew.
 3  */
 4 int crew_create (crew_t *crew, int crew_size)
 5 {
 6     int crew_index;
 7     int status;
 8
 9     /*
10      * We won't create more than CREW_SIZE members.
11      */
```

```
12          if (crew_size > CREW_SIZE)
13              return EINVAL;
14
15          crew->crew_size = crew_size;
16          crew->work_count = 0;
17          crew->first = NULL;
18          crew->last = NULL;
19
20          /*
21           * Initialize synchronization objects.
22           */
23          status = pthread_mutex_init (&crew->mutex, NULL);
24          if (status != 0)
25              return status;
26          status = pthread_cond_init (&crew->done, NULL);
27          if (status != 0)
28              return status;
29          status = pthread_cond_init (&crew->go, NULL);
30          if (status != 0)
31              return status;
32
33          /*
34           * Create the worker threads.
35           */
36          for (crew_index = 0; crew_index < CREW_SIZE; crew_index++) {
37              crew->crew[crew_index].index = crew_index;
38              crew->crew[crew_index].crew = crew;
39              status = pthread_create (&crew->crew[crew_index].thread,
40                  NULL, worker_routine, (void*)&crew->crew[crew_index]);
41              if (status != 0)
42                  err_abort (status, "Create worker");
43          }
44          return 0;
45      }
```

■ crew.c   part 3   crew_create

Part 4 shows the crew_start function, which is called to assign a new path name and search string to the work crew. The function is synchronous—that is, after assigning the task it waits for the crew members to complete the task before returning to the caller. The crew_start function assumes that the crew_t structure has been previously created by calling crew_create, shown in part 3, but does not attempt to validate the structure.

20-26   Wait for the crew members to finish any previously assigned work. Although crew_start is synchronous, the crew may be processing a task assigned by another thread. On creation, the crew's work_count is set to 0, so the first call to crew_start will not need to wait.

28-43   Get the proper values of `path_max` and `name_max` for the file system specified by the file path we'll be reading. The `pathconf` function may return a value of −1 without setting `errno`, if the requested value for the file system is "unlimited." To detect this, we need to clear `errno` before making the call. If `pathconf` returns −1 without setting `errno`, assume reasonable values.

47-48   The values returned by `pathconf` don't include the terminating null character of a string—so add one character to both.

49-67   Allocate a work queue entry (`work_t`) and fill it in. Add it to the end of the request queue.

68-75   We've queued a single work request, so awaken one of the waiting work crew members by signaling the condition variable. If the attempt fails, free the work request, clear the work queue, and return with the error.

76-80   Wait for the crew to complete the task. The crew members handle all output, so when they're done we simply return to the caller.

■ `crew.c`   part 4   `crew_start`

```
 1  /*
 2   * Pass a file path to a work crew previously created
 3   * using crew_create
 4   */
 5  int crew_start (
 6      crew_p crew,
 7      char *filepath,
 8      char *search)
 9  {
10      work_p request;
11      int status;
12
13      status = pthread_mutex_lock (&crew->mutex);
14      if (status != 0)
15          return status;
16
17      /*
18       * If the crew is busy, wait for them to finish.
19       */
20      while (crew->work_count > 0) {
21          status = pthread_cond_wait (&crew->done, &crew->mutex);
22          if (status != 0) {
23              pthread_mutex_unlock (&crew->mutex);
24              return status;
25          }
26      }
27
28      errno = 0;
29      path_max = pathconf (filepath, _PC_PATH_MAX);
```

```
30          if (path_max == -1) {
31              if (errno == 0)
32                  path_max = 1024;                   /* "No limit" */
33              else
34                  errno_abort ("Unable to get PATH_MAX");
35          }
36          errno = 0;
37          name_max = pathconf (filepath, _PC_NAME_MAX);
38          if (name_max == -1) {
39              if (errno == 0)
40                  name_max = 256;                    /* "No limit" */
41              else
42                  errno_abort ("Unable to get NAME_MAX");
43          }
44          DPRINTF ((
45              "PATH_MAX for %s is %ld, NAME_MAX is %ld\n",
46              filepath, path_max, name_max));
47          path_max++;                                /* Add null byte */
48          name_max++;                                /* Add null byte */
49          request = (work_p)malloc (sizeof (work_t));
50          if (request == NULL)
51              errno_abort ("Unable to allocate request");
52          DPRINTF (("Requesting %s\n", filepath));
53          request->path = (char*)malloc (path_max);
54          if (request->path == NULL)
55              errno_abort ("Unable to allocate path");
56          strcpy (request->path, filepath);
57          request->string = search;
58          request->next = NULL;
59          if (crew->first == NULL) {
60              crew->first = request;
61              crew->last = request;
62          } else {
63              crew->last->next = request;
64              crew->last = request;
65          }
66
67          crew->work_count++;
68          status = pthread_cond_signal (&crew->go);
69          if (status != 0) {
70              free (crew->first);
71              crew->first = NULL;
72              crew->work_count = 0;
73              pthread_mutex_unlock (&crew->mutex);
74              return status;
75          }
76          while (crew->work_count > 0) {
77              status = pthread_cond_wait (&crew->done, &crew->mutex);
```

```
78                 if (status != 0)
79                     err_abort (status, "waiting for crew to finish");
80             }
81         status = pthread_mutex_unlock (&crew->mutex);
82         if (status != 0)
83             err_abort (status, "Unlock crew mutex");
84         return 0;
85     }
```

■ crew.c   part 4   crew_start

Part 5 shows the initial thread (main) for the little work crew sample.

10-13   The program requires three arguments—the program name, a string for which to search, and a path name. For example, "crew butenhof ~"

15-23   On a Solaris system, call thr_setconcurrency to ensure that at least one LWP (kernel execution context) is created for each crew member. The program will work without this call, but, on a uniprocessor, you would not see any concurrency. See Section 5.6.3 for more information on "many to few" scheduling models, and Section 10.1.3 for information on "set concurrency" functions.

24-30   Create a work crew, and assign to it the concurrent file search.

■ crew.c   part 5   main

```
1   /*
2    * The main program to "drive" the crew...
3    */
4   int main (int argc, char *argv[])
5   {
6       crew_t my_crew;
7       char line[128], *next;
8       int status;
9
10      if (argc < 3) {
11          fprintf (stderr, "Usage: %s string path\n", argv[0]);
12          return -1;
13      }
14
15  #ifdef sun
16      /*
17       * On Solaris 2.5, threads are not timesliced. To ensure
18       * that our threads can run concurrently, we need to
19       * increase the concurrency level to CREW_SIZE.
20       */
21      DPRINTF (("Setting concurrency level to %d\n", CREW_SIZE));
22      thr_setconcurrency (CREW_SIZE);
23  #endif
24      status = crew_create (&my_crew, CREW_SIZE);
25      if (status != 0)
26          err_abort (status, "Create crew");
```

```
27
28       status = crew_start (&my_crew, argv[2], argv[1]);
29       if (status != 0)
30           err_abort (status, "Start crew");
31
32       return 0;
33  }
```

■ crew.c   part 5   main

4.3 Client/Server

But the Judge said he never had summed up before;
So the Snark undertook it instead,
And summed it so well that it came to far more
Than the Witnesses ever had said!
    —Lewis Carroll, The Hunting of the Snark

In a client/server system, a "client" requests that a "server" perform some operation on a set of data (Figure 4.3). The server performs the operation independently—the client can either wait for the server or proceed in parallel and look for the result at a later time when the result is required. Although it is simplest to have the client wait for the server, that's rarely very useful—it certainly doesn't

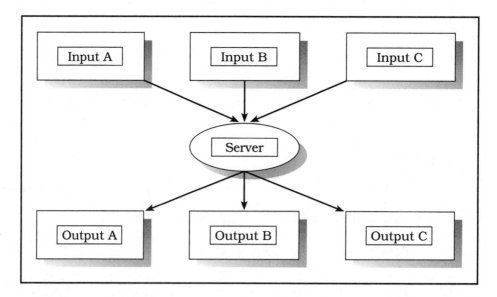

FIGURE 4.3 *Client/Server*

provide a speed advantage to the client. On the other hand, it can be an easy way to manage synchronization for some common resource.

If a set of threads all need to read input from stdin, it might be confusing for them to each issue independent prompt–and–read operations. Imagine that two threads each writes its prompt using printf, and then each reads the response using gets—you would have no way of knowing to which thread you were responding. If one thread asks "OK to send mail?" and the other asks "OK to delete root directory?" you'd probably like to know which thread will receive your response. Of course there are ways to keep the prompt and response "connected" without introducing a server thread; for example, by using the flockfile and funlockfile functions to lock both stdin and stdout around the prompt–and–read sequences, but a server thread is more interesting—and certainly more relevant to this section.

In the following program, server.c, each of four threads will repeatedly read, and then echo, input lines. When the program is run you should see the threads prompt in varying orders, and another thread may prompt before the echo. But you'll never see a prompt or an echo between the prompt and read performed by the "prompt server."

7-9   These symbols define the commands that can be sent to the "prompt server." It can be asked to *read* input, *write* output, or *quit*.

14-22   The request_t structure defines each request to the server. The outstanding requests are linked in a list using the next member. The operation member contains one of the request codes (read, write, or quit). The synchronous member is nonzero if the client wishes to wait for the operation to be completed (synchronous), or 0 if it does not wish to wait (asynchronous).

27-33   The tty_server_t structure provides the context for the server thread. It has the synchronization objects (mutex and request), a flag denoting whether the server is running, and a list of requests that have been made and not yet processed (first and last).

35-37   This program has a single server, and the control structure (tty_server) is statically allocated and initialized here. The list of requests is empty, and the server is not running. The mutex and condition variable are statically initialized.

43-45   The main program and client threads coordinate their shutdown using these synchronization objects (client_mutex and clients_done) rather than using pthread_join.

■ server.c   part 1   definitions

```
1  #include <pthread.h>
2  #include <math.h>
3  #include "errors.h"
4
5  #define CLIENT_THREADS  4            /* Number of clients */
6
7  #define REQ_READ        1            /* Read with prompt */
8  #define REQ_WRITE       2            /* Write */
```

```
 9  #define REQ_QUIT          3                  /* Quit server */
10
11  /*
12   * Internal to server "package" -- one for each request.
13   */
14  typedef struct request_tag {
15      struct request_tag  *next;              /* Link to next */
16      int                 operation;          /* Function code */
17      int                 synchronous;        /* Nonzero if synchronous */
18      int                 done_flag;          /* Predicate for wait */
19      pthread_cond_t      done;               /* Wait for completion */
20      char                prompt[32];         /* Prompt string for reads */
21      char                text[128];          /* Read/write text */
22  } request_t;
23
24  /*
25   * Static context for the server
26   */
27  typedef struct tty_server_tag {
28      request_t           *first;
29      request_t           *last;
30      int                 running;
31      pthread_mutex_t     mutex;
32      pthread_cond_t      request;
33  } tty_server_t;
34
35  tty_server_t tty_server = {
36      NULL, NULL, 0,
37      PTHREAD_MUTEX_INITIALIZER, PTHREAD_COND_INITIALIZER};
38
39  /*
40   * Main program data
41   */
42
43  int client_threads;
44  pthread_mutex_t client_mutex = PTHREAD_MUTEX_INITIALIZER;
45  pthread_cond_t clients_done = PTHREAD_COND_INITIALIZER;
```

■ server.c   part 1   definitions

Part 2 shows the server thread function, tty_server_routine. It loops, processing requests continuously until asked to quit.

25-30   The server waits for a request to appear using the request condition variable.

31-34   Remove the first request from the queue—if the queue is now empty, also clear the pointer to the last entry (tty_server.last).

43-66   The switch statement performs the requested work, depending on the operation given in the request packet. REQ_QUIT tells the server to shut down. REQ_READ tells the server to read, with an optional prompt string. REQ_WRITE tells the server to write a string.

67-79   If a request is marked "synchronous" (synchronous flag is nonzero), the server sets done_flag and signals the done condition variable. When the request is synchronous, the client is responsible for freeing the request packet. If the request was asynchronous, the server frees request on completion.

80-81   If the request was REQ_QUIT, terminate the server thread by breaking out of the while loop, to the return statement.

■ server.c   part 2   tty_server_routine

```
1   /*
2    * The server start routine. It waits for a request to appear
3    * in tty_server.requests using the request condition variable.
4    * It processes requests in FIFO order. If a request is marked
5    * "synchronous" (synchronous != 0), the server will set done_flag
6    * and signal the request's condition variable. The client is
7    * responsible for freeing the request. If the request was not
8    * synchronous, the server will free the request on completion.
9    */
10  void *tty_server_routine (void *arg)
11  {
12      static pthread_mutex_t prompt_mutex = PTHREAD_MUTEX_INITIALIZER;
13      request_t *request;
14      int operation, len;
15      int status;
16
17      while (1) {
18          status = pthread_mutex_lock (&tty_server.mutex);
19          if (status != 0)
20              err_abort (status, "Lock server mutex");
21
22          /*
23           * Wait for data
24           */
25          while (tty_server.first == NULL) {
26              status = pthread_cond_wait (
27                  &tty_server.request, &tty_server.mutex);
28              if (status != 0)
29                  err_abort (status, "Wait for request");
30          }
31          request = tty_server.first;
32          tty_server.first = request->next;
33          if (tty_server.first == NULL)
34              tty_server.last = NULL;
35          status = pthread_mutex_unlock (&tty_server.mutex);
36          if (status != 0)
37              err_abort (status, "Unlock server mutex");
38
39          /*
40           * Process the data
41           */
```

```
42              operation = request->operation;
43              switch (operation) {
44                  case REQ_QUIT:
45                      break;
46                  case REQ_READ:
47                      if (strlen (request->prompt) > 0)
48                          printf (request->prompt);
49                      if (fgets (request->text, 128, stdin) == NULL)
50                          request->text[0] = '\0';
51                      /*
52                       * Because fgets returns the newline, and we don't
53                       * want it, we look for it, and turn it into a null
54                       * (truncating the input) if found. It should be the
55                       * last character, if it is there.
56                       */
57                      len = strlen (request->text);
58                      if (len > 0 && request->text[len-1] == '\n')
59                          request->text[len-1] = '\0';
60                      break;
61                  case REQ_WRITE:
62                      puts (request->text);
63                      break;
64                  default:
65                      break;
66              }
67              if (request->synchronous) {
68                  status = pthread_mutex_lock (&tty_server.mutex);
69                  if (status != 0)
70                      err_abort (status, "Lock server mutex");
71                  request->done_flag = 1;
72                  status = pthread_cond_signal (&request->done);
73                  if (status != 0)
74                      err_abort (status, "Signal server condition");
75                  status = pthread_mutex_unlock (&tty_server.mutex);
76                  if (status != 0)
77                      err_abort (status, "Unlock server mutex");
78              } else
79                  free (request);
80              if (operation == REQ_QUIT)
81                  break;
82          }
83      return NULL;
84  }
```

■ server.c   part 2   tty_server_routine

Part 3 shows the function that is called to initiate a request to the tty server thread. The caller specifies the desired operation (REQ_QUIT, REQ_READ, or REQ_WRITE), whether the operation is synchronous or not (sync), an optional prompt string (prompt) for REQ_READ operations, and the pointer to a string (input for REQ_WRITE, or a buffer to return the result of an REQ_READ operation).

16-40   If a tty server thread is not already running, start one. A temporary thread attributes object (detached_attr) is created, and the *detachstate* attribute is set to PTHREAD_CREATE_DETACHED. Thread attributes will be explained later in Section 5.2.3. In this case, we are just saying that we will not need to use the thread identifier after creation.

45-76   Allocate and initialize a server request (request_t) packet. If the request is synchronous, initialize the condition variable (done) in the request packet—otherwise the condition variable isn't used. The new request is linked onto the request queue.

81-83   Wake the server thread to handle the queued request.

88-105   If the request is synchronous, wait for the server to set done_flag and signal the done condition variable. If the operation is REQ_READ, copy the result string into the output buffer. Finally, destroy the condition variable, and free the request packet.

■ server.c   part 3   tty_server_request

```
1   /*
2    * Request an operation
3    */
4   void tty_server_request (
5       int           operation,
6       int           sync,
7       const char    *prompt,
8       char          *string)
9   {
10      request_t *request;
11      int status;
12
13      status = pthread_mutex_lock (&tty_server.mutex);
14      if (status != 0)
15          err_abort (status, "Lock server mutex");
16      if (!tty_server.running) {
17          pthread_t thread;
18          pthread_attr_t detached_attr;
19
20          status = pthread_attr_init (&detached_attr);
21          if (status != 0)
22              err_abort (status, "Init attributes object");
23          status = pthread_attr_setdetachstate (
24              &detached_attr, PTHREAD_CREATE_DETACHED);
25          if (status != 0)
26              err_abort (status, "Set detach state");
27          tty_server.running = 1;
28          status = pthread_create (&thread, &detached_attr,
29              tty_server_routine, NULL);
```

```
30          if (status != 0)
31              err_abort (status, "Create server");
32
33          /*
34           * Ignore an error in destroying the attributes object.
35           * It's unlikely to fail, there's nothing useful we can
36           * do about it, and it's not worth aborting the program
37           * over it.
38           */
39          pthread_attr_destroy (&detached_attr);
40      }
41
42      /*
43       * Create and initialize a request structure.
44       */
45      request = (request_t*)malloc (sizeof (request_t));
46      if (request == NULL)
47          errno_abort ("Allocate request");
48      request->next = NULL;
49      request->operation = operation;
50      request->synchronous = sync;
51      if (sync) {
52          request->done_flag = 0;
53          status = pthread_cond_init (&request->done, NULL);
54          if (status != 0)
55              err_abort (status, "Init request condition");
56      }
57      if (prompt != NULL)
58          strncpy (request->prompt, prompt, 32);
59      else
60          request->prompt[0] = '\0';
61      if (operation == REQ_WRITE && string != NULL)
62          strncpy (request->text, string, 128);
63      else
64          request->text[0] = '\0';
65
66      /*
67       * Add the request to the queue, maintaining the first and
68       * last pointers.
69       */
70      if (tty_server.first == NULL) {
71          tty_server.first = request;
72          tty_server.last = request;
73      } else {
74          (tty_server.last)->next = request;
75          tty_server.last = request;
76      }
77
78      /*
```

```
79          * Tell the server that a request is available.
80          */
81         status = pthread_cond_signal (&tty_server.request);
82         if (status != 0)
83             err_abort (status, "Wake server");
84
85         /*
86          * If the request was "synchronous", then wait for a reply.
87          */
88         if (sync) {
89             while (!request->done_flag) {
90                 status = pthread_cond_wait (
91                     &request->done, &tty_server.mutex);
92                 if (status != 0)
93                     err_abort (status, "Wait for sync request");
94             }
95             if (operation == REQ_READ) {
96                 if (strlen (request->text) > 0)
97                     strcpy (string, request->text);
98                 else
99                     string[0] = '\0';
100            }
101            status = pthread_cond_destroy (&request->done);
102            if (status != 0)
103                err_abort (status, "Destroy request condition");
104            free (request);
105        }
106        status = pthread_mutex_unlock (&tty_server.mutex);
107        if (status != 0)
108            err_abort (status, "Unlock mutex");
109    }
```

■ server.c   part 3   tty_server_request

Part 4 shows the thread start function for the client threads, which repeatedly queue tty operation requests to the server.

12-22   Read a line through the tty server. If the resulting string is empty, break out of the loop and terminate. Otherwise, loop four times printing the result string, at one-second intervals. Why four? It just "mixes things up" a little.

26-31   Decrease the count of client threads, and wake the main thread if this is the last client thread to terminate.

■ server.c   part 4   client_routine

```
1  /*
2   * Client routine -- multiple copies will request server.
3   */
4  void *client_routine (void *arg)
```

```
 5  {
 6      int my_number = (int)arg, loops;
 7      char prompt[32];
 8      char string[128], formatted[128];
 9      int status;
10
11      sprintf (prompt, "Client %d> ", my_number);
12      while (1) {
13          tty_server_request (REQ_READ, 1, prompt, string);
14          if (strlen (string) == 0)
15              break;
16          for (loops = 0; loops < 4; loops++) {
17              sprintf (
18                  formatted, "(%d#%d) %s", my_number, loops, string);
19              tty_server_request (REQ_WRITE, 0, NULL, formatted);
20              sleep (1);
21          }
22      }
23      status = pthread_mutex_lock (&client_mutex);
24      if (status != 0)
25          err_abort (status, "Lock client mutex");
26      client_threads--;
27      if (client_threads <= 0) {
28          status = pthread_cond_signal (&clients_done);
29          if (status != 0)
30              err_abort (status, "Signal clients done");
31      }
32      status = pthread_mutex_unlock (&client_mutex);
33      if (status != 0)
34          err_abort (status, "Unlock client mutex");
35      return NULL;
36  }
```

■ server.c   part 4   client_routine

Part 5 shows the main program for server.c. It creates a set of client threads to utilize the tty server, and waits for them.

7-15   On a Solaris system, set the concurrency level to the number of client threads by calling thr_setconcurrency. Because all the client threads will spend some of their time blocked on condition variables, we don't really need to increase the concurrency level for this program—however, it will provide less predictable execution behavior.

20-26   Create the client threads.

27-35   This construct is much like pthread_join, except that it completes only when all of the client threads have terminated. As I have said elsewhere, pthread_join is nothing magical, and there is no reason to use it to detect thread termination unless it does exactly what you want. Joining multiple threads in a loop with pthread_join is rarely exactly what you want, and a "multiple join" like that shown here is easy to construct.

```
1  int main (int argc, char *argv[])
2  {
3      pthread_t thread;
4      int count;
5      int status;
6
7  #ifdef sun
8      /*
9       * On Solaris 2.5, threads are not timesliced. To ensure
10      * that our threads can run concurrently, we need to
11      * increase the concurrency level to CLIENT_THREADS.
12      */
13     DPRINTF (("Setting concurrency level to %d\n", CLIENT_THREADS));
14     thr_setconcurrency (CLIENT_THREADS);
15 #endif
16
17     /*
18      * Create CLIENT_THREADS clients.
19      */
20     client_threads = CLIENT_THREADS;
21     for (count = 0; count < client_threads; count++) {
22         status = pthread_create (&thread, NULL,
23             client_routine, (void*)count);
24         if (status != 0)
25             err_abort (status, "Create client thread");
26     }
27     status = pthread_mutex_lock (&client_mutex);
28     if (status != 0)
29         err_abort (status, "Lock client mutex");
30     while (client_threads > 0) {
31         status = pthread_cond_wait (&clients_done, &client_mutex);
32         if (status != 0)
33             err_abort (status, "Wait for clients to finish");
34     }
35     status = pthread_mutex_unlock (&client_mutex);
36     if (status != 0)
37         err_abort (status, "Unlock client mutex");
38     printf ("All clients done\n");
39     tty_server_request (REQ_QUIT, 1, NULL, NULL);
40     return 0;
41 }
```

5 Advanced threaded programming

"Take some more tea," the March Hare said to Alice, very earnestly.
"I've had nothing yet," Alice replied in an offended tone:
   "so I ca'n't take more."
*"You mean you ca'n't take **less**," said the Hatter:*
   *"it's very easy to take **more** than nothing."*
   —Lewis Carroll, Alice's Adventures in Wonderland

The Pthreads standard provides many capabilities that aren't needed by many programs. To keep the sections dealing with synchronization and threads relatively simple, the more advanced capabilities are collected into this additional section.

Section 5.1 describes a facility to manage initialization of data, particularly within a library, in a multithreaded environment.

Section 5.2 describes "attributes objects," a way to control various characteristics of your threads, mutexes, and condition variables when you create them.

Section 5.3 describes cancellation, a way to ask your threads to "go away" when you don't need them to continue.

Section 5.4 describes thread-specific data, a sort of database mechanism that allows a library to associate data with individual threads that it encounters and to retrieve that data later.

Section 5.5 describes the Pthreads facilities for realtime scheduling, to help your program interact with the cold, cruel world in a predictable way.

5.1 One-time initialization

"'Tis the voice of the Jubjub!" he suddenly cried.
(This man, that they used to call "Dunce.")
"As the Bellman would tell you," he added with pride,
"I have uttered that sentiment once."
   —Lewis Carroll, The Hunting of the Snark

```
pthread_once_t once_control = PTHREAD_ONCE_INIT;
int pthread_once (pthread_once_t *once_control,
    void (*init_routine) (void));
```

Some things need to be done once and only once, no matter what. When you are initializing an application, it is often easiest to do all that from main, before calling anything else that might depend on the initialization—and, in particular, before creating any threads that might depend on having initialized mutexes, created thread-specific data keys, and so forth.

If you are writing a library, you usually don't have that luxury. But you must still be sure that the necessary initialization has been completed before you can use anything that needs to be initialized. Statically initialized mutexes can help a lot, but sometimes you may find this "one-time initialization" feature more convenient.

In traditional sequential programming, one-time initialization is often managed by a boolean variable. A control variable is statically initialized to 0, and any code that depends on the initialization can test the variable. If the value is still 0 it can perform the initialization and then set the variable to 1. Later checks will skip the initialization.

When you are using multiple threads, it is not that easy. If more than one thread executes the initialization sequence concurrently, two threads may both find initializer to be 0, and both perform the initialization, which, presumably, should have been performed only once. The state of initialization is a shared *invariant* that must be protected by a mutex.

You can code your own one-time initialization using a boolean variable and a statically initialized mutex. In many cases this will be more convenient than pthread_once, and it will always be more efficient. The main reason for pthread_once is that you were not originally allowed to statically initialize a mutex. Thus, to use a mutex, you had to first call pthread_mutex_init. You must initialize a mutex only once, so the initialization call must be made in one-time initialization code. The pthread_once function solved this recursive problem. When static initialization of mutexes was added to the standard, pthread_once was retained as a convenience function. If it's convenient, use it, but remember that you don't have to use it.

First, you declare a control variable of type pthread_once_t. The control variable *must* be statically initialized using the PTHREAD_ONCE_INIT macro, as shown in the following program, called once.c. You must also create a function containing the code to perform all initialization that is to be associated with the control variable. Now, at any time, a thread may call pthread_once, specifying a pointer to the control variable and a pointer to the associated initialization function.

The pthread_once function first checks the control variable to determine whether the initialization has already completed. If so, pthread_once simply returns. If initialization has not yet been started, pthread_once calls the initialization function (with no arguments), and then records that initialization has been completed. If a thread calls pthread_once while initialization is in progress in another thread, the calling thread will wait until that other thread completes initialization, and then return. In other words, when any call to pthread_once returns successfully, the caller can be certain that all states initialized by the associated initialization function are ready to go.

13-20   The function once_init_routine initializes the mutex when called—the use of
         pthread_once ensures that it will be called exactly one time.

29   The thread function thread_routine calls pthread_once before using mutex,
         to ensure that it exists even if it had not already been created by main.

51   The main program also calls pthread_once before using mutex, so that the
         program will execute correctly regardless of when thread_routine runs. Notice
         that, while I normally stress that all shared data must be initialized before creat-
         ing any thread that uses it, in this case, the only critical shared data is really the
         once_block—it is irrelevant that the mutex is not initialized, because the use of
         pthread_once ensures proper synchronization.

■   once.c

```
1   #include <pthread.h>
2   #include "errors.h"
3
4   pthread_once_t once_block = PTHREAD_ONCE_INIT;
5   pthread_mutex_t mutex;
6
7   /*
8    * This is the one-time initialization routine. It will be
9    * called exactly once, no matter how many calls to pthread_once
10   * with the same control structure are made during the course of
11   * the program.
12   */
13  void once_init_routine (void)
14  {
15      int status;
16
17      status = pthread_mutex_init (&mutex, NULL);
18      if (status != 0)
19          err_abort (status, "Init Mutex");
20  }
21
22  /*
23   * Thread start routine that calls pthread_once.
24   */
25  void *thread_routine (void *arg)
26  {
27      int status;
28
29      status = pthread_once (&once_block, once_init_routine);
30      if (status != 0)
31          err_abort (status, "Once init");
32      status = pthread_mutex_lock (&mutex);
33      if (status != 0)
34          err_abort (status, "Lock mutex");
35      printf ("thread_routine has locked the mutex.\n");
```

```
36          status = pthread_mutex_unlock (&mutex);
37          if (status != 0)
38              err_abort (status, "Unlock mutex");
39          return NULL;
40      }
41
42      int main (int argc, char *argv[])
43      {
44          pthread_t thread_id;
45          char *input, buffer[64];
46          int status;
47
48          status = pthread_create (&thread_id, NULL, thread_routine, NULL);
49          if (status != 0)
50              err_abort (status, "Create thread");
51          status = pthread_once (&once_block, once_init_routine);
52          if (status != 0)
53              err_abort (status, "Once init");
54          status = pthread_mutex_lock (&mutex);
55          if (status != 0)
56              err_abort (status, "Lock mutex");
57          printf ("Main has locked the mutex.\n");
58          status = pthread_mutex_unlock (&mutex);
59          if (status != 0)
60              err_abort (status, "Unlock mutex");
61          status = pthread_join (thread_id, NULL);
62          if (status != 0)
63              err_abort (status, "Join thread");
64          return 0;
65      }
```

■   once.c

5.2 Attributes objects

The fifth is ambition. It next will be right
To describe each particular batch:
Distinguishing those that have feathers, and bite,
From those that have whiskers, and scratch.
  —Lewis Carroll, The Hunting of the Snark

So far, when we created threads, or dynamically initialized mutexes and condition variables, we have usually used the pointer value NULL as the second argument. That argument is actually a pointer to an *attributes object*. The value

NULL indicates that Pthreads should assume the default value for all attributes—just as it does when statically initializing a mutex or condition variable.

An attributes object is an extended argument list provided when you initialize an object. It allows the main interfaces (for example, `pthread_create`) to be relatively simple, while allowing "expert" capability when you need it. Later POSIX standards will be able to add options without requiring source changes to existing code. In addition to standard attributes provided by Pthreads, an implementation can provide specialized options without creating nonstandard parameters.

You can think of an attributes object as a private structure. You read or write the "members" of the structure by calling special functions, rather than by accessing public member names. For example, you read the *stacksize* attribute from a thread attributes object by calling `pthread_attr_getstacksize`, or write it by calling `pthread_attr_setstacksize`.

In a simple implementation of Pthreads the type `pthread_attr_t` might be a `typedef struct` and the get and set functions might be macros to read or write members of the variable. Another implementation might allocate memory when you initialize an attributes object, and it may implement the get and set operations as real functions that perform validity checking.

Threads, mutexes, and condition variables each have their own special attributes object type. Respectively, the types are `pthread_attr_t`, `pthread_mutexattr_t`, and `pthread_condattr_t`.

5.2.1 Mutex attributes

```
pthread_mutexattr_t attr;
int pthread_mutexattr_init (pthread_mutexattr_t *attr);
int pthread_mutexattr_destroy (
    pthread_mutexattr_t *attr);
#ifdef _POSIX_THREAD_PROCESS_SHARED
int pthread_mutexattr_getpshared (
    pthread_mutexattr_t *attr, int *pshared);
int pthread_mutexattr_setpshared (
    pthread_mutexattr_t *attr, int pshared);
#endif
```

Pthreads defines the following attributes for mutex creation: *pshared, protocol,* and *prioceiling.* No system is required to implement any of these attributes, however, so check the system documentation before using them.

You initialize a mutex attributes object by calling `pthread_mutexattr_init`, specifying a pointer to a variable of type `pthread_mutexattr_t`, as in `mutex_attr.c`, shown next. You use that attributes object by passing its address to `pthread_mutex_init` instead of the NULL value we've been using so far.

If your system provides the `_POSIX_THREAD_PROCESS_SHARED` option, then it supports the *pshared* attribute, which you can set by calling the function `pthread_mutexattr_setpshared`. If you set the *pshared* attribute to the value `PTHREAD_PROCESS_SHARED`, you can use the mutex to synchronize threads within separate processes that have access to the memory where the mutex (`pthread_mutex_t`) is initialized. The default value for this attribute is `PTHREAD_PROCESS_PRIVATE`.

The `mutex_attr.c` program shows how to set a mutex attributes object to create a mutex using the *pshared* attribute. This example uses the default value, `PTHREAD_PROCESS_PRIVATE`, to avoid the additional complexity of creating shared memory and forking a process. The other mutex attributes, *protocol* and *prioceiling*, will be discussed later in Section 5.5.5.

■ mutex_attr.c

```
1  #include <pthread.h>
2  #include "errors.h"
3
4  pthread_mutex_t mutex;
5
6  int main (int argc, char *argv[])
7  {
8      pthread_mutexattr_t mutex_attr;
9      int status;
10
11     status = pthread_mutexattr_init (&mutex_attr);
12     if (status != 0)
13         err_abort (status, "Create attr");
14 #ifdef _POSIX_THREAD_PROCESS_SHARED
15     status = pthread_mutexattr_setpshared (
16         &mutex_attr, PTHREAD_PROCESS_PRIVATE);
17     if (status != 0)
18         err_abort (status, "Set pshared");
19 #endif
20     status = pthread_mutex_init (&mutex, &mutex_attr);
21     if (status != 0)
22         err_abort (status, "Init mutex");
23     return 0;
24 }
```

■ mutex_attr.c

5.2.2 Condition variable attributes

```
pthread_condattr_t attr;
int pthread_condattr_init (pthread_condattr_t *attr);
int pthread_condattr_destroy (
    pthread_condattr_t *attr);
#ifdef _POSIX_THREAD_PROCESS_SHARED
int pthread_condattr_getpshared (
    pthread_condattr_t *attr, int *pshared);
int pthread_condattr_setpshared (
    pthread_condattr_t *attr, int pshared);
#endif
```

Pthreads defines only one attribute for condition variable creation, pshared. No system is required to implement this attribute, so check the system documentation before using it. You initialize a condition variable attributes object using pthread_condattr_init, specifying a pointer to a variable of type pthread_condattr_t, as in cond_attr.c, shown next. You use that attributes object by passing its address to pthread_cond_init instead of the NULL value we've been using so far.

If your system defines _POSIX_THREAD_PROCESS_SHARED then it supports the *pshared* attribute. You set the *pshared* attribute by calling the function pthread_condattr_setpshared. If you set the *pshared* attribute to the value PTHREAD_PROCESS_SHARED, the condition variable can be used by threads in separate processes that have access to the memory where the condition variable (pthread_cond_t) is initialized. The default value for this attribute is PTHREAD_PROCESS_PRIVATE.

The cond_attr.c program shows how to set a condition variable attributes object to create a condition variable using the *pshared* attribute. This example uses the default value, PTHREAD_PROCESS_PRIVATE, to avoid the additional complexity of creating shared memory and forking a process.

■ cond_attr.c

```
1  #include <pthread.h>
2  #include "errors.h"
3
4  pthread_cond_t cond;
5
6  int main (int argc, char *argv[])
7  {
8      pthread_condattr_t cond_attr;
9      int status;
10
```

```
11        status = pthread_condattr_init (&cond_attr);
12        if (status != 0)
13            err_abort (status, "Create attr");
14   #ifdef _POSIX_THREAD_PROCESS_SHARED
15        status = pthread_condattr_setpshared (
16            &cond_attr, PTHREAD_PROCESS_PRIVATE);
17        if (status != 0)
18            err_abort (status, "Set pshared");
19   #endif
20        status = pthread_cond_init (&cond, &cond_attr);
21        if (status != 0)
22            err_abort (status, "Init cond");
23        return 0;
24   }
```

■ cond_attr.c

To make use of a PTHREAD_PROCESS_SHARED condition variable, you must also use a PTHREAD_PROCESS_SHARED mutex. That's because two threads that synchronize using a condition variable must also use the same mutex. Waiting for a condition variable automatically unlocks, and then locks, the associated mutex. So if the mutex isn't also created with PTHREAD_PROCESS_SHARED, the synchronization won't work.

5.2.3 Thread attributes

```
pthread_attr_t attr;
int pthread_attr_init (pthread_attr_t *attr);
int pthread_attr_destroy (pthread_attr_t *attr);
int pthread_attr_getdetachstate (
    pthread_attr_t *attr, int *detachstate);
int pthread_attr_setdetachstate (
    pthread_attr_t *attr, int detachstate);
#ifdef _POSIX_THREAD_ATTR_STACKSIZE
int pthread_attr_getstacksize (
    pthread_attr_t *attr, size_t *stacksize);
int pthread_attr_setstacksize (
    pthread_attr_t *attr, size_t stacksize);
#endif
#ifdef _POSIX_THREAD_ATTR_STACKADDR
int pthread_attr_getstackaddr (
    pthread_attr_t *attr, void *stackaddr);
int pthread_attr_setstackaddr (
    pthread_attr_t *attr, void **stackaddr);
#endif
```

POSIX defines the following attributes for thread creation: *detachstate, stacksize, stackaddr, scope, inheritsched, schedpolicy,* and *schedparam.* Some systems won't support all of these attributes, so you need to check the system documentation before using them. You initialize a thread attributes object using `pthread_attr_init`, specifying a pointer to a variable of type `pthread_attr_t`, as in the program `thread_attr.c`, shown later. You use the attributes object you've created by passing its address as the second argument to `pthread_create` instead of the `NULL` value we've been using so far.

All Pthreads systems support the *detachstate* attribute. The value of this attribute can be either `PTHREAD_CREATE_JOINABLE` or `PTHREAD_CREATE_DETACHED`. By default, threads are created *joinable,* which means that the thread identification created by `pthread_create` can be used to join with the thread and retrieve its return value, or to cancel it. If you set the *detachstate* attribute to `PTHREAD_CREATE_DETACHED`, the identification of threads created using that attributes object can't be used. It also means that when the thread terminates, any resources it used can immediately be reclaimed by the system.

When you create threads that you know you won't need to cancel, or join with, you should create them detached. Remember that, in many cases, even if you want to know when a thread terminates, or receive some return value from it, you may not need to use `pthread_join`. If you provide your own notification mechanism, for example, using a condition variable, you can still create your threads detached.

❚ Setting the size of a stack is not very portable.

If your system defines the symbol `_POSIX_THREAD_ATTR_STACKSIZE`, then you can set the *stacksize* attribute to specify the minimum size for the stack of a thread created using the attributes object. Most systems will support this option, but you should use it with caution because stack size isn't portable. The amount of stack space you'll need depends on the calling standards and data formats used by each system.

Pthreads defines the symbol `PTHREAD_STACK_MIN` as the minimum stack size required for a thread: If you really need to specify a stack size, you might be best off calculating your requirements in terms of the minimum required by the implementation. Or, you could base your requirements on the default *stacksize* attribute selected by the implementation—for example, twice the default, or half the default. The program `thread_attr.c` shows how to read the default *stacksize* attribute value of an initialized attribute by calling `pthread_attr_getstacksize`.

❚ Setting the address of a stack is less portable!

If your system defines the symbol `_POSIX_THREAD_ATTR_STACKADDR`, then you can set the *stackaddr* attribute to specify a region of memory to be used as a stack by any thread created using this attributes object. The stack must be at least as large as `PTHREAD_STACK_MIN`. You may need to specify an area of memory with an address that's aligned to some required granularity. On a machine where the stack grows downward from higher addresses to lower addresses, the address you specify should be the highest address in the stack, not the lowest. If the stack grows up, you need to specify the lowest address.

You also need to be aware of whether the machine increments (or decrements) the stack before or after writing a new value—this determines whether the address you specify should be "inside" or "outside" the stack you've allocated. The system can't tell whether you allocated enough space, or specified the right address, so it has to trust you. If you get it wrong, undesirable things will occur.

Use the *stackaddr* attribute only with great caution, and beware that it may well be the least portable aspect of Pthreads. While a reasonable value for the *stacksize* attribute will probably work on a wide range of machines, it is little more than a wild coincidence if any particular value of the *stackaddr* attribute works on any two machines. Also, you must remember that you can create only one thread with any value of the *stackaddr* attribute. If you create two concurrent threads with the same *stackaddr* attribute value, the threads will run on the same stack. (That would be bad.)

The `thread_attr.c` program that follows shows some of these attributes in action, with proper conditionalization to avoid using the *stacksize* attribute if it is not supported by your system. If *stacksize* is supported (and it will be on most UNIX systems), the program will print the default and minimum stack size, and set *stacksize* to a value twice the minimum. The code also creates the thread *detached*, which means no thread can join with it to determine when it completes. Instead, `main` exits by calling `pthread_exit`, which means that the process will terminate when the last thread exits.

This example does not include the priority scheduling attributes, which are discussed (and demonstrated) in Section 5.5.2. It also does not demonstrate use of the *stackaddr* attribute—as I said, there is no way to use *stackaddr* in any remotely portable way and, although I have mentioned it for completeness, I strongly discourage use of *stackaddr* in any program.

■   `thread_attr.c`

```
1   #include <limits.h>
2   #include <pthread.h>
3   #include "errors.h"
4
5   /*
6    * Thread start routine that reports it ran, and then exits.
7    */
8   void *thread_routine (void *arg)
9   {
10      printf ("The thread is here\n");
11      return NULL;
12   }
13
14   int main (int argc, char *argv[])
```

```
15  {
16      pthread_t thread_id;
17      pthread_attr_t thread_attr;
18      struct sched_param thread_param;
19      size_t stack_size;
20      int status;
21
22      status = pthread_attr_init (&thread_attr);
23      if (status != 0)
24          err_abort (status, "Create attr");
25
26      /*
27       * Create a detached thread.
28       */
29      status = pthread_attr_setdetachstate (
30          &thread_attr, PTHREAD_CREATE_DETACHED);
31      if (status != 0)
32          err_abort (status, "Set detach");
33  #ifdef _POSIX_THREAD_ATTR_STACKSIZE
34      /*
35       * If supported, determine the default stack size and report
36       * it, and then select a stack size for the new thread.
37       *
38       * Note that the standard does not specify the default stack
39       * size, and the default value in an attributes object need
40       * not be the size that will actually be used.  Solaris 2.5
41       * uses a value of 0 to indicate the default.
42       */
43      status = pthread_attr_getstacksize (&thread_attr, &stack_size);
44      if (status != 0)
45          err_abort (status, "Get stack size");
46      printf ("Default stack size is %u; minimum is %u\n",
47          stack_size, PTHREAD_STACK_MIN);
48      status = pthread_attr_setstacksize (
49          &thread_attr, PTHREAD_STACK_MIN*2);
50      if (status != 0)
51          err_abort (status, "Set stack size");
52  #endif
53      status = pthread_create (
54          &thread_id, &thread_attr, thread_routine, NULL);
55      if (status != 0)
56          err_abort (status, "Create thread");
57      printf ("Main exiting\n");
58      pthread_exit (NULL);
59      return 0;
60  }
```

■ *thread_attr.c*

5.3 Cancellation

"Now, I give you fair warning,"
> *shouted the Queen, stamping on the ground as she spoke;*
> *"either you or your head must be off,*
> *and that in about half no time! Take your choice!"*
The Duchess took her choice, and was gone in a moment.

> —Lewis Carroll, Alice's Adventures in Wonderland

```
int pthread_cancel (pthread_t thread);
int pthread_setcancelstate (int state, int *oldstate);
int pthread_setcanceltype (int type, int *oldtype);
void pthread_testcancel (void);
void pthread_cleanup_push (
    void (*routine)(void *), void *arg);
void pthread_cleanup_pop (int execute);
```

Most of the time each thread runs independently, finishes a specific job, and exits on its own. But sometimes a thread is created to do something that doesn't necessarily need to be finished. The user might press a CANCEL button to stop a long search operation. Or the thread might be part of a redundant algorithm and is no longer useful because some other thread succeeded. What do you do when you just want a thread to go away? That's what the Pthreads cancellation interfaces are for.

Cancelling a thread is a lot like telling a human to stop something they're doing. Say that one of the bailing programmers has become maniacally obsessed with reaching land, and refuses to stop rowing until reaching safety (Figure 5.1). When the boat finally runs up onto the beach, he's become so fixated that he fails to realize he's done. The other programmers must roughly shake him, and forcibly remove the oars from his blistered hands to stop him—but clearly he must be stopped. That's cancellation. Sort of. I can think of other analogies for cancellation within the bailing programmer story, but I choose to ignore them. Perhaps you can, too.

Cancellation allows you to tell a thread to shut itself down. You don't need it often, but it can sometimes be extremely useful. Cancellation isn't an arbitrary external termination. It is more like a polite (though not necessarily "friendly") request. You're most likely to want to cancel a thread when you've found that something you set it off to accomplish is no longer necessary. You should never use cancellation unless you really want the target thread to go away. It is a termination mechanism, not a communication channel. So, why would you want to do that to a thread that you presumably created for some reason?

An application might use threads to perform long-running operations, perhaps in the background, while the user continues working. Such operations

FIGURE 5.1 *Thread cancellation analogy*

might include saving a large document, preparing to print a document, or sorting a large list. Most such interfaces probably will need to have some way for the user to cancel an operation, whether it is pressing the ESC key or Ctrl-C, or clicking a stop sign icon on the screen. The thread receiving the user interface cancel request would then determine that one or more background operations were in progress, and use pthread_cancel to cancel the appropriate threads.

Often, threads are deployed to "explore" a data set in parallel for some heuristic solution. For example, solving an equation for a local minimum or maximum. Once you've gotten one answer that's good enough, the remaining threads may no longer be needed. If so, you can cancel them to avoid wasting processor time and get on to other work.

Pthreads allows each thread to control its own termination. It can restore program invariants and unlock mutexes. It can even defer cancellation while it completes some important operation. For example, when two write operations must *both* complete if either completes, a cancellation between the two is not acceptable.

Pthreads supports three cancellation modes, described in Table 5.1, which are encoded as two binary values called "cancellation state" and "cancellation

Mode	State	Type	Meaning
Off	disabled	may be either	Cancellation remains pending until enabled.
Deferred	enabled	deferred	Cancellation occurs at next *cancellation point.*
Asynchronous	enabled	asynchronous	Cancellation may be processed at any time.

TABLE 5.1   *Cancellation states*

type." Each essentially can be on or off. (While that technically gives four modes, one of them is redundant.) As shown in the table, cancellation state is said to be *enabled* or *disabled,* and cancellation type is said to be *deferred* or *asynchronous.*

By default, cancellation is *deferred,* and can occur only at specific points in the program that check whether the thread has been requested to terminate, called *cancellation points.* Most functions that can wait for an unbounded time should be deferred cancellation points. Deferred cancellation points include waiting on a condition variable, reading or writing a file, and other functions where the thread may be blocked for a substantial period of time. There is also a special function called `pthread_testcancel` that is nothing but a deferred cancellation point. It will return immediately if the thread hasn't been asked to terminate, which allows you to turn any of your functions into cancellation points.

Some systems provide a function to *terminate* a thread immediately. Although that sounds useful, it is difficult to use such a function safely. In fact, it is nearly impossible in a normal modular programming environment. If a thread is terminated with a mutex locked, for example, the next thread trying to lock that mutex will be stuck waiting forever.

It might seem that the thread system could automatically release the mutex; but most of the time that's no help. Threads lock mutexes because they're modifying shared data. No other thread can know what data has been modified or what the thread was trying to change, which makes it difficult to fix the data. Now the program is broken. When the mutex is left locked, you can usually tell that something's broken because one or more threads will hang waiting for the mutex.

The only way to recover from terminating a thread with a locked mutex is for the application to be able to analyze all shared data and repair it to achieve a consistent and correct state. That is not impossible, and it is worth substantial effort when an application must be fail-safe. However, it is generally not practical for anything but an embedded system where the application designers control every bit of shared state in the process. You would have to rebuild not only your own program or library state, but also the state affected by any library functions that might be called by the thread (for example, the ANSI C library).

To cancel a thread, you need the thread's identifier, the `pthread_t` value returned to the creator by `pthread_create` or returned to the thread itself by `pthread_self`. Cancelling a thread is asynchronous—that is, when the call to pthread_cancel returns, the thread has not necessarily been canceled, it may have only been notified that a cancel request is *pending* against it. If you need to know when the thread has actually terminated, you must *join* with it by calling pthread_join after cancelling it.

If the thread had asynchronous cancelability type set, or when the thread next reaches a deferred cancellation point, the cancel request will be *delivered* by the system. When that happens, the system will set the thread's cancelability type to PTHREAD_CANCEL_DEFERRED and the cancelability state to PTHREAD_CANCEL_DISABLE. That is, the thread can clean up and terminate without having to worry about being canceled again.

When a function that is a cancellation point detects a pending cancel request, the function does not return to the caller. The active cleanup handlers will be called, if there are any, and the thread will terminate. There is no way to "handle" cancellation and continue execution—the thread must either defer cancellation entirely or terminate. This is analogous to C++ object destructors, rather than C++ exceptions—the object is allowed to clean up after itself, but it is not allowed to avoid destruction.

The following program, called cancel.c, shows how to write a thread that responds "reasonably quickly" to deferred cancellation, by calling pthread_testcancel within a loop.

11-19 The thread function thread_routine loops indefinitely, until canceled, testing periodically for a pending cancellation request. It minimizes the overhead of calling pthread_testcancel by doing so only every 1000 iterations (line 17).

27-35 On a Solaris system, set the thread concurrency level to 2, by calling thr_setconcurrency. Without the call to thr_setconcurrency, this program will hang on Solaris because thread_routine is "compute bound" and will not block. The main program would never have another chance to run once thread_routine started, and could not call pthread_cancel.

36-54 The main program creates a thread running thread_routine, sleeps for two seconds, and then cancels the thread. It joins with the thread, and checks the return value, which should be PTHREAD_CANCELED to indicate that it was canceled, rather than terminated normally.

■ cancel.c
───

```
1  #include <pthread.h>
2  #include "errors.h"
3
4  static int counter;
5
6  /*
7   * Loop until canceled. The thread can be canceled only
8   * when it calls pthread_testcancel, which it does each 1000
9   * iterations.
10  */
```

```
11  void *thread_routine (void *arg)
12  {
13      DPRINTF (("thread_routine starting\n"));
14      for (counter = 0; ; counter++)
15          if ((counter % 1000) == 0) {
16              DPRINTF (("calling testcancel\n"));
17              pthread_testcancel ();
18          }
19  }
20
21  int main (int argc, char *argv[])
22  {
23      pthread_t thread_id;
24      void *result;
25      int status;
26
27  #ifdef sun
28      /*
29       * On Solaris 2.5, threads are not timesliced. To ensure
30       * that our two threads can run concurrently, we need to
31       * increase the concurrency level to 2.
32       */
33      DPRINTF (("Setting concurrency level to 2\n"));
34      thr_setconcurrency (2);
35  #endif
36      status = pthread_create (
37          &thread_id, NULL, thread_routine, NULL);
38      if (status != 0)
39          err_abort (status, "Create thread");
40      sleep (2);
41
42      DPRINTF (("calling cancel\n"));
43      status = pthread_cancel (thread_id);
44      if (status != 0)
45          err_abort (status, "Cancel thread");
46
47      DPRINTF (("calling join\n"));
48      status = pthread_join (thread_id, &result);
49      if (status != 0)
50          err_abort (status, "Join thread");
51      if (result == PTHREAD_CANCELED)
52          printf ("Thread canceled at iteration %d\n", counter);
53      else
54          printf ("Thread was not canceled\n");
55      return 0;
56  }
```

■ cancel.c

A thread can disable cancellation around sections of code that need to complete without interruption, by calling `pthread_setcancelstate`. For example, if a database update operation takes two separate `write` calls, you wouldn't want to complete the first and have the second canceled. If you request that a thread be canceled while cancellation is disabled, the thread remembers that it was canceled but won't do anything about it until after cancellation is enabled again. Because enabling cancellation isn't a *cancellation point*, you also need to test for a pending cancel request if you want a cancel processed immediately.

When a thread may be canceled while it holds private resources, such as a locked mutex or heap storage that won't ever be freed by any other thread, those resources need to be released when the thread is canceled. If the thread has a mutex locked, it may also need to "repair" shared data to restore program invariants. *Cleanup handlers* provide the mechanism to accomplish the cleanup, somewhat like process `atexit` handlers. After acquiring a resource, and before any cancellation points, declare a cleanup handler by calling `pthread_cleanup_push`. Before releasing the resource, but after any cancellation points, remove the cleanup handler by calling `pthread_cleanup_pop`.

If you don't have a thread's identifier, you can't cancel the thread. That means that, at least using portable POSIX functions, you can't write an "idle thread killer" that will arbitrarily terminate threads in the process. You can only cancel threads that you created, or threads for which the creator (or the thread itself) gave you an identifier. That generally means that cancellation is restricted to operating within a subsystem.

5.3.1 Deferred cancelability

"Deferred cancelability" means that the thread's cancelability type has been set to `PTHREAD_CANCEL_DEFERRED` and the thread's cancelability enable has been set to `PTHREAD_CANCEL_ENABLE`. The thread will only respond to cancellation requests when it reaches one of a set of "cancellation points."

The following functions are always cancellation points on any Pthreads system:

`pthread_cond_wait`	`fsync`	`sigwaitinfo`
`pthread_cond_timedwait`	`mq_receive`	`sigsuspend`
`pthread_join`	`mq_send`	`sigtimedwait`
`pthread_testcancel`	`msync`	`sleep`
`sigwait`	`nanosleep`	`system`
`aio_suspend`	`open`	`tcdrain`
`close`	`pause`	`wait`
`creat`	`read`	`waitpid`
`fcntl (F_SETLCKW)`	`sem_wait`	`write`

The following list of functions may be cancellation points. You should write your code so that it will function correctly if any of these are cancellation points and also so that it will not break if any of them are not. If you depend upon any particular behavior, you may limit the portability of your code. You'll have to look at the conformance documentation to find out which, if any, are cancellation points for the system you are using:

closedir	getc_unlocked	printf
ctermid	getchar	putc
fclose	getchar_unlocked	putc_unlocked
fcntl (except F_SETLCKW)	getcwd	putchar
fflush	getgrgid	putchar_unlocked
fgetc	getgrgid_r	puts
fgets	getrtnam	readdir
fopen	getgrnam_r	remove
fprintf	getlogin	rename
fputc	getlogin_r	rewind
fputs	getpwnam	rewinddir
fread	getpwnam_r	scanf
freopen	getpwuid	tmpfile
fscanf	getpwuid_r	tmpname
fseek	gets	ttyname
ftell	lseek	ttyname_r
fwrite	opendir	ungetc
getc	perror	

Pthreads specifies that any ANSI C or POSIX function not specified in one of the two lists cannot be a cancellation point. However, your system probably has many additional cancellation points. That's because few UNIX systems are "POSIX." That is, they support other programming interfaces as well—such as BSD 4.3, System V Release 4, UNIX95, and so forth. POSIX doesn't recognize the existence of functions such as select or poll, and therefore it can't say whether or not they are cancellation points. Yet clearly both are functions that may block for an arbitrary period of time, and programmers using them with cancellation would reasonably expect them to behave as cancellation points. X/Open is currently addressing this problem for UNIX98 (*X/Open System Interfaces, Issue 5*), by extending the Pthreads list of cancellation points.

Most cancellation points involve I/O operations that may block the thread for an "unbounded" time. They're cancelable so that the waits can be interrupted. When a thread reaches a cancellation point the system determines whether a cancel is *pending* for the current ("target") thread. A cancel will be pending if another thread has called pthread_cancel for the target thread since the last time the target thread returned from a cancellation point. If a cancel is pending, the system will immediately begin calling cleanup functions, and then the thread will terminate.

If no cancel is currently pending, the function will proceed. If another thread requests that the thread be canceled while the thread is waiting for something (such as I/O) then the wait will be interrupted and the thread will begin its cancellation cleanup.

If you need to ensure that cancellation can't occur at a particular cancellation point, or during some sequence of cancellation points, you can temporarily disable cancellation in that region of code. The following program, called `cancel_disable.c`, is a variant of `cancel.c`. The "target" thread periodically calls `sleep`, and does not want the call to be cancelable.

23-32 After each cycle of 755 iterations, `thread_routine` will call `sleep` to wait a second. (The value 755 is just an arbitrary number that popped into my head. Do arbitrary numbers ever pop into your head?) Prior to sleeping, `thread_routine` disables cancellation by setting the cancelability state to `PTHREAD_CANCEL_DISABLE`. After `sleep` returns, it restores the saved cancelability state by calling `pthread_setcancelstate` again.

33-35 Just as in `cancel.c`, test for a pending cancel every 1000 iterations.

■ cancel_disable.c

```
1  #include <pthread.h>
2  #include "errors.h"
3
4  static int counter;
5
6  /*
7   * Thread start routine.
8   */
9  void *thread_routine (void *arg)
10 {
11     int state;
12     int status;
13
14     for (counter = 0; ; counter++) {
15
16         /*
17          * Each 755 iterations, disable cancellation and sleep
18          * for one second.
19          *
20          * Each 1000 iterations, test for a pending cancel by
21          * calling pthread_testcancel().
22          */
23         if ((counter % 755) == 0) {
24             status = pthread_setcancelstate (
25                 PTHREAD_CANCEL_DISABLE, &state);
26             if (status != 0)
27                 err_abort (status, "Disable cancel");
28             sleep (1);
29             status = pthread_setcancelstate (
30                 state, &state);
31             if (status != 0)
32                 err_abort (status, "Restore cancel");
```

```
33              } else
34                  if ((counter % 1000) == 0)
35                      pthread_testcancel ();
36          }
37  }
38
39  int main (int argc, char *argv[])
40  {
41      pthread_t thread_id;
42      void *result;
43      int status;
44
45      status = pthread_create (
46          &thread_id, NULL, thread_routine, NULL);
47      if (status != 0)
48          err_abort (status, "Create thread");
49      sleep (2);
50      status = pthread_cancel (thread_id);
51      if (status != 0)
52          err_abort (status, "Cancel thread");
53
54      status = pthread_join (thread_id, &result);
55      if (status != 0)
56          err_abort (status, "Join thread");
57      if (result == PTHREAD_CANCELED)
58          printf ("Thread canceled at iteration %d\n", counter);
59      else
60          printf ("Thread was not canceled\n");
61      return 0;
62  }
```

■ cancel_disable.c

5.3.2 Asynchronous cancelability

Asynchronous cancellation is useful because the "target thread" doesn't need to poll for cancellation requests by using cancellation points. That can be valuable for a thread that runs a tight compute-bound loop (for example, searching for a prime number factor) where the overhead of calling pthread_testcancel might be severe.

| Avoid asynchronous cancellation!
| It is difficult to use correctly and is rarely useful.

The problem is that you're limited in what you can do with asynchronous cancellation enabled. You can't acquire any resources, for example, including locking a mutex. That's because the cleanup code would have no way to determine whether the mutex had been locked. Asynchronous cancellation can occur at any hardware instruction. On some computers it may even be possible to interrupt some instructions in the middle. That makes it really difficult to determine what the canceled thread was doing.

For example, when you call `malloc` the system allocates some heap memory for you, stores a pointer to that memory somewhere (possibly in a hardware register), and then returns to your code, which probably moves the return value into some local storage for later use. There are lots of places that `malloc` might be interrupted by an asynchronous cancel, with varying effects. It might be interrupted before the memory was allocated. Or it might be interrupted after allocating storage but before it stored the address for return. Or it might even return to your code, but get interrupted before the return value could be copied to a local variable. In any of those cases the variable where your code expects to find a pointer to the allocated memory will be uninitialized. You can't tell whether the memory really was allocated yet. You can't free the memory, so that memory (if it was allocated to you) will remain allocated for the life of the program. That's a memory leak, which is not a desirable feature.

Or when you call `pthread_mutex_lock`, the system might be interrupted within a function call either before or after locking the mutex. Again, there's no way for your program to find out, because the interrupt may have occurred between any two instructions, even within the `pthread_mutex_lock` function, which might leave the mutex unusable. If the mutex is locked, the application will likely end up hanging because it will never be *unlocked*.

| Call no code with asynchronous cancellation enabled unless you wrote it to be async-cancel safe—and even then, think twice!

You are not allowed to call any function that acquires resources while asynchronous cancellation is enabled. In fact, you should never call *any* function while asynchronous cancellation is enabled unless the function is documented as "async-cancel safe." The only functions required to be async safe by Pthreads are `pthread_cancel`, `pthread_setcancelstate`, and `pthread_setcanceltype`. (And there is no reason to call `pthread_cancel` with asynchronous cancelability enabled.) No other POSIX or ANSI C functions need be async-cancel safe, and you should never call them with asynchronous cancelability enabled.

Pthreads suggests that all library functions should document whether or not they are async-cancel safe. However if the description of a function does not specifically say it is async-cancel safe you should always assume that it is not. The consequences of asynchronous cancellation in a function that is not async-cancel safe can be severe. And worse, the effects are sensitive to timing—so a function that appears to be async-cancel safe during experimentation may in fact cause all sorts of problems later when it ends up being canceled in a slightly different place.

The following program, `cancel_async.c`, shows the use of asynchronous cancellation in a compute-bound loop. Use of asynchronous cancellation makes this loop "more responsive" than the deferred cancellation loop in cancel.c. However, the program would become unreliable if any function calls were made within the loop, whereas the deferred cancellation version would continue to function correctly. In most cases, synchronous cancellation is preferable.

24-28   To keep the thread running awhile with something more interesting than an empty loop, cancel_async.c uses a simple matrix multiply nested loop. The matrixa and matrixb arrays are initialized with, respectively, their major or minor array index.

34-36   The cancellation type is changed to PTHREAD_CANCEL_ASYNCHRONOUS, allowing asynchronous cancellation within the matrix multiply loops.

39-44   The thread repeats the matrix multiply until canceled, on each iteration replacing the first source array (matrixa) with the result of the previous multiplication (matrixc).

66-74   Once again, on a Solaris system, set the thread concurrency level to 2, allowing the main thread and thread_routine to run concurrently on a uniprocessor. The program will hang without this step, since user mode threads are not timesliced on Solaris.

■   cancel_async.c
───

```
 1  #include <pthread.h>
 2  #include "errors.h"
 3
 4  #define SIZE    10      /* array size */
 5
 6  static int matrixa[SIZE][SIZE];
 7  static int matrixb[SIZE][SIZE];
 8  static int matrixc[SIZE][SIZE];
 9
10  /*
11   * Loop until canceled. The thread can be canceled at any
12   * point within the inner loop, where asynchronous cancellation
13   * is enabled. The loop multiplies the two matrices matrixa
14   * and matrixb.
15   */
16  void *thread_routine (void *arg)
17  {
18      int cancel_type, status;
19      int i, j, k, value = 1;
20
21      /*
22       * Initialize the matrices to something arbitrary.
23       */
24      for (i = 0; i < SIZE; i++)
25          for (j = 0; j < SIZE; j++) {
26              matrixa[i][j] = i;
27              matrixb[i][j] = j;
28          }
29
```

```
30      while (1) {
31          /*
32           * Compute the matrix product of matrixa and matrixb.
33           */
34          status = pthread_setcanceltype (
35                  PTHREAD_CANCEL_ASYNCHRONOUS,
36                  &cancel_type);
37          if (status != 0)
38              err_abort (status, "Set cancel type");
39          for (i = 0; i < SIZE; i++)
40              for (j = 0; j < SIZE; j++) {
41                  matrixc[i][j] = 0;
42                  for (k = 0; k < SIZE; k++)
43                      matrixc[i][j] += matrixa[i][k] * matrixb[k][j];
44              }
45          status = pthread_setcanceltype (
46                  cancel_type,
47                  &cancel_type);
48          if (status != 0)
49              err_abort (status, "Set cancel type");
50
51          /*
52           * Copy the result (matrixc) into matrixa to start again
53           */
54          for (i = 0; i < SIZE; i++)
55              for (j = 0; j < SIZE; j++)
56                  matrixa[i][j] = matrixc[i][j];
57      }
58  }
59
60  int main (int argc, char *argv[])
61  {
62      pthread_t thread_id;
63      void *result;
64      int status;
65
66  #ifdef sun
67      /*
68       * On Solaris 2.5, threads are not timesliced. To ensure
69       * that our two threads can run concurrently, we need to
70       * increase the concurrency level to 2.
71       */
72      DPRINTF (("Setting concurrency level to 2\n"));
73      thr_setconcurrency (2);
74  #endif
75      status = pthread_create (
76          &thread_id, NULL, thread_routine, NULL);
77      if (status != 0)
78          err_abort (status, "Create thread");
79      sleep (1);
```

```
80      status = pthread_cancel (thread_id);
81      if (status != 0)
82          err_abort (status, "Cancel thread");
83      status = pthread_join (thread_id, &result);
84      if (status != 0)
85          err_abort (status, "Join thread");
86      if (result == PTHREAD_CANCELED)
87          printf ("Thread canceled\n");
88      else
89          printf ("Thread was not canceled\n");
90      return 0;
91  }
```

■ cancel_async.c

❙ Warning: do not let "DCE threads'" habits carry over to Pthreads!

I'll end this section with a warning. DCE threads, a critical component of the
Open Software Foundation's Distributed Computing Environment, was designed
to be independent of the underlying UNIX kernel. Systems with no thread support
at all often emulated "thread synchronous" I/O in user mode, using nonblocking
I/O mode, so that a thread attempting I/O on a busy file was blocked on a condition variable until a later select or poll showed that the I/O could complete.
DCE listener threads might block indefinitely on a socket read, and it was important to be able to cancel that read.

When DCE was ported to newer kernels that had thread support, but not
Pthreads support, the user mode I/O wrappers were usually omitted, resulting in
a thread blocked within a kernel that did not support deferred cancellation. Users
discovered that, in many cases, these systems implemented asynchronous cancellation in such a way that, quite by coincidence, a kernel wait might be
canceled "safely" if the thread switched to asynchronous cancellation immediately before the kernel call, and switched back to deferred cancellation
immediately after. This observation was publicized in DCE documentation, but it
is a very dangerous hack, even on systems where it seems to work. You should
never try this on any Pthreads system! If your system conforms to POSIX
1003.1c–1995 (or POSIX 1003.1, 1996 edition, or later), it supports deferred cancellation of, at minimum, kernel functions such as read and write. You do not
need asynchronous cancellation, and using it can be extremely dangerous.

5.3.3 Cleaning up

❙ When you write any library code, design it to handle deferred
cancellation gracefully. Disable cancellation where it is not
appropriate, and always use cleanup handlers at cancellation points.

If a section of code needs to restore some state when it is canceled, it must use cleanup handlers. When a thread is canceled while waiting for a condition variable, it will wake up with the mutex locked. Before the thread terminates it usually needs to restore invariants, and it always needs to release the mutex.

Each thread may be considered to have a stack of active cleanup handlers. Cleanup handlers are added to the stack by calling `pthread_cleanup_push`, and the most recently added cleanup handler is removed by calling `pthread_cleanup_pop`. When the thread is canceled or when it exits by calling `pthread_exit`, Pthreads calls each active cleanup handler in turn, beginning with the most recently added cleanup handler. When all active cleanup handlers have returned, the thread is terminated.

Pthreads cleanup handlers are designed so that you can often use the cleanup handler even when the thread wasn't canceled. It is often useful to run the same cleanup function regardless of whether your code is canceled or completes normally. When `pthread_cleanup_pop` is called with a nonzero value, the cleanup handler is executed even if the thread was not canceled.

You cannot push a cleanup handler in one function and pop it in another function. The `pthread_cleanup_push` and `pthread_cleanup_pop` operations may be defined as macros, such that `pthread_cleanup_push` contains the opening brace "{" of a block, while `pthread_cleanup_pop` contains the matching closing brace "}" of the block. You must always keep this restriction in mind while using cleanup handlers, if you wish your code to be portable.

The following program, `cancel_cleanup.c`, shows the use of a cleanup handler to release a mutex when a condition variable wait is canceled.

10-17   The control structure (`control`) is used by all threads to maintain shared synchronization objects and invariants. Each thread increases the member `counter` by one when it starts, and decreases it at termination. The member `busy` is used as a dummy condition wait predicate—it is initialized to 1, and never cleared, which means that the condition wait loops will never terminate (in this example) until the threads are canceled.

24-34   The function `cleanup_handler` is installed as the cancellation cleanup handler for each thread. It is called on normal termination as well as through cancellation, to decrease the count of active threads and unlock the mutex.

47   The function `thread_routine` establishes `cleanup_handler` as the active cancellation cleanup handler.

54-58   Wait until the `control` structure's `busy` member is set to 0, which, in this example, will never occur. The condition wait loop will exit only when the wait is canceled.

60   Although the condition wait loop in this example will not exit, the function cleans up by removing the active cleanup handler. The nonzero argument to `pthread_cleanup_pop`, remember, means that the cleanup handler will be called even though cancellation did not occur.

In some cases, you may omit "unreachable statements" like this `pthread_cleanup_pop` call. However, in this case, your code might not compile without it. The `pthread_cleanup_push` and `pthread_cleanup_pop` macros are special, and may expand to form, respectively, the beginning and ending of a block. Digital

UNIX does this, for example, to implement cancellation on top of the common structured exception handling provided by the operating system.

■ cancel_cleanup.c

```
1   #include <pthread.h>
2   #include "errors.h"
3
4   #define THREADS 5
5
6   /*
7    * Control structure shared by the test threads, containing
8    * the synchronization and invariant data.
9    */
10  typedef struct control_tag {
11      int                 counter, busy;
12      pthread_mutex_t     mutex;
13      pthread_cond_t      cv;
14  } control_t;
15
16  control_t control =
17      {0, 1, PTHREAD_MUTEX_INITIALIZER, PTHREAD_COND_INITIALIZER};
18
19  /*
20   * This routine is installed as the cancellation cleanup
21   * handler around the cancelable condition wait. It will
22   * be called by the system when the thread is canceled.
23   */
24  void cleanup_handler (void *arg)
25  {
26      control_t *st = (control_t *)arg;
27      int status;
28
29      st->counter--;
30      printf ("cleanup_handler: counter == %d\n", st->counter);
31      status = pthread_mutex_unlock (&st->mutex);
32      if (status != 0)
33          err_abort (status, "Unlock in cleanup handler");
34  }
35
36  /*
37   * Multiple threads are created running this routine (controlled
38   * by the THREADS macro). They maintain a "counter" invariant,
39   * which expresses the number of running threads. They specify a
40   * nonzero value to pthread_cleanup_pop to run the same
41   * "finalization" action when cancellation does not occur.
42   */
43  void *thread_routine (void *arg)
44  {
45      int status;
```

```
46
47      pthread_cleanup_push (cleanup_handler, (void*)&control);
48
49      status = pthread_mutex_lock (&control.mutex);
50      if (status != 0)
51          err_abort (status, "Mutex lock");
52      control.counter++;
53
54      while (control.busy) {
55          status = pthread_cond_wait (&control.cv, &control.mutex);
56          if (status != 0)
57              err_abort (status, "Wait on condition");
58      }
59
60      pthread_cleanup_pop (1);
61      return NULL;
62  }
63
64  int main (int argc, char *argv[])
65  {
66      pthread_t thread_id[THREADS];
67      int count;
68      void *result;
69      int status;
70
71      for (count = 0; count < THREADS; count++) {
72          status = pthread_create (
73              &thread_id[count], NULL, thread_routine, NULL);
74          if (status != 0)
75              err_abort (status, "Create thread");
76      }
77
78      sleep (2);
79
80      for (count = 0; count < THREADS; count++) {
81          status = pthread_cancel (thread_id[count]);
82          if (status != 0)
83              err_abort (status, "Cancel thread");
84
85          status = pthread_join (thread_id[count], &result);
86          if (status != 0)
87              err_abort (status, "Join thread");
88          if (result == PTHREAD_CANCELED)
89              printf ("thread %d canceled\n", count);
90          else
91              printf ("thread %d was not canceled\n", count);
92      }
93      return 0;
94  }
```

■ cancel_cleanup.c

If one of your threads creates a set of threads to "subcontract" some function, say, a parallel arithmetic operation, and the "contractor" is canceled while the function is in progress, you probably won't want to leave the subcontractor threads running. Instead, you could "pass on" the cancellation to each subcontrator thread, letting them handle their own termination independently.

If you had originally intended to join with the subcontractors, remember that they will continue to consume some resources until they have been joined or detached. When the contractor thread cancels them, you should not delay cancellation by joining with the subcontractors. Instead, you can cancel each thread and immediately detach it using `pthread_detach`. The subcontractor resources can then be recycled immediately as they finish, while the contractor can wrap things up independently.

The following program, `cancel_subcontract.c`, shows one way to propagate cancellation to subcontractors.

9–12   The `team_t` structure defines the state of the team of subcontractor threads. The `join_i` member records the index of the last subcontractor with which the contractor had joined, so on cancellation from within `pthread_join`, it can cancel the threads it had not yet joined. The `workers` member is an array recording the thread identifiers of the subcontractor threads.

18–25   The subcontractor threads are started running the `worker_routine` function. This function loops until canceled, calling `pthread_testcancel` every 1000 iterations.

31–46   The `cleanup` function is established as the active cleanup handler within the contractor thread. When the contractor is canceled, `cleanup` iterates through the remaining (unjoined) subcontractors, cancelling and detaching each. Note that it does not join the subcontractors—in general, it is not a good idea to wait in a cleanup handler. The thread, after all, is expected to clean up and terminate, not to wait around for something to happen. But if your cleanup handler really needs to wait for something, don't be afraid, it will work just fine.

53–76   The contractor thread is started running `thread_routine`. This function creates a set of subcontractors, then joins with each subcontractor. As it joins each thread, it records the current index within the `workers` array in the `team_t` member `join_i`. The cleanup handler is established with a pointer to the team structure so that it can determine the last offset and begin cancelling the remaining subcontractors.

78–104   The main program creates the contractor thread, running `thread_routine`, and then sleeps for five seconds. When it wakes up, it cancels the contractor thread, and waits for it to terminate.

■ `cancel_subcontract.c`
_____

```
1   #include <pthread.h>
2   #include "errors.h"
3
4   #define THREADS 5
5
```

```
 6  /*
 7   * Structure that defines the threads in a "team."
 8   */
 9  typedef struct team_tag {
10      int          join_i;                    /* join index */
11      pthread_t    workers[THREADS];          /* thread identifiers */
12  } team_t;
13
14  /*
15   * Start routine for worker threads. They loop waiting for a
16   * cancellation request.
17   */
18  void *worker_routine (void *arg)
19  {
20      int counter;
21
22      for (counter = 0; ; counter++)
23          if ((counter % 1000) == 0)
24              pthread_testcancel ();
25  }
26
27  /*
28   * Cancellation cleanup handler for the contractor thread. It
29   * will cancel and detach each worker in the team.
30   */
31  void cleanup (void *arg)
32  {
33      team_t *team = (team_t *)arg;
34      int count, status;
35
36      for (count = team->join_i; count < THREADS; count++) {
37          status = pthread_cancel (team->workers[count]);
38          if (status != 0)
39              err_abort (status, "Cancel worker");
40
41          status = pthread_detach (team->workers[count]);
42          if (status != 0)
43              err_abort (status, "Detach worker");
44          printf ("Cleanup: canceled %d\n", count);
45      }
46  }
47
48  /*
49   * Thread start routine for the contractor. It creates a team of
50   * worker threads, and then joins with them. When canceled, the
51   * cleanup handler will cancel and detach the remaining threads.
52   */
53  void *thread_routine (void *arg)
```

```
54  {
55      team_t team;                        /* team info */
56      int count;
57      void *result;                       /* Return status */
58      int status;
59
60      for (count = 0; count < THREADS; count++) {
61          status = pthread_create (
62              &team.workers[count], NULL, worker_routine, NULL);
63          if (status != 0)
64              err_abort (status, "Create worker");
65      }
66      pthread_cleanup_push (cleanup, (void*)&team);
67
68      for (team.join_i = 0; team.join_i < THREADS; team.join_i++) {
69          status = pthread_join (team.workers[team.join_i], &result);
70          if (status != 0)
71              err_abort (status, "Join worker");
72      }
73
74      pthread_cleanup_pop (0);
75      return NULL;
76  }
77
78  int main (int argc, char *argv[])
79  {
80      pthread_t thread_id;
81      int status;
82
83  #ifdef sun
84      /*
85       * On Solaris 2.5, threads are not timesliced. To ensure
86       * that our threads can run concurrently, we need to
87       * increase the concurrency level to at least 2 plus THREADS
88       * (the number of workers).
89       */
90      DPRINTF (("Setting concurrency level to %d\n", THREADS+2));
91      thr_setconcurrency (THREADS+2);
92  #endif
93      status = pthread_create (&thread_id, NULL, thread_routine, NULL);
94      if (status != 0)
95          err_abort (status, "Create team");
96      sleep (5);
97      printf ("Cancelling...\n");
98      status = pthread_cancel (thread_id);
99      if (status != 0)
100         err_abort (status, "Cancel team");
```

```
101        status = pthread_join (thread_id, NULL);
102        if (status != 0)
103            err_abort (status, "Join team");
104  }
```

■ cancel_subcontract.c

5.4 Thread-specific data

No, I've made up my mind about it: if I'm Mabel, I'll stay down here. It'll be
no use their putting their heads down and saying "Come up again,
dear!" I shall only look up and say "Who am I, then? Tell me that first, and
then, if I like being that person, I'll come up: if not, I'll stay down here till
I'm somebody else."
—Lewis Carroll, *Alice's Adventures in Wonderland*

When a function in a single threaded program needs to create private data that persists across calls to that function, the data can be allocated statically in memory. The name's scope can be limited to the function or file that uses it (static) or it can be made global (extern).

It is not quite that simple when you use threads. All threads within a process share the same address space, which means that any variable declared as static or extern, or in the process heap, may be read and written by all threads within the process. That has several important implications for code that wants to store "persistent" data between a series of function calls within a thread:

- The value in a static or extern variable, or in the heap, will be the value last written by any thread. In some cases this may be what you want, for example, to maintain the seed of a pseudorandom number sequence. In other cases, it may not be what you want.
- The only storage a thread has that's truly "private" are processor registers. Even stack addresses can be shared, although only if the "owner" deliberately exposes an address to another thread. In any event, neither registers nor "private" stack can replace uses of persistent static storage in non-threaded code.

So when you need a private variable, you must first decide whether all threads share the same value, or whether each thread should have its own value. If they share, then you can use static or extern data, just as you could in a single threaded program; however, you must synchronize access to the shared data across multiple threads, usually by adding one or more mutexes.

If each thread needs its own value for a private variable, then you must store all the values somewhere, and each thread must be able to locate the proper value. In some cases you might be able to use static data, for example, a table where you can search for a value unique to each thread, such as the thread's `pthread_t`. In many interesting cases you cannot predict how many threads might call the function—imagine you were implementing a thread-safe library that could be called by arbitrary code, in any number of threads.

The most general solution is to `malloc` some heap in each thread and store the values there, but your code will need to be able to find the proper private data in any thread. You could create a linked list of all the private values, storing the creating thread's identifier (`pthread_t`) so it could be found again, but that will be slow if there are many threads. You need to search the list to find the proper value, and it would be difficult to recover the storage that was allocated by terminated threads—your function cannot know when a thread terminates.

> ❙ New interfaces should not rely on implicit persistent storage!

When you are designing new interfaces, there's a better solution. You should require the caller to allocate the necessary persistent state, and tell you where it is. There are many advantages to this model, including, most importantly:

- In many cases, you can avoid internal synchronization using this model, and, in rare cases where the caller wishes to share the persistent state between threads, the caller can supply the needed synchronization.
- The caller can instead choose to allocate more than one state buffer for use within a single thread. The result is several independent sequences of calls to your function within the same thread, with no conflict.

The problem is that you often need to support *implicit* persistent states. You may be making an existing interface thread-safe, and cannot add an argument to the functions, or require that the caller maintain a new data structure for your benefit. That's where thread-specific data comes in.

Thread-specific data allows each thread to have a separate copy of a variable, as if each thread has an array of thread-specific data values, which is indexed by a common "key" value. Imagine that the bailing programmers are wearing their corporate ID badges, clipped to their shirt pockets (Figure 5.2). While the information is different for each programmer, you can find the information easily without already knowing which programmer you're examining.

The program creates a *key* (sort of like posting a corporate regulation that employee identification badges always be displayed clipped to the left breast pocket of the employee's shirt or jacket) and each thread can then independently set or get its own value for that key (although the badge is always on the left pocket, each employee has a unique badge number, and, in most cases, a unique name). The *key* is the same for all threads, but each thread can associate its own independent *value* with that shared key. Each thread can change its private value for a key at any time, without affecting the key or any value other threads may have for the key.

FIGURE 5.2 *Thread-specific data analogy*

5.4.1 Creating thread-specific data

```
pthread_key_t key;
int pthread_key_create (
    pthread_key_t *key, void (*destructor)(void *));
int pthread_key_delete (pthread_key_t key);
```

A thread-specific data key is represented in your program by a variable of type `pthread_key_t`. Like most Pthreads types, `pthread_key_t` is *opaque* and you should never make any assumptions about the structure or content. The easiest way to create a thread-specific data key is to call `pthread_key_create` before any threads try to use the key, for example early in the program's `main` function.

If you need to create a thread-specific data key later, you have to ensure that `pthread_key_create` is called only once for each `pthread_key_t` variable. That's because if you create a key twice, you are really creating two different keys. The second key will overwrite the first, which will be lost forever along with the values any threads might have set for the first key.

When you can't add code to `main`, the easiest way to ensure that a thread-specific data key is created only once is to use `pthread_once`, the one-time initialization function, as shown in the following program, `tsd_once.c`.

7-10   The `tsd_t` structure is used to contain per-thread data. Each thread allocates a private `tsd_t` structure, and stores a pointer to that structure as its value for the thread-specific data key `tsd_key`. The `thread_id` member holds the thread's identifier (`pthread_t`), and the `string` member holds the pointer to a "name" string for the thread. The variable `tsd_key` holds the thread-specific data key used to access the `tsd_t` structures.

19-27   One-time initialization (`pthread_once`) is used to ensure that the key `tsd_key` is created before the first access.

33-56   The threads begin in the thread start function `thread_routine`. The argument (`arg`) is a pointer to a character string naming the thread. Each thread calls `pthread_once` to ensure that the thread-specific data key has been created. The thread then allocates a `tsd_t` structure, initializes the `thread_id` member with the thread's identifier, and copies its argument to the `string` member.

The thread gets the current thread-specific data value by calling `pthread_getspecific`, and prints a message using the thread's name. It then sleeps for a few seconds and prints another message to demonstrate that the thread-specific data value remains the same, even though another thread has assigned a different `tsd_t` structure address to the same thread-specific data key.

■   tsd_once.c
───

```
1   #include <pthread.h>
2   #include "errors.h"
3
4   /*
5    * Structure used as the value for thread-specific data key.
6    */
7   typedef struct tsd_tag {
8       pthread_t    thread_id;
9       char         *string;
10  } tsd_t;
11
12  pthread_key_t tsd_key;                /* Thread-specific data key */
13  pthread_once_t key_once = PTHREAD_ONCE_INIT;
14
15  /*
16   * One-time initialization routine used with the pthread_once
17   * control block.
18   */
19  void once_routine (void)
20  {
21      int status;
22
23      printf ("initializing key\n");
24      status = pthread_key_create (&tsd_key, NULL);
25      if (status != 0)
26          err_abort (status, "Create key");
27  }
```

```
28
29   /*
30    * Thread start routine that uses pthread_once to dynamically
31    * create a thread-specific data key.
32    */
33   void *thread_routine (void *arg)
34   {
35       tsd_t *value;
36       int status;
37
38       status = pthread_once (&key_once, once_routine);
39       if (status != 0)
40           err_abort (status, "Once init");
41       value = (tsd_t*)malloc (sizeof (tsd_t));
42       if (value == NULL)
43           errno_abort ("Allocate key value");
44       status = pthread_setspecific (tsd_key, value);
45       if (status != 0)
46           err_abort (status, "Set tsd");
47       printf ("%s set tsd value %p\n", arg, value);
48       value->thread_id = pthread_self ();
49       value->string = (char*)arg;
50       value = (tsd_t*)pthread_getspecific (tsd_key);
51       printf ("%s starting...\n", value->string);
52       sleep (2);
53       value = (tsd_t*)pthread_getspecific (tsd_key);
54       printf ("%s done...\n", value->string);
55       return NULL;
56   }
57
58   void main (int argc, char *argv[])
59   {
60       pthread_t thread1, thread2;
61       int status;
62
63       status = pthread_create (
64           &thread1, NULL, thread_routine, "thread 1");
65       if (status != 0)
66           err_abort (status, "Create thread 1");
67       status = pthread_create (
68           &thread2, NULL, thread_routine, "thread 2");
69       if (status != 0)
70           err_abort (status, "Create thread 2");
71       pthread_exit (NULL);
72   }
```

■ tsd_once.c

Pthreads allows you to *destroy* a thread-specific data key when your program no longer needs it, by calling `pthread_key_delete`. The Pthreads standard guarantees only 128 thread-specific data keys at any one time, so it may be useful to destroy a key that you know you aren't using and won't need again. The actual number of keys supported by your Pthreads system is specified by the value of the symbol `PTHREAD_KEYS_MAX` defined in `<limits.h>`.

When you destroy a thread-specific data key, it does not affect the current value of that key in any thread, not even in the calling thread. That means your code is completely responsible for freeing any memory that you have associated with the thread-specific data key, in all threads. Of course, any use of the deleted thread-specific data key (`pthread_key_t`) results in undefined behavior.

> Delete thread-specific data keys only when you
> are sure no thread has a value for that key!
>
> Or ... don't destroy them at all.

You should never destroy a key while some thread still has a value for that key. Some later call to `pthread_key_create`, for example, might reuse the `pthread_key_t` identifier that had been assigned to a deleted key. When an existing thread that had set a value for the old key requests the value of the new key, it will receive the old value. The program will likely react badly to receiving this incorrect data, so you should never delete a thread-specific data key until you are sure that no existing threads have a value for that key, for example, by maintaining a "reference count" for the key, as shown in the program `tsd_destructor.c`, in Section 5.4.3.

Even better, don't destroy thread-specific data keys. There's rarely any need to do so, and if you try you will almost certainly run into difficulties. Few programs will require even the minimum Pthreads limit of 128 thread-specific data keys. Rarely will you use more than a few. In general, each component that uses thread-specific data will have a small number of keys each maintaining pointers to data structures that contain related data. It would take a lot of components to exhaust the available keys!

5.4.2 Using thread-specific data

```
int pthread_setspecific (
    pthread_key_t key, const void *value);
void *pthread_getspecific (pthread_key_t key);
```

You can use the `pthread_getspecific` function to determine the thread's current value for a key, or `pthread_setspecific` to change the current value. Take a look at Section 7.3.1 for ideas on using thread-specific data to adapt old libraries that rely on static data to be thread-safe.

A thread-specific data value of NULL means something special to Pthreads—do not set a thread-specific data value of NULL unless you really mean it.

The initial value for any new key (in all threads) is NULL. Also, Pthreads sets the thread-specific data value for a key to NULL before calling that key's destructor (passing the previous value of the key) when a thread terminates.[*] If your thread-specific data value is the address of heap storage, for example, and you want to free that storage in your destructor, you must use the argument passed to the destructor rather than calling pthread_getspecific.

Pthreads will not call the destructor for a thread-specific data key if the terminating thread has a value of NULL for that key. NULL is special, meaning "this key has no value." If you ever use pthread_setspecific to set the value of a thread-specific data key to NULL, you need to remember that you are not setting the value NULL, but rather stating that the key no longer has a value in the current thread.

Destructor functions are called only when the thread terminates, not when the value of a thread-specific data key is changed.

Another important thing to remember is that thread-specific data key destructor functions are not called when you replace an existing value for that key. That is, if you allocate a structure in heap and assign a pointer to that structure as the value of a thread-specific data key, and then later allocate a new structure and assign a pointer to that new structure to the same thread-specific data key, in the same thread, you are responsible for freeing the old structure. Pthreads will not free the old structure, nor will it call your destructor function with a pointer to the old structure.

5.4.3 Using destructor functions

When a thread exits while it has a value defined for some thread-specific data key, you usually need to do something about it. If your key's value is a pointer to heap memory, you will need to free the memory to avoid a memory leak each time a thread terminates. Pthreads allows you to define a *destructor* function

---

[*]That is, unfortunately, not what the standard says. This is one of the problems with formal standards—they say what they say, not what they were intended to say. Somehow, an error crept in, and the sentence specifying that "the implementation clears the thread-specific data value before calling the destructor" was deleted. Nobody noticed, and the standard was approved with the error. So the standard says (by omission) that if you want to write a portable application using thread-specific data, that will not hang on thread termination, you must call pthread_setspecific within your destructor function to change the value to NULL. This would be silly, and any serious implementation of Pthreads will violate the standard in this respect. Of course, the standard will be fixed, probably by the 1003.1n amendment (assorted corrections to 1003.1c–1995), but that will take a while.

when you create a thread-specific data key. When a thread terminates with a non-NULL value for a thread-specific data key, the key's destructor (if any) is called with the current value of the key.

▌ Thread-specific data destructors are called in "unspecified order."

Pthreads checks all thread-specific data keys in the process when a thread exits, and for each thread-specific data key with a value that's not NULL, it sets the value to NULL and then calls the key's destructor function. Going back to our analogy, someone might collect the identity badges of all programmers by removing whatever is hanging from each programmer's left shirt pocket, safe in the knowledge that it will always be the programmer's badge. Be careful, because the order in which destructors are called is undefined. Try to make each destructor as independent as possible.

Thread-specific data destructors can set a new value for the key for which a value is being destroyed or for any other key. You should never do this directly, but it can easily happen indirectly if you call other functions from your destructor. For example, the ANSI C library's destructors might be called before yours—and calling an ANSI C function, for example, using fprintf to write a log message to a file, could cause a new value to be assigned to a thread-specific data key. The system must recheck the list of thread-specific data values for you after all destructors have been called.

▌ If your thread-specific data destructor creates a new thread-specific
▌ data value, you will get another chance. Maybe too many chances!

The standard requires that a Pthreads implementation may recheck the list some fixed number of times and then give up. When it gives up, the final thread-specific data value is not destroyed. If the value is a pointer to heap memory, the result may be a memory leak, so be careful. The <limits.h> header defines _PTHREAD_DESTRUCTOR_ITERATIONS to the number of times the system will check, and the value must be at least 4. Alternately, the system is allowed to keep checking forever, so a destructor function that always sets thread-specific data values may cause an infinite loop.

Usually, new thread-specific data values are set within a destructor only when subsystem 1 uses thread-specific data that depends on another independent subsystem 2 that also uses thread-specific data. Because the order in which destructor functions run is unspecified, the two may be called in the wrong order. If the subsystem 1 destructor needs to call into subsystem 2, it may inadvertently result in allocating new thread-specific data for subsystem 2. Although the subsystem 2 destructor will need to be called again to free the new data, the subsystem 1 thread-specific data remains NULL, so the loop will terminate.

The following program, tsd_destructor.c, demonstrates using thread-specific data destructors to release memory when a thread terminates. It also keeps track of how many threads are using the thread-specific data, and deletes the thread-specific data key when the destructor is run for the final thread. This program is similar in structure to `tsd_once.c`, from Section 5.3, so only the relevant differences will be annotated here.

12-14   In addition to the key value (`identity_key`), the program maintains a count of threads that are using the key (`identity_key_counter`), which is protected by a mutex (`identity_key_mutex`).

22-42   The function `identity_key_destructor` is the thread-specific data key's destructor function. It begins by printing a message so we can observe when it runs in each thread. It frees the storage used to maintain thread-specific data, the `private_t` structure. Then it locks the mutex associated with the thread-specific data key (`identity_key_mutex`) and decreases the count of threads using the key. If the count reaches 0, it deletes the key and prints a message.

48-63   The function `identity_key_get` can be used anywhere (in this example, it is used only once per thread) to get the value of `identity_key` for the calling thread. If there is no current value (the value is NULL), then it allocates a new `private_t` structure and assigns it to the key for future reference.

68-78   The function `thread_routine` is the thread start function used by the example. It acquires a value for the key by calling `identity_key_get`, and sets the members of the structure. The `string` member is set to the thread's argument, creating a global "name" for the thread, which can be used for printing messages.

80-114   The main program creates the thread-specific data key `tsd_key`. Notice that, unlike `tsd_once.c`, this program does not bother to use `pthread_once`. As I mentioned in the annotation for that example, in a main program it is perfectly safe, and more efficient, to create the key inside `main`, before creating any threads.

101   The main program initializes the reference counter (`identity_key_counter`) to 3. It is critical that you define in advance how many threads will reference a key that will be deleted based on a reference count, as we intend to do. The counter must be set before any thread using the key can possibly terminate.

    You cannot, for example, code `identity_key_get` so that it dynamically increases the counter when it first assigns a thread-specific value for `identity_key`. That is because one thread might assign a thread-specific value for `identity_key` and then terminate before another thread using the key had a chance to start. If that happened, the first thread's destructor would find no remaining references to the key, and it would delete the key. Later threads would then fail when trying to set thread-specific data values.

■ tsd_destructor.c

```
1   #include <pthread.h>
2   #include "errors.h"
3
4   /*
5    * Structure used as value of thread-specific data key.
6    */
```

```
 7  typedef struct private_tag {
 8      pthread_t    thread_id;
 9      char         *string;
10  } private_t;
11
12  pthread_key_t identity_key;              /* Thread-specific data key */
13  pthread_mutex_t identity_key_mutex = PTHREAD_MUTEX_INITIALIZER;
14  long identity_key_counter = 0;
15
16  /*
17   * This routine is called as each thread terminates with a value
18   * for the thread-specific data key. It keeps track of how many
19   * threads still have values, and deletes the key when there are
20   * no more references.
21   */
22  void identity_key_destructor (void *value)
23  {
24      private_t *private = (private_t*)value;
25      int status;
26
27      printf ("thread \"%s\" exiting...\n", private->string);
28      free (value);
29      status = pthread_mutex_lock (&identity_key_mutex);
30      if (status != 0)
31          err_abort (status, "Lock key mutex");
32      identity_key_counter--;
33      if (identity_key_counter <= 0) {
34          status = pthread_key_delete (identity_key);
35          if (status != 0)
36              err_abort (status, "Delete key");
37          printf ("key deleted...\n");
38      }
39      status = pthread_mutex_unlock (&identity_key_mutex);
40      if (status != 0)
41          err_abort (status, "Unlock key mutex");
42  }
43
44  /*
45   * Helper routine to allocate a new value for thread-specific
46   * data key if the thread doesn't already have one.
47   */
48  void *identity_key_get (void)
49  {
50      void *value;
51      int status;
52
53      value = pthread_getspecific (identity_key);
```

```
54      if (value == NULL) {
55          value = malloc (sizeof (private_t));
56          if (value == NULL)
57              errno_abort ("Allocate key value");
58          status = pthread_setspecific (identity_key, (void*)value);
59          if (status != 0)
60              err_abort (status, "Set TSD");
61      }
62      return value;
63  }
64
65  /*
66   * Thread start routine to use thread-specific data.
67   */
68  void *thread_routine (void *arg)
69  {
70      private_t *value;
71
72      value = (private_t*)identity_key_get ();
73      value->thread_id = pthread_self ();
74      value->string = (char*)arg;
75      printf ("thread \"%s\" starting...\n", value->string);
76      sleep (2);
77      return NULL;
78  }
79
80  void main (int argc, char *argv[])
81  {
82      pthread_t thread_1, thread_2;
83      private_t *value;
84      int status;
85
86      /*
87       * Create the TSD key, and set the reference counter to
88       * the number of threads that will use it (two thread_routine
89       * threads plus main). This must be done before creating
90       * the threads! Otherwise, if one thread runs the key's
91       * destructor before any other thread uses the key, it will
92       * be deleted.
93       *
94       * Note that there's rarely any good reason to delete a
95       * thread-specific data key.
96       */
97      status = pthread_key_create (
98          &identity_key, identity_key_destructor);
99      if (status != 0)
100         err_abort (status, "Create key");
```

```
101        identity_key_counter = 3;
102        value = (private_t*)identity_key_get ();
103        value->thread_id = pthread_self ();
104        value->string = "Main thread";
105        status = pthread_create (&thread_1, NULL,
106            thread_routine, "Thread 1");
107        if (status != 0)
108            err_abort (status, "Create thread 1");
109        status = pthread_create (&thread_2, NULL,
110            thread_routine, "Thread 2");
111        if (status != 0)
112            err_abort (status, "Create thread 2");
113        pthread_exit (NULL);
114    }
```

■ tsd_destructor.c

5.5 Realtime scheduling

"Well, it's no use your talking about waking him," said Tweedledum,
  "when you're only one of the things in his dream. You know
  very well you're not real."
"I am real!" said Alice, and began to cry.
"You wo'n't make yourself a bit realler by crying," Tweedledee remarked:
  "there's nothing to cry about."
  —Lewis Carroll, Through the Looking-Glass

Once upon a time, realtime programming was considered an arcane and rare art. Realtime programmers were doing unusual things, outside of the programming mainstream, like controlling nuclear reactors or airplane navigational systems. But the POSIX.1b realtime extension defines *realtime* as "the ability of the operating system to provide a required level of service in a bounded response time." What applies to the operating system also applies to your application or library.

"Bounded" response time does not necessarily mean "fast" response, but it does mean "predictable" response. There must be some way to define a span of time during which a sequence of operations is guaranteed to complete. A system controlling a nuclear reactor has more strict response requirements than most programs you will write, and certainly the consequences of failing to meet the reactor's response requirements are more severe. But a lot of code you write will need to provide some "required level of service" within some "bounded response time." Realtime programming just means that the software lives in the real world.

Realtime programming covers such a vast area that it is common to divide it into two separate categories. "Hard realtime" is the traditional sort most people think of. When your nuclear reactor will go critical if a fuel rod adjustment is delayed by a microsecond or your airplane will crash if the navigation system takes a half second to respond to a wind sheer, that's *hard* realtime. Hard realtime is unforgiving, because the required level of service and bounded response time are defined by physics or something equally unyielding. "Soft realtime" means that you need to meet your schedule most of the time, but the consequences of failing to meet the schedule are not severe.

Many systems that interact with humans should be designed according to soft realtime principles. Although humans react slowly, in computer terms, they're sensitive to response time. Make your users wait too often while the screen redraws before accepting the next mouse click, and they'll be annoyed. Nobody likes a "busy cursor"—most people expect response to be at least predictable, even when it cannot be fast.

Threads are useful for all types of realtime programming, because coding for predictable response is far easier when you can keep the operations separate. Your "user input function" doesn't have to wait for your sort operation or for your screen update operation because it executes independently.

Achieving predictability requires a lot more than just separating operations into different threads, however. For one thing, you need to make sure that the thread you need to run "soon" won't be left sitting on a run queue somewhere while another thread uses the processor. Most systems, by default, will try to distribute resources more or less fairly between threads. That's nice for a lot of things—but realtime isn't fair. Realtime means carefully giving precedence to the parts of the program that limit external response time.

5.5.1 POSIX realtime options

The POSIX standards are flexible, because they're designed to be useful in a wide range of environments. In particular, since traditional UNIX systems don't support any form of realtime scheduling control, all of the tools for controlling realtime response are optional. The fact that a given implementation of UNIX "conforms to 1003.1c–1995" does not mean you can write predictable realtime programs.

If the system defines _POSIX_THREAD_PRIORITY_SCHEDULING, it provides support for assigning realtime scheduling priorities to threads. The POSIX priority scheduling model is a little more complicated than the traditional UNIX priority model, but the principle is similar. Priority scheduling allows the programmer to give the system an idea of how important any two threads are, relative to each other. Whenever more than one thread is ready to execute, the system will choose the thread with the highest priority.

5.5.2 Scheduling policies and priorities

```
int sched_get_priority_max (int policy);
int sched_get_priority_min (int policy);
int pthread_attr_getinheritsched (
    const pthread_attr_t *attr, int *inheritsched);
int pthread_attr_setinheritsched (
    pthread_attr_t *attr, int inheritsched);
int pthread_attr_getschedparam (
    const pthread_attr_t *attr,
    struct sched_param *param);
int pthread_attr_setschedparam (
    pthread_attr_t *attr,
    const struct sched_param *param);
int pthread_attr_getschedpolicy (
    const pthread_attr_t *attr, int *policy);
int pthread_attr_setschedpolicy (
    pthread_attr_t *attr, int policy);
int pthread_getschedparam (pthread_t thread,
    int *policy, struct sched_param *param);
int pthread_setschedparam (
    pthread_t thread, int policy,
    const struct sched_param *param);
```

A Pthreads system that supports _POSIX_THREAD_PRIORITY_SCHEDULING must provide a definition of the struct sched_param structure that includes at least the member sched_priority. The sched_priority member is the only scheduling parameter used by the standard Pthreads scheduling policies, SCHED_FIFO and SCHED_RR. The minimum and maximum priority values (sched_priority member) that are allowed for each scheduling policy can be determined by calling sched_get_priority_min or sched_get_priority_max, respectively, for the scheduling policy. Pthreads systems that support additional, nonstandard scheduling policies may include additional members.

The SCHED_FIFO (*first in, first out*) policy allows a thread to run until another thread with a higher priority becomes *ready,* or until it blocks voluntarily. When a thread with SCHED_FIFO scheduling policy becomes *ready,* it begins executing immediately unless a thread with equal or higher priority is already executing.

The SCHED_RR (*round-robin*) policy is much the same, except that if a thread with SCHED_RR policy executes for more than a fixed period of time (the *timeslice interval*) without blocking, and another thread with SCHED_RR or SCHED_FIFO policy and the same priority is *ready,* the *running* thread will be preempted so the *ready* thread can be executed.

When threads with SCHED_FIFO or SCHED_RR policy wait on a condition variable or wait to lock a mutex, they will be awakened in priority order. That is, if a low-priority SCHED_FIFO thread and a high-priority SCHED_FIFO thread are both waiting to lock the same mutex, the high-priority thread will always be unblocked first when the mutex is unlocked.

Pthreads defines the name of an additional scheduling policy, called SCHED_OTHER. Pthreads, however, says nothing at all regarding what this scheduling policy does. This is an illustration of an unofficial POSIX philosophy that has been termed "a standard way to be nonstandard" (or, alternately, "a portable way to be nonportable"). That is, when you use any implementation of Pthreads that supports the priority scheduling option, you can write a portable program that creates threads running in SCHED_OTHER policy, but the behavior of that program is nonportable. (The official explanation of SCHED_OTHER is that it provides a portable way for a program to declare that it does not need a realtime scheduling policy.)

The SCHED_OTHER policy may be an alias for SCHED_FIFO, or it may be SCHED_RR, or it may be something entirely different. The real problem with this ambiguity is not that you don't know what SCHED_OTHER does, but that you have no way of knowing what scheduling parameters it might require. Because the meaning of SCHED_OTHER is undefined, it does not necessarily use the sched_priority member of the struct sched_param structure, and it may require additional, nonstandard members that an implementation may add to the structure. If there's any point to this, it is simply that SCHED_OTHER is not portable. If you write any code that uses SCHED_OTHER you should be aware that the code is not portable—you are, by definition, depending on the SCHED_OTHER of the particular Pthreads implementation for which you wrote the code.

The *schedpolicy* and *schedparam* attributes, set respectively by pthread_attr_setschedpolicy and pthread_attr_setschedparam, specify the explicit scheduling policy and parameters for the attributes object. Pthreads does not specify a default value for either of these attributes, which means that each implementation may choose some "appropriate" value. A realtime operating system intended for embedded controller applications, for example, might choose to create threads by default with SCHED_FIFO policy, and, perhaps, some medium-range priority.

Most multiuser operating systems are more likely to use a nonstandard "time-share" scheduling policy by default, causing threads to be scheduled more or less as processes have always been scheduled. The system may, for example, temporarily reduce the priority of "CPU hogs" so that they cannot prevent other threads from making progress.

One example of a multiuser operating system is Digital UNIX, which supports two nonstandard timeshare scheduling policies. The *foreground* policy (SCHED_FG_NP), which is the default, is used for normal interactive activity, and corresponds to the way nonthreaded processes are scheduled. The *background* policy (SCHED_BG_NP) can be used for less important support activities.

When you set the scheduling policy or priority attributes in an attributes object, you must also set the inheritsched attribute!

The *inheritsched* attribute, which you can set by calling `pthread_attr_setinheritsched`, controls whether a thread you create inherits scheduling information from the creating thread, or uses the explicit scheduling information in the *schedpolicy* and *schedparam* attributes. Pthreads does not specify a default value for *inheritsched*, either, so if you care about the policy and scheduling parameters of your thread, you must always set this attribute.

Set the *inheritsched* attribute to `PTHREAD_INHERIT_SCHED` to cause a new thread to inherit the scheduling policy and parameters of the creating thread. Scheduling inheritance is useful when you're creating "helper" threads that are working on behalf of the creator—it generally makes sense for them to run at the same policy and priority. Whenever you need to control the scheduling policy or parameters of a thread you create, you must set the *inheritsched* attribute to `PTHREAD_EXPLICIT_SCHED`.

58-118   The following program, `sched_attr.c`, shows how to use an attributes object to create a thread with an explicit scheduling policy and priority. Notice that it uses conditional code to determine whether the priority scheduling feature of Pthreads is supported at compilation time. It will print a message if the option is not supported and continue, although the program in that case will not do much. (It creates a thread with default scheduling behavior, which can only say that it ran.)

Although Solaris 2.5 defines `_POSIX_THREAD_PRIORITY_SCHEDULING`, it does not support the POSIX realtime scheduling policies, and attempting to set the policy attribute to `SCHED_RR` would fail. This program treats Solaris as if it did not define the `_POSIX_THREAD_PRIORITY_SCHEDULING` option.

■   sched_attr.c

```
1  #include <unistd.h>
2  #include <pthread.h>
3  #include <sched.h>
4  #include "errors.h"
5
6  /*
7   * Thread start routine. If priority scheduling is supported,
8   * report the thread's scheduling attributes.
9   */
10 void *thread_routine (void *arg)
11 {
12     int my_policy;
13     struct sched_param my_param;
14     int status;
15
16     /*
17      * If the priority scheduling option is not defined, then we
18      * can do nothing with the output of pthread_getschedparam,
19      * so just report that the thread ran, and exit.
20      */
```

```
21  #if defined (_POSIX_THREAD_PRIORITY_SCHEDULING) && !defined (sun)
22      status = pthread_getschedparam (
23          pthread_self (), &my_policy, &my_param);
24      if (status != 0)
25          err_abort (status, "Get sched");
26      printf ("thread_routine running at %s/%d\n",
27          (my_policy == SCHED_FIFO ? "FIFO"
28              : (my_policy == SCHED_RR ? "RR"
29              : (my_policy == SCHED_OTHER ? "OTHER"
30              : "unknown"))),
31          my_param.sched_priority);
32  #else
33      printf ("thread_routine running\n");
34  #endif
35      return NULL;
36  }
37
38  int main (int argc, char *argv[])
39  {
40      pthread_t thread_id;
41      pthread_attr_t thread_attr;
42      int thread_policy;
43      struct sched_param thread_param;
44      int status, rr_min_priority, rr_max_priority;
45
46      status = pthread_attr_init (&thread_attr);
47      if (status != 0)
48          err_abort (status, "Init attr");
49
50      /*
51       * If the priority scheduling option is defined, set various
52       * scheduling parameters. Note that it is particularly important
53       * that you remember to set the inheritsched attribute to
54       * PTHREAD_EXPLICIT_SCHED, or the policy and priority that you've
55       * set will be ignored! The default behavior is to inherit
56       * scheduling information from the creating thread.
57       */
58  #if defined (_POSIX_THREAD_PRIORITY_SCHEDULING) && !defined (sun)
59      status = pthread_attr_getschedpolicy (
60          &thread_attr, &thread_policy);
61      if (status != 0)
62          err_abort (status, "Get policy");
63      status = pthread_attr_getschedparam (
64          &thread_attr, &thread_param);
65      if (status != 0)
66          err_abort (status, "Get sched param");
67      printf (
68          "Default policy is %s, priority is %d\n",
69          (thread_policy == SCHED_FIFO ? "FIFO"
```

```
70              : (thread_policy == SCHED_RR ? "RR"
71                : (thread_policy == SCHED_OTHER ? "OTHER"
72                  : "unknown"))),
73          thread_param.sched_priority);
74
75      status = pthread_attr_setschedpolicy (
76          &thread_attr, SCHED_RR);
77      if (status != 0)
78          printf ("Unable to set SCHED_RR policy.\n");
79      else {
80          /*
81           * Just for the sake of the exercise, we'll use the
82           * middle of the priority range allowed for
83           * SCHED_RR. This should ensure that the thread will be
84           * run, without blocking everything else. Because any
85           * assumptions about how a thread's priority interacts
86           * with other threads (even in other processes) are
87           * nonportable, especially on an implementation that
88           * defaults to System contention scope, you may have to
89           * adjust this code before it will work on some systems.
90           */
91          rr_min_priority = sched_get_priority_min (SCHED_RR);
92          if (rr_min_priority == -1)
93              errno_abort ("Get SCHED_RR min priority");
94          rr_max_priority = sched_get_priority_max (SCHED_RR);
95          if (rr_max_priority == -1)
96              errno_abort ("Get SCHED_RR max priority");
97          thread_param.sched_priority =
98              (rr_min_priority + rr_max_priority)/2;
99          printf (
100             "SCHED_RR priority range is %d to %d: using %d\n",
101             rr_min_priority,
102             rr_max_priority,
103             thread_param.sched_priority);
104         status = pthread_attr_setschedparam (
105             &thread_attr, &thread_param);
106         if (status != 0)
107             err_abort (status, "Set params");
108         printf (
109             "Creating thread at RR/%d\n",
110             thread_param.sched_priority);
111         status = pthread_attr_setinheritsched (
112             &thread_attr, PTHREAD_EXPLICIT_SCHED);
113         if (status != 0)
114             err_abort (status, "Set inherit");
115     }
116 #else
117     printf ("Priority scheduling not supported\n");
```

```
118  #endif
119      status = pthread_create (
120          &thread_id, &thread_attr, thread_routine, NULL);
121      if (status != 0)
122          err_abort (status, "Create thread");
123      status = pthread_join (thread_id, NULL);
124      if (status != 0)
125          err_abort (status, "Join thread");
126      printf ("Main exiting\n");
127      return 0;
128  }
```

■ sched_attr.c

The next program, sched_thread.c, shows how to modify the realtime scheduling policy and parameters for a running thread. When changing the scheduling policy and parameters in a thread attributes object, remember, you use two separate operations: one to modify the scheduling policy and the other to modify the scheduling parameters.

You cannot modify the scheduling policy of a running thread separately from the thread's parameters, because the policy and parameters must always be consistent for scheduling to operate correctly. Each scheduling policy may have a unique range of valid scheduling priorities, and a thread cannot operate at a priority that isn't valid for its current policy. To ensure consistency of the policy and parameters, they are set with a single call.

55   Unlike sched_attr.c, sched_thread.c does not check the compile-time feature macro _POSIX_THREAD_PRIORITY_SCHEDULING. That means it will probably not compile, and almost certainly won't run correctly, on a system that does not support the option. There's nothing wrong with writing a program that way—in fact, that's what you are likely to do most of the time. If you need priority scheduling, you would document that your application requires the _POSIX_THREAD_ PRIORITY_SCHEDULING option, and use it.

57–62   Solaris 2.5, despite defining _POSIX_THREAD_PRIORITY_SCHEDULING, does not support realtime scheduling policies. For this reason, the ENOSYS from sched_ get_priority_min is handled as a special case.

■ sched_thread.c

```
1  #include <unistd.h>
2  #include <pthread.h>
3  #include <sched.h>
4  #include "errors.h"
5
6  #define THREADS 5
7
8  /*
9   * Structure describing each thread.
10  */
```

```
11  typedef struct thread_tag {
12      int         index;
13      pthread_t   id;
14  } thread_t;
15
16  thread_t        threads[THREADS];
17  int             rr_min_priority;
18
19  /*
20   * Thread start routine that will set its own priority.
21   */
22  void *thread_routine (void *arg)
23  {
24      thread_t *self = (thread_t*)arg;
25      int my_policy;
26      struct sched_param my_param;
27      int status;
28
29      my_param.sched_priority = rr_min_priority + self->index;
30      DPRINTF ((
31          "Thread %d will set SCHED_FIFO, priority %d\n",
32          self->index, my_param.sched_priority));
33      status = pthread_setschedparam (
34          self->id, SCHED_RR, &my_param);
35      if (status != 0)
36          err_abort (status, "Set sched");
37      status = pthread_getschedparam (
38          self->id, &my_policy, &my_param);
39      if (status != 0)
40          err_abort (status, "Get sched");
41      printf ("thread_routine %d running at %s/%d\n",
42          self->index,
43          (my_policy == SCHED_FIFO ? "FIFO"
44              : (my_policy == SCHED_RR ? "RR"
45              : (my_policy == SCHED_OTHER ? "OTHER"
46              : "unknown"))),
47          my_param.sched_priority);
48      return NULL;
49  }
50
51  int main (int argc, char *argv[])
52  {
53      int count, status;
54
55      rr_min_priority = sched_get_priority_min (SCHED_RR);
56      if (rr_min_priority == -1) {
57  #ifdef sun
58          if (errno == ENOSYS) {
59              fprintf (stderr, "SCHED_RR is not supported.\n");
```

```
60                  exit (0);
61          }
62 #endif
63          errno_abort ("Get SCHED_RR min priority");
64      }
65      for (count = 0; count < THREADS; count++) {
66          threads[count].index = count;
67          status = pthread_create (
68              &threads[count].id, NULL,
69              thread_routine, (void*)&threads[count]);
70          if (status != 0)
71              err_abort (status, "Create thread");
72      }
73      for (count = 0; count < THREADS; count++) {
74          status = pthread_join (threads[count].id, NULL);
75          if (status != 0)
76              err_abort (status, "Join thread");
77      }
78      printf ("Main exiting\n");
79      return 0;
80 }
```

■ sched_thread.c

5.5.3 Contention scope and allocation domain

```
int pthread_attr_getscope (
    const pthread_attr_t *attr, int *contentionscope);
int pthread_attr_setscope (
    pthread_attr_t *attr, int contentionscope);
```

Besides scheduling policy and parameters, two other controls are important in realtime scheduling. Unless you are writing a realtime application, they probably don't matter. If you are writing a realtime application, you will need to find out which settings of these controls are supported by a system.

The first control is called *contention scope*. It is a description of how your threads compete for processor resources. *System contention scope* means that your thread competes for processor resources against threads outside your process. A high-priority system contention scope thread in your process can keep system contention scope threads in other processes from running (or vice versa). *Process contention scope* means that your threads compete only among themselves. Usually, process contention scope means that the operating system chooses a process to execute, possibly using only the traditional UNIX priority, and some additional scheduler within the process applies the POSIX scheduling rules to determine which thread to execute.

Pthreads provides the thread *scope* attribute so that you can specify whether each thread you create should have process or system contention scope. A Pthreads system may choose to support PTHREAD_SCOPE_PROCESS, PTHREAD_SCOPE_SYSTEM, or both. If you try to create a thread with a scope that is not supported by the system, pthread_attr_setscope will return ENOTSUP.

The second control is *allocation domain.* An allocation domain is the set of processors within the system for which threads may compete. A system may have one or more allocation domains, each containing one or more processors. In a uniprocessor system, an allocation domain will contain only one processor, but you may still have more than one allocation domain. On a multiprocessor, each allocation domain may contain from one processor to the number of processors in the system.

There is no Pthreads interface to set a thread's allocation domain. The POSIX.14 (Multiprocessor Profile) working group considered proposing standard interfaces, but the effort was halted by the prospect of dealing with the wide range of hardware architectures and existing software interfaces. Despite the lack of a standard, any system supporting multiprocessors will have interfaces to affect the allocation domain of a thread.

Because there is no standard interface to control allocation domain, there is no way to describe precisely all the effects of any particular hypothetical situation. Still, you may need to be concerned about these things if you use a system that supports multiprocessors. A few things to think about:

1. How do system contention scope threads and process contention scope threads, within the same allocation domain, interact with each other? They are competing for resources in some manner, but the behavior is not defined by the standard.
2. If the system supports "overlapping" allocation domains, in other words, if a processor can appear in more than one allocation domain within the system, and you have one system contention scope thread in each of two overlapping allocation domains, what happens?

System contention scope is *predictable.*

Process contention scope is *cheap.*

On most systems, you will get better performance, and lower cost, by using only *process* contention scope. Context switches between system contention scope threads usually require at least one call into the kernel, and those calls are relatively expensive compared to the cost of saving and restoring thread state in user mode. Each system contention scope thread will be permanently associated with one "kernel entity," and the number of kernel entities is usually more limited than the number of Pthreads threads. Process contention scope threads may share one kernel entity, or some small number of kernel entities. On a given system configuration, for example, you may be able to create thousands of process contention scope threads, but only hundreds of system contention scope threads.

On the other hand, process contention scope gives you no real control over the scheduling priority of your thread—while a high priority may give it precedence over other threads in the process, it has no advantage over threads in other processes with lower priority. System contention scope gives you better predictability by allowing control, often to the extent of being able to make your thread "more important" than threads running within the operating system kernel.

> System contention scope is less predictable with an allocation domain greater than one.

When a thread is assigned to an allocation domain with more than a single processor, the application can no longer rely on completely predictable scheduling behavior. Both high- and low-priority threads may run at the same time, for example, because the scheduler will not allow processors to be idle just because a high-priority thread is running. The uniprocessor behavior would make little sense on a multiprocessor.

When thread 1 awakens thread 2 by unlocking a mutex, and thread 2 has a higher priority than thread 1, thread 2 will preempt thread 1 and begin running immediately. However, if thread 1 and thread 2 are running simultaneously in an allocation domain greater than one, and thread 1 awakens thread 3, which has lower priority than thread 1 but higher priority than thread 2, thread 3 may not immediately preempt thread 2. Thread 3 may remain *ready* until thread 2 blocks.

For some applications, the predictability afforded by guaranteed preemption in the case outlined in the previous paragraph may be important. In most cases, it is not that important as long as thread 3 will eventually run. Although POSIX does not require any Pthreads system to implement this type of "cross processor preemption," you are more likely to find it when you use system contention scope threads. If predictability is critical, of course, you should be using system contention scope anyway.

5.5.4 Problems with realtime scheduling

One of the problems of relying on realtime scheduling is that it is not modular. In real applications you will generally be working with libraries from a variety of sources, and those libraries may rely on threads for important functions like network communication and resource management. Now, it may seem reasonable to make "the most important thread" in your library run with SCHED_FIFO policy and maximum priority. The resulting thread, however, isn't just the most important thread for your library—it is (or, at least, behaves as) the most important thread in the entire process, including the main program and any other libraries. Your high-priority thread may prevent all other libraries, and in some cases even the operating system, from performing work on which the application relies.

Another problem, which really isn't a problem with priority scheduling, but with the way many people think about priority scheduling, is that it doesn't do what many people expect. Many people think that "realtime priority" threads somehow "go faster" than other threads, and that's not true. Realtime priority threads may actually go slower, because there is more overhead involved in making all of the required preemption checks at all the right times—especially on a multiprocessor.

A more severe problem with fixed priority scheduling is called *priority inversion*. Priority inversion is when a low-priority thread can prevent a high-priority thread from running—a nasty interaction between *scheduling* and *synchronization*. Scheduling rules state that one thread should run, but synchronization requires that another thread run, so that the priorities of the two threads appear to be reversed.

Priority inversion occurs when low-priority thread acquires a shared resource (such as a mutex), and is preempted by a high-priority thread that then blocks on that same resource. With only two threads, the low-priority thread would then be allowed to run, eventually (we assume) releasing the mutex. However, if a third thread with a priority between those two is ready to run, it can prevent the low-priority thread from running. Because the low-priority thread holds the mutex that the high-priority thread needs, the middle-priority thread is also keeping the higher-priority thread from running.

There are a number of ways to prevent priority inversion. The simplest is to avoid using realtime scheduling, but that's not always practical. Pthreads provides several mutex locking protocols that help avoid priority inversion, *priority ceiling* and *priority inheritance*. These are discussed in Section 5.5.5.

❚ Most threaded programs do not need realtime scheduling.

A final problem is that priority scheduling isn't completely portable. Pthreads defines the priority scheduling features under an option, and many implementations that are not primarily intended for realtime programming may choose not to support the option. Even if the option is supported, there are many important aspects of priority scheduling that are not covered by the standard. When you use system contention scope, for example, where your threads may compete directly against threads within the operating system, setting a high priority on your threads might prevent kernel I/O drivers from functioning on some systems.

Pthreads does not specify a thread's default scheduling policy or priority, or how the standard scheduling policies interact with nonstandard policies. So when you set the scheduling policy and priority of your thread, using "portable" interfaces, the standard provides no way to predict how that setting will affect any other threads in the process or the system itself.

If you really need priority scheduling, then use it—and be aware that it has special requirements beyond simply Pthreads. If you need priority scheduling, keep the following in mind:

1. Process contention scope is "nicer" than system contention scope, because you will not prevent a thread in another process, or in the kernel, from running.
2. SCHED_RR is "nicer" than SCHED_FIFO, and slightly more portable, because SCHED_RR threads will be preempted at intervals to share the available processor time with other threads at the same priority.
3. Lower priorities for SCHED_FIFO and SCHED_RR policies are nicer than higher priorities, because you are less likely to interfere with something else that's important.

Unless your code really needs priority scheduling, avoid it. In most cases, introducing priority scheduling will cause more problems than it will solve.

5.5.5 Priority-aware mutexes

```
#if defined (_POSIX_THREAD_PRIO_PROTECT) \
  || defined (_POSIX_THREAD_PRIO_INHERIT)
int pthread_mutexattr_getprotocol (
    const pthread_mutexattr_t *attr, int *protocol);
int pthread_mutexattr_setprotocol (
    pthread_mutexattr_t *attr, int protocol);
#endif
#ifdef _POSIX_THREAD_PRIO_PROTECT
int pthread_mutexattr_getprioceiling (
    const pthread_attr_t *attr, int *prioceiling);
int pthread_mutexattr_setprioceiling (
    pthread_mutexattr_t *attr, int prioceiling);
int pthread_mutex_getprioceiling (
    const pthread_mutex_t *mutex, int *prioceiling);
int pthread_mutex_setprioceiling (
    pthread_mutex_t *mutex,
    int prioceiling, int *old_ceiling);
#endif
```

Pthreads provides several special mutex attributes that can help to avoid priority inversion deadlocks. Locking, or waiting for, a mutex with one of these attributes may change the priority of the thread—or the priority of other threads—to ensure that the thread that owns the mutex cannot be preempted by another thread that needs to lock the same mutex.

These mutex attributes may not be supported by your implementation of Pthreads, because they are optional features. If your code needs to function with or without these options, you can conditionally compile references based on the feature test macros _POSIX_THREAD_PRIO_PROTECT or _POSIX_THREAD_PRIO_INHERIT, defined in <unistd.h>, or you can call sysconf during program execution to check for _SC_THREAD_PRIO_PROTECT or _SC_THREAD_PRIO_INHERIT.

Once you've created a mutex using one of these attributes, you can lock and unlock the mutex exactly like any other mutex. As a consequence, you can easily convert any mutex you create by changing the code that initializes the mutex. (You must call `pthread_mutex_init`, however, because you cannot statically initialize a mutex with nondefault attributes.)

> "Priority ceiling" protocol means that while a thread owns the mutex, it runs at the specified priority.

If your system defines `_POSIX_THREAD_PRIO_PROTECT` then it supports the *protocol* and *prioceiling* attributes. You set the *protocol* attribute by calling `pthread_mutexattr_setprotocol`. If you set the *protocol* attribute to the value `PTHREAD_PRIO_PROTECT`, then you can also specify the priority ceiling for mutexes created using the attributes object by setting the *prioceiling* attribute.

You set the *prioceiling* attribute by calling the function `pthread_mutexattr_setprioceiling`. When any thread locks a mutex defined with such an attributes object, the thread's priority will be set to the priority ceiling of the mutex, unless the thread's priority is already the same or higher. Note that locking the mutex in a thread running at a priority above the priority ceiling of the mutex breaks the protocol, removing the protection against priority inversion.

> "Priority inheritance" means that when a thread waits on a mutex owned by a lower-priority thread, the priority of the owner is increased to that of the waiter.

If your system defines `_POSIX_THREAD_PRIO_INHERIT` then it supports the *protocol* attribute. If you set the *protocol* attribute to the value `PTHREAD_PRIO_INHERIT`, then no thread holding the mutex can be preempted by another thread with a priority lower than that of any thread waiting for the mutex. When any thread attempts to lock the mutex while a lower-priority thread holds the mutex, the priority of the thread currently holding the mutex will be raised to the priority of the waiter as long as it owns the mutex.

If your system does not define either `_POSIX_THREAD_PRIO_PROTECT` or `_POSIX_THREAD_PRIO_INHERIT` then the *protocol* attribute may not be defined. The default value of the *protocol* attribute (or the effective value if the attribute isn't defined) is `POSIX_PRIO_NONE`, which means that thread priorities are not modified by the act of locking (or waiting for) a mutex.

5.5.5.1 Priority ceiling mutexes

The simplest of the two types of "priority aware" mutexes is the *priority ceiling* (or "priority protection") protocol (Figure 5.3). When you create a mutex using a priority ceiling, you specify the highest priority at which a thread will ever be running when it locks the mutex. Any thread locking that mutex will have its

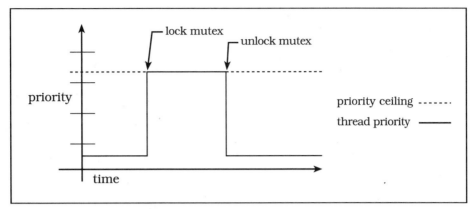

FIGURE 5.3 *Priority ceiling mutex operation*

priority automatically raised to that value, which will allow it to finish with the mutex before it can be preempted by any other thread that might try to lock the mutex. You can also examine or modify the priority ceiling of a mutex that was created with the priority ceiling (*protect*) protocol.

A priority ceiling mutex is not useful within a library that can be called by threads you don't control. If any thread that is running at a priority above the ceiling locks the priority ceiling mutex, the protocol is broken. This doesn't necessarily guarantee a priority inversion, but it removes all protection against priority inversion. Since the priority ceiling protocol adds overhead to each mutex operation compared to a normal "unprotected" mutex, you may have wasted processor time accomplishing nothing.

Priority ceiling is perfect for an embedded realtime application where the developers control all synchronization within the system. The priority ceiling can be safely determined when the code is designed, and you can avoid priority inversion with a relatively small cost in performance compared to more general solutions. Of course it is always most efficient to avoid priority inversion, either by avoiding priority scheduling or by using any given mutex only within threads of equal priority. Equally, of course, these alternatives rarely prove practical when you need them most.

You can use priority ceiling within almost any main program, even when you don't control the code in libraries you use. That's because while it is common for threads that call into library functions to lock library mutexes, it is not common for threads created by a library to call into application code and lock application mutexes. If you use a library that has "callbacks" into your code, you must either ensure that those callbacks (and any functions they call) don't use the priority ceiling mutexes or that no thread in which the callback might be invoked will run at a priority above the ceiling priority of the mutex.

5.5.5.2 Priority inheritance mutexes

The other Pthreads mutex protocol is *priority inheritance.* In the priority inheritance protocol, when a thread locks a mutex the thread's priority is controlled through the mutex (Figure 5.4). When another thread needs to block on that mutex, it looks at the priority of the thread that owns the mutex. If the thread that owns the mutex has a lower priority than the thread attempting to block on the mutex, the priority of the owner is raised to the priority of the blocking thread.

The priority increase ensures that the thread that has the mutex locked cannot be preempted unless the waiting thread would also have been preempted—in a sense, the thread owning the mutex is working on behalf of the higher-priority thread. When the thread unlocks the mutex, the thread's priority is automatically lowered to its normal priority and the highest-priority waiter is awakened. If a second thread of even higher priority blocks on the mutex, the thread that has the mutex blocked will again have its priority increased. The thread will still be returned to its original priority when the mutex is unlocked.

The priority inheritance protocol is more general and powerful than priority ceiling, but also more complicated and expensive. If a library package must make use of priority scheduling, and cannot avoid use of a mutex from threads of different priority, then priority inheritance is the only currently available solution. If you are writing a main program, and know that none of your mutexes can be locked by threads created within a library, then priority ceiling will accomplish the same result as priority inheritance, and with less overhead.

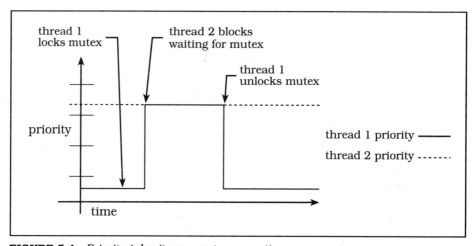

FIGURE 5.4   *Priority inheritance mutex operation*

5.6 Threads and kernel entities

> *"Two lines!" cried the Mock Turtle. "Seals, turtles, salmon, and so on:*
>   *then, when you've cleared all the jelly-fish out of the way—"*
> *"That generally takes some time," interrupted the Gryphon.*
> *"—you advance twice—"*
> *"Each with a lobster as a partner!" cried the Gryphon.*
>   —Lewis Carroll, *Alice's Adventures in Wonderland*

Pthreads deliberately says very little about implementation details. This leaves each vendor free to make decisions based on the needs of their users and to allow the state of the art to advance by permitting innovation. The standard places a few essential requirements on the implementation—enough that you can write strictly conforming POSIX applications[*] that do useful work with threads and will be able to run correctly on all conforming implementations of the standard.

Any Pthreads implementation must ensure that "system services invoked by one thread do not suspend other threads" so that you do not need to worry that calling `read` might block all threads in the process on some systems. On the other hand, this does not mean that your process will always have the maximum possible level of concurrency.

Nevertheless, when using a system it is often useful to understand the ways in which the system may be implemented. When writing ANSI C expressions, for example, it is often helpful to understand what the code generator, and even the hardware, will do with those expressions. With that in mind, the following sections describe, briefly, a few of the main variations you're likely to encounter.

The important terms used in these sections are "Pthreads thread," "kernel entity," and "processor." "Pthreads thread" means a thread that you created by calling `pthread_create`, represented by an identifier of type `pthread_t`. These are the threads that you control using Pthreads interfaces. By "processor," I refer to the physical hardware, the particular thing of which a "multiprocessor" has more than one.

Most operating systems have at least one additional level of abstraction between "Pthreads thread" and "processor" and I refer to that as a "kernel entity," because that is the term used by Pthreads. In some systems, "kernel entity" may be a traditional UNIX process. It may be a Digital UNIX Mach thread, or a Solaris 2.x LWP, or an IRIX *sproc* process. The exact meaning of "kernel entity," and how it interacts with the Pthreads thread, is the crucial difference between the three models described in the following sections.

---

[*] *Strictly conforming* is used by POSIX to mean something quite specific: a strictly conforming application is one that does not rely on any options or extensions to the standard and requires only the specified minimum value for all implementation limits (but will work correctly with any allowed value).

5.6.1 Many-to-one (user level)

The many-to-one method is also sometimes called a "library implementation." In general, "many-to-one" implementations are designed for operating systems with no support for threads. Pthreads implementations that run on generic UNIX kernels usually fall into this category—for example, the classic DCE threads reference implementation, or the SunOS 4.x LWP package (no relation to the Solaris 2.x LWP, which is a kernel entity).

Many-to-one implementations cannot take advantage of parallelism on a multiprocessor, and any blocking system service, for example, a call to read, will block all threads in the process. Some implementations may help you avoid this problem by using features such as UNIX nonblocking I/O, or POSIX.1b asynchronous I/O, where available. However, these features have limitations; for example, not all device drivers support nonblocking I/O, and traditional UNIX disk file system response is usually considered "instantaneous" and will ignore the nonblocking I/O mode.

Some many-to-one implementations may not be tightly integrated with the ANSI C library's support functions, and that can cause serious trouble. The *stdio* functions, for example, might block the entire process (and all threads) while one thread waits for you to enter a command. Any many-to-one implementation that conforms to the Pthreads standard, however, has gotten around these problems, perhaps by including a special version of *stdio* and other functions.

When you require concurrency but do not need parallelism, a many-to-one implementation may provide the best thread creation performance, as well as the best context switch performance for voluntary blocking using mutexes and condition variables. It is fast because the Pthreads library saves and restores thread context entirely in user mode. You can, for example, create a lot of threads and block most of them on condition variables (waiting for some external event) very quickly, without involving the kernel at all.

Figure 5.5 shows the mapping of Pthreads threads (left column) to the kernel entity (middle column), which is a process, to physical processors (right column). In this case, the process has four Pthreads threads, labeled "Pthread 1" through "Pthread 4." The Pthreads library schedules the four threads onto the single process in user mode by swapping register state (SP, general registers, and so forth). The library may use a timer to preempt a Pthreads thread that runs too long. The kernel schedules the process onto one of the two physical processors, labeled "processor 1" and "processor 2." The important characteristics of this model are shown in Table 5.2.

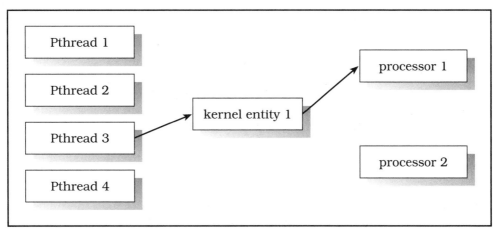

FIGURE 5.5 *Many-to-one thread mapping*

Advantages	Disadvantages
Fastest context switch time.	Potentially long latency during system service blocking.
Simple; the implementation may even be (mostly) portable.*	Single-process applications cannot take advantage of multiprocessor hardware.

* The DCE threads user-mode scheduler can usually be ported to new operating systems in a few days, involving primarily new assembly language for the register context switching routines. We use the motto "Some Assembly Required."

TABLE 5.2 *Many-to-one thread scheduling*

5.6.2 One-to-one (kernel level)

One-to-one thread mapping is also sometimes called a "kernel thread" implementation. The Pthreads library assigns each thread to a kernel entity. It generally must use blocking kernel functions to wait on mutexes and condition variables. While synchronization may occur either within the kernel or in user mode, thread scheduling occurs within the kernel.

Pthreads threads can take full advantage of multiprocessor hardware in a one-to-one implementation without any extra effort on your part, for example, separating your code into multiple processes. When a thread blocks in the kernel, it does not affect other threads any more than the blocking of a normal UNIX process affects other processes. One thread can even process a page fault without affecting other threads.

One-to-one implemenations suffer from two main problems. The first is that they do not scale well. That is, each thread in your application is a kernel entity. Because kernel memory is precious, kernel objects such as processes and threads are often limited by preallocated arrays, and most implementations will limit the number of threads you can create. It will also limit the number of threads that can be created on the entire system—so depending on what other processes are doing, your process may not be able to reach its own limit.

The second problem is that blocking on a mutex and waiting on a condition variable, which happen frequently in many applications, are substantially more expensive on most one-to-one implementations, because they require entering the machine's protected kernel mode. Note that locking a mutex, when it was not already locked, or unlocking a mutex, when there are no waiting threads, may be no more expensive than on a many-to-one implementation, because on most systems those functions can be completed in user mode.

A one-to-one implementation can be a good choice for CPU-bound applications, which don't block very often. Many high-performance parallel applications begin by creating a worker thread for each physical processor in the system, and, once started, the threads run independently for a substantial time period. Such applications will work well because they do not strain the kernel by creating a lot of threads, and they don't require a lot of calls into the kernel to block and unblock their threads.

Figure 5.6 shows the mapping of Pthreads threads (left column) to kernel entities (middle column) to physical processors (right column). In this case, the process has four Pthreads threads, labeled "Pthread 1" through "Pthread 4." Each Pthreads thread is permanently bound to the corresponding kernel entity. The kernel schedules the four kernel entities (along with those from other processes) onto the two physical processors, labeled "processor 1" and "processor 2." The important characteristics of this model are shown in Table 5.3.

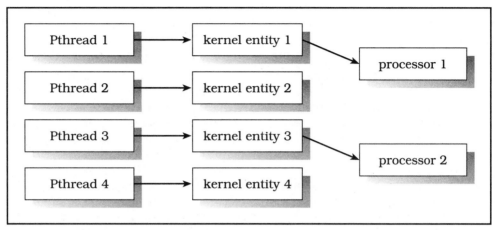

FIGURE 5.6 *One-to-one thread mapping*

Advantages	Disadvantages
Can take advantage of multiprocessor hardware within a single process.	Relatively slow thread context switch (calls into kernel).
No latency during system service blocking.	Poor scaling when many threads are used, because each Pthreads thread takes kernel resources from the system.

TABLE 5.3 *One-to-one thread scheduling*

5.6.3 Many-to-few (two level)

The many-to-few model tries to merge the advantages of both the many-to-one and one-to-one models, while avoiding their disadvantages. This model requires cooperation between the user-level Pthreads library and the kernel. They share scheduling responsibilities and may communicate information about the threads between each other.

When the Pthreads library needs to switch between two threads, it can do so directly, in user mode. The new Pthreads thread runs on the same kernel entity without intervention from the kernel. This gains the performance benefit of many-to-one implementations for the most common cases, when a thread blocks on a mutex or condition variable, and when a thread terminates.

When the kernel needs to block a thread, to wait for an I/O or other resource, it does so. The kernel may inform the Pthreads library, as in Digital UNIX 4.0, so that the library can preserve process concurrency by immediately scheduling a new Pthreads thread, somewhat like the original "scheduler activations" model proposed by the famous University of Washington research [Anderson, 1991]. Or, the kernel may simply block the kernel entity, in which case it may allow programmers to increase the number of kernel entities that are allocated to the process, as in Solaris 2.5—otherwise the process could be stalled when all kernel entities have blocked, even though other user threads are ready to run.

Many-to-few implementations excel in most real-world applications, because in most applications, threads perform a mixture of CPU-bound and I/O-bound operations, and block both in I/O and in Pthreads synchronization. Most applications also create more threads than there are physical processors, either directly or because an application that creates a few threads also uses a parallel library that creates a few threads, and so forth.

Figure 5.7 shows the mapping of Pthreads threads (left column) to kernel entities (middle column) to physical processors (right column). In this case, the process has four Pthreads threads, labeled "Pthread 1" through "Pthread 4." The Pthreads library creates some number of kernel entities at initialization (and may create more later). Typically, the library will start with one kernel entity (labeled "kernel entity 1" and "kernel entity 2") for each physical processor. The kernel schedules these kernel entities (along with those from other processes) onto the

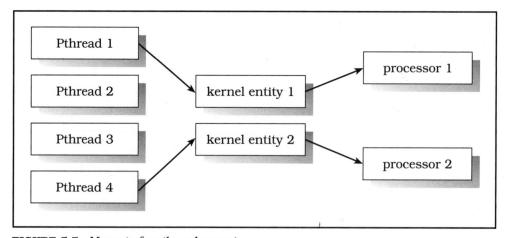

FIGURE 5.7 *Many-to-few thread mapping*

two physical processors, labeled "processor 1" and "processor 2." The important characteristics of this model are shown in Table 5.4.

Advantages	Disadvantages
Can take advantage of multiprocessor hardware within a process.	More complicated than other models.
Most context switches are in user mode (fast).	Programmers lose direct control over kernel entities, since the thread's priority may be meaningful only in user mode.
Scales well; a process may use one kernel entity per physical processor, or "a few" more.	
Little latency during system service blocking.	

TABLE 5.4 *Many-to-few thread scheduling*

6 POSIX adjusts to threads

"Who are you?" said the Caterpillar.
This was not an encouraging opening for a conversation.
Alice replied, rather shyly, "I—I hardly know, Sir,
   just at present—at least I know who I was when I got up this morning, but
   I think I must have been changed several times since then."
—Lewis Carroll, Alice's Adventures in Wonderland

Pthreads changes the meaning of a number of traditional POSIX process functions. Most of the changes are obvious, and you'd probably expect them even if the standard hadn't added specific wording. When a thread blocks for I/O, for example, only the calling thread blocks, while other threads in the process can continue to run.

But there's another class of POSIX functions that doesn't extend into the threaded world quite so unambiguously. For example, when you `fork` a threaded process, what happens to the threads? What does `exec` do in a threaded process? What happens when one of the threads in a threaded process calls `exit`?

6.1 `fork`

| Avoid using `fork` in a threaded program (if you can)
| unless you intend to `exec` a new program immediately.

When a threaded process calls `fork` to create a child process, Pthreads specifies that only the thread calling `fork` exists in the child. Although only the calling thread exists on return from `fork` in the child process, all other Pthreads states remain as they were at the time of the call to `fork`. In the child process, the thread has the same thread state as in the parent. It owns the same mutexes, has the same value for all thread-specific data keys, and so forth. All mutexes and condition variables exist, although any threads that were waiting on a synchronization object at the time of the `fork` are no longer waiting. (They don't exist in the child process, so how could they be waiting?)

Pthreads does not "terminate" the other threads in a forked process, as if they exited with `pthread_exit` or even as if they were canceled. They simply cease to exist. That is, the threads do not run thread-specific data destructors or cleanup handlers. This is not a problem if the child process is about to call `exec` to run a new program, but if you use `fork` to clone a threaded program, beware that you may lose access to memory, especially heap memory stored only as thread-specific data values.

> The state of mutexes is not affected by a `fork`. If it was locked in the parent it is locked in the child!

If a mutex was locked at the time of the call to `fork`, then it is still locked in the child. Because a locked mutex is *owned* by the thread that locked it, the mutex can be unlocked in the child only if the thread that locked the mutex was the one that called `fork`. This is important to remember—if another thread has a mutex locked when you call `fork`, you will lose access to that mutex and any data controlled by that mutex.

Despite the complications, you can `fork` a child that continues running and even continues to use Pthreads. You must use fork handlers carefully to protect your mutexes and the shared data that the mutexes are protecting. Fork handlers are described in Section 6.1.1.

Because thread-specific data destructors and cleanup handlers are not called, you may need to worry about memory leaks. One possible solution would be to cancel threads created by your subsystem in the *prepare* fork handler, and wait for them to terminate before allowing the `fork` to continue (by returning), and then create new threads in the *parent* handler that is called after `fork` completes. This could easily become messy, and I am not recommending it as a solution. Instead, take another look at the warning back at the beginning of this section: Avoid using `fork` in threaded code except where the child process will immediately `exec` a new program.

POSIX specifies a small set of functions that may be called safely from within signal-catching functions ("async-signal safe" functions), and `fork` is one of them. However, none of the POSIX threads functions is async-signal safe (and there are good reasons for this, because being async-signal safe generally makes a function substantially more expensive). With the introduction of fork handlers, however, a call to `fork` is also a call to some set of fork handlers.

The purpose of a fork handler is to allow threaded code to protect synchronization state and data invariants across a `fork`, and in most cases that requires locking mutexes. But you cannot lock mutexes from a signal-catching function. So while it is legal to call `fork` from within a signal-catching function, doing so may (beyond the control or knowledge of the caller) require performing other operations that cannot be performed within a signal-catching function.

This is an inconsistency in the POSIX standard that will need to be fixed. Nobody yet knows what the eventual solution will be. My advice is to avoid using `fork` in a signal-catching function.

6.1.1 Fork handlers

```
int pthread_atfork (void (*prepare)(void),
    void (*parent)(void), void (*child)(void));
```

Pthreads added the `pthread_atfork` "fork handler" mechanism to allow your code to protect data invariants across `fork`. This is somewhat analogous to `atexit`, which allows a program to perform cleanup when a process terminates. With `pthread_atfork` you supply three separate handler addresses. The *prepare* fork handler is called before the fork takes place in the parent process. The *parent* fork handler is called after the fork in the parent process, and the *child* fork handler is called after the fork in the child process.

> If you write a subsystem that uses mutexes and does not establish fork handlers, then that subsystem will not function correctly in a child process after a `fork`.

Normally a *prepare* fork handler locks all mutexes used by the associated code (for a library or an application) in the correct order to prevent deadlocks. The thread calling `fork` will *block* in the *prepare* fork handler until it has locked all the mutexes. That ensures that no other threads can have the mutexes locked or be modifying data that the child might need. The *parent* fork handler need only unlock all of those mutexes, allowing the parent process and all threads to continue normally.

The *child* fork handler may often be the same as the *parent* fork handler; but sometimes you'll need to reset the program or library state. For example, if you use "daemon" threads to perform functions in the background you'll need to either record the fact that those threads no longer exist or create new threads to perform the same function in the child. You may need to reset counters, free heap memory, and so forth.

> Your fork handlers are only as good as everyone else's fork handlers.

The system will run all *prepare* fork handlers declared in the process when any thread calls `fork`. If you code your *prepare* and *child* fork handlers correctly then, in principle, you will be able to continue operating in the child process. But what if someone else didn't supply fork handlers or didn't do it right? The ANSI C library on a threaded system, for example, must use a set of mutexes to synchronize internal data, such as *stdio* file streams.

If you use an ANSI C library that doesn't supply fork handlers to prepare those mutexes properly for a fork, for example, then, sometimes, you may find that your child process hangs when it calls `printf`, because another thread in the parent process had the mutex locked when your thread called `fork`. There's often nothing you can do about this type of problem except to file a problem report against the system. These mutexes are usually private to the library, and aren't visible to your code—you can't lock them in your *prepare* handler or before calling `fork`.

The program `atfork.c` shows the use of fork handlers. When run with no argument, or with a nonzero argument, the program will install fork handlers. When run with a zero argument, such as `atfork 0`, it will not.

With fork handlers installed, the result will be two output lines reporting the result of the `fork` call and, in parentheses, the pid of the current process. Without fork handlers, the child process will be created while the initial thread owns the mutex. Because the initial thread does not exist in the child, the mutex cannot be unlocked, and the child process will hang—only the parent process will print its message.

13-25   Function `fork_prepare` is the *prepare* handler. This will be called by `fork`, in the parent process, before creating the child process. Any state changed by this function, in particular, mutexes that are locked, will be copied into the child process. The `fork_prepare` function locks the program's mutex.

31-42   Function `fork_parent` is the *parent* handler. This will be called by `fork`, in the parent process, after creating the child process. In general, a *parent* handler should undo whatever was done in the *prepare* handler, so that the parent process can continue normally. The `fork_parent` function unlocks the mutex that was locked by `fork_prepare`.

48-60   Function `fork_child` is the *child* handler. This will be called by `fork`, in the child process. In most cases, the *child* handler will need to do whatever was done in the `fork_parent` handler to "unlock" the state so that the child can continue. It may also need to perform additional cleanup, for example, `fork_child` sets the `self_pid` variable to the child process's pid as well as unlocking the process mutex.

65-91   After creating a child process, which will continue executing the `thread_routine` code, the `thread_routine` function locks the mutex. When run with fork handlers, the fork call will be blocked (when the *prepare* handler locks the mutex) until the mutex is available. Without fork handlers, the thread will `fork` before `main` unlocks the mutex, and the thread will hang in the child at this point.

99-106   The main program declares fork handlers unless the program is run with an argument of 0.

108-123   The main program locks the mutex before creating the thread that will fork. It then sleeps for several seconds, to ensure that the thread will be able to call `fork` while the mutex is locked, and then unlocks the mutex. The thread running `thread_routine` will always succeed in the parent process, because it will simply block until `main` releases the lock.

However, without the fork handlers, the child process will be created while the mutex is locked. The thread (`main`) that locked the mutex does not exist in the child, and cannot unlock the mutex in the child process. Mutexes can be unlocked in the child only if they were locked by the thread that called fork—and fork handlers provide the best way to ensure that.

■ atfork.c
_____

```
1  #include <sys/types.h>
2  #include <pthread.h>
3  #include <sys/wait.h>
4  #include "errors.h"
5
6  pid_t self_pid;                              /* pid of current process */
7  pthread_mutex_t mutex = PTHREAD_MUTEX_INITIALIZER;
8
9  /*
10  * This routine will be called prior to executing the fork,
11  * within the parent process.
12  */
13 void fork_prepare (void)
14 {
15     int status;
16
17     /*
18      * Lock the mutex in the parent before creating the child,
19      * to ensure that no other thread can lock it (or change any
20      * associated shared state) until after the fork completes.
21      */
22     status = pthread_mutex_lock (&mutex);
23     if (status != 0)
24         err_abort (status, "Lock in prepare handler");
25 }
26
27 /*
28  * This routine will be called after executing the fork, within
29  * the parent process
30  */
31 void fork_parent (void)
32 {
33     int status;
34
35     /*
36      * Unlock the mutex in the parent after the child has been
37      * created.
38      */
39     status = pthread_mutex_unlock (&mutex);
40     if (status != 0)
41         err_abort (status, "Unlock in parent handler");
42 }
43
```

```
44   /*
45    * This routine will be called after executing the fork, within
46    * the child process.
47    */
48   void fork_child (void)
49   {
50       int status;
51
52       /*
53        * Update the file scope "self_pid" within the child process, and
54        * unlock the mutex.
55        */
56       self_pid = getpid ();
57       status = pthread_mutex_unlock (&mutex);
58       if (status != 0)
59           err_abort (status, "Unlock in child handler");
60   }
61
62   /*
63    * Thread start routine, which will fork a new child process.
64    */
65   void *thread_routine (void *arg)
66   {
67       pid_t child_pid;
68       int status;
69
70       child_pid = fork ();
71       if (child_pid == (pid_t)-1)
72           errno_abort ("Fork");
73
74       /*
75        * Lock the mutex -- without the atfork handlers, the mutex will
76        * remain locked in the child process and this lock attempt will
77        * hang (or fail with EDEADLK) in the child.
78        */
79       status = pthread_mutex_lock (&mutex);
80       if (status != 0)
81           err_abort (status, "Lock in child");
82       status = pthread_mutex_unlock (&mutex);
83       if (status != 0)
84           err_abort (status, "Unlock in child");
85       printf ("After fork: %d (%d)\n", child_pid, self_pid);
86       if (child_pid != 0) {
87           if ((pid_t)-1 == waitpid (child_pid, (int*)0, 0))
88               errno_abort ("Wait for child");
89       }
90       return NULL;
91   }
92
93   int main (int argc, char *argv[])
```

```
94  {
95      pthread_t fork_thread;
96      int atfork_flag = 1;
97      int status;
98
99      if (argc > 1)
100         atfork_flag = atoi (argv[1]);
101     if (atfork_flag) {
102         status = pthread_atfork (
103             fork_prepare, fork_parent, fork_child);
104         if (status != 0)
105             err_abort (status, "Register fork handlers");
106     }
107     self_pid = getpid ();
108     status = pthread_mutex_lock (&mutex);
109     if (status != 0)
110         err_abort (status, "Lock mutex");
111     /*
112      * Create a thread while the mutex is locked. It will fork a
113      * process, which (without atfork handlers) will run with the
114      * mutex locked.
115      */
116     status = pthread_create (
117         &fork_thread, NULL, thread_routine, NULL);
118     if (status != 0)
119         err_abort (status, "Create thread");
120     sleep (5);
121     status = pthread_mutex_unlock (&mutex);
122     if (status != 0)
123         err_abort (status, "Unlock mutex");
124     status = pthread_join (fork_thread, NULL);
125     if (status != 0)
126         err_abort (status, "Join thread");
127     return 0;
128 }
```

■ atfork.c

Now, imagine you are writing a library that manages network server connections, and you create a thread for each network connection that listens for service requests. In your *prepare* fork handler you lock all of the library's mutexes to make sure the child's state is consistent and recoverable. In your *parent* fork handler you unlock those mutexes and return. When designing the *child* fork handler, you need to decide exactly what a fork means to your library. If you want to retain all network connections in the child, then you would create a new listener thread for each connection and record their identifiers in the appropriate data structures before releasing the mutexes. If you want the child to begin with no open connections, then you would locate the existing parent connection data structures and free them, closing the associated files that were propagated by fork.

6.2   exec

The exec function isn't affected much by the presence of threads. The function of exec is to wipe out the current program context and replace it with a new program. A call to exec immediately terminates all threads in the process except the thread calling exec. They do not execute cleanup handlers or thread-specific data destructors—the threads simply cease to exist.

All synchronization objects also vanish, except for *pshared* mutexes (mutexes created using the PTHREAD_PROCESS_SHARED attribute value) and *pshared* condition variables, which remain usable as long as the shared memory is mapped by some process. You should, however, unlock any *pshared* mutexes that the current process may have locked—the system will not unlock them for you.

6.3   Process exit

In a nonthreaded program, an explicit call to the exit function has the same effect as returning from the program's main function. The process exits. Pthreads adds the pthread_exit function, which can be used to cause a single thread to exit while the process continues. In a threaded program, therefore, you call exit when you want the process to exit, or pthread_exit when you want only the calling thread to exit.

In a threaded program, main is effectively the "thread start function" for the process's initial thread. Although returning from the start function of any other thread terminates that thread just as if it had called pthread_exit, returning from main terminates the *process*. All memory (and threads) associated with the process evaporate. Threads do not run cleanup handlers or thread-specific data destructors. Calling exit has the same effect.

When you don't want to make use of the initial thread or make it wait for other threads to complete, you can exit from main by calling pthread_exit rather than by returning or calling exit. Calling pthread_exit from main will terminate the initial thread without affecting the other threads in the process, allowing them to continue and complete normally.

The exit function provides a simple way to shut down the entire process. For example, if a thread determines that data has been severely corrupted by some error, it may be dangerous to allow the program to continue to operate on the data. When the program is somehow broken, it might be dangerous to attempt to shut down the application threads cleanly. In that case, you might call exit to stop all processing immediately.

6.4   *Stdio*

Pthreads specifies that the ANSI C standard I/O (*stdio*) functions are thread-safe. Because the *stdio* package requires static storage for output buffers and file state, *stdio* implementations will use synchronization, such as mutexes or semaphores.

6.4.1 `flockfile` and `funlockfile`

```
void flockfile (FILE *file);
int ftrylockfile (FILE *file);
void funlockfile (FILE *file);
```

In some cases, it is important that a sequence of *stdio* operations occur in uninterrupted sequence; for example, a prompt followed by a read from the terminal, or two writes that need to appear together in the output file even if another thread attempts to write data between the two *stdio* calls. Therefore, Pthreads adds a mechanism to lock a file and specifies how file locking interacts with internal *stdio* locking. To write a prompt string to `stdin` and read a response from `stdout` without allowing another thread to read from `stdin` or write to `stdout` between the two, you would need to lock both `stdin` and `stdout` around the two calls as shown in the following program, `flock.c`.

19-20   This is the important part: Two separate calls to `flockfile` are made, one for each of the two file streams. To avoid possible deadlock problems within *stdio*, Pthreads recommends always locking input streams before output streams, when you must lock both. That's good advice, and I've taken it by locking `stdin` before `stdout`.

29-30   The two calls to `funlockfile` must, of course, be made in the opposite order. Despite the specialized call, you are effectively locking mutexes within the *stdio* library, and you should respect a consistent lock hierarchy.

■ `flock.c`

```
1   #include <pthread.h>
2   #include "errors.h"
3
4   /*
5    * This routine writes a prompt to stdout (passed as the thread's
6    * "arg"), and reads a response. All other I/O to stdin and stdout
7    * is prevented by the file locks until both prompt and fgets are
8    * complete.
9    */
10  void *prompt_routine (void *arg)
11  {
12      char *prompt = (char*)arg;
13      char *string;
14      int len;
15
16      string = (char*)malloc (128);
```

```
17          if (string == NULL)
18              errno_abort ("Alloc string");
19          flockfile (stdin);
20          flockfile (stdout);
21          printf (prompt);
22          if (fgets (string, 128, stdin) == NULL)
23              string[0] = '\0';
24          else {
25              len = strlen (string);
26              if (len > 0 && string[len-1] == '\n')
27                  string[len-1] = '\0';
28          }
29          funlockfile (stdout);
30          funlockfile (stdin);
31          return (void*)string;
32      }
33
34      int main (int argc, char *argv[])
35      {
36          pthread_t thread1, thread2, thread3;
37          char *string;
38          int status;
39
40      #ifdef sun
41          /*
42           * On Solaris 2.5, threads are not timesliced. To ensure
43           * that our threads can run concurrently, we need to
44           * increase the concurrency level.
45           */
46          DPRINTF (("Setting concurrency level to 4\n"));
47          thr_setconcurrency (4);
48      #endif
49          status = pthread_create (
50              &thread1, NULL, prompt_routine, "Thread 1> ");
51          if (status != 0)
52              err_abort (status, "Create thread");
53          status = pthread_create (
54              &thread2, NULL, prompt_routine, "Thread 2> ");
55          if (status != 0)
56              err_abort (status, "Create thread");
57          status = pthread_create (
58              &thread3, NULL, prompt_routine, "Thread 3> ");
59          if (status != 0)
60              err_abort (status, "Create thread");
61          status = pthread_join (thread1, (void**)&string);
62          if (status != 0)
63              err_abort (status, "Join thread");
64          printf ("Thread 1: \"%s\"\n", string);
65          free (string);
66          status = pthread_join (thread2, (void**)&string);
```

```
67      if (status != 0)
68          err_abort (status, "Join thread");
69      printf ("Thread 1: \"%s\"\n", string);
70      free (string);
71      status = pthread_join (thread3, (void**)&string);
72      if (status != 0)
73          err_abort (status, "Join thread");
74      printf ("Thread 1: \"%s\"\n", string);
75      free (string);
76      return 0;
77  }
```

■ flock.c

You can also use the flockfile and funlockfile functions to ensure that a series of writes is not interrupted by a file access from some other thread. The ftrylockfile function works like pthread_mutex_trylock in that it attempts to lock the file and, if the file is already locked, returns an error status instead of blocking.

6.4.2 getchar_unlocked and putchar_unlocked

```
int getc_unlocked (FILE *stream);
int getchar_unlocked (void);
int putc_unlocked (int c, FILE *stream);
int putchar_unlocked (int c);
```

ANSI C provides functions to get and put single characters efficiently into *stdio* buffers. The functions getchar and putchar operate on stdin and stdout, respectively, and getc and putc can be used on any *stdio* file stream. These are traditionally implemented as macros for maximum performance, directly reading or writing the file stream's data buffer. Pthreads, however, requires these functions to lock the *stdio* stream data, to prevent code from accidentally corrupting the *stdio* buffers.

The overhead of locking and unlocking mutexes will probably vastly exceed the time spent performing the character copy, so these functions are no longer high performance. Pthreads could have defined new functions that provided the locked variety rather than redefining the existing functions; however, the result would be that existing code would be unsafe for use in threads. The working group decided that it was preferable to make existing code slower, rather than to make it incorrect.

Pthreads adds new functions that replace the old high-performance macros with essentially the same implementation as the traditional macros. The functions getc_unlocked, putc_unlocked, getchar_unlocked, and putchar_unlocked do not perform any locking, so you must use flockfile and funlockfile around any sequence of these operations. If you want to read or write a single character, you should usually use the locked variety rather than locking the file stream, calling the new unlocked get or put function, and then unlocking the file stream.

If you want to perform a sequence of fast character accesses, where you would have previously used getchar and putchar, you can now use getchar_unlocked and putchar_unlocked. The following program, putchar.c, shows the difference between using putchar and using a sequence of putchar_unlocked calls within a file lock.

9-20   When the program is run with a nonzero argument or no argument at all, it creates threads running the lock_routine function. This function locks the stdout file stream, and then writes its argument (a string) to stdout one character at a time using putchar_unlocked.

28-37   When the program is run with a zero argument, it creates threads running the unlock_routine function. This function writes its argument to stdout one character at a time using putchar. Although putchar is internally synchronized to ensure that the *stdio* buffer is not corrupted, the individual characters may appear in any order.

■   putchar.c
───

```
1   #include <pthread.h>
2   #include "errors.h"
3
4   /*
5    * This function writes a string (the function's arg) to stdout,
6    * by locking the file stream and using putchar_unlocked to write
7    * each character individually.
8    */
9   void *lock_routine (void *arg)
10  {
11      char *pointer;
12
13      flockfile (stdout);
14      for (pointer = arg; *pointer != '\0'; pointer++) {
15          putchar_unlocked (*pointer);
16          sleep (1);
17      }
18      funlockfile (stdout);
19      return NULL;
20  }
21
22  /*
23   * This function writes a string (the function's arg) to stdout,
24   * by using putchar to write each character individually.
25   * Although the internal locking of putchar prevents file stream
26   * corruption, the writes of various threads may be interleaved.
27   */
28  void *unlock_routine (void *arg)
```

```
29   {
30       char *pointer;
31
32       for (pointer = arg; *pointer != '\0'; pointer++) {
33           putchar (*pointer);
34           sleep (1);
35       }
36       return NULL;
37   }
38
39   int main (int argc, char *argv[])
40   {
41       pthread_t thread1, thread2, thread3;
42       int flock_flag = 1;
43       void *(*thread_func)(void *);
44       int status;
45
46       if (argc > 1)
47           flock_flag = atoi (argv[1]);
48       if (flock_flag)
49           thread_func = lock_routine;
50       else
51           thread_func = unlock_routine;
52       status = pthread_create (
53           &thread1, NULL, thread_func, "this is thread 1\n");
54       if (status != 0)
55           err_abort (status, "Create thread");
56       status = pthread_create (
57           &thread2, NULL, thread_func, "this is thread 2\n");
58       if (status != 0)
59           err_abort (status, "Create thread");
60       status = pthread_create (
61           &thread3, NULL, thread_func, "this is thread 3\n");
62       if (status != 0)
63           err_abort (status, "Create thread");
64       pthread_exit (NULL);
65   }
```

■ putchar.c

6.5 Thread-safe functions

Although ANSI C and POSIX 1003.1–1990 were not developed with threads in mind, most of the functions they define can be made thread-safe without changing the external interface. For example, although malloc and free must be changed to support threads, code calling these functions need not be aware of the changes. When you call malloc, it locks a mutex (or perhaps several mutexes) to perform the operation, or may use other equivalent synchronization mechanisms. But your code just calls `malloc` as it always has, and it does the same thing as always.

In two main classes of functions, this is not true:

- Functions that traditionally return pointers to internal static buffers, for example, `asctime`. An internal mutex wouldn't help, since the caller will read the formatted time string some time after the function returns and, therefore, after the mutex has been unlocked.
- Functions that require static context between a series of calls, for example, `strtok`, which stores the current position within the token string in a local static variable. Again, using a mutex within `strtok` wouldn't help, because other threads would be able to overwrite the current location between two calls.

In these cases, Pthreads has defined variants of the existing functions that are thread-safe, which are designated by the suffix "_r" at the end of the function name. These variants move context outside the library, under the caller's control. When each thread uses a private buffer or context, the functions are thread-safe. You can also share context between threads if you want—but the caller must provide synchronization between the threads. If you want two threads to search a directory in parallel, you must synchronize their use of the shared `struct dirent` passed to `readdir_r`.

A few existing functions, such as `ctermid`, are already thread-safe as long as certain restrictions are placed on parameters. These restrictions are noted in the following sections.

6.5.1 User and terminal identification

```
int getlogin_r (char *name, size_t namesize);
char *ctermid (char *s);
int ttyname_r (int fildes,
    char *name, size_t namesize);
```

These functions return data to a caller-specified buffer. For `getlogin_r`, `namesize` must be at least `LOGIN_NAME_MAX` characters. For `ttyname_r`, `namesize` must be at least `TTY_NAME_MAX` characters. Either function returns a value of 0 on success, or an error number on failure. In addition to errors that might be returned by `getlogin` or `ttyname`, `getlogin_r` and `ttyname_r` may return `ERANGE` to indicate that the `name` buffer is too small.

Pthreads requires that when `ctermid` (which has not changed) is used in a threaded environment, the `s` return argument must be specified as a pointer to a character buffer having at least L_ctermid bytes. It was felt that this restriction was sufficient, without defining a new variant to also specify the size of the buffer. Program getlogin.c shows how to call these functions. Notice that these functions do not depend on threads, or <pthread.h>, in any way, and may even be provided on systems that don't support threads.

■ getlogin.c

```
1  #include <limits.h>
2  #include "errors.h"
3
4  /*
5   * If either TTY_NAME_MAX or LOGIN_NAME_MAX are undefined
6   * (this means they are "indeterminate" values), assume a
7   * reasonable size (for simplicity) rather than using sysconf
8   * and dynamically allocating the buffers.
9   */
10 #ifndef TTY_NAME_MAX
11 # define TTY_NAME_MAX     128
12 #endif
13 #ifndef LOGIN_NAME_MAX
14 # define LOGIN_NAME_MAX   32
15 #endif
16
17 int main (int argc, char *argv[])
18 {
19     char login_str[LOGIN_NAME_MAX];
20     char stdin_str[TTY_NAME_MAX];
21     char cterm_str[L_ctermid], *cterm_str_ptr;
22     int status;
23
24     status = getlogin_r (login_str, sizeof (login_str));
25     if (status != 0)
26         err_abort (status, "Get login");
27     cterm_str_ptr = ctermid (cterm_str);
28     if (cterm_str_ptr == NULL)
29         errno_abort ("Get cterm");
30     status = ttyname_r (0, stdin_str, sizeof (stdin_str));
31     if (status != 0)
32         err_abort (status, "Get stdin");
33     printf ("User: %s, cterm: %s, fd 0: %s\n",
34         login_str, cterm_str, stdin_str);
35     return 0;
36 }
```

■ getlogin.c

6.5.2 Directory searching

```
int readdir_r (DIR *dirp, struct dirent *entry,
    struct dirent **result);
```

This function performs essentially the same action as `readdir`. That is, it returns the next directory entry in the directory stream specified by `dirp`. The difference is that instead of returning a pointer to that entry, it copies the entry into the buffer specified by `entry`. On success, it returns 0 and sets the pointer specified by `result` to the buffer `entry`. On reaching the end of the directory stream, it returns 0 and sets `result` to `NULL`. On failure, it returns an error number such as `EBADF`.

Refer to program `pipe.c`, in Section 4.1, for a demonstration of using `readdir_r` to allow your threads to search multiple directories concurrently.

6.5.3 String token

```
char *strtok_r (
    char *s, const char *sep, char **lasts);
```

This function returns the next token in the string `s`. Unlike `strtok`, the context (the current pointer within the original string) is maintained in `lasts`, which is specified by the caller, rather than in a static pointer internal to the function.

In the first call of a series, the argument `s` gives a pointer to the string. In subsequent calls to return successive tokens of that string, `s` must be specified as `NULL`. The value `lasts` is set by `strtok_r` to maintain the function's position within the string, and on each subsequent call you must return that same value of `lasts`. The `strtok_r` function returns a pointer to the next token, or `NULL` when there are no more tokens to be found in the original string.

6.5.4 Time representation

```
char *asctime_r (const struct tm *tm, char *buf);
char *ctime_r (const time_t *clock, char *buf);
struct tm *gmtime_r (
    const time_t *clock, struct tm *result);
struct tm *localtime_r (
    const time_t *clock, struct tm *result);
```

The output buffers (buf and result) are supplied by the caller, instead of returning a pointer to static storage internal to the functions. Otherwise, they are identical to the traditional variants. The asctime_r and ctime_r routines, which return ASCII character representations of a system time, both require that their buf argument point to a character string of at least 26 bytes.

6.5.5 Random number generation

```
int rand_r (unsigned int *seed);
```

The seed is maintained in caller-supplied storage (seed) rather than using static storage internal to the function. The main problem with this interface is that it is not usually practical to have a single seed shared by all application and library code within a program. As a result, the application and each library will generally have a separate "stream" of random numbers. Thus, a program converted to use rand_r instead of rand is likely to generate different results, even if no threads are created. (Creating threads would probably change the order of calls to rand, and therefore change results anyway.)

6.5.6 Group and user database

Group database:
```
int getgrgid_r (
    gid_t gid, struct group *grp, char *buffer,
    size_t bufsize, struct group **result);
int getgrnam_r (
    const char *name, struct group *grp,
    char *buffer, size_t bufsize,
    struct group **result);
```

User database:
```
int getpwuid_r (
    uid_t uid, struct passwd *pwd, char *buffer,
    size_t bufsize, struct passwd **result);
int getpwnam_r (
    const char *name, struct passwd *pwd,
    char *buffer, size_t bufsize,
    struct passwd **result);
```

These functions store a copy of the group or user record (grp or pwd, respectively) for the specified group or user (gid, uid, or name) in a buffer designated by the arguments `buffer` and `bufsize`. The function return value is in each case either 0 for success, or an error number (such as `ERANGE` when the buffer is too small) to designate an error. If the requested record is not present in the group or `passwd` database, the functions may return success but store the value `NULL` into the `result` pointer. If the record is found and the buffer is large enough, `result` becomes a pointer to the `struct group` or `struct passwd` record within `buffer`.

The maximum required size for `buffer` can be determined by calling `sysconf` with the argument `_SC_GETGR_R_SIZE_MAX` (for group data) or with the argument `_SC_GETPW_R_SIZE_MAX` (for user data).

6.6 Signals

Beware the Jabberwock, my son!
The jaws that bite, the claws that catch!
Beware the Jubjub bird, and shun
The frumious Bandersnatch!
    —Lewis Carroll, Through the Looking-Glass

The history of the Pthreads signal-handling model is the most convoluted and confusing part of the standard. There were several different viewpoints, and it was difficult to devise a compromise that would satisfy everyone in the working group (much less the larger and more diverse balloting group). This isn't surprising, since signals are complicated anyway, and have a widely divergent history in the industry.

There were two primary conflicting goals:

- First, "signals should be completely compatible with traditional UNIX." That means signal handlers and masks should remain associated with the process. That makes them virtually useless with multiple threads, which is as it should be since signals have complicating semantics that make it difficult for signals and threads to coexist peacefully. Tasks should be accomplished synchronously using threads rather than asynchronously using signals.

- Second, "signals should be completely compatible with traditional UNIX." This time, "compatible" means signal handlers and masks should be completely thread-private. Most existing UNIX code would then function essentially the same running within a thread as it had within a process. Code migration would be simplified.

The problem is that the definitions of "compatible" were incompatible. Although many people involved in the negotiation may not agree with the final result, nearly everyone would agree that those who devised the compromise did an extraordinarily good job, and that they were quite courageous to attempt the feat.

> When writing threaded code, treat signals as Jabberwocks—
> curious and potentially dangerous creatures to be
> approached with caution, if at all.

It is always best to avoid using signals in conjunction with threads. At the same time, it is often not possible or practical to keep them separate. When signals and threads meet, beware. If at all possible, use only pthread_sigmask to mask signals in the main thread, and sigwait to handle signals synchronously within a single thread dedicated to that purpose. If you must use sigaction (or equivalent) to handle synchronous signals (such as SIGSEGV) within threads, be especially cautious. Do as little work as possible within the signal-catching function.

6.6.1 Signal actions

All signal actions are process-wide. A program must coordinate any use of sigaction between threads. This is nonmodular, but also relatively simple, and signals have never been modular. A function that dynamically modifies signal actions, for example, to catch or ignore SIGFPE while it performs floating-point operations, or SIGPIPE while it performs network I/O, will be tricky to code on a threaded system.

While modifying the process signal action for a signal number is itself thread-safe, there is no protection against some other thread setting a new signal action immediately afterward. Even if the code tries to be "good" by saving the original signal action and restoring it, it may be foiled by another thread, as shown in Figure 6.1.

Signals that are not "tied" to a specific hardware execution context are delivered to one arbitrary thread within the process. That means a SIGCHLD raised by a child process termination, for example, may not be delivered to the thread that created the child. Similarly, a call to kill results in a signal that may be delivered to any thread.

Thread 1	Thread 2	Comments
sigaction(SIGFPE)		Thread 1's signal action active.
	sigaction(SIGFPE)	Thread 2's signal action active.
Generate SIGFPE		Thread 1 signal is handled by the thread 2 signal action (but still in the context of thread 1).
Restore action		Thread 1 restores original signal action.
	restore action	Thread 2 restores thread 1's signal action—original action is lost.

FIGURE 6.1 *Nonmodularity of signal actions*

The synchronous "hardware context" signals, including SIGFPE, SIGSEGV, and SIGTRAP, are delivered to the thread that caused the hardware condition, never to another thread.

> You cannot kill a thread by sending it a SIGKILL or stop a thread by sending it a SIGSTOP.

Any signal that affected a process still affects the process when multiple threads are active, which means that sending a SIGKILL to a process or to any specific thread in the process (using pthread_kill, which we'll get to in Section 6.6.3) will terminate the process. Sending a SIGSTOP will cause all threads to stop until a SIGCONT is received. This ensures that existing process control functions continue to work—otherwise most threads in a process could continue running when you stopped a command by sending a SIGSTOP. This also applies to the default action of the other signals, for example, SIGSEGV, if not handled, will terminate the process and generate a core file—it will not terminate only the thread that generated the SIGSEGV.

What does this mean to a programmer? It has always been common wisdom that library code should not change signal actions—that this is exclusively the province of the main program. This philosophy becomes even more wise when you are programming with threads. Signal actions must always be under the control of a single component, at least, and to assign that responsibility to the main program makes the most sense in nearly all situations.

6.6.2 Signal masks

```
int pthread_sigmask (int how,
    const sigset_t *set, sigset_t *oset);
```

Each thread has its own private signal mask, which is modified by calling pthread_sigmask. Pthreads does not specify what sigprocmask does within a threaded process—it may do nothing. Portable threaded code does not call sigprocmask. A thread can block or unblock signals without affecting the ability of other threads to handle the signal. This is particularly important for synchronous signals. It would be awkward if thread A were unable to process a SIGFPE because thread B was currently processing its own SIGFPE or, even worse, because thread C had blocked SIGFPE. When a thread is created, it inherits the signal mask of the thread that created it—if you want a signal to be masked everywhere, mask it first thing in main.

6.6.3 pthread_kill

```
int pthread_kill (pthread_t thread, int sig);
```

Within a process, one thread can send a signal to a specific thread (including itself) by calling pthread_kill. When calling pthread_kill, you specify not only the signal number to be delivered, but also the pthread_t identifier for the thread to which you want the signal sent. You cannot use pthread_kill to send a signal to a thread in another process, however, because a thread identifier (pthread_t) is meaningful only within the process that created it.

The signal sent by pthread_kill is handled like any other signal. If the "target" thread has the signal masked, it will be marked pending against that thread. If the thread is waiting for the signal in sigwait (covered in Section 6.6.4), the thread will receive the signal. If the thread does not have the signal masked, and is not blocked in sigwait, the current signal action will be taken.

Remember that, aside from signal-catching functions, signal actions affect the process. Sending the SIGKILL signal to a specific thread using pthread_kill will kill the process, not just the specified thread. Use pthread_cancel to get rid of a particular thread (see Section 5.3). Sending SIGSTOP to a thread will stop all threads in the process until a SIGCONT is sent by some other process.

The raise function specified by ANSI C has traditionally been mapped to a kill for the current process. That is, raise (SIGABRT) is usually the same as kill (getpid (), SIGABRT).

With multiple threads, code calling raise is most likely to intend that the signal be sent to the calling thread, rather than to some arbitrary thread within the process. Pthreads specifies that raise (SIGABRT) is the same as pthread_kill (pthread_self (), SIGABRT).

The following program, susp.c, uses pthread_kill to implement a portable "suspend and resume" (or, equivalently, "suspend and continue") capability much like that provided by the Solaris "UI threads" interfaces thr_suspend and thr_continue.* You call the thd_suspend function with the pthread_t of a thread, and when the function returns, the specified thread has been *suspended* from execution. The thread cannot execute until a later call to thd_continue is made with the same pthread_t.

A request to suspend a thread that is already suspended has no effect. Calling thd_continue a single time for a suspended thread will cause it to resume execution, even if it had been suspended by multiple calls to thd_suspend. Calling thd_continue for a thread that is not currently suspended has no effect.

---

*The algorithm (and most of the code) for susp.c was developed by a coworker of mine, Brian Silver. The code shown here is a simplified version for demonstration purposes.

Suspend and resume are commonly used to solve some problems, for example, multithread garbage collectors, and may even work sometimes if the programmer is very careful. This emulation of suspend and resume may therefore be valuable to the few programmers who really need these functions. Beware, however, that should you suspend a thread while it holds some resource (such as a mutex), application deadlock can easily result.

6   The symbol ITERATIONS defines how many times the "target" threads will loop. If this value is set too small, some or all of the threads will terminate before the main thread has been able to suspend and continue them as it desires. If that happens, the program will fail with an error message—increase the value of ITERATIONS until the problem goes away.

12   The variable sentinel is used to synchronize between a signal-catching function and another thread. "Oh?" you may ask, incredulously. This mechanism is not perfect—the suspending thread (the one calling thd_suspend) waits in a loop, yielding the processor until this sentinel changes state. The volatile storage attribute ensures that the signal-catching function will write the value to memory.* Remember, you cannot use a mutex within a signal-catching function.

22-40   The suspend_signal_handler function will be established as the signal-catching function for the "suspend" signal, SIGUSR1. It initializes a signal mask to block all signals except SIGUSR2, which is the "resume" signal, and then waits for that signal by calling sigsuspend. Just before suspending itself, it sets the sentinel variable to inform the suspending thread that it is no longer executing user code—for most practical purposes, it is already suspended.

The purpose for this synchronization between the signal-catching function and thd_suspend is that, to be most useful, the thread calling thd_suspend must be able to know when the target thread has been successfully suspended. Simply calling pthread_kill is not enough, because the system might not deliver the signal for a substantial period of time; we need to know when the signal has been received.

47-51   The resume_signal_handler function will be established as the signal-catching function for the "resume" signal, SIGUSR1. The function isn't important, since the signal is sent only to interrupt the call to sigsuspend in suspend_signal_handler.

■ susp.c   part1   signal-catchingfunctions

```
1  #include <pthread.h>
2  #include <signal.h>
3  #include "errors.h"
4
5  #define THREAD_COUNT    20
6  #define ITERATIONS      40000
```

---

*A semaphore, as described later in Section 6.6.6, would provide cleaner, and somewhat safer, synchronization. The thd_suspend would call sem_wait on a semaphore with an initial value of 0, and the signal-catching function would call sem_post to wake it.

```
 7
 8  unsigned long thread_count = THREAD_COUNT;
 9  unsigned long iterations = ITERATIONS;
10  pthread_mutex_t the_mutex = PTHREAD_MUTEX_INITIALIZER;
11  pthread_mutex_t mut = PTHREAD_MUTEX_INITIALIZER;
12  volatile int sentinel = 0;
13  pthread_once_t once = PTHREAD_ONCE_INIT;
14  pthread_t *array = NULL, null_pthread = {0};
15  int bottom = 0;
16  int inited = 0;
17
18  /*
19   * Handle SIGUSR1 in the target thread, to suspend it until
20   * receiving SIGUSR2 (resume).
21   */
22  void
23  suspend_signal_handler (int sig)
24  {
25      sigset_t signal_set;
26
27      /*
28       * Block all signals except SIGUSR2 while suspended.
29       */
30      sigfillset (&signal_set);
31      sigdelset (&signal_set, SIGUSR2);
32      sentinel = 1;
33      sigsuspend (&signal_set);
34
35      /*
36       * Once I'm here, I've been resumed, and the resume signal
37       * handler has been run to completion.
38       */
39      return;
40  }
41
42  /*
43   * Handle SIGUSR2 in the target thread, to resume it. Note that
44   * the signal handler does nothing. It exists only because we need
45   * to cause sigsuspend() to return.
46   */
47  void
48  resume_signal_handler (int sig)
49  {
50      return;
51  }
```

The `suspend_init_routine` function dynamically initializes the suspend/resume package when the first call to `thd_suspend` is made. It is actually called indirectly by `pthread_once`.

15-16   It allocates an initial array of thread identifiers, which is used to record the identifiers of all threads that have been suspended. This array is used to ensure that multiple calls to `thd_suspend` have no additional effect on the target thread, and that calling `thd_continue` for a thread that is not suspended has no effect.

21-35   It sets up signal actions for the `SIGUSR1` and `SIGUSR2` signals, which will be used, respectively, to suspend and resume threads.

■ susp.c   part 2   initialization

```
1   /*
2    * Dynamically initialize the "suspend package" when first used
3    * (called by pthread_once).
4    */
5   void
6   suspend_init_routine (void)
7   {
8       int status;
9       struct sigaction sigusr1, sigusr2;
10
11      /*
12       * Allocate the suspended threads array. This array is used
13       * to guarentee idempotency
14       */
15      bottom = 10;
16      array = (pthread_t*) calloc (bottom, sizeof (pthread_t));
17
18      /*
19       * Install the signal handlers for suspend/resume.
20       */
21      sigusr1.sa_flags = 0;
22      sigusr1.sa_handler = suspend_signal_handler;
23
24      sigemptyset (&sigusr1.sa_mask);
25      sigusr2.sa_flags = 0;
26      sigusr2.sa_handler = resume_signal_handler;
27      sigusr2.sa_mask = sigusr1.sa_mask;
28
29      status = sigaction (SIGUSR1, &sigusr1, NULL);
30      if (status == -1)
31          errno_abort ("Installing suspend handler");
32
33      status = sigaction (SIGUSR2, &sigusr2, NULL);
34      if (status == -1)
35          errno_abort ("Installing resume handler");
```

```
36
37        inited = 1;
38        return;
39    }
```

9-40   The thd_suspend function suspends a thread, and returns when that thread has ceased to execute user code. It first ensures that the suspend/resume package is initialized by calling pthread_once. Under protection of a mutex, it searches for the target thread's identifier in the array of suspended thread identifiers. If the thread is already suspended, thd_suspend returns successfully.

47-60   Determine whether there is an empty entry in the array of suspended threads and, if not, realloc the array with an extra entry.

65-78   The sentinel variable is initialized to 0, to detect when the target thread suspension occurs. The thread is sent a SIGUSR1 signal by calling pthread_kill, and thd_suspend loops, calling sched_yield to avoid monopolizing a processor, until the target thread responds by setting sentinel. Finally, the suspended thread's identifier is stored in the array.

```
 1    /*
 2     * Suspend a thread by sending it a signal (SIGUSR1), which will
 3     * block the thread until another signal (SIGUSR2) arrives.
 4     *
 5     * Multiple calls to thd_suspend for a single thread have no
 6     * additional effect on the thread -- a single thd_continue
 7     * call will cause it to resume execution.
 8     */
 9    int
10    thd_suspend (pthread_t target_thread)
11    {
12        int status;
13        int i = 0;
14
15        /*
16         * The first call to thd_suspend will initialize the
17         * package.
18         */
19        status = pthread_once (&once, suspend_init_routine);
20        if (status != 0)
21            return status;
22
23        /*
24         * Serialize access to suspend, makes life easier.
25         */
```

```
26      status = pthread_mutex_lock (&mut);
27      if (status != 0)
28          return status;
29
30      /*
31       * Threads that are suspended are added to the target_array;
32       * a request to suspend a thread already listed in the array
33       * is ignored. Sending a second SIGUSR1 would cause the
34       * thread to resuspend itself as soon as it is resumed.
35       */
36      while (i < bottom)
37          if (array[i++] == target_thread) {
38              status = pthread_mutex_unlock (&mut);
39              return status;
40          }
41
42      /*
43       * Ok, we really need to suspend this thread. So, let's find
44       * the location in the array that we'll use. If we run off
45       * the end, realloc the array for more space.
46       */
47      i = 0;
48      while (array[i] != 0)
49          i++;
50
51      if (i == bottom) {
52          array = (pthread_t*) realloc (
53              array, (++bottom * sizeof (pthread_t)));
54          if (array == NULL) {
55              pthread_mutex_unlock (&mut);
56              return errno;
57          }
58
59          array[bottom] = null_pthread;    /* Clear new entry */
60      }
61
62      /*
63       * Clear the sentinel and signal the thread to suspend.
64       */
65      sentinel = 0;
66      status = pthread_kill (target_thread, SIGUSR1);
67      if (status != 0) {
68          pthread_mutex_unlock (&mut);
69          return status;
70      }
71
72      /*
73       * Wait for the sentinel to change.
74       */
```

```
75      while (sentinel == 0)
76          sched_yield ();
77
78      array[i] = target_thread;
79
80      status = pthread_mutex_unlock (&mut);
81      return status;
82  }
```

■ susp.c   part 3   thd_suspend

23-26   The thd_continue function first checks whether the suspend/resume package has been initialized (inited is not 0). If it has not been initialized, then no threads are suspended, and thd_continue returns with success.

33-39   If the specified thread identifier is not found in the array of suspended threads, then it is not suspended—again, return with success.

45-51   Send the resume signal, SIGUSR2. There's no need to wait—the thread will resume whenever it can, and the thread calling thd_continue doesn't need to know.

■ susp.c   part 4   thd_continue

```
1  /*
2   * Resume a suspended thread by sending it SIGUSR2 to break
3   * it out of the sigsuspend() in which it's waiting. If the
4   * target thread isn't suspended, return with success.
5   */
6  int
7  thd_continue (pthread_t target_thread)
8  {
9      int status;
10     int i = 0;
11
12     /*
13      * Serialize access to suspend, makes life easier.
14      */
15     status = pthread_mutex_lock (&mut);
16     if (status != 0)
17         return status;
18
19     /*
20      * If we haven't been initialized, then the thread must be
21      * "resumed"; it couldn't have been suspended!
22      */
23     if (!inited) {
24         status = pthread_mutex_unlock (&mut);
25         return status;
26     }
27
```

```
28          /*
29           * Make sure the thread is in the suspend array. If not, it
30           * hasn't been suspended (or it has already been resumed) and
31           * we can just carry on.
32           */
33          while (array[i] != target_thread && i < bottom)
34              i++;
35
36          if (i >= bottom) {
37              pthread_mutex_unlock (&mut);
38              return 0;
39          }
40
41          /*
42           * Signal the thread to continue, and remove the thread from
43           * the suspended array.
44           */
45          status = pthread_kill (target_thread, SIGUSR2);
46          if (status != 0) {
47              pthread_mutex_unlock (&mut);
48              return status;
49          }
50
51          array[i] = 0;                    /* Clear array element */
52          status = pthread_mutex_unlock (&mut);
53          return status;
54      }
```

■ susp.c   part 4   thd_continue

2-25   The thread_routine function is the thread start routine for each of the "target"
        threads created by the program. It simply loops for a substantial period of time,
        periodically printing a status message. On each iteration, it yields to other threads
        to ensure that the processor time is apportioned "fairly" across all the threads.
            Notice that instead of calling printf, the function formats a message with
        sprintf and then displays it on stdout (file descriptor 1) by calling write. This
        illustrates one of the problems with using suspend and resume (thd_suspend and
        thd_continue) for synchronization. Suspend and resume are scheduling func-
        tions, not synchronization functions, and using scheduling and synchronization
        controls together can have severe consequences.

        ▮ Incautious use of suspend and resume can deadlock your application.

            In this case, if a thread were suspended while modifying a *stdio* stream, all other
        threads that tried to modify that *stdio* stream might block, waiting for a mutex that
        is locked by the suspended thread. The write function, on the other hand, is usu-
        ally a call to the kernel—the kernel is atomic with respect to signals, and therefore
        can't be suspended. Use of write, therefore, cannot cause a deadlock.

In general, you cannot suspend a thread that may possibly hold any resource, if that resource may be required by some other thread before the suspended thread is resumed. In particular, the result is a *deadlock* if the thread that would resume the suspended thread first needs to acquire the resource. This prohibition includes, especially, mutexes used by libraries you call—such as the mutexes used by `malloc` and `free`, or the mutexes used by *stdio*.

36–42   Threads are created with an attributes object set to create threads detached, rather than joinable. The result is that threads will cease to exist as soon as they terminate, rather than remaining until main calls `pthread_join`. The `pthread_kill` function does not necessarily fail if you attempt to send a signal to a terminated thread (the standard is silent on this point), and you may be merely setting a pending signal in a thread that will never be able to act on it. If this were to occur, the `thd_suspend` routine would hang waiting for the thread to respond. Although `pthread_kill` may not fail when sending to a terminated thread, it will fail when sending to a thread that doesn't exist—so this attribute converts a possible hang, when the program is run with ITERATIONS set too low, into an abort with an error message.

51–85   The main thread sleeps for two seconds after creating the threads to allow them to reach a "steady state." It then loops through the first half of the threads, suspending each of them. It waits an additional two seconds and then resumes each of the threads it had suspended. It waits another two seconds, suspends each of the remaining threads (the second half), and then after another two seconds resumes them.

By watching the status messages printed by the individual threads, you can see the pattern of output change as the threads are suspended and resumed.

■ susp.c   part 5   sampleprogram

```
1   static void *
2   thread_routine (void *arg)
3   {
4       int number = (int)arg;
5       int status;
6       int i;
7       char buffer[128];
8
9       for (i = 1; i <= iterations; i++) {
10          /*
11           * Every time each thread does 5000 interations, print
12           * a progress report.
13           */
14          if (i % 2000 == 0) {
15              sprintf (
16                  buffer, "Thread %02d: %d\n",
17                  number, i);
18              write (1, buffer, strlen (buffer));
19          }
20
```

```
21                    sched_yield ();
22          }
23
24          return (void *)0;
25  }
26
27  int
28  main (int argc, char *argv[])
29  {
30          pthread_t threads[THREAD_COUNT];
31          pthread_attr_t detach;
32          int status;
33          void *result;
34          int i;
35
36          status = pthread_attr_init (&detach);
37          if (status != 0)
38              err_abort (status, "Init attributes object");
39          status = pthread_attr_setdetachstate (
40              &detach, PTHREAD_CREATE_DETACHED);
41          if (status != 0)
42              err_abort (status, "Set create-detached");
43
44          for (i = 0; i< THREAD_COUNT; i++) {
45              status = pthread_create (
46                  &threads[i], &detach, thread_routine, (void *)i);
47              if (status != 0)
48                  err_abort (status, "Create thread");
49          }
50
51          sleep (2);
52
53          for (i = 0; i < THREAD_COUNT/2; i++) {
54              printf ("Suspending thread %d.\n", i);
55              status = thd_suspend (threads[i]);
56              if (status != 0)
57                  err_abort (status, "Suspend thread");
58          }
59
60          printf ("Sleeping ...\n");
61          sleep (2);
62
63          for (i = 0; i < THREAD_COUNT/2; i++) {
64              printf ("Continuing thread %d.\n", i);
65              status = thd_continue (threads[i]);
66              if (status != 0)
67                  err_abort (status, "Suspend thread");
68          }
69
```

```
70          for (i = THREAD_COUNT/2; i < THREAD_COUNT; i++) {
71              printf ("Suspending thread %d.\n", i);
72              status = thd_suspend (threads[i]);
73              if (status != 0)
74                  err_abort (status, "Suspend thread");
75          }
76
77          printf ("Sleeping ...\n");
78          sleep (2);
79
80          for (i = THREAD_COUNT/2; i < THREAD_COUNT; i++) {
81              printf ("Continuing thread %d.\n", i);
82              status = thd_continue (threads[i]);
83              if (status != 0)
84                  err_abort (status, "Continue thread");
85          }
86
87          pthread_exit (NULL);            /* Let threads finish */
88      }
```

■ susp.c   part 5   sampleprogram

6.6.4 sigwait and sigwaitinfo

```
int sigwait (const sigset_t *set, int *sig);
#ifdef _POSIX_REALTIME_SIGNALS
int sigwaitinfo (
    const sigset_t *set, siginfo_t *info);
int sigtimedwait (
    const sigset_t *set, siginfo_t *info,
    const struct timespec *timeout);
#endif
```

> Always use `sigwait` to work with asynchronous signals within threaded code.

Pthreads adds a function to allow threaded programs to deal with "asynchronous" signals synchronously. That is, instead of allowing a signal to interrupt a thread at some arbitrary point, a thread can choose to receive a signal synchronously. It does this by calling `sigwait`, or one of `sigwait`'s siblings.

> The signals for which you `sigwait` must be masked in the sigwaiting thread, and should usually be masked in all threads.

The `sigwait` function takes a signal set as its argument, and returns a signal number when any signal in that set occurs. You can create a thread that waits for some signal, for example, SIGINT, and causes some application activity when it occurs. The nonobvious rule is that the signals for which you wait must be masked before calling sigwait. In fact, you should ideally mask these signals in main, at the start of the program. Because signal masks are inherited by threads you create, all threads will (by default) have the signal masked. This ensures that the signal will never be delivered to any thread except the one that calls sigwait.

Signals are delivered only once. If two threads are blocked in sigwait, only one of them will receive a signal that's sent to the process. This means you can't, for example, have two independent subsystems using sigwait that catch SIGINT. It also means that the signal will not be caught by sigwait in one thread and also delivered to some signal-catching function in another thread. That's not so bad, since you couldn't do that in the old nonthreaded model either—only one signal action can be active at a time.

While sigwait, a Pthreads function, reports errors by returning an error number, its siblings, sigwaitinfo and sigtimedwait, were added to POSIX prior to Pthreads, and use the older errno mechanism. This is confusing and awkward, and that is unfortunate. The problem is that they deal with the additional information supplied by the POSIX realtime signals option (<unistd.h> defines the symbol _POSIX_REALTIME_SIGNALS), and the POSIX realtime amendment, POSIX.1b, was completed before the Pthreads amendment.

Both sigwaitinfo and sigtimedwait return the realtime signal information, siginfo_t, for signals received. In addition, sigtimedwait allows the caller to specify that sigtimedwait should return with the error EAGAIN in the event that none of the selected signals is received within the specified interval.

The sigwait.c program creates a "sigwait thread" that handles SIGINT.

23-41   The signal_waiter thread repeatedly calls sigwait, waiting for a SIGINT signal. It counts five occurrences of SIGINT (printing a message each time), and then signals a condition variable on which main is waiting. At that time, main will exit.

61-65   The main program begins by masking SIGINT. Because all threads inherit their initial signal mask from their creator, SIGINT will be masked in all threads. This prevents SIGINT from being delivered at any time except when the signal_ waiter thread is blocked in sigwait and ready to receive the signal.

■   sigwait.c
───

```
1   #include <sys/types.h>
2   #include <unistd.h>
3   #include <pthread.h>
4   #include <signal.h>
5   #include "errors.h"
6
7   pthread_mutex_t mutex = PTHREAD_MUTEX_INITIALIZER;
8   pthread_cond_t cond = PTHREAD_COND_INITIALIZER;
9   int interrupted = 0;
10  sigset_t signal_set;
11
```

```
12    /*
13     * Wait for the SIGINT signal. When it has occurred 5 times, set the
14     * "interrupted" flag (the main thread's wait predicate) and signal a
15     * condition variable. The main thread will exit.
16     */
17    void *signal_waiter (void *arg)
18    {
19        int sig_number;
20        int signal_count = 0;
21        int status;
22
23        while (1) {
24            sigwait (&signal_set, &sig_number);
25            if (sig_number == SIGINT) {
26                printf ("Got SIGINT (%d of 5)\n", signal_count+1);
27                if (++signal_count >= 5) {
28                    status = pthread_mutex_lock (&mutex);
29                    if (status != 0)
30                        err_abort (status, "Lock mutex");
31                    interrupted = 1;
32                    status = pthread_cond_signal (&cond);
33                    if (status != 0)
34                        err_abort (status, "Signal condition");
35                    status = pthread_mutex_unlock (&mutex);
36                    if (status != 0)
37                        err_abort (status, "Unlock mutex");
38                    break;
39                }
40            }
41        }
42        return NULL;
43    }
44
45    int main (int argc, char *argv[])
46    {
47        pthread_t signal_thread_id;
48        int status;
49
50        /*
51         * Start by masking the "interesting" signal, SIGINT in the
52         * initial thread. Because all threads inherit the signal mask
53         * from their creator, all threads in the process will have
54         * SIGINT masked unless one explicitly unmasks it. The
55         * semantics of sigwait requires that all threads (including
56         * the thread calling sigwait) have the signal masked, for
57         * reliable operation. Otherwise, a signal that arrives
58         * while the sigwaiter is not blocked in sigwait might be
59         * delivered to another thread.
60         */
```

```
61          sigemptyset (&signal_set);
62          sigaddset (&signal_set, SIGINT);
63          status = pthread_sigmask (SIG_BLOCK, &signal_set, NULL);
64          if (status != 0)
65              err_abort (status, "Set signal mask");
66
67          /*
68           * Create the sigwait thread.
69           */
70          status = pthread_create (&signal_thread_id, NULL,
71              signal_waiter, NULL);
72          if (status != 0)
73              err_abort (status, "Create sigwaiter");
74
75          /*
76           * Wait for the sigwait thread to receive SIGINT and signal
77           * the condition variable.
78           */
79          status = pthread_mutex_lock (&mutex);
80          if (status != 0)
81              err_abort (status, "Lock mutex");
82          while (!interrupted) {
83              status = pthread_cond_wait (&cond, &mutex);
84              if (status != 0)
85                  err_abort (status, "Wait for interrupt");
86          }
87          status = pthread_mutex_unlock (&mutex);
88          if (status != 0)
89              err_abort (status, "Unlock mutex");
90          printf ("Main terminating with SIGINT\n");
91          return 0;
92      }
```

■ sigwait.c

6.6.5 SIGEV_THREAD

Some of the functions in the POSIX.1b realtime standard, which provide for asynchronous notification, allow the programmer to give specific instructions about how that notification is to be accomplished. For example, when initiating an asynchronous device read or write using aio_read or aio_write, the programmer specifies a struct aiocb, which contains, among other members, a struct sigevent. Other functions that accept a struct sigevent include timer_create (which creates a per-process timer) and sigqueue (which queues a signal to a process).

The `struct sigevent` structure in POSIX.1b provides a "notification mechanism" that allows the programmer to specify whether a signal is to be generated, and, if so, what signal number should be used. Pthreads adds a new notification mechanism called `SIGEV_THREAD`. This new notification mechanism causes the signal notification function to be run as if it were the start routine of a thread.

Pthreads adds several members to the POSIX.1b `struct sigevent` structure. The new members are `sigev_notify_function`, a pointer to a thread start function; and `sigev_notify_attributes`, a pointer to a thread attributes object (`pthread_attr_t`) containing the desired thread creation attributes. If `sigev_notify_attributes` is `NULL`, the notify thread is created as if the *detachstate* attribute was set to `PTHREAD_CREATE_DETACHED`. This avoids a memory leak—in general, the notify thread's identifier won't be available to any other thread. Furthermore, Pthreads says that the result of specifying an attributes object that has the *detachstate* attribute set to `PTHREAD_CREATE_JOINABLE` is "undefined." (Most likely, the result will be a memory leak because the thread cannot be joined—if you are lucky, the system may override your choice and create it detached anyway.)

The `SIGEV_THREAD` notification function may not actually be run in a new thread—Pthreads carefully specifies that it behaves as if it were run in a new thread, just as I did a few paragraphs ago. The system may, for example, queue `SIGEV_THREAD` events and call the start routines, serially, in some internal "server thread." The difference is effectively indistinguishable to the application. A system that uses a server thread must be very careful about the attributes specified for the notification thread—for example, scheduling policy and priority, contention scope, and minimum stack size must all be taken into consideration.

The `SIGEV_THREAD` feature is not available to any of the "traditional" signal generation mechanisms, such as `setitimer`, or for `SIGCHLD`, `SIGINT`, and so forth. Those who are programming using the POSIX.1b "realtime signal" interfaces, including timers and asynchronous I/O, may find this new capability useful.

The following program, `sigev_thread.c`, shows how to use the `SIGEV_THREAD` notification mechanism for a POSIX.1b timer.

20-37 The function `timer_thread` is specified as the "notification function" (thread start routine) for the `SIGEV_THREAD` timer. The function will be called each time the timer expires. It counts expirations, and wakes the main thread after five. Notice that, unlike a signal-catching function, the `SIGEV_THREAD` notification function can make full use of Pthreads synchronization operations. This can be a substantial advantage in many situations.

45-51 Unfortunately, neither Solaris 2.5 nor Digital UNIX 4.0 correctly implemented `SIGEV_THREAD`. Thus, unlike all other examples in this book, this code will not compile on Solaris 2.5. This `#ifdef` block allows the code to compile, and to fail gracefully if the resulting program is run, with an error message. Although the program will compile on Digital UNIX 4.0, it will not run. The implementation of `SIGEV_THREAD` has been fixed in Digital UNIX 4.0D, which should be available by the time you read this, and it should also be fixed in Solaris 2.6.

56-59   These statements initialize the `sigevent` structure, which describes how the
system should notify the application when an event occurs. In this case, we are
telling it to call `timer_thread` when the timer expires, and to use default
attributes.

■ sigev_thread.c

```
1  #include <pthread.h>
2  #include <sys/signal.h>
3  #include <sys/time.h>
4  #include "errors.h"
5
6  timer_t timer_id;
7  pthread_mutex_t mutex = PTHREAD_MUTEX_INITIALIZER;
8  pthread_cond_t cond = PTHREAD_COND_INITIALIZER;
9  int counter = 0;
10
11 /*
12  * Thread start routine to notify the application when the
13  * timer expires. This routine is run "as if" it were a new
14  * thread, each time the timer expires.
15  *
16  * When the timer has expired 5 times, the main thread will
17  * be awakened, and will terminate the program.
18  */
19 void
20 timer_thread (void *arg)
21 {
22     int status;
23
24     status = pthread_mutex_lock (&mutex);
25     if (status != 0)
26         err_abort (status, "Lock mutex");
27     if (++counter >= 5) {
28         status = pthread_cond_signal (&cond);
29         if (status != 0)
30             err_abort (status, "Signal condition");
31     }
32     status = pthread_mutex_unlock (&mutex);
33     if (status != 0)
34         err_abort (status, "Unlock mutex");
35
36     printf ("Timer %d\n", counter);
37 }
38
39 main()
```

```
40  {
41      int status;
42      struct itimerspec ts;
43      struct sigevent se;
44
45  #ifdef sun
46      fprintf (
47          stderr,
48          "This program cannot compile on Solaris 2.5.\n"
49          "To build and run on Solaris 2.6, remove the\n"
50          "\"#ifdef sun\" block in main().\n");
51  #else
52      /*
53       * Set the sigevent structure to cause the signal to be
54       * delivered by creating a new thread.
55       */
56      se.sigev_notify = SIGEV_THREAD;
57      se.sigev_value.sival_ptr = &timer_id;
58      se.sigev_notify_function = timer_thread;
59      se.sigev_notify_attributes = NULL;
60
61      /*
62       * Specify a repeating timer that fires every 5 seconds.
63       */
64      ts.it_value.tv_sec = 5;
65      ts.it_value.tv_nsec = 0;
66      ts.it_interval.tv_sec = 5;
67      ts.it_interval.tv_nsec = 0;
68
69      DPRINTF (("Creating timer\n"));
70      status = timer_create(CLOCK_REALTIME, &se, &timer_id);
71      if (status == -1)
72          errno_abort ("Create timer");
73
74      DPRINTF ((
75          "Setting timer %d for 5-second expiration...\n", timer_id));
76      status = timer_settime(timer_id, 0, &ts, 0);
77      if (status == -1)
78          errno_abort ("Set timer");
79
80      status = pthread_mutex_lock (&mutex);
81      if (status != 0)
82          err_abort (status, "Lock mutex");
83      while (counter < 5) {
84          status = pthread_cond_wait (&cond, &mutex);
85          if (status != 0)
86              err_abort (status, "Wait on condition");
87      }
```

```
88          status = pthread_mutex_unlock (&mutex);
89          if (status != 0)
90              err_abort (status, "Unlock mutex");
91
92      #endif /* Sun */
93          return 0;
94      }
```

■ sigev_thread.c

6.6.6 Semaphores: synchronizing with a signal-catching function

```
#ifdef _POSIX_SEMAPHORES
int sem_init (sem_t *sem,
    int pshared, unsigned int value);
int sem_destroy (sem_t *sem);
int sem_wait (sem_t *sem);
int sem_trywake (sem_t *sem);
int sem_post (sem_t *sem);
int sem_getvalue (sem_t *sem, int *sval);
#endif
```

Although mutexes and condition variables provide an ideal solution to most synchronization needs, they cannot meet all needs. One example of this is a need to communicate between a POSIX signal-catching function and a thread waiting for some asynchronous event. In new code, it is best to use sigwait or sigwait-info rather than relying on a signal-catching function, and this neatly avoids this problem. However, the use of asynchronous POSIX signal-catching functions is well established and widespread, and most programmers working with threads and existing code will probably encounter this situation.

To awaken a thread from a POSIX signal-catching function, you need a mechanism that's reentrant with respect to POSIX signals (async-signal safe). POSIX provides relatively few of these functions, and none of the Pthreads functions is included. That's primarily because an async-signal safe mutex lock operation would be many times slower than one that isn't async-signal safe. Outside of the kernel, making a function async-signal safe usually requires that the function mask (block) signals while it runs—and that is expensive.

In case you're curious, here is the full list of POSIX 1003.1–1996 functions that are async-signal safe (some of these functions exist only when certain POSIX options are defined, such as _POSIX_ASYNCHRONOUS_IO or _POSIX_TIMERS):

access	getoverrun	sigismember
aio_error	getgroups	sigpending
aio_return	getpgrp	sigprocmask
aio_suspend	getpid	sigqueue
alarm	getppid	sigsuspend
cfgetispeed	getuid	sleep
cfgetospeed	kill	stat
cfsetispeed	link	sysconf
cfsetospeed	lseek	tcdrain
chdir	mkdir	tcflow
chmod	mkfifo	tcflush
chown	open	tcgetattr
clock_gettime	pathconf	tcgetpgrp
close	pause	tcsendbreak
creat	pipe	tcsetattr
dup2	read	tcsetpgrp
dup	rename	time
execle	rmdir	timer_getoverrun
execve	sem_post	timer_gettime
_exit	setgid	timer_settime
fcntl	setpgid	times
fdatasync	setsid	umask
fork	setuid	uname
fstat	sigaction	unlink
fsync	sigaddset	utime
getegid	sigdelset	wait
geteuid	sigemptyset	waitpid
getgid	sigfillset	write

POSIX.1b provides counting semaphores, and most systems that support Pthreads also support POSIX.1b semaphores. You may notice that the sem_post function, which wakes threads waiting on a semaphore, appears in the list of async-signal safe functions. If your system supports POSIX semaphores (<unistd.h> defines the _POSIX_SEMAPHORES option), then Pthreads adds the ability to use semaphores between threads within a process. That means you can *post* a semaphore, from within a POSIX signal-catching function, to wake a thread in the same process or in another process.

A semaphore is a different kind of synchronization object—it is a little like a mutex, a little like a condition variable. The differences can make semaphores a little harder to use for many common tasks, but they make semaphores substantially easier to use for certain specialized purposes. In particular, semaphores can be *posted* (unlocked or signaled) from a POSIX signal-catching function.

> Semaphores are a general synchronization mechanism.
>
> We just have no reason to use them that way.

I am emphasizing the use of semaphores to pass information from a signal-catching function, rather than for general use, for a couple of reasons. One reason is that semaphores are part of a different standard. As I said, most systems that support Pthreads will also support POSIX.1b, but there is no such requirement anywhere in the standard. So you may well find yourself without access to semaphores, and you shouldn't feel dependent on them. (Of course, you may also find yourself *with* semaphores and *without* threads—but in that case, you should be reading a different book.)

Another reason for keeping semaphores here with signals is that, although semaphores are a completely general synchronization mechanism, it can be more difficult to solve many problems using semaphores—mutexes and condition variables are simpler. If you've got Pthreads, you only *need* semaphores to handle this one specialized function—waking a waiting thread from a signal-catching function. Just remember that you *can* use them for other things when they're convenient and available.

POSIX semaphores contain a count, but no "owner," so although they can be used essentially as a lock, they can also be used to wait for events. The terminology used in the POSIX semaphore operations stresses the "wait" behavior rather than the "lock" behavior. Don't be confused by the names, though; there's no difference between "waiting" on a semaphore and "locking" the semaphore.

A thread waits on a semaphore (to lock a resource, or wait for an event) by calling sem_wait. If the semaphore counter is greater than zero, sem_wait decrements the counter and returns immediately. Otherwise, the thread blocks. A thread can post a semaphore (to unlock a resource, or awaken a waiter) by calling sem_post. If one or more threads are waiting on the semaphore, sem_post will wake one waiter (the highest priority, or earliest, waiter). If no threads are waiting, the semaphore counter is incremented.

The initial value of the semaphore counter is the distinction between a "lock" semaphore and a "wait" semaphore. By creating a semaphore with an initial count of 1, you allow one thread to complete a sem_wait operation without blocking—this "locks" the semaphore. By creating a semaphore with an initial count of 0, you force all threads that call sem_wait to block until some thread calls sem_post.

The differences in how semaphores work give the semaphore two important advantages over mutexes and condition variables that may be of use in threaded programs:

1. Unlike mutexes, semaphores have no concept of an "owner." This means that any thread may release threads blocked on a semaphore, much as if any thread could unlock a mutex that some thread had locked. (Although this is usually not a good programming model, there are times when it is handy.)

2. Unlike condition variables, semaphores can be independent of any external state. Condition variables depend on a shared predicate and a mutex for waiting—semaphores do not.

A semaphore is represented in your program by a variable of type sem_t. You should never make a copy of a sem_t variable—the result of using a copy of a sem_t variable in the sem_wait, sem_trywait, sem_post, and sem_destroy functions is undefined. For our purposes, a sem_t variable is initialized by calling the sem_init function. POSIX.1b provides other ways to create a "named" semaphore that can be shared between processes without sharing memory, but there is no need for this capability when using a semaphore within a single process.

Unlike Pthreads functions, the POSIX semaphore functions use errno to report errors. That is, success is designated by returning the value 0, and errors are designated by returning the value –1 and setting the variable errno to an error code.

If you have a section of code in which you want up to two threads to execute simultaneously while others wait, you can use a semaphore without any additional state. Initialize the semaphore to the value 2; then put a sem_wait at the beginning of the code and a sem_post at the end. Two threads can then *wait* on the semaphore without blocking, but a third thread will find the semaphore's counter at 0, and block. As each thread exits the region of code it *posts* the semaphore, releasing one waiter (if any) or restoring the counter.

The sem_getvalue function returns the current value of the semaphore counter if there are no threads waiting. If threads are waiting, sem_getvalue returns a negative number. The absolute value of that number tells how many threads are waiting on the semaphore. Keep in mind that the value it returns may already be incorrect—it can change at any time due to the action of some other thread.

The best use for sem_getvalue is as a way to wake multiple waiters, somewhat like a condition variable broadcast. Without sem_getvalue, you have no way of knowing how many threads might be blocked on a semaphore. To "broadcast" a semaphore, you could call sem_getvalue and sem_post in a loop until sem_getvalue reports that there are no more waiters.

But remember that other threads can call sem_post during this loop, and there is no synchronization between the various concurrent calls to sem_post and sem_getvalue. You can easily end up issuing one or more extra calls to sem_post, which will cause the next thread that calls sem_wait to find a value greater than 0, and return immediately without blocking.

The program below, semaphore_signal.c, uses a semaphore to awaken threads from within a POSIX signal-catching function. Notice that the sem_init call sets the initial value to 0 so that each thread calling sem_wait will block. The main program then requests an interval timer, with a POSIX signal-catching function that will wake one waiting thread by calling sem_post. Each occurrence of the POSIX timer signal will awaken one waiting thread. The program will exit when each thread has been awakened five times.

32-35   Notice the code to check for EINTR return status from the sem_wait call. The POSIX timer signal in this program will always occur while one or more threads are blocked in sem_wait. When a signal occurs for a process (such as a timer signal), the system may deliver that signal within the context of any thread within the process. Likely "victims" include threads that the kernel knows to be waiting, for example, on a semaphore. So there is a fairly good chance that the sem_wait thread will be chosen, at least sometimes. If that occurs, the call to sem_wait will return with EINTR. The thread must then retry the call. Treating an EINTR return as "success" would make it appear that two threads had been awakened by each call to sem_post: the thread that was interrupted, and the thread that was awakened by the sem_post call.

■ semaphore_signal.c

```
 1  #include <sys/types.h>
 2  #include <unistd.h>
 3  #include <pthread.h>
 4  #include <semaphore.h>
 5  #include <signal.h>
 6  #include <time.h>
 7  #include "errors.h"
 8
 9  sem_t    semaphore;
10
11  /*
12   * Signal-catching function.
13   */
14  void signal_catcher (int sig)
15  {
16      if (sem_post (&semaphore) == -1)
17          errno_abort ("Post semaphore");
18  }
19
20  /*
21   * Thread start routine which waits on the semaphore.
22   */
23  void *sem_waiter (void *arg)
24  {
25      int number = (int)arg;
26      int counter;
27
28      /*
29       * Each thread waits 5 times.
30       */
31      for (counter = 1; counter <= 5; counter++) {
32          while (sem_wait (&semaphore) == -1) {
```

```
33                  if (errno != EINTR)
34                      errno_abort ("Wait on semaphore");
35              }
36          printf ("%d waking (%d)...\n", number, counter);
37      }
38      return NULL;
39  }
40
41  int main (int argc, char *argv[])
42  {
43      int thread_count, status;
44      struct sigevent sig_event;
45      struct sigaction sig_action;
46      sigset_t sig_mask;
47      timer_t timer_id;
48      struct itimerspec timer_val;
49      pthread_t sem_waiters[5];
50
51  #if !defined(_POSIX_SEMAPHORES) || !defined(_POSIX_TIMERS)
52  # if !defined(_POSIX_SEMAPHORES)
53      printf ("This system does not support POSIX semaphores\n");
54  # endif
55  # if !defined(_POSIX_TIMERS)
56      printf ("This system does not support POSIX timers\n");
57  # endif
58      return -1;
59  #else
60      sem_init (&semaphore, 0, 0);
61
62      /*
63       * Create 5 threads to wait on a semaphore.
64       */
65      for (thread_count = 0; thread_count < 5; thread_count++) {
66          status = pthread_create (
67                  &sem_waiters[thread_count], NULL,
68                  sem_waiter, (void*)thread_count);
69          if (status != 0)
70              err_abort (status, "Create thread");
71      }
72
73      /*
74       * Set up a repeating timer using signal number SIGRTMIN,
75       * set to occur every 2 seconds.
76       */
77      sig_event.sigev_value.sival_int = 0;
78      sig_event.sigev_signo = SIGRTMIN;
79      sig_event.sigev_notify = SIGEV_SIGNAL;
```

```
80      if (timer_create (CLOCK_REALTIME, &sig_event, &timer_id) == -1)
81          errno_abort ("Create timer");
82      sigemptyset (&sig_mask);
83      sigaddset (&sig_mask, SIGRTMIN);
84      sig_action.sa_handler = signal_catcher;
85      sig_action.sa_mask = sig_mask;
86      sig_action.sa_flags = 0;
87      if (sigaction (SIGRTMIN, &sig_action, NULL) == -1)
88          errno_abort ("Set signal action");
89      timer_val.it_interval.tv_sec = 2;
90      timer_val.it_interval.tv_nsec = 0;
91      timer_val.it_value.tv_sec = 2;
92      timer_val.it_value.tv_nsec = 0;
93      if (timer_settime (timer_id, 0, &timer_val, NULL) == -1)
94          errno_abort ("Set timer");
95
96      /*
97       * Wait for all threads to complete.
98       */
99      for (thread_count = 0; thread_count < 5; thread_count++) {
100         status = pthread_join (sem_waiters[thread_count], NULL);
101         if (status != 0)
102             err_abort (status, "Join thread");
103     }
104     return 0;
105 #endif
106 }
```

■ semaphore_signal.c

7 "Real code"

"When we were still little," the Mock Turtle went on at last, more calmly,
though still sobbing a little now and then, "we went to school in the sea.
The master was an old Turtle—we used to call him Tortoise—"
"Why did you call him Tortoise, if he wasn't one?" Alice asked.
"We called him Tortoise because he taught us," said the
Mock Turtle angrily.
—Lewis Carroll, Through the Looking-Glass

This section builds on most of the earlier sections of the book, but principally on the mutex and condition variable sections. You should already understand how to create both types of synchronization objects and how they work. I will demonstrate the design and construction of *barrier* and *read/write lock* synchronization mechanisms that are built from mutexes, condition variables, and a dash of data. Both barriers and read/write locks are in common use, and have been proposed for standardization in the near future. I will follow up with a *work queue server* that lets you parcel out tasks to a pool of threads.

The purpose of all this is to teach you more about the subtleties of using all these new threaded programming tools (that is, mutexes, condition variables, and threads). The library packages may be useful to you as is or as templates. Primarily, though, they are here to give me something to talk about in this section, and I have omitted some complication that may be valuable in real code. The error detection and recovery code, for example, is fairly primitive.

7.1 Extended synchronization

Mutexes and condition variables are flexible and efficient synchronization tools. You can build just about any form of synchronization you need using those two things. But you shouldn't build them from scratch every time you need them. It is nice to start with a general, modular implementation that doesn't need to be debugged every time. This section shows some common and useful tools that you won't have to redesign every time you write an application that needs them.

First we'll build a *barrier*. The function of a barrier is about what you might guess—it stops threads. A barrier is initialized to stop a certain number of threads—when the required number of threads have reached the barrier, all are allowed to continue.

Then we'll build something called a *read/write lock*. A read/write lock allows multiple threads to read data simultaneously, but prevents any thread from modifying data that is being read or modified by another thread.

7.1.1 Barriers

A barrier is a way to keep the members of a group together. If our intrepid "bailing programmers" washed up on a deserted island, for example, and they ventured into the jungle to explore, they would want to remain together, for the illusion of safety in numbers, if for no other reason (Figure 7.1). Any exploring programmer finding himself very far in front of the others would therefore wait for them before continuing.

A barrier is usually employed to ensure that all threads cooperating in some parallel algorithm reach a specific point in that algorithm before any can pass. This is especially common in code that has been *decomposed* automatically by creating fine-grained parallelism within compiled source code. All threads may execute the same code, with threads processing separate portions of a shared data set (such as an array) in some areas and processing private data in parallel

FIGURE 7.1 *Barrier analogy*

in other areas. Still other areas must be executed by only one thread, such as setup or cleanup for the parallel regions. The boundaries between these areas are often implemented using barriers. Thus, threads completing a matrix computation may wait at a barrier until all have finished. One may then perform setup for the next parallel segment while the others skip ahead to another barrier. When the setup thread reaches that barrier, all threads begin the next parallel region.

Figure 7.2 shows the operation of a barrier being used to synchronize three threads, called thread 1, thread 2, and thread 3. The figure is a sort of timing diagram, with time increasing from left to right. Each of the lines beginning at the labels in the upper left designates the behavior of a specific thread—solid for thread 1, dotted for thread 2, and dashed for thread 3. When the lines drop within the rounded rectangle, they are interacting with the barrier. If the line drops below the center line, it shows that the thread is blocked waiting for other threads to reach the barrier. The line that stops above the center line represents the final thread to reach the barrier, awakening all waiters.

In this example, thread 1 and then thread 2 wait on the barrier. At a later time, thread 3 waits on the barrier, finds that the barrier is now full, and awakens all the waiters. All three threads then return from the barrier wait.

The core of a barrier is a *counter*. The counter is initialized to the number of threads in the "tour group," the number of threads that must wait on a barrier before all the waiters return. I'll call that the "threshold," to give it a simple one-word name. When each thread reaches the barrier, it decreases the counter. If the value hasn't reached 0, it waits. If the value has reached 0, it wakes up the waiting threads.

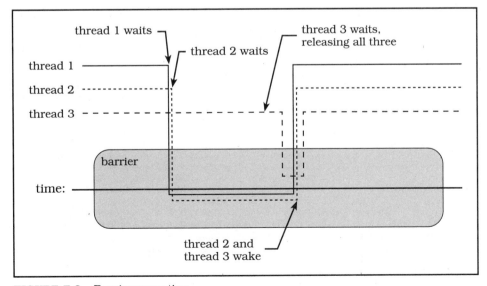

FIGURE 7.2 *Barrier operation*

Because the counter will be modified by multiple threads, it has to be protected by a mutex. Because threads will be waiting for some event (a counter value of 0), the barrier needs to have a condition variable and a predicate expression. When the counter reaches 0 and the barrier drops open, we need to reset the counter, which means the barrier must store the original threshold.

The obvious predicate is to simply wait for the counter to reach 0, but that complicates the process of resetting the barrier. When can we reset the count to the original value? We can't reset it when the counter reaches 0, because at that point most of the threads are waiting on the condition variable. The counter must be 0 when they wake up, or they'll continue waiting. Remember that condition variable waits occur in loops that retest the predicate.

The best solution is to add a separate variable for the predicate. We will use a "cycle" variable that is logically inverted each time some thread determines that one cycle of the barrier is complete. That is, whenever the counter value is reset, before broadcasting the condition variable, the thread inverts the cycle flag. Threads wait in a loop as long as the cycle flag remains the same as the value seen on entry, which means that each thread must save the initial value.

The header file `barrier.h` and the C source file `barrier.c` demonstrate an implementation of barriers using standard Pthreads mutexes and condition variables. This is a portable implementation that is relatively easy to understand. One could, of course, create a much more efficient implementation for any specific system based on knowledge of nonportable hardware and operating system characteristics.

6-13   Part 1 shows the structure of a barrier, represented by the type `barrier_t`. You can see the mutex (`mutex`) and the condition variable (`cv`). The `threshhold` member is the number of threads in the group, whereas `counter` is the number of threads that have yet to join the group at the barrier. And `cycle` is the flag discussed in the previous paragraph. It is used to ensure that a thread awakened from a barrier wait will immediately return to the caller, but will block in the barrier if it calls the wait operation again before all threads have resumed execution.

15   The `BARRIER_VALID` macro defines a "magic number," which we store into the `valid` member and then check to determine whether an address passed to other barrier interfaces is "reasonably likely to be" a barrier. This is an easy, quick check that will catch the most common errors.[*]

---

[*] I always like to define magic numbers using hexadecimal constants that can be pronounced as English words. For barriers, I invented my own restaurant called the "DB cafe," or, in C syntax, `0xdbcafe`. Many interesting (or at least mildly amusing) English words can be spelled using only the letters *a* through *f*. There are even more possibilities if you allow the digit 1 to stand in for the letter l. and the digit 0 to stand in for the letter o. (Whether you like the results will depend a lot on the typeface in which you commonly read your code.)

■ `barrier.h`   part 1   `barrier_t`

```
 1  #include <pthread.h>
 2
 3  /*
 4   * Structure describing a barrier.
 5   */
 6  typedef struct barrier_tag {
 7      pthread_mutex_t     mutex;      /* Control access to barrier */
 8      pthread_cond_t      cv;         /* wait for barrier */
 9      int                 valid;      /* set when valid */
10      int                 threshold;  /* number of threads required */
11      int                 counter;    /* current number of threads */
12      int                 cycle;      /* alternate cycles (0 or 1) */
13  } barrier_t;
14
15  #define BARRIER_VALID   0xdbcafe
```

■ `barrier.h`   part 1   `barrier_t`

Part 2 shows definitions and prototypes that allow you to do something with the `barrier_t` structure. First, you will want to initialize a new barrier.

4-6   You can initialize a static barrier at compile time by using the macro BARRIER_ INITIALIZER. You can instead dynamically initialize a barrier by calling the function `barrier_init`.

11-13   Once you have initialized a barrier, you will want to be able to use it, and the main thing to be done with a barrier is to wait on it. When we're done with a barrier, it would be nice to be able to destroy the barrier and reclaim the resources it used. We'll call these operations `barrier_init`, `barrier_wait`, and `barrier_ destroy`. All the operations need to specify upon which barrier they will operate. Because barriers are synchronization objects, and contain both a mutex and a condition variable (neither of which can be copied), we always pass a pointer to a barrier. Only the initialization operation requires a second parameter, the number of waiters required before the barrier opens.

To be consistent with Pthreads conventions, the functions all return an integer value, representing an error number defined in <errno.h>. The value 0 represents success.

■ `barrier.h`   part 2   `interfaces`

```
 1  /*
 2   * Support static initialization of barriers.
 3   */
 4  #define BARRIER_INITIALIZER(cnt) \
 5      {PTHREAD_MUTEX_INITIALIZER, PTHREAD_COND_INITIALIZER, \
 6      BARRIER_VALID, cnt, cnt, 0}
 7
```

```
 8  /*
 9   * Define barrier functions
10   */
11  extern int barrier_init (barrier_t *barrier, int count);
12  extern int barrier_destroy (barrier_t *barrier);
13  extern int barrier_wait (barrier_t *barrier);
```

■ barrier.h   part 2   interfaces

Now that you know the interface definition, you could write a program using barriers. But then, the point of this section is not to tell you how to use barriers, but to help improve your understanding of threaded programming by showing how to build a barrier. The following examples show the functions provided by barrier.c, to implement the interfaces we've just seen in barrier.h.

Part 1 shows barrier_init, which you would call to dynamically initialize a barrier, for example, if you allocate a barrier with malloc.

12   Both the counter and threshold are set to the same value. The counter is the "working counter" and will be reset to threshold for each barrier cycle.

14-16   If mutex initialization fails, barrier_init returns the failing status to the caller.

17-21   If condition variable (cv) initialization fails, barrier_init destroys the mutex it had already created and returns the failure status—the status of pthread_mutex_destroy is ignored because the failure to create the condition variable is more important than the failure to destroy the mutex.

22   The barrier is marked valid only after all initialization is complete. This does not completely guarantee that another thread erroneously trying to wait on that barrier will detect the invalid barrier rather than failing in some less easily diagnosable manner, but at least it is a token attempt.

■ barrier.c   part 1   barrier_init

```
 1  #include <pthread.h>
 2  #include "errors.h"
 3  #include "barrier.h"
 4
 5  /*
 6   * Initialize a barrier for use.
 7   */
 8  int barrier_init (barrier_t *barrier, int count)
 9  {
10      int status;
11
12      barrier->threshold = barrier->counter = count;
13      barrier->cycle = 0;
14      status = pthread_mutex_init (&barrier->mutex, NULL);
15      if (status != 0)
16          return status;
17      status = pthread_cond_init (&barrier->cv, NULL);
```

```
18      if (status != 0) {
19          pthread_mutex_destroy (&barrier->mutex);
20          return status;
21      }
22      barrier->valid = BARRIER_VALID;
23      return 0;
24  }
```

■ barrier.c   part 1   barrier_init

Part 2 shows the barrier_destroy function, which destroys the mutex and condition variable (cv) in the barrier_t structure. If we had allocated any additional resources for the barrier, we would need to release those resources also.

8-9   First check that the barrier appears to be valid, and initialized, by looking at the valid member. We don't lock the mutex first, because that will fail, possibly with something nasty like a segmentation fault, if the mutex has been destroyed or hasn't been initialized. Because we do not lock the mutex first, the validation check is not entirely reliable, but it is better than nothing, and will only fail to detect some race conditions where one thread attempts to destroy a barrier while another is initializing it, or where two threads attempt to destroy a barrier at nearly the same time.

19-22 If any thread is currently waiting on the barrier, return EBUSY.

24-27 At this point, the barrier is "destroyed"—all that's left is cleanup. To minimize the chances of confusing errors should another thread try to wait on the barrier before we're done, mark the barrier "not valid" by clearing valid, before changing any other state. Then, unlock the mutex, since we cannot destroy it while it is locked.

33-35 Destroy the mutex and condition variable. If the mutex destruction fails, return the status; otherwise, return the status of the condition variable destruction. Or, to put it another way, return an error status if either destruction failed; otherwise, return success.

■ barrier.c   part 2   barrier_destroy

```
1  /*
2   * Destroy a barrier when done using it.
3   */
4  int barrier_destroy (barrier_t *barrier)
5  {
6      int status, status2;
7
8      if (barrier->valid != BARRIER_VALID)
9          return EINVAL;
10
11     status = pthread_mutex_lock (&barrier->mutex);
12     if (status != 0)
13         return status;
14
```

```
15      /*
16       * Check whether any threads are known to be waiting; report
17       * "BUSY" if so.
18       */
19      if (barrier->counter != barrier->threshold) {
20          pthread_mutex_unlock (&barrier->mutex);
21          return EBUSY;
22      }
23
24      barrier->valid = 0;
25      status = pthread_mutex_unlock (&barrier->mutex);
26      if (status != 0)
27          return status;
28
29      /*
30       * If unable to destroy either 1003.1c synchronization
31       * object, return the error status.
32       */
33      status = pthread_mutex_destroy (&barrier->mutex);
34      status2 = pthread_cond_destroy (&barrier->cv);
35      return (status == 0 ? status : status2);
36  }
```

■ barrier.c   part 2   barrier_destroy

Finally, part 3 shows the implementation of barrier_wait.

10-11   First we verify that the argument barrier appears to be a valid barrier_t. We perform this check before locking the mutex, so that barrier_destroy can safely destroy the mutex once it has cleared the valid member. This is a simple attempt to minimize the damage if one thread attempts to wait on a barrier while another thread is simultaneously either initializing or destroying that barrier.

We cannot entirely avoid problems, since without the mutex, barrier_wait has no guarantee that it will see the correct (up-to-date) value of valid. The valid check may succeed when the barrier is being made invalid, or fail when the barrier is being made valid. Locking the mutex first would do no good, because the mutex may not exist if the barrier is not fully initialized, or if it is being destroyed. This isn't a problem as long as you use the barrier correctly—that is, you initialize the barrier before any thread can possibly try to use it, and do not destroy the barrier until you are sure no thread will try to use it again.

17   Copy the current value of the barrier's cycle into a local variable. The comparison of our local cycle against the barrier_t structure's cycle member becomes our condition wait predicate. The predicate ensures that all currently waiting threads will return from barrier_wait when the last waiter broadcasts the condition variable, but that any thread that calls barrier_wait again will wait for the next broadcast. (This is the "tricky part" of correctly implementing a barrier.)

19-22   Now we decrease `counter`, which is the number of threads that are required but haven't yet waited on the barrier. When `counter` reaches 0, no more threads are needed—they're all here and waiting anxiously to continue to the next attraction. Now all we need to do is tell them to wake up. We advance to the next `cycle`, reset the `counter`, and broadcast the barrier's condition variable.

28-29   Earlier, I mentioned that a program often needs one thread to perform some cleanup or setup between parallel regions. Each thread could lock a mutex and check a flag so that only one thread would perform the setup. However, the setup may not need additional synchronization, for example, because the other threads will wait at a barrier for the next parallel region, and, in that case, it would be nice to avoid locking an extra mutex.

     The `barrier_wait` function has this capability built into it. One and only one thread will return with the special value of -1 while the others return 0. In this particular implementation, the one that waits last and wakes the others will take the honor, but in principle it is "unspecified" which thread returns -1. The thread that receives -1 can perform the setup, while others race ahead. If you do not need the special return status, treat -1 as another form of success. The proposed POSIX.1j standard has a similar capability—one (unspecified) thread completing a barrier will return the status `BARRIER_SERIAL_THREAD`.

35   Any threaded code that uses condition variables should always either support deferred cancellation or disable cancellation. Remember that there are two distinct *types* of cancellation: *deferred* and *asynchronous*. Code that deals with asynchronous cancellation is rare. In general it is difficult or impossible to support asynchronous cancellation in any code that acquires resources (including locking a mutex). Programmers can't assume any function supports asynchronous cancellation unless its documentation specifically says so. Therefore we do not need to worry about asynchronous cancellation.

     We could code `barrier_wait` to deal with deferred cancellation, but that raises difficult questions. How, for example, will the barrier wait ever be satisfied if one of the threads has been canceled? And if it won't be satisfied, what happens to all the other threads that have already waited (or are about to wait) on that barrier? There are various ways to answer these questions. One would be for `barrier_wait` to record the thread identifiers of all threads waiting on the barrier, and for any thread that's canceled within the wait to cancel all other waiters.

     Or we might handle cancellation by setting some special error flag and broadcasting the condition variable, and modifying `barrier_wait` to return a special error when awakened in that way. However, it makes little sense to cancel one thread that's using a barrier. We're going to disallow it, by disabling cancellation prior to the wait, and restoring the previous state of cancellation afterward. This is the same approach taken by the proposed POSIX.1j standard, by the way—barrier waits are not cancellation points.

42-46   If there are more threads that haven't reached the barrier, we need to wait for them. We do that by waiting on the condition variable until the barrier has advanced to the next cycle—that is, the barrier's `cycle` no longer matches the local copy.

■ barrier.c   part 3   barrier_wait

```
1  /*
2   * Wait for all members of a barrier to reach the barrier. When
3   * the count (of remaining members) reaches 0, broadcast to wake
4   * all threads waiting.
5   */
6  int barrier_wait (barrier_t *barrier)
7  {
8      int status, cancel, tmp, cycle;
9
10     if (barrier->valid != BARRIER_VALID)
11         return EINVAL;
12
13     status = pthread_mutex_lock (&barrier->mutex);
14     if (status != 0)
15         return status;
16
17     cycle = barrier->cycle;    /* Remember which cycle we're on */
18
19     if (--barrier->counter == 0) {
20         barrier->cycle = !barrier->cycle;
21         barrier->counter = barrier->threshold;
22         status = pthread_cond_broadcast (&barrier->cv);
23         /*
24          * The last thread into the barrier will return status
25          * -1 rather than 0, so that it can be used to perform
26          * some special serial code following the barrier.
27          */
28         if (status == 0)
29             status = -1;
30     } else {
31         /*
32          * Wait with cancellation disabled, because barrier_wait
33          * should not be a cancellation point.
34          */
35         pthread_setcancelstate (PTHREAD_CANCEL_DISABLE, &cancel);
36
37         /*
38          * Wait until the barrier's cycle changes, which means
39          * that it has been broadcast, and we don't want to wait
40          * anymore.
41          */
42         while (cycle == barrier->cycle) {
43             status = pthread_cond_wait (
44                     &barrier->cv, &barrier->mutex);
45             if (status != 0) break;
46         }
47
```

```
48              pthread_setcancelstate (cancel, &tmp);
49      }
50      /*
51       * Ignore an error in unlocking. It shouldn't happen, and
52       * reporting it here would be misleading -- the barrier wait
53       * completed, after all, whereas returning, for example,
54       * EINVAL would imply the wait had failed. The next attempt
55       * to use the barrier *will* return an error, or hang, due
56       * to whatever happened to the mutex.
57       */
58      pthread_mutex_unlock (&barrier->mutex);
59      return status;              /* error, -1 for waker, or 0 */
60  }
```

■ barrier.c   part 3   barrier_wait

Finally, barrier_main.c is a simple program that uses barriers. Each thread loops on calculations within a private array.

35,47   At the beginning and end of each iteration, the threads, running function thread_routine, all wait on a barrier to synchronize the operation.

56-61   At the end of each iteration, the "lead thread" (the one receiving a –1 result from barrier_wait) will modify the data of all threads, preparing them for the next iteration. The others go directly to the top of the loop and wait on the barrier at line 35.

■ barrier_main.c

```
1  #include <pthread.h>
2  #include "barrier.h"
3  #include "errors.h"
4
5  #define THREADS 5
6  #define ARRAY 6
7  #define INLOOPS 1000
8  #define OUTLOOPS 10
9
10  /*
11   * Keep track of each thread.
12   */
13  typedef struct thread_tag {
14      pthread_t    thread_id;
15      int          number;
16      int          increment;
17      int          array[ARRAY];
18      } thread_t;
19
20  barrier_t barrier;
21  thread_t thread[THREADS];
22
```

```
23  /*
24   * Start routine for threads.
25   */
26  void *thread_routine (void *arg)
27  {
28      thread_t *self = (thread_t*)arg;     /* Thread's thread_t */
29      int in_loop, out_loop, count, status;
30
31      /*
32       * Loop through OUTLOOPS barrier cycles.
33       */
34      for (out_loop = 0; out_loop < OUTLOOPS; out_loop++) {
35          status = barrier_wait (&barrier);
36          if (status > 0)
37              err_abort (status, "Wait on barrier");
38
39          /*
40           * This inner loop just adds a value to each element in
41           * the working array.
42           */
43          for (in_loop = 0; in_loop < INLOOPS; in_loop++)
44              for (count = 0; count < ARRAY; count++)
45                  self->array[count] += self->increment;
46
47          status = barrier_wait (&barrier);
48          if (status > 0)
49              err_abort (status, "Wait on barrier");
50
51          /*
52           * The barrier causes one thread to return with the
53           * special return status -1. The thread receiving this
54           * value increments each element in the shared array.
55           */
56          if (status == -1) {
57              int thread_num;
58
59              for (thread_num = 0; thread_num < THREADS; thread_num++)
60                  thread[thread_num].increment += 1;
61          }
62      }
63      return NULL;
64  }
65
66  int main (int arg, char *argv[])
67  {
68      int thread_count, array_count;
69      int status;
70
71      barrier_init (&barrier, THREADS);
72
```

```
73        /*
74         * Create a set of threads that will use the barrier.
75         */
76        for (thread_count = 0; thread_count < THREADS; thread_count++) {
77            thread[thread_count].increment = thread_count;
78            thread[thread_count].number = thread_count;
79
80            for (array_count = 0; array_count < ARRAY; array_count++)
81                thread[thread_count].array[array_count] = array_count + 1;
82
83            status = pthread_create (&thread[thread_count].thread_id,
84                NULL, thread_routine, (void*)&thread[thread_count]);
85            if (status != 0)
86                err_abort (status, "Create thread");
87        }
88
89        /*
90         * Now join with each of the threads.
91         */
92        for (thread_count = 0; thread_count < THREADS; thread_count++) {
93            status = pthread_join (thread[thread_count].thread_id, NULL);
94            if (status != 0)
95                err_abort (status, "Join thread");
96
97            printf ("%02d: (%d) ",
98                thread_count, thread[thread_count].increment);
99
100           for (array_count = 0; array_count < ARRAY; array_count++)
101               printf ("%010u ",
102                   thread[thread_count].array[array_count]);
103           printf ("\n");
104       }
105
106       /*
107        * To be thorough, destroy the barrier.
108        */
109       barrier_destroy (&barrier);
110       return 0;
111   }
```

■ barrier_main.c

7.1.2 Read/write locks

A read/write lock is a lot like a mutex. It is another way to prevent more than one thread from modifying shared data at the same time. But unlike a mutex it distinguishes between *reading* data and *writing* data. A mutex excludes all other threads, while a read/write lock allows more than one thread to *read* the data, as long as none of them needs to change it.

Read/write locks are used to protect information that you need to read frequently but usually don't need to modify. For example, when you build a cache of recently accessed information, many threads may simultaneously examine the cache without conflict. When a thread needs to update the cache, it must have exclusive access.

When a thread locks a read/write lock, it chooses *shared read access* or *exclusive write access.* A thread that wants read access can't continue while any thread currently has write access. A thread trying to gain write access can't continue when another thread currently has either write access or read access.

When both readers and writers are waiting for access at the same time, the readers are given precedence when the write lock is released. *Read* precedence favors concurrency because it potentially allows many threads to accomplish work simultaneously. *Write* precedence on the other hand would ensure that pending modifications to the shared data are completed before the data is used. There's no absolute right or wrong policy, and if you don't find the implementation here appropriate for you, it is easy to change.

Figure 7.3 shows the operation of a read/write lock being used to synchronize three threads, called thread 1, thread 2, and thread 3. The figure is a sort of timing diagram, with time increasing from left to right. Each of the lines beginning at the labels in the upper left designates the behavior of a specific thread—solid for thread 1, dotted for thread 2, and dashed for thread 3. When the lines drop within the rounded rectangle, they are interacting with the read/write lock. If the

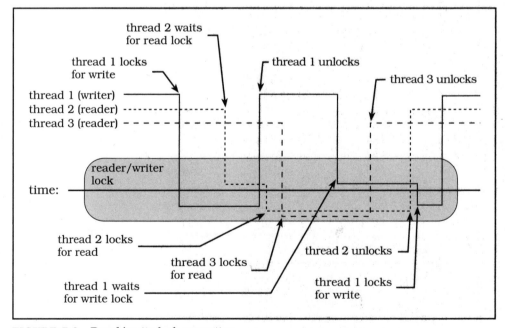

FIGURE 7.3   *Read/write lock operation*

line drops below the center line, it shows that the thread has the read/write lock locked, either for exclusive write or for shared read. Lines that hover above the center line represent threads waiting for the lock.

In this example, thread 1 locks the read/write lock for exclusive write. Thread 2 tries to lock the read/write lock for shared read and, finding it already locked for exclusive write, blocks. When thread 1 releases the lock, it awakens thread 2, which then succeeds in locking the read/write lock for shared read. Thread 3 then tries to lock the read/write lock for shared read and, because the read/write lock is already locked for shared read, it succeeds immediately. Thread 1 then tries to lock the read/write lock again for exclusive write access, and blocks because the read/write lock is already locked for read access. When thread 3 unlocks the read/write lock, it cannot awaken thread 1, because there is another reader. Only when thread 2 also unlocks the read/write lock, and the lock becomes unlocked, can thread 1 be awakened to lock the read/write lock for exclusive write access.

The header file `rwlock.h` and the C source file `rwlock.c` demonstrate an implementation of read/write locks using standard Pthreads mutexes and condition variables. This is a portable implementation that is relatively easy to understand. One could, of course, create a much more efficient implementation for any specific system based on knowledge of nonportable hardware and operating system characteristics.

The rest of this section shows the details of a read/write lock package. First, `rwlock.h` describes the interfaces, and then `rwlock.c` provides the implementation. Part 1 shows the structure of a read/write lock, represented by the type `rwlock_t`.

7-9   Of course, there's a `mutex` to serialize access to the structure. We'll use two separate condition variables, one to wait for read access (called `read`) and one to wait for write access (called, surprisingly, `write`).

10   The `rwlock_t` structure has a `valid` member to easily detect common usage errors, such as trying to lock a read/write lock that hasn't been initialized. The member is set to a magic number when the read/write lock is initialized, just as in `barrier_init`.

11-12   To enable us to determine whether either condition variable has waiters, we'll keep a count of active readers (`r_active`) and a flag to indicate an active writer (`w_active`).

13-14   We also keep a count of the number of threads waiting for read access (`r_wait`) and for write access (`w_wait`).

17   Finally, we need a "magic number" for our `valid` member. (See the footnote in Section 7.1.1 if you missed this part of the barrier example.)

■ `rwlock.h`   `part 1`   `rwlock_t`

```
1  #include <pthread.h>
2
3  /*
4   * Structure describing a read/write lock.
5   */
```

```
 6  typedef struct rwlock_tag {
 7       pthread_mutex_t      mutex;
 8       pthread_cond_t       read;           /* wait for read */
 9       pthread_cond_t       write;          /* wait for write */
10       int                  valid;          /* set when valid */
11       int                  r_active;       /* readers active */
12       int                  w_active;       /* writer active */
13       int                  r_wait;         /* readers waiting */
14       int                  w_wait;         /* writers waiting */
15  } rwlock_t;
16
17  #define RWLOCK_VALID      0xfacade
```

■ rwlock.h   part 1   rwlock_t

We could have saved some space and simplified the code by using a single condition variable, with readers and writers waiting using separate predicate expressions. We will use one condition variable for each predicate, because it is more efficient. This is a common trade-off. The main consideration is that when two predicates share a condition variable, you must always wake them using pthread_cond_broadcast, which would mean waking all waiters each time the read/write lock is unlocked.

We keep track of a boolean variable for "writer active," since there can only be one. There are also counters for "readers active," "readers waiting," and "writers waiting." We could get by without counters for readers and writers waiting. All readers are awakened simultaneously using a broadcast, so it doesn't matter how many there are. Writers are awakened only if there are no readers, so we could dispense with keeping track of whether there are any threads waiting to write (at the cost of an occasional wasted condition variable signal when there are no waiters).

We count the number of threads waiting for read access because the condition variable waits might be canceled. Without cancellation, we could use a simple flag—"threads are waiting for read" or "no threads are waiting for read." Each thread could set it before waiting, and we could clear it before broadcasting to wake all waiting readers. However, because we can't count the threads waiting on a condition variable, we wouldn't know whether to clear that flag when a waiting reader was canceled. This information is critical, because if there are no readers waiting when the read/write lock is unlocked, we must wake a writer—but we cannot wake a writer if there are waiting readers. A count of waiting readers, which we can decrease when a waiter is canceled, solves the problem.

The consequences of "getting it wrong" are less important for writers than for readers. Because we check for readers first, we don't really need to know whether there are writers. We could signal a "potential writer" anytime the read/write lock was released with no waiting readers. But counting waiting writers allows us to avoid a condition variable signal when no threads are waiting.

Part 2 shows the rest of the definitions and the function prototypes.

4-6   The RWLOCK_INITIALIZER macro allows you to statically initialize a read/write lock.

11-18   Of course, you must also be able to initialize a read/write lock that you cannot allocate statically, so we provide rwl_init to initialize dynamically, and rwl_destroy to destroy a read/write lock once you're done with it. In addition, there are functions to lock and unlock the read/write lock for either read or write access. You can "try to lock" a read/write lock, either for read or write access, by calling rwl_readtrylock or rwl_writetrylock., just as you can try to lock a mutex by calling pthread_mutex_trylock.

■ rwlock.h   part 2   interfaces

```
1  /*
2   * Support static initialization of barriers.
3   */
4  #define RWL_INITIALIZER \
5      {PTHREAD_MUTEX_INITIALIZER, PTHREAD_COND_INITIALIZER, \
6      PTHREAD_COND_INITIALIZER, RWLOCK_VALID, 0, 0, 0, 0}
7
8  /*
9   * Define read/write lock functions.
10  */
11 extern int rwl_init (rwlock_t *rwlock);
12 extern int rwl_destroy (rwlock_t *rwlock);
13 extern int rwl_readlock (rwlock_t *rwlock);
14 extern int rwl_readtrylock (rwlock_t *rwlock);
15 extern int rwl_readunlock (rwlock_t *rwlock);
16 extern int rwl_writelock (rwlock_t *rwlock);
17 extern int rwl_writetrylock (rwlock_t *rwlock);
18 extern int rwl_writeunlock (rwlock_t *rwlock);
```

■ rwlock.h   part 2   interfaces

The file rwlock.c contains the implementation of read/write locks. The following examples break down each of the functions used to implement the rwlock.h interfaces.

Part 1 shows rwl_init, which initializes a read/write lock. It initializes the Pthreads synchronization objects, initializes the counters and flags, and finally sets the valid sentinel to make the read/write lock recognizable to the other interfaces. If we are unable to initialize the read condition variable, we destroy the mutex that we'd already created. Similarly, if we are unable to initialize the write condition variable, we destroy both the mutex and the read condition variable.

■ rwlock.c   part 1   rwl_init

```
1  #include <pthread.h>
2  #include "errors.h"
```

```
 3   #include "rwlock.h"
 4
 5   /*
 6    * Initialize a read/write lock.
 7    */
 8   int rwl_init (rwlock_t *rwl)
 9   {
10       int status;
11
12       rwl->r_active = 0;
13       rwl->r_wait = rwl->w_wait = 0;
14       rwl->w_active = 0;
15       status = pthread_mutex_init (&rwl->mutex, NULL);
16       if (status != 0)
17           return status;
18       status = pthread_cond_init (&rwl->read, NULL);
19       if (status != 0) {
20           /* if unable to create read CV, destroy mutex */
21           pthread_mutex_destroy (&rwl->mutex);
22           return status;
23       }
24       status = pthread_cond_init (&rwl->write, NULL);
25       if (status != 0) {
26           /* if unable to create write CV, destroy read CV and mutex */
27           pthread_cond_destroy (&rwl->read);
28           pthread_mutex_destroy (&rwl->mutex);
29           return status;
30       }
31       rwl->valid = RWLOCK_VALID;
32       return 0;
33   }
```

■   rwlock.c   part 1   rwl_init

Part 2 shows the rwl_destroy function, which destroys a read/write lock.

8-9   We first try to verify that the read/write lock was properly initialized by check-ing the valid member. This is not a complete protection against incorrect usage, but it is cheap, and it will catch some of the most common errors. See the anno-tation for barrier.c, part 2, for more about how the valid member is used.

10-30   Check whether the read/write lock is in use. We look for threads that are using or waiting for either read or write access. Using two separate if statements makes the test slightly more readable, though there's no other benefit.

36-39   As in barrier_destroy, we destroy all Pthreads synchronization objects, and store each status return. If any of the destruction calls fails, returning a nonzero value, rwl_destroy will return that status, and if they all succeed it will return 0 for success.

```
1   /*
2    * Destroy a read/write lock.
3    */
4   int rwl_destroy (rwlock_t *rwl)
5   {
6       int status, status1, status2;
7
8       if (rwl->valid != RWLOCK_VALID)
9           return EINVAL;
10      status = pthread_mutex_lock (&rwl->mutex);
11      if (status != 0)
12          return status;
13
14      /*
15       * Check whether any threads own the lock; report "BUSY" if
16       * so.
17       */
18      if (rwl->r_active > 0 || rwl->w_active) {
19          pthread_mutex_unlock (&rwl->mutex);
20          return EBUSY;
21      }
22
23      /*
24       * Check whether any threads are known to be waiting; report
25       * EBUSY if so.
26       */
27      if (rwl->r_wait != 0 || rwl->w_wait != 0) {
28          pthread_mutex_unlock (&rwl->mutex);
29          return EBUSY;
30      }
31
32      rwl->valid = 0;
33      status = pthread_mutex_unlock (&rwl->mutex);
34      if (status != 0)
35          return status;
36      status = pthread_mutex_destroy (&rwl->mutex);
37      status1 = pthread_cond_destroy (&rwl->read);
38      status2 = pthread_cond_destroy (&rwl->write);
39      return (status == 0 ? status
40          : (status1 == 0 ? status1 : status2));
41  }
```

Part 3 shows the code for `rwl_readcleanup` and `rwl_writecleanup`, two cancellation cleanup handlers used in locking the read/write lock for read and write access, respectively. As you may infer from this, read/write locks, unlike barriers, are cancellation points. When a wait is canceled, the waiter needs to decrease the count of threads waiting for either a read or write lock, as appropriate, and unlock the mutex.

■ rwlock.c   part 3   cleanuphandlers

```
1  /*
2   * Handle cleanup when the read lock condition variable
3   * wait is canceled.
4   *
5   * Simply record that the thread is no longer waiting,
6   * and unlock the mutex.
7   */
8  static void rwl_readcleanup (void *arg)
9  {
10     rwlock_t    *rwl = (rwlock_t *)arg;
11
12     rwl->r_wait--;
13     pthread_mutex_unlock (&rwl->mutex);
14 }
15
16 /*
17  * Handle cleanup when the write lock condition variable
18  * wait is canceled.
19  *
20  * Simply record that the thread is no longer waiting,
21  * and unlock the mutex.
22  */
23 static void rwl_writecleanup (void *arg)
24 {
25     rwlock_t *rwl = (rwlock_t *)arg;
26
27     rwl->w_wait--;
28     pthread_mutex_unlock (&rwl->mutex);
29 }
```

■ rwlock.c   part 3   cleanuphandlers

10-26   Part 4 shows `rwl_readlock`, which locks a read/write lock for read access. If a writer is currently active (`w_active` is nonzero), we wait for it to broadcast the read condition variable. The `r_wait` member counts the number of threads waiting to read. This could be a simple boolean variable, except for one problem—when a waiter is canceled, we need to know whether there are any remaining waiters. Maintaining a count makes this easy, since the cleanup handler only needs to decrease the count.

This is one of the places where the code must be changed to convert our read/ write lock from "reader preference" to "writer preference," should you choose to do that. To implement writer preference, a reader must block while there are waiting writers (w_wait > 0), not merely while there are active writers, as we do here.

15,21   Notice the use of the cleanup handler around the condition wait. Also, notice that we pass the argument 0 to pthread_cleanup_pop so that the cleanup code is called only if the wait is canceled. We need to perform slightly different actions when the wait is not canceled. If the wait is not canceled, we need to increase the count of active readers before unlocking the mutex.

■ rwlock.c   part 4   rwl_readlock

```
1  /*
2   * Lock a read/write lock for read access.
3   */
4  int rwl_readlock (rwlock_t *rwl)
5  {
6      int status;
7
8      if (rwl->valid != RWLOCK_VALID)
9          return EINVAL;
10     status = pthread_mutex_lock (&rwl->mutex);
11     if (status != 0)
12         return status;
13     if (rwl->w_active) {
14         rwl->r_wait++;
15         pthread_cleanup_push (rwl_readcleanup, (void*)rwl);
16         while (rwl->w_active) {
17             status = pthread_cond_wait (&rwl->read, &rwl->mutex);
18             if (status != 0)
19                 break;
20         }
21         pthread_cleanup_pop (0);
22         rwl->r_wait--;
23     }
24     if (status == 0)
25         rwl->r_active++;
26     pthread_mutex_unlock (&rwl->mutex);
27     return status;
28 }
```

■ rwlock.c   part 4   rwl_readlock

Part 5 shows rwl_readtrylock. This function is nearly identical to rwl_read-lock, except that, instead of waiting for access if a writer is active, it returns EBUSY. It doesn't need a cleanup handler, and has no need to increase the count of waiting readers.

This function must also be modified to implement "writer preference" read/write locks, by returning EBUSY when a writer is waiting, not just when a writer is active.

■ rwlock.c   part 5   rwl_readtrylock

```
 1  /*
 2   * Attempt to lock a read/write lock for read access (don't
 3   * block if unavailable).
 4   */
 5  int rwl_readtrylock (rwlock_t *rwl)
 6  {
 7      int status, status2;
 8
 9      if (rwl->valid != RWLOCK_VALID)
10          return EINVAL;
11      status = pthread_mutex_lock (&rwl->mutex);
12      if (status != 0)
13          return status;
14      if (rwl->w_active)
15          status = EBUSY;
16      else
17          rwl->r_active++;
18      status2 = pthread_mutex_unlock (&rwl->mutex);
19      return (status2 != 0 ? status2 : status);
20  }
```

■ rwlock.c   part 5   rwl_readtrylock

---

13   Part 6 shows rwl_readunlock. This function essentially reverses the effect of rwl_readlock or rwl_tryreadlock, by decreasing the count of active readers (r_active).

14-15   If there are no more active readers, and at least one thread is waiting for write access, signal the write condition variable to unblock one. Note that there is a race here, and whether you should be concerned about it depends on your notion of what should happen. If another thread that is interested in read access calls rwl_readlock or rwl_tryreadlock before the awakened writer can run, the reader may "win," despite the fact that we just selected a writer.

Because our version of read/write locks has "reader preference," this is what we usually want to happen—the writer will determine that it has failed and will resume waiting. (It received a spurious wakeup.) If the implementation changes to prefer writers, the spurious wakeup will not occur, because the potential reader would have to block. The waiter we just unblocked cannot decrease w_wait until it actually claims the lock.

■ `rwlock.c`   part 6   `rwl_readunlock`

```
 1  /*
 2   * Unlock a read/write lock from read access.
 3   */
 4  int rwl_readunlock (rwlock_t *rwl)
 5  {
 6      int status, status2;
 7
 8      if (rwl->valid != RWLOCK_VALID)
 9          return EINVAL;
10      status = pthread_mutex_lock (&rwl->mutex);
11      if (status != 0)
12          return status;
13      rwl->r_active--;
14      if (rwl->r_active == 0 && rwl->w_wait > 0)
15          status = pthread_cond_signal (&rwl->write);
16      status2 = pthread_mutex_unlock (&rwl->mutex);
17      return (status2 == 0 ? status : status2);
18  }
```

■ `rwlock.c`   part 6   `rwl_readunlock`

13   Part 7 shows `rwl_writelock`. This function is much like `rwl_readlock`, except for the predicate condition on the condition variable wait. In part 1, I explained that, to convert from "preferred read" to "preferred write," a potential reader would have to wait until there were no active or waiting writers, whereas currently it waits only for active writers. The predicate in `rwl_writelock` is the converse of that condition. Because we support "preferred read," in theory, we must wait here if there are any active or waiting readers. In fact, it is a bit simpler, because if there are any active readers, there cannot be any waiting readers—the whole point of a read/write lock is that multiple threads can have read access at the same time. On the other hand, we do have to wait if there are any active writers, because we allow only one writer at a time.

25   Unlike `r_active`, which is a counter, `w_active` is treated as a boolean. Or is it a counter? There's really no semantic difference, since the value of 1 can be considered a boolean TRUE or a count of 1—there can be only one active writer at any time.

■ `rwlock.c`   part 7   `rwl_writelock`

```
 1  /*
 2   * Lock a read/write lock for write access.
 3   */
 4  int rwl_writelock (rwlock_t *rwl)
```

```
 5  {
 6      int status;
 7
 8      if (rwl->valid != RWLOCK_VALID)
 9          return EINVAL;
10      status = pthread_mutex_lock (&rwl->mutex);
11      if (status != 0)
12          return status;
13      if (rwl->w_active || rwl->r_active > 0) {
14          rwl->w_wait++;
15          pthread_cleanup_push (rwl_writecleanup, (void*)rwl);
16          while (rwl->w_active || rwl->r_active > 0) {
17              status = pthread_cond_wait (&rwl->write, &rwl->mutex);
18              if (status != 0)
19                  break;
20          }
21          pthread_cleanup_pop (0);
22          rwl->w_wait--;
23      }
24      if (status == 0)
25          rwl->w_active = 1;
26      pthread_mutex_unlock (&rwl->mutex);
27      return status;
28  }
```

■ rwlock.c   part 7   rwl_writelock

Part 8 shows rwl_writetrylock. This function is much like rwl_writelock, except that it returns EBUSY if the read/write lock is currently in use (either by a reader or by a writer) rather than waiting for it to become free.

■ rwlock.c   part 8   rwl_writetrylock

```
 1  /*
 2   * Attempt to lock a read/write lock for write access. Don't
 3   * block if unavailable.
 4   */
 5  int rwl_writetrylock (rwlock_t *rwl)
 6  {
 7      int status, status2;
 8
 9      if (rwl->valid != RWLOCK_VALID)
10          return EINVAL;
11      status = pthread_mutex_lock (&rwl->mutex);
12      if (status != 0)
13          return status;
14      if (rwl->w_active || rwl->r_active > 0)
15          status = EBUSY;
```

```
16        else
17            rwl->w_active = 1;
18        status2 = pthread_mutex_unlock (&rwl->mutex);
19        return (status != 0 ? status : status2);
20  }
```

■ rwlock.c   part 8   rwl_writetrylock

Finally, part 9 shows rwl_writeunlock. This function is called by a thread
with a write lock, to release the lock.

13-19   When a writer releases the read/write lock, it is always free; if there are any
threads waiting for access, we must wake one. Because we implement "preferred
read" access, we first look for threads that are waiting for read access. If there are
any, we broadcast the read condition variable to wake them all.

20-26   If there were no waiting readers, but there are one or more waiting writers,
wake one of them by signaling the write condition variable.

To implement a "preferred write" lock, you would reverse the two tests, waking
a waiting writer, if any, before looking for waiting readers.

■ rwlock.c   part 9   rwl_writeunlock

```
1   /*
2    * Unlock a read/write lock from write access.
3    */
4   int rwl_writeunlock (rwlock_t *rwl)
5   {
6       int status;
7
8       if (rwl->valid != RWLOCK_VALID)
9           return EINVAL;
10      status = pthread_mutex_lock (&rwl->mutex);
11      if (status != 0)
12          return status;
13      rwl->w_active = 0;
14      if (rwl->r_wait > 0) {
15          status = pthread_cond_broadcast (&rwl->read);
16          if (status != 0) {
17              pthread_mutex_unlock (&rwl->mutex);
18              return status;
19          }
20      } else if (rwl->w_wait > 0) {
21          status = pthread_cond_signal (&rwl->write);
22          if (status != 0) {
23              pthread_mutex_unlock (&rwl->mutex);
24              return status;
25          }
26      }
```

```
27        status = pthread_mutex_unlock (&rwl->mutex);
28        return status;
29    }
```

■ rwlock.c   part 9   writelock

Now that we have all the pieces, rwlock_main.c shows a program that uses read/write locks.

11–17   Each thread is described by a structure of type thread_t. The thread_num member is the thread's index within the array of thread_t structures. The thread_id member is the pthread_t (thread identifier) returned by pthread_create when the thread was created. The updates and reads members are counts of the number of read lock and write lock operations performed by the thread. The interval member is generated randomly as each thread is created, to determine how many iterations the thread will read before it performs a write.

22–26   The threads cycle through an array of data_t elements. Each element has a read/write lock, a data element, and a count of how many times some thread has updated the element.

48–58   The program creates a set of threads running the thread_routine function. Each thread loops ITERATIONS times, practicing use of the read/write lock. It cycles through the array of data elements in sequence, resetting the index (element) to 0 when it reaches the end. At intervals specified by each thread's interval member, the thread will modify the current data element instead of reading it. The thread locks the read/write lock for write access, stores its thread_num as the new data value, and increases the updates counter.

59–73   On all other iterations, thread_routine reads the current data element, locking the read/write lock for read access. It compares the data value against its thread_num to determine whether it was the most recent thread to update that data element, and, if so, it increments a counter.

95–103   On Solaris systems, increase the thread concurrency level to generate more interesting activity. Without timeslicing of user threads, each thread would tend to execute sequentially otherwise.

■ rwlock_main.c

```
 1    #include "rwlock.h"
 2    #include "errors.h"
 3
 4    #define THREADS        5
 5    #define DATASIZE       15
 6    #define ITERATIONS     10000
 7
 8    /*
 9     * Keep statistics for each thread.
10     */
11    typedef struct thread_tag {
12        int            thread_num;
```

```
13      pthread_t    thread_id;
14      int          updates;
15      int          reads;
16      int          interval;
17 } thread_t;
18
19 /*
20  * Read/write lock and shared data.
21  */
22 typedef struct data_tag {
23      rwlock_t    lock;
24      int         data;
25      int         updates;
26 } data_t;
27
28 thread_t threads[THREADS];
29 data_t data[DATASIZE];
30
31 /*
32  * Thread start routine that uses read/write locks.
33  */
34 void *thread_routine (void *arg)
35 {
36     thread_t *self = (thread_t*)arg;
37     int repeats = 0;
38     int iteration;
39     int element = 0;
40     int status;
41
42     for (iteration = 0; iteration < ITERATIONS; iteration++) {
43         /*
44          * Each "self->interval" iterations, perform an
45          * update operation (write lock instead of read
46          * lock).
47          */
48         if ((iteration % self->interval) == 0) {
49             status = rwl_writelock (&data[element].lock);
50             if (status != 0)
51                 err_abort (status, "Write lock");
52             data[element].data = self->thread_num;
53             data[element].updates++;
54             self->updates++;
55             status = rwl_writeunlock (&data[element].lock);
56             if (status != 0)
57                 err_abort (status, "Write unlock");
58         } else {
59             /*
60              * Look at the current data element to see whether
61              * the current thread last updated it. Count the
```

```
62                 * times, to report later.
63                 */
64                status = rwl_readlock (&data[element].lock);
65                if (status != 0)
66                    err_abort (status, "Read lock");
67                self->reads++;
68                if (data[element].data == self->thread_num)
69                    repeats++;
70                status = rwl_readunlock (&data[element].lock);
71                if (status != 0)
72                    err_abort (status, "Read unlock");
73            }
74            element++;
75            if (element >= DATASIZE)
76                element = 0;
77        }
78
79    if (repeats > 0)
80        printf (
81            "Thread %d found unchanged elements %d times\n",
82            self->thread_num, repeats);
83    return NULL;
84 }
85
86 int main (int argc, char *argv[])
87 {
88    int count;
89    int data_count;
90    int status;
91    unsigned int seed = 1;
92    int thread_updates = 0;
93    int data_updates = 0;
94
95 #ifdef sun
96    /*
97     * On Solaris 2.5, threads are not timesliced. To ensure
98     * that our threads can run concurrently, we need to
99     * increase the concurrency level to THREADS.
100     */
101    DPRINTF (("Setting concurrency level to %d\n", THREADS));
102    thr_setconcurrency (THREADS);
103 #endif
104
105    /*
106     * Initialize the shared data.
107     */
108    for (data_count = 0; data_count < DATASIZE; data_count++) {
109        data[data_count].data = 0;
110        data[data_count].updates = 0;
```

```
111         status = rwl_init (&data[data_count].lock);
112         if (status != 0)
113             err_abort (status, "Init rw lock");
114     }
115
116     /*
117      * Create THREADS threads to access shared data.
118      */
119     for (count = 0; count < THREADS; count++) {
120         threads[count].thread_num = count;
121         threads[count].updates = 0;
122         threads[count].reads = 0;
123         threads[count].interval = rand_r (&seed) % 71;
124         status = pthread_create (&threads[count].thread_id,
125             NULL, thread_routine, (void*)&threads[count]);
126         if (status != 0)
127             err_abort (status, "Create thread");
128     }
129
130     /*
131      * Wait for all threads to complete, and collect
132      * statistics.
133      */
134     for (count = 0; count < THREADS; count++) {
135         status = pthread_join (threads[count].thread_id, NULL);
136         if (status != 0)
137             err_abort (status, "Join thread");
138         thread_updates += threads[count].updates;
139         printf ("%02d: interval %d, updates %d, reads %d\n",
140             count, threads[count].interval,
141             threads[count].updates, threads[count].reads);
142     }
143
144     /*
145      * Collect statistics for the data.
146      */
147     for (data_count = 0; data_count < DATASIZE; data_count++) {
148         data_updates += data[data_count].updates;
149         printf ("data %02d: value %d, %d updates\n",
150             data_count, data[data_count].data,
151             data[data_count].updates);
152         rwl_destroy (&data[data_count].lock);
153     }
154
155     printf ("%d thread updates, %d data updates\n",
156         thread_updates, data_updates);
157     return 0;
158 }
```

■ rwlock_main.c

7.2 Work queue manager

I've already briefly outlined the various models of thread cooperation. These include pipelines, work crews, client/servers, and so forth. In this section, I present the development of a "work queue," a set of threads that accepts work requests from a common queue, processing them (potentially) in parallel.

The work *queue* manager could also be considered a work *crew* manager, depending on your reference point. If you think of it as a way to feed work to a set of threads, then "work crew" might be more appropriate. I prefer to think of it as a queue that magically does work for you in the background, since the presence of the work crew is almost completely invisible to the caller.

When you create the work queue, you can specify the maximum level of parallelism that you need. The work queue manager interprets that as the maximum number of "engine" threads that it may create to process your requests. Threads will be started and stopped as required by the amount of work. A thread that finds nothing to do will wait a short time and then terminate. The optimal "short time" depends on how expensive it is to create a new thread on your system, the cost in system resources to keep a thread going that's not doing anything, and how likely it is that you'll need the thread again soon. I've chosen two seconds, which is probably much too long.

The header file `workq.h` and the C source file `workq.c` demonstrate an implementation of a work queue manager. Part 1 shows the two structure types used by the work queue package. The `workq_t` type is the external representation of a work queue, and the `workq_ele_t` is an internal representation of work items that have been queued.

6–9 The `workq_ele_t` structure is used to maintain a linked list of work items. It has a link element (called `next`) and a `data` value, which is stored when the work item is queued and passed to the caller's "engine function" with no interpretation.

14–16 Of course, there's a mutex to serialize access to the `workq_t`, and a condition variable (cv) on which the engine threads wait for work to be queued.

17 The `attr` member is a thread attributes object, used when creating new engine threads. The attributes object could instead have been a static variable within `workq.c`, but I chose to add a little memory overhead to each work queue, rather than add the minor complexity of one-time initialization of a static data item.

18 The `first` member points to the first item on the work queue. As an optimization to make it easier to queue new items at the end of the queue, the `last` member points to the last item on the queue.

19–24 These members record assorted information about the work queue. The `valid` member is a magic number that's set when the work queue is initialized, as we've seen before in barriers and read/write locks. (In this case, the magic number is the month and year of my daughter's birthday.) The `quit` member is a flag that allows the "work queue manager" to tell engine threads to terminate as soon as the queue is empty. The `parallelism` member records how many threads the creator chose to allow the work queue to utilize, `counter` records the number of threads created, and `idle` records the current number of threads that are waiting for work. The `engine` member is the user's "engine function," supplied when the work queue was created. As you can see, the engine function takes an "untyped" (`void *`) argument, and has no return value.

```
1  #include <pthread.h>
2
3  /*
4   * Structure to keep track of work queue requests.
5   */
6  typedef struct workq_ele_tag {
7      struct workq_ele_tag      *next;
8      void                      *data;
9  } workq_ele_t;
10
11 /*
12  * Structure describing a work queue.
13  */
14 typedef struct workq_tag {
15     pthread_mutex_t     mutex;              /* control access to queue */
16     pthread_cond_t      cv;                 /* wait for work */
17     pthread_attr_t      attr;               /* create detached threads */
18     workq_ele_t         *first, *last;      /* work queue */
19     int                 valid;              /* valid */
20     int                 quit;               /* workq should quit */
21     int                 parallelism;        /* maximum threads */
22     int                 counter;            /* current threads */
23     int                 idle;               /* number of idle threads */
24     void                (*engine)(void *arg);   /* user engine */
25 } workq_t;
26
27 #define WORKQ_VALID     0xdec1992
```

Part 2 shows the interfaces we'll create for our work queue. We need to create and destroy work queue managers, so we'll define `workq_init` and `workq_destroy`. Both take a pointer to a `workq_t` structure. In addition, the initializer needs the maximum number of threads the manager is allowed to create to service the queue, and the engine function. Finally, the program needs to be able to queue work items for processing—we'll call the interface for this `workq_add`. It takes a pointer to the `workq_t` and the argument that should be passed to the engine function.

■ workq.h   part 2   interfaces

```
1   /*
2    * Define work queue functions.
3    */
4   extern int workq_init (
5       workq_t     *wq,
6       int         threads,                /* maximum threads */
7       void        (*engine)(void *));     /* engine routine */
8   extern int workq_destroy (workq_t *wq);
9   extern int workq_add (workq_t *wq, void *data);
```

■ workq.h   part 2   interfaces

The file workq.c contains the implementation of our work queue. The following examples break down each of the functions used to implement the workq.h interfaces.

Part 1 shows the workq_init function, which initializes a work queue. We create the Pthreads synchronization objects that we need, and fill in the remaining members.

14–22   Initialize the thread attributes object attr so that the engine threads we create will run detached. That means we do not need to keep track of their thread identifier values, or worry about joining with them.

34–40   We're not ready to quit yet (we've hardly started!), so clear the quit flag. The parallelism member records the maximum number of threads we are allowed to create, which is the workq_init parameter threads. The counter member will record the current number of active engine threads, initially 0, and idle will record the number of active threads waiting for more work. And of course, finally, we set the valid member.

■ workq.c   part 1   workq_init

```
1   #include <pthread.h>
2   #include <stdlib.h>
3   #include <time.h>
4   #include "errors.h"
5   #include "workq.h"
6
7   /*
8    * Initialize a work queue.
9    */
10  int workq_init (workq_t *wq, int threads, void (*engine)(void *arg))
11  {
12      int status;
13
14      status = pthread_attr_init (&wq->attr);
15      if (status != 0)
16          return status;
17      status = pthread_attr_setdetachstate (
```

```
18                   &wq->attr, PTHREAD_CREATE_DETACHED);
19          if (status != 0) {
20              pthread_attr_destroy (&wq->attr);
21              return status;
22          }
23          status = pthread_mutex_init (&wq->mutex, NULL);
24          if (status != 0) {
25              pthread_attr_destroy (&wq->attr);
26              return status;
27          }
28          status = pthread_cond_init (&wq->cv, NULL);
29          if (status != 0) {
30              pthread_mutex_destroy (&wq->mutex);
31              pthread_attr_destroy (&wq->attr);
32              return status;
33          }
34          wq->quit = 0;                        /* not time to quit */
35          wq->first = wq->last = NULL;         /* no queue entries */
36          wq->parallelism = threads;           /* max servers */
37          wq->counter = 0;                     /* no server threads yet */
38          wq->idle = 0;                        /* no idle servers */
39          wq->engine = engine;
40          wq->valid = WORKQ_VALID;
41          return 0;
42      }
```

■ workq.c   part 1   workq_init

Part 2 shows the workq_destroy function. The procedure for shutting down a work queue is a little different than the others we've seen. Remember that the Pthreads mutex and condition variable destroy function fail, returning EBUSY, when you try to destroy an object that is in use. We used the same model for barriers and read/write locks. But we cannot do the same for work queues—the calling program cannot know whether the work queue is in use, because the caller only queues requests that are processed asynchronously.

The work queue manager will accept a request to shut down at any time, but it will wait for all existing engine threads to complete their work and terminate. Only when the last work queue element has been processed and the last engine thread has exited will workq_destroy return successfully.

24   If the work queue has no threads, either it was never used or all threads have timed out and shut down since it was last used. That makes things easy, and we can skip all the shutdown complication.

25-33   If there are engine threads, they are asked to shut down by setting the quit flag in the workq_t structure and broadcasting the condition variable to awaken any waiting (idle) engine threads. Each engine thread will eventually run and see this flag. When they see it and find no more work, they'll shut themselves down.

44-50   The last thread to shut down will wake up the thread that's waiting in workq_ destroy, and the shutdown will complete. Instead of creating a condition variable that's used only to wake up workq_destroy, the last thread will signal the same condition variable used to inform idle engine threads of new work. At this point, all waiters have already been awakened by a broadcast, and they won't wait again because the quit flag is set. Shutdown occurs only once during the life of the work queue manager, so there's little point to creating a separate condition variable for this purpose.

■ workq.c   part 2   workq_destroy

```
 1  /*
 2   * Destroy a work queue.
 3   */
 4  int workq_destroy (workq_t *wq)
 5  {
 6      int status, status1, status2;
 7
 8      if (wq->valid != WORKQ_VALID)
 9          return EINVAL;
10      status = pthread_mutex_lock (&wq->mutex);
11      if (status != 0)
12          return status;
13      wq->valid = 0;                    /* prevent any other operations */
14
15      /*
16       * Check whether any threads are active, and run them down:
17       *
18       * 1.       set the quit flag
19       * 2.       broadcast to wake any servers that may be asleep
20       * 4.       wait for all threads to quit (counter goes to 0)
21       *          Because we don't use join, we don't need to worry
22       *          about tracking thread IDs.
23       */
24      if (wq->counter > 0) {
25          wq->quit = 1;
26          /* if any threads are idling, wake them. */
27          if (wq->idle > 0) {
28              status = pthread_cond_broadcast (&wq->cv);
29              if (status != 0) {
30                  pthread_mutex_unlock (&wq->mutex);
31                  return status;
32              }
33          }
34
35          /*
36           * Just to prove that every rule has an exception, I'm
37           * using the "cv" condition for two separate predicates
38           * here. That's OK, since the case used here applies
39           * only once during the life of a work queue -- during
40           * rundown. The overhead is minimal and it's not worth
41           * creating a separate condition variable that would
```

```
42              * wait and be signaled exactly once!
43              */
44             while (wq->counter > 0) {
45                 status = pthread_cond_wait (&wq->cv, &wq->mutex);
46                 if (status != 0) {
47                     pthread_mutex_unlock (&wq->mutex);
48                     return status;
49                 }
50             }
51         }
52         status = pthread_mutex_unlock (&wq->mutex);
53         if (status != 0)
54             return status;
55         status = pthread_mutex_destroy (&wq->mutex);
56         status1 = pthread_cond_destroy (&wq->cv);
57         status2 = pthread_attr_destroy (&wq->attr);
58         return (status ? status : (status1 ? status1 : status2));
59     }
```

■ `workq.c`   part 2   `workq_destroy`

Part 3 shows `workq_add`, which accepts work for the queue manager system.

16-35   It allocates a new work queue element and initializes it from the parameters. It queues the element, updating the `first` and `last` pointers as necessary.

40-45   If there are idle engine threads, which were created but ran out of work, signal the condition variable to wake one.

46-59   If there are no idle engine threads, and the value of `parallelism` allows for more, create a new engine thread. If there are no idle threads and it can't create a new engine thread, `workq_add` returns, leaving the new element for the next thread that finishes its current assignment.

■ `workq.c`   part 3   `workq_add`

```
1  /*
2   * Add an item to a work queue.
3   */
4  int workq_add (workq_t *wq, void *element)
5  {
6      workq_ele_t *item;
7      pthread_t id;
8      int status;
9
10     if (wq->valid != WORKQ_VALID)
11         return EINVAL;
12
13     /*
14      * Create and initialize a request structure.
15      */
16     item = (workq_ele_t *)malloc (sizeof (workq_ele_t));
```

```
17          if (item == NULL)
18              return ENOMEM;
19          item->data = element;
20          item->next = NULL;
21          status = pthread_mutex_lock (&wq->mutex);
22          if (status != 0) {
23              free (item);
24              return status;
25          }
26
27          /*
28           * Add the request to the end of the queue, updating the
29           * first and last pointers.
30           */
31          if (wq->first == NULL)
32              wq->first = item;
33          else
34              wq->last->next = item;
35          wq->last = item;
36
37          /*
38           * if any threads are idling, wake one.
39           */
40          if (wq->idle > 0) {
41              status = pthread_cond_signal (&wq->cv);
42              if (status != 0) {
43                  pthread_mutex_unlock (&wq->mutex);
44                  return status;
45              }
46          } else if (wq->counter < wq->parallelism) {
47              /*
48               * If there were no idling threads, and we're allowed to
49               * create a new thread, do so.
50               */
51              DPRINTF (("Creating new worker\n"));
52              status = pthread_create (
53                  &id, &wq->attr, workq_server, (void*)wq);
54              if (status != 0) {
55                  pthread_mutex_unlock (&wq->mutex);
56                  return status;
57              }
58              wq->counter++;
59          }
60          pthread_mutex_unlock (&wq->mutex);
61          return 0;
62      }
```

That takes care of all the external interfaces, but we will need one more function, the start function for the engine threads. The function, shown in part 4, is called workq_server. Although we could start a thread running the caller's engine with the appropriate argument for each request, this is more efficient. The workq_server function will dequeue the next request and pass it to the engine function, then look for new work. It will wait if necessary and shut down only when a certain period of time passes without any new work appearing, or when told to shut down by workq_destroy.

Notice that the server begins by locking the work queue mutex, and the "matching" unlock does not occur until the engine thread is ready to terminate. Despite this, the thread spends most of its life with the mutex unlocked, either waiting for work in the condition variable wait or within the caller's engine function.

29–62   When a thread completes the condition wait loop, either there is work to be done or the work queue is shutting down (wq->quit is nonzero).

67–80   First, we check for work and process the work queue element if there is one. There could still be work queued when workq_destroy is called, and it must all be processed before any engine thread terminates.

The user's engine function is called with the mutex unlocked, so that the user's engine can run a long time, or block, without affecting the execution of other engine threads. That does not necessarily mean that engine functions can run in parallel—the caller-supplied engine function is responsible for ensuring whatever synchronization is needed to allow the desired level of concurrency or parallelism. Ideal engine functions would require little or no synchronization and would run in parallel.

86–104   When there is no more work and the queue is being shut down, the thread terminates, awakening workq_destroy if this was the last engine thread to shut down.

110–114   Finally we check whether the engine thread timed out looking for work, which would mean the engine has waited long enough. If there's still no work to be found, the engine thread exits.

■ workq.c   part 4   workq_server

```
1   /*
2    * Thread start routine to serve the work queue.
3    */
4   static void *workq_server (void *arg)
5   {
6       struct timespec timeout;
7       workq_t *wq = (workq_t *)arg;
8       workq_ele_t *we;
9       int status, timedout;
10
11      /*
12       * We don't need to validate the workq_t here... we don't
```

```
13          * create server threads until requests are queued (the
14          * queue has been initialized by then!) and we wait for all
15          * server threads to terminate before destroying a work
16          * queue.
17          */
18         DPRINTF (("A worker is starting\n"));
19         status = pthread_mutex_lock (&wq->mutex);
20         if (status != 0)
21             return NULL;
22
23         while (1) {
24             timedout = 0;
25             DPRINTF (("Worker waiting for work\n"));
26             clock_gettime (CLOCK_REALTIME, &timeout);
27             timeout.tv_sec += 2;
28
29             while (wq->first == NULL && !wq->quit) {
30                 /*
31                  * Server threads time out after spending 2 seconds
32                  * waiting for new work, and exit.
33                  */
34                 status = pthread_cond_timedwait (
35                         &wq->cv, &wq->mutex, &timeout);
36                 if (status == ETIMEDOUT) {
37                     DPRINTF (("Worker wait timed out\n"));
38                     timedout = 1;
39                     break;
40                 } else if (status != 0) {
41                     /*
42                      * This shouldn't happen, so the work queue
43                      * package should fail. Because the work queue
44                      * API is asynchronous, that would add
45                      * complication. Because the chances of failure
46                      * are slim, I choose to avoid that
47                      * complication. The server thread will return,
48                      * and allow another server thread to pick up
49                      * the work later. Note that if this were the
50                      * only server thread, the queue wouldn't be
51                      * serviced until a new work item is
52                      * queued. That could be fixed by creating a new
53                      * server here.
54                      */
55                     DPRINTF ((
56                         "Worker wait failed, %d (%s)\n",
57                         status, strerror (status)));
58                     wq->counter--;
59                     pthread_mutex_unlock (&wq->mutex);
60                     return NULL;
61                 }
62             }
```

```
63              DPRINTF (("Work queue: %#lx, quit: %d\n",
64                  wq->first, wq->quit));
65          we = wq->first;
66
67          if (we != NULL) {
68              wq->first = we->next;
69              if (wq->last == we)
70                  wq->last = NULL;
71              status = pthread_mutex_unlock (&wq->mutex);
72              if (status != 0)
73                  return NULL;
74              DPRINTF (("Worker calling engine\n"));
75              wq->engine (we->data);
76              free (we);
77              status = pthread_mutex_lock (&wq->mutex);
78              if (status != 0)
79                  return NULL;
80          }
81
82          /*
83           * If there are no more work requests, and the servers
84           * have been asked to quit, then shut down.
85           */
86          if (wq->first == NULL && wq->quit) {
87              DPRINTF (("Worker shutting down\n"));
88              wq->counter--;
89
90              /*
91               * NOTE: Just to prove that every rule has an
92               * exception, I'm using the "cv" condition for two
93               * separate predicates here.  That's OK, since the
94               * case used here applies only once during the life
95               * of a work queue -- during rundown. The overhead
96               * is minimal and it's not worth creating a separate
97               * condition variable that would wait and be
98               * signaled exactly once!
99               */
100             if (wq->counter == 0)
101                 pthread_cond_broadcast (&wq->cv);
102             pthread_mutex_unlock (&wq->mutex);
103             return NULL;
104         }
105
106         /*
107          * If there's no more work, and we wait for as long as
108          * we're allowed, then terminate this server thread.
109          */
110         if (wq->first == NULL && timedout) {
111             DPRINTF (("engine terminating due to timeout.\n"));
```

```
112              wq->counter--;
113              break;
114          }
115      }
116
117      pthread_mutex_unlock (&wq->mutex);
118      DPRINTF (("Worker exiting\n"));
119      return NULL;
120  }
```

■ workq.c   part 4   workq_server

Finally, workq_main.c is a sample program that uses our work queue manager. Two threads queue work elements to the work queue in parallel. The engine function is designed to gather some statistics about engine usage. To accomplish this, it uses thread-specific data. When the sample run completes, main collects all of the thread-specific data and reports some statistics.

15-19   Each engine thread has an engine_t structure associated with the thread-specific data key engine_key. The engine function gets the calling thread's value of this key, and if the current value is NULL, creates a new engine_t structure and assigns it to the key. The calls member of engine_t structure records the number of calls to the engine function within each thread.

29-37   The thread-specific data key's destructor function, destructor, adds the terminating thread's engine_t to a list (engine_list_head), where main can find it later to generate the final report.

43-68   The engine function's work is relatively boring. The argument is a pointer to a power_t structure, containing the members value and power. It uses a trivial loop to multiply value by itself power times. The result is discarded in this example, and the power_t structure is freed.

73-98   A thread is started, by main, running the thread_routine function. In addition, main calls thread_routine. The thread_routine function loops for some number of iterations, determined by the macro ITERATIONS, creating and queuing work queue elements. The value and power members of the power_t structure are determined semirandomly using rand_r. The function sleeps for a random period of time, from zero to four seconds, to occasionally allow engine threads to time out and terminate. Typically when you run this program you would expect to see summary messages reporting some small number of engine threads, each of which processed some number of calls—which total 50 calls (25 each from the two threads).

■ workq_main.c

```
1  #include <pthread.h>
2  #include <stdlib.h>
3  #include <stdio.h>
4  #include <time.h>
5  #include "workq.h"
```

```
 6  #include "errors.h"
 7
 8  #define ITERATIONS      25
 9
10  typedef struct power_tag {
11      int         value;
12      int         power;
13  } power_t;
14
15  typedef struct engine_tag {
16      struct engine_tag   *link;
17      pthread_t           thread_id;
18      int                 calls;
19  } engine_t;
20
21  pthread_key_t engine_key;        /* Keep track of active engines */
22  pthread_mutex_t engine_list_mutex = PTHREAD_MUTEX_INITIALIZER;
23  engine_t *engine_list_head = NULL;
24  workq_t workq;
25
26  /*
27   * Thread-specific data destructor routine for engine_key.
28   */
29  void destructor (void *value_ptr)
30  {
31      engine_t *engine = (engine_t*)value_ptr;
32
33      pthread_mutex_lock (&engine_list_mutex);
34      engine->link = engine_list_head;
35      engine_list_head = engine;
36      pthread_mutex_unlock (&engine_list_mutex);
37  }
38
39  /*
40   * This is the routine called by the work queue servers to
41   * perform operations in parallel.
42   */
43  void engine_routine (void *arg)
44  {
45      engine_t *engine;
46      power_t *power = (power_t*)arg;
47      int result, count;
48      int status;
49
50      engine = pthread_getspecific (engine_key);
51      if (engine == NULL) {
52          engine = (engine_t*)malloc (sizeof (engine_t));
53          status = pthread_setspecific (
54              engine_key, (void*)engine);
```

```
55              if (status != 0)
56                  err_abort (status, "Set tsd");
57              engine->thread_id = pthread_self ();
58              engine->calls = 1;
59          } else
60              engine->calls++;
61          result = 1;
62          printf (
63              "Engine: computing %d^%d\n",
64              power->value, power->power);
65          for (count = 1; count <= power->power; count++)
66              result *= power->value;
67          free (arg);
68      }
69
70      /*
71       * Thread start routine that issues work queue requests.
72       */
73      void *thread_routine (void *arg)
74      {
75          power_t *element;
76          int count;
77          unsigned int seed = (unsigned int)time (NULL);
78          int status;
79
80          /*
81           * Loop, making requests.
82           */
83          for (count = 0; count < ITERATIONS; count++) {
84              element = (power_t*)malloc (sizeof (power_t));
85              if (element == NULL)
86                  errno_abort ("Allocate element");
87              element->value = rand_r (&seed) % 20;
88              element->power = rand_r (&seed) % 7;
89              DPRINTF ((
90                  "Request: %d^%d\n",
91                  element->value, element->power));
92              status = workq_add (&workq, (void*)element);
93              if (status != 0)
94                  err_abort (status, "Add to work queue");
95              sleep (rand_r (&seed) % 5);
96          }
97          return NULL;
98      }
99
100     int main (int argc, char *argv[])
101     {
102         pthread_t thread_id;
103         engine_t *engine;
```

```
104        int count = 0, calls = 0;
105        int status;
106
107        status = pthread_key_create (&engine_key, destructor);
108        if (status != 0)
109            err_abort (status, "Create key");
110        status = workq_init (&workq, 4, engine_routine);
111        if (status != 0)
112            err_abort (status, "Init work queue");
113        status = pthread_create (&thread_id, NULL, thread_routine, NULL);
114        if (status != 0)
115            err_abort (status, "Create thread");
116        (void)thread_routine (NULL);
117        status = pthread_join (thread_id, NULL);
118        if (status != 0)
119            err_abort (status, "Join thread");
120        status = workq_destroy (&workq);
121        if (status != 0)
122            err_abort (status, "Destroy work queue");
123
124        /*
125         * By now, all of the engine_t structures have been placed
126         * on the list (by the engine thread destructors), so we
127         * can count and summarize them.
128         */
129        engine = engine_list_head;
130        while (engine != NULL) {
131            count++;
132            calls += engine->calls;
133            printf ("engine %d: %d calls\n", count, engine->calls);
134            engine = engine->link;
135        }
136        printf ("%d engine threads processed %d calls\n",
137            count, calls);
138        return 0;
139  }
```

■ `workq_main.c`

7.3 But what about existing libraries?

> *"The great art of riding, as I was saying is—*
> *to keep your balance properly. Like this, you know—"*
> *He let go the bridle, and stretched out both his arms to*
> *show Alice what he meant, and this time he fell flat on*
> *his back, right under the horse's feet.*
>
> —Lewis Carroll, Through the Looking-Glass

When you create a new library, all it takes is careful design to ensure that the library will be thread-safe. As you decide what state is needed for the function, you can determine which state needs to be shared between threads, which state should be managed by the caller through external context handles, which state can be kept in local variables within a function, and so forth. You can define the interfaces to the functions to support that state in the most efficient manner. But when you're modifying an existing library to work with threads, you usually don't have that luxury. And when you are using someone else's library, you may need simply to "make do."

7.3.1 Modifying libraries to be thread-safe

Many functions rely on static storage across a sequence of calls, for example, strtok or getpwd. Others depend on returning a pointer to static storage, for example, asctime. This section points out some techniques that can help when you need to make "legacy" libraries thread-safe, using some well-known examples in the ANSI C run-time library.

The simplest technique is to assign a mutex to each subsystem. At any call into the subsystem you lock the mutex; at any exit from the subsystem you unlock the mutex. Because this single mutex covers the entire subsystem, we often refer to such a mechanism as a "big mutex" (see Section 3.2.4). The mutex prevents more than one thread from executing within the subsystem at a time. Note that this fixes only *synchronization races*, not *sequence races* (Section 8.1.2 describes the distinction between the two). The best candidates for this approach are functions that do little except maintain some internal database. That includes functions such as malloc and free that manage an internal resource pool but grant limited (or no) external visibility into that pool.

One problem with using the "big mutex" approach is that you have to be careful about your definition of "subsystem." You need to include all functions that share data or that call each other. If malloc and free have one mutex while realloc uses another, then you've got a race as soon as one thread calls realloc while another thread is in malloc or free.

And what if realloc is implemented to call malloc, copy data, and then call free on the old pointer? The realloc function would lock the heap mutex and call malloc. The malloc function would immediately try to lock the heap mutex itself, resulting in a deadlock. There are several ways to solve this. One is to carefully separate each of the external interfaces into an internal "engine" function that does the actual work and an external entry point that locks the subsystem mutex and calls the engine. Other entry points within the subsystem that need the same engine function would call it directly rather than using the normal entry point. That's often the most efficient solution, but it is also harder to do. Another possibility is to construct a "recursive" mutex that allows the subsystem to relock its own mutex without deadlock.[*] Now `malloc` and `free` are allowed to relock the mutex held by `realloc`, but another thread trying to call any of them will be blocked until `realloc` completely unlocks the recursive mutex.

Most functions with persistent state require more substantial changes than just a "big mutex," especially to avoid altering the interface. The `asctime` function, for example, returns a pointer to the character string representation of a binary time. Traditionally, the string is formatted into a static buffer declared within the `asctime` function, and the function returns a pointer to that buffer.

Locking a mutex within `asctime` isn't enough to protect the data. In fact, it is not even particularly useful. After `asctime` returns, the mutex has been unlocked. The caller needs to read the buffer, and there is nothing to prevent another thread from calling `asctime` (and "corrupting" the first thread's result) before the first thread has finished reading or copying it. To solve this problem using a mutex, the *caller* would need to lock a mutex before calling `asctime`, and then unlock it only after it had finished with the data or copied the returned buffer somewhere "safe."

The problem can instead be fixed by recoding `asctime` to allocate a heap buffer using `malloc`, formatting the time string into that buffer, and returning its address. The function can use a thread-specific data key to keep track of the heap address so that it can be reused on the next call within that thread. When the thread terminates, a destructor function can `free` the storage.

It would be more efficient to avoid using `malloc` and thread-specific data, but that requires changing the interface to `asctime`. Pthreads adds a new thread-safe alternative to `asctime`, called `asctime_r`, which requires the caller to pass the address and length of a buffer. The `asctime_r` function formats the time string into the caller's buffer. This allows the caller to manage the buffer in any way that's convenient. It can be on the thread's stack, in heap, or can even be shared between threads. Although in a way this is "giving up" on the existing function and defining a new function, it is often the best way (and sometimes the only practical way) to make a function thread-safe.

7.3.2 Living with legacy libraries

Sometimes you have to work with code you didn't write, and can't change. A lot of code is now being made thread-safe, and most operating systems that support threads can be expected to supply thread-safe implementations of the

---

[*] It is easy to construct a "recursive" mutex using a mutex, a condition variable, the `pthread_t` value of the current owner (if any), and a count of the owner's "recursion depth." The depth is 0 when the recursive mutex is not locked, and greater than 0 when it is locked. The mutex protects access to the depth and owner members, and the condition variable is used to wait for the depth to become 0, should a thread wish to lock the recursive mutex while another thread has it locked.

common bundled library packages. The "inner circle" of thread-safe libraries will gradually increase to become the rule rather than the exception as more application and library developers demand thread-safety.

But inevitably you'll find that a library you need hasn't been made thread-safe, for example, an older version of the X Windows windowing system, or a database engine, or a simulation package. And you won't have source code. Of course you'll immediately complain to the supplier of the library and convince them to make the next version fully thread-safe. But what can you do until the new version arrives?

If you really need the library, the answer is "use it anyway." There are a number of techniques you can use, from simple to complex. The appropriate level of complexity required depends entirely on the library's interface and how (as well as how much) you use the library in your code.

   ❙ Make the unsafe library into a server thread.

In some cases, you may find it convenient to restrict use of the library to one thread, making that thread a "server" for the capabilities provided by the unsafe library. This technique is commonly applied, for example, when using versions of the X11 protocol client library that are not thread-safe. The main thread or some other thread created for the purpose processes queued X11 requests on behalf of other threads. Only the server thread makes calls into the X11 library, so it does not matter whether X11 is thread-safe.

   ❙ Write your own "big mutex" wrappers around the interfaces.

If the function you need has a "thread-safe interface" but not a "thread-safe implementation," then you may be able to encapsulate each call inside a wrapper function (or a macro) that locks a mutex, calls the function, and then unlocks the mutex. This is just an external version of the "big mutex" approach. By "thread-safe interface" I mean that the function relies on the static state, but that any data returned to the caller isn't subject to alteration by later calls. For example, `malloc` fits that category. The allocation of memory involves static data that needs to be protected, but once a block has been allocated and returned to a caller, that address (and the memory to which it points) will not be affected by later calls to `malloc`. The external "big mutex" is not a good solution for libraries that may block for substantial periods of time—like X11 or any other network protocol. While the result may be safe, it will be very inefficient unless you rarely use the library, because other threads may be locked out for long periods of time while remote operations are taking place.

   ❙ Extend the implementation with external state.

A big mutex won't fix a function like `asctime` that writes data into a static buffer and returns the address: The returned data must be protected until the caller is finished using it, and the data is used outside the wrapper. For a function like strtok the data is in use until the entire *sequence* of tokens has been parsed. In general, functions that have persistent static data are more difficult to encapsulate.

A function like asctime can be encapsulated by creating a wrapper function that locks a mutex, calls the function, copies the return value into a thread-safe buffer, unlocks the mutex, and then returns. The thread-safe buffer can be dynamically allocated by the wrapper function using malloc, for instance. You can require the caller to free the buffer when done, which changes the interface, or you can make the wrapper keep track of a per-thread buffer using thread-specific data.

Alternatively, you could invent a new interface that requires the caller to supply a buffer. The caller can use a stack buffer, or a buffer in heap, or, if properly synchronized (by the caller), it can share the buffer between threads. Remember that if the wrapper uses thread-specific data to keep track of a per-thread heap buffer, the wrapper can be made compatible with the original interface. The other variants require interface changes: The caller must supply different inputs or it must be aware of the need to free the returned buffer.

A function that keeps persistent state across a sequence of calls is more difficult to encapsulate neatly. The static data must be protected throughout. The easiest way to do this is simply to change the caller to lock a mutex before the first call and keep it locked until after the final call of a sequence. But remember that no other thread can use the function until the mutex is unlocked. If the caller does a substantial amount of processing between calls, a major processing bottleneck can occur. Of course, this may also be difficult or impossible to integrate into a simple wrapper—the wrapper would have to be able to recognize the first and last of any series of calls.

A better, but harder, way is to find some way to encapsulate the function (or a set of related functions) into a new thread-safe interface. There is no general model for this transformation, and in many cases it may be impossible. But often you just need to be creative, and possibly apply some constraints. While the library function may not be easy to encapsulate, you may be able to encapsulate "special cases" that you use. While strtok, for example, allows you to alter the token delimiters at each call, most code does not take advantage of this flexibility. Without the complication of varying delimiters, you could define a new token parsing model on top of strtok where all tokens in a string are found by a thread-safe setup function and stored where they can be retrieved one by one without calling strtok again. Thus, while the setup function would lock a common mutex and serialize access across all threads, the information retrieval function could run without any serialization.

8 Hints to avoid debugging

"Other maps are such shapes, with their islands and capes!
But we've got our brave Captain to thank"
(So the crew would protest) "that he's bought us the best—
A perfect and absolute blank!"
　　—Lewis Carroll, The Hunting of the Snark

Writing a complicated threaded program is a lot harder than writing a simple synchronous program, but once you learn the rules it is not much harder than writing a complicated synchronous program. Writing a threaded program to perform a complicated *asynchronous* function will usually be easier than writing the same program using more traditional asynchronous programming techniques.

The complications begin when you need to debug or analyze your threaded program. That's not so much because using threads is hard, but rather because the tools for debugging and analyzing threaded code are less well developed and understood than the programming interfaces. You may feel as if you are navigating from a blank map. That doesn't mean you can't utilize the power of threaded programming right now, but it does mean that you need to be careful, and maybe a little more creative, in avoiding the rocks and shoals of the uncharted waters.

Although this chapter mentions some thread debugging and analysis tools and suggests what you can accomplish with them, my goal isn't to tell you about tools you can use to solve problems. Instead, I will describe some of the common problems that you may encounter and impart something resembling "sage advice" on avoiding those problems before you have to debug them—or, perhaps more realistically, how to recognize which problems you may be encountering.

❙ Check your assumptions at the door.

Threaded programming is probably new to you. Asynchronous programming may be new to you. If so, you'll need to be careful about your assumptions. You've crossed a bridge, and behavior that's acceptable—or even required—in Synchronous Land can be dangerous across the river in Asynchronous Land. You can learn the new rules without a lot of trouble, and with practice you'll probably even feel comfortable with them. But you have to start by being constantly aware that something's changed.

8.1 Avoiding incorrect code

"For instance, now," she went on, sticking a large piece of plaster on her fin-
   ger as she spoke, "there's the King's Messenger. He's in prison now,
   being punished: and the trial doesn't even begin till next Wednesday:
   and of course the crime comes last of all."
"Suppose he never commits the crime?" said Alice.
"That would be all the better, wouldn't it?" the Queen said, as she bound the
   plaster round her finger with a bit of ribbon.
   —Lewis Carroll, Through the Looking-Glass

Pthreads doesn't provide much assistance in debugging your threaded code. That is not surprising, since POSIX does not recognize the concept of debugging at all, even in explaining why the nearly universal SIGTRAP signal is not included in the standard. There is no standard way to interact with your program or observe its behavior as it runs, although every threaded system will provide some form of debugging tool. Even in the unlikely event that the developers of the system had no concern for you, the poor programmer, they needed to debug their own code.

A vendor that provides threads with an operating system will provide at least a basic thread "observation window" in a debugging utility. You should expect at minimum the ability to display a list of the running threads and their current state, the state of mutexes and condition variables, and the stack trace of all threads. You should also be able to set breakpoints in specified threads and specify a "current thread" to examine registers, variables, and stack traces.

Because implementations of Pthreads are likely to maintain a lot of state in user mode, within the process, debugging using traditional UNIX mechanisms such as ptrace or the proc file system can be difficult. A common solution is to provide a special library that is called by the debugger, which knows how to search through the address space of the process being debugged to find the state of threads and synchronization objects. Solaris, for example, provides the libthread_db.so shared library, and Digital UNIX provides libpthreaddebug.so.

A thread package placed on top of an operating system by a third party will not be able to provide much integration with a debugger. For example, the portable "DCE threads" library provides a built-in debug command parser that you can invoke from the debugger using the **print** or **call** command to report the state of threads and synchronization objects within the process.* This limited debugging support is at best inconvenient—you can't analyze thread state within a core file after a program has failed, and it cannot understand (or report) the symbolic names of program variables.

---

* For historical reasons, the function is called cma_debug. Should you find yourself stuck with DCE threads code, try calling it, and enter the **help** command for a list of additional commands.

The following sections describe some of the most common classes of threaded programming errors, with the intention of helping you to avoid these problems while designing, as well as possibly making it easier to recognize them while debugging.

8.1.1 Avoid relying on "thread inertia"

Always, *always*, remember that threads are asynchronous. That's especially important to keep in mind when you develop code on uniprocessor systems where threads may be "slightly synchronous." Nothing happens simultaneously on a uniprocessor, where *ready* threads are serially timesliced at relatively predictable intervals. When you create a new thread on a uniprocessor or unblock a thread waiting for a mutex or condition variable, it cannot run immediately unless it has a higher priority than the creator or waker.

The same phenomenon may occur even on a multiprocessor, if you have reached the "concurrency limit" of the process, for example, when you have more *ready* threads than there are processors. The creator, or the thread waking another thread, given equal priority, will continue running until it blocks or until the next timeslice (which may be many nanoseconds away).

This means that the thread that currently has a processor has an advantage. It tends to remain in motion, exhibiting behavior vaguely akin to physical inertia. As a result, you may get away with errors that will cause your code to break in mysterious ways when the newly created or awakened thread is able to run immediately—when there are free processors. The following program, `inertia.c`, demonstrates how this phenomenon can disrupt your program.

27-41   The question is one of whether the thread function `printer_thread` will see the value of `stringPtr` that was set before the call to `pthread_create`, or the value set after the call to `pthread_create`. The desired value is "After value." This is a very common class of programming error. Of course, in most cases the problem is less obvious than in this simple example. Often, the variable is uninitialized, not set to some benign value, and the result may be data corruption or a segmentation fault.

39   Now, notice the delay loop. Even on a multiprocessor, this program won't break all the time. The program will usually be able to change `stringPtr` before the new thread can begin executing—it takes time for a newly created thread to get into your code, after all, and the "window of opportunity" in this particular program is only a few instructions. The loop allows me to demonstrate the problem by delaying the `main` thread long enough to give the `printer` thread time to start. If you make this loop long enough, you will see the problem even on a uniprocessor, if `main` is eventually timesliced.

■ `inertia.c`

```
1    #include <pthread.h>
2    #include "errors.h"
```

```
 3
 4  void *printer_thread (void *arg)
 5  {
 6      char *string = *(char**)arg;
 7
 8      printf ("%s\n", string);
 9      return NULL;
10  }
11
12  int main (int argc, char *argv[])
13  {
14      pthread_t printer_id;
15      char *string_ptr;
16      int i, status;
17
18  #ifdef sun
19      /*
20       * On Solaris 2.5, threads are not timesliced. To ensure
21       * that our two threads can run concurrently, we need to
22       * increase the concurrency level to 2.
23       */
24      DPRINTF (("Setting concurrency level to 2\n"));
25      thr_setconcurrency (2);
26  #endif
27      string_ptr = "Before value";
28      status = pthread_create (
29          &printer_id, NULL, printer_thread, (void*)&string_ptr);
30      if (status != 0)
31          err_abort (status, "Create thread");
32
33      /*
34       * Give the thread a chance to get started if it's going to run
35       * in parallel, but not enough that the current thread is likely
36       * to be timesliced. (This is a tricky balance, and the loop may
37       * need to be adjusted on your system before you can see the bug.)
38       */
39      for (i = 0; i < 10000000; i++);
40
41      string_ptr = "After value";
42      status = pthread_join (printer_id, NULL);
43      if (status != 0)
44          err_abort (status, "Join thread");
45      return 0;
46  }
```

■ inertia.c

The way to fix inertia.c is to set the "After value," the one you want the threads to see, before creating the thread. That's not so hard, is it? There may still be a "Before value," whether it is uninitialized storage or a value that was previously used for some other purpose, but the thread you create can't see it. By the memory visibility rules given in Section 3.4, the new thread sees all memory writes that occurred prior to the call into `pthread_create`. Always design your code so that threads aren't started until after all the resources they need have been created and initialized exactly the way you want the thread to see them.

> ❘ Never assume that a thread you create will wait for you.

You can cause yourself as many problems by assuming a thread will run "soon" as by assuming it won't run "too soon." Creating a thread that relies on "temporary storage" in the creator thread is almost always a bad idea. I have seen code that creates a series of threads, passing a pointer to the same local structure to each, changing the structure member values each time. The problem is that you can't assume threads will start in any specific order. All of those threads may start after your last creation call, in which case they all get the last value of the data. Or the threads might start a little bit out of order, so that the first and second thread get the same data, but the others get what you intended them to get.

Thread inertia is a special case of thread races. Although thread races are covered much more extensively in Section 8.1.2, thread inertia is a subtle effect, and many people do not recognize it as a race. So test your code thoroughly on a multiprocessor, if at all possible. Do this as early as possible during development, and continuously throughout development. Do this despite the fact that, especially without a perfect threaded debugger, testing on a multiprocessor will be more difficult than debugging on a uniprocessor. And, of course, you should carefully read the following section.

8.1.2 Never bet your mortgage on a thread race

A race occurs when two or more threads try to get someplace or do something at the same time. Only one can win. Which thread wins is determined by a lot of factors, not all of which are under your control. The outcome may be affected by how many processors are on the system, how many other processes are running, how much network overhead the system is handling, and other things like that. That's a nondeterministic race. It probably won't come out the same if you run the same program twice in a row. You don't want to bet on races like that.[*]

> | When you write threaded code, assume that at any arbitrary point,
> | within any statement of your program, each thread may go to sleep for
> | an unbounded period of time.

---

[*] My daughter had this figured out by the time she was three—when she wanted to race, she told me ahead of time whether my job was to win or lose. There's really no point to leaving these important things to chance!

Processors may execute your threads at differing rates, depending on processor load, interrupts, and so forth. Timeslicing on a processor may interrupt a thread at any point for an unspecified duration. During the time that a thread isn't running, any other thread may run and do anything that synchronization protocols in your code don't specifically prevent it from doing, which means that between any two instructions a thread may find an entirely different picture of memory, with an entirely different set of threads active. The way to protect a thread's view of the world from surprises is to rely only on explicit synchronization between threads.

Most synchronization problems will probably show up pretty quickly if you're debugging on a multiprocessor. Threads with insufficient synchronization will compete for the honor of reaching memory last. It is a minor irony of thread races that the "loser" generally wins because the memory system will keep the last value written to an address. Sometimes, you won't notice a race at all. But sometimes you'll get a mystifying wrong result, and sometimes you'll get a segmentation fault.

Races are usually difficult to diagnose. The problem often won't occur at all on a uniprocessor system because races require concurrent execution. The level of concurrency on a uniprocessor, even with timeslicing, is fairly low, and often an unsynchronized sequence of writes will complete before another thread gets a chance to read the inconsistent data. Even on a multiprocessor, races may be difficult to reproduce, and they often refuse to reveal themselves to a debugger. Races depend on the relative timing of thread execution—something a debugger is likely to change.

Some races have more to do with memory visibility than with synchronization of multiple writes. Remember the basic rules of memory visibility (see Section 3.4): A thread can always see changes to memory that were performed by a thread previously running on the same processor. On a uniprocessor all threads run on the same processor, which makes it difficult to detect memory visibility problems during debugging. On a multiprocessor, you may see visibility races only when the threads are scheduled on different processors while executing specific vulnerable sections of code.

> No ordering exists between threads
> unless you cause ordering.
>
> Bill Gallmeister's corollary:
> "Threads will run in the most evil order possible."

You don't want to find yourself debugging thread races. You may never see the same outcome twice. The symptoms will change when you try to debug the code—possibly by masquerading as an entirely different kind of problem, not just as the same problem in a different place. Even worse, the problem may never occur at all until a customer runs the code, and then it may fail every time, but only in the customer's immense, monolithic application, and only after it has been running for days. It will be running on a secured system with no network access, they will be unable to show you the proprietary code, and will be unable to reproduce the problem with a simple test program.

❚ "Scheduling" is not the same as "synchronization."

It may appear at first that setting a thread to the SCHED_FIFO scheduling policy and maximum priority would allow you to avoid using expensive synchronization mechanisms by guaranteeing that no other thread can run until the thread blocks itself or lowers its priority. There are several problems with this, but the main problem is that it won't work on a multiprocessor. The SCHED_FIFO policy prevents preemption by another thread, but on a multiprocessor other threads can run without any form of preemption.

Scheduling exists to tell the system how important a specific job (thread) is to your application so it can schedule the job you need the most. Synchronization exists to tell the system that no other thread can be allowed into the critical section until the calling thread is done.

In real life, a deterministic race, where the winner is guaranteed from the beginning, isn't very exciting (except to a three year old). But a deterministic race represents a substantially safer bet, and that's the kind of race you want to design into your programs. A deterministic race, as you can guess, isn't much of a race at all. It is more like waiting in line—nice, organized, and predictable. Excitement is overrated, especially when it comes to debugging complicated threaded applications.

The simplest form of race is when more than one thread tries to write shared state without proper synchronization, for example, when two threads increment a shared counter. The two threads may fetch the same value from memory, increment it independently, and store the same result into memory; the counter has been incremented by one rather than by two, and both threads have the same result value.

A slightly more subtle race occurs when one thread is writing some set of shared data while another thread reads that data. If the reads occur in a different order, or if the reader catches up to the writer, then the reader may get inconsistent results. For example, one thread increments a shared array index and then writes data into the array element at that index. Another thread fetches the shared index before the writer has filled in the entire element and reads that element. The reader finds inconsistent data because the element hasn't been completely set up yet. It may take an unexpected code path because of something it sees there or it may follow a bad pointer.

Always design and code assuming that threads are more asynchronous than you can imagine. Anyone who's written a lot of code knows that computers have little creatures that enjoy annoying you. Remember that when you code with threads there are lots of them loose at the same time. Take no chances, make no assumptions. Make sure any shared state is set up and visible before creating the thread that will use it; or create it using static mutexes or pthread_once. Use a mutex to ensure that threads can't read inconsistent data. If you must share stack data between threads, be sure all threads that use the data have terminated before returning from the function that allocated the storage.

"Sequence races" may occur when you assume some ordering of events, but that ordering isn't coded into the application. Sequence races can occur even when you carefully apply synchronization control to ensure data consistency. You can only avoid this kind of race by ensuring that ordering isn't important, or by adding code that forces everything to happen in the order it needs to happen.

For example, imagine that three threads share a counter variable. Each will store a private copy of the current value and increment the shared counter. If the three threads are performing the same function, and none of them cares which value of the counter they get, then it is enough to lock a mutex around the fetch and increment operation. The mutex guarantees that each thread gets a distinct value, and no values are skipped. There's no race because none of the threads cares who wins.

But if it matters which value each thread receives, that simple code will not do the job. For example, you might imagine that threads are guaranteed to start in the order in which they are created, so that the first thread gets the value 1, the second gets the value 2, and so forth. Once in a while (probably while you're debugging), the threads will get the value you expect, and everything will work, and at other times, the threads will happen to run in a different order.

There are several ways to solve this. For example, you could assign each of the threads the proper value to begin with, by incrementing the counter in the thread that creates them and passing the appropriate value to each thread in a data structure. The best solution, though, is to avoid the problem by designing the code so that startup order doesn't matter. The more symmetrical your threads are, and the fewer assumptions they make about their environment, the less chance that this kind of race will happen.

Races aren't always way down there at the level of memory address references, though. They can be anywhere. The traditional ANSI C library, for example, allows a number of sequence races when you use certain functions in an application with multiple threads. The readdir function, for example, relies on static storage within the function to maintain context across a series of identical calls to readdir. If one thread calls readdir while another thread is in the middle of a sequence of its own calls to readdir, the static storage will be overwritten with a new context.

> "Sequence races" can occur even when all your code uses mutexes to protect shared data!

This race occurs even if readdir is "thread aware" and locks a mutex to protect the static storage. It is not a synchronization race, it is a sequence race. Thread A might call readdir to scan directory /usr/bin, for example, which locks the mutex, returns the first entry, and then unlocks the mutex. Thread B might then call readdir to scan directory /usr/include, which also locks the mutex, returns the first entry, and then unlocks the mutex. Now thread A calls `readdir` again expecting the second entry in `/usr/bin`; but instead it gets the second entry in `/usr/include`. No interface has behaved improperly, but the end result is wrong. The interface to `readdir` simply is not appropriate for use by threads.

That's why Pthreads specifies a set of new *reentrant* functions, including `readdir_r`, which has an additional argument that is used to maintain context across calls. The additional argument solves the sequence race by avoiding any need for shared data. The call to `readdir_r` in thread A returns the first entry from `/usr/bin` in thread A's buffer, and the call to `readdir_r` in thread B returns the first entry from `/usr/include` in thread B's buffer . . . and the second call in thread A returns the second entry from `/usr/bin` in thread A's buffer. Refer to `pipe.c`, in Section 4.1, for a program that uses `readdir_r`.

Sequence races can also be found at higher levels of coding. File descriptors in a process, for example, are shared across all threads. If two threads attempt to `getc` from the same file, each character in the file can go to only one thread. Even though `getc` itself is thread-safe, the sequence of characters seen by each thread is not deterministic—it depends on the ordering of each thread's independent calls to `getc`. They may alternate, each getting every second character throughout the file. Or one may get 2 or 100 characters in a row and then the other might get 1 character before being preempted for some reason.

There are a number of ways you can resolve the `getc` race. You can open the file under two separate file descriptors and assign one to each thread. In that way, each thread sees every character, in order. That solves the race by removing the dependency on ordering. Or you can lock the file across the entire sequence of `gets` operations in each thread, which solves the race by enforcing the desired order. The program `putchar.c`, back in Section 6.4.2, shows a similar situation.

Usually a program that doesn't *care* about ordering will run more efficiently than a program that enforces some particular ordering, first, because enforcing the ordering will always introduce computational overhead that's not directly related to getting the job done. Remember Amdahl's law. "Unordered" programs are more efficient because the greatest power of threaded programming is that things can happen concurrently, and synchronization prevents concurrency. Running an application on a multiprocessor system doesn't help much if most processors spend their time waiting for one to finish something.

8.1.3 Cooperate to avoid deadlocks

Like races, deadlocks are the result of synchronization problems in a program. While races are resource conflicts caused by insufficient synchronization, deadlocks are usually conflicts in the use of synchronization. A deadlock can happen when any two threads share resources. Essentially a deadlock occurs when thread A has resource 1 and can't continue until it has resource 2, while thread B has resource 2 and can't continue until it has resource 1.

The most common type of deadlock in a Pthreads program is *mutex deadlock,* where both resources are mutexes. There is one really important advantage of a deadlock over a race: It is much easier to debug the problem. In a race, the threads do something incorrectly and move on. The problem shows up sometime later, usually as a side effect. But in a deadlock the threads are still there waiting, and always will be—if they could go anywhere, it wouldn't be a deadlock. So when you attach to the process with the debugger or look at a crash dump, you can see what resources are involved. With a little detective work you can often determine why it happened.

The most likely cause is a resource ordering inconsistency. The study of deadlocks goes way back to the early days of operating system design. Anyone who's taken computer science courses has probably run into the classic *dining philosophers* problem. Some philosophers sit at a round table with plates of spaghetti; each alternately eats and discusses philosophy. Although no utensils are required to discuss philosophy, each philosopher requires two forks to eat. The table is set with a single fork between each pair. The philosophers need to synchronize their eating and discussion to prevent deadlock. The most obvious form of deadlock is when all philosophers simultaneously pick up one fork each and refuse to put it down.

There's always a way to make sure that your philosophers can all eat, eventually. For example, a philosopher can take the fork to her right, and then look to her left. If the fork is available, she can take it and eat. If not, she should return the fork she's holding to the table and chat awhile. (That is the mutex backoff strategy discussed in Section 3.2.5.1.) Since the philosophers are all in a good mood and none has recently published papers severely critical of adjoining colleagues, those who get to eat will in reasonably short order return both of their forks to the table so that their colleagues on each side can proceed.

A more reliable (and more sanitary) solution is to skip the spaghetti and serve a dish that can be eaten with one fork. Mutex deadlocks can't happen if each thread has only one mutex locked at a time. It is a good idea to avoid calling functions with a mutex locked. First, if that function (or something it calls) locks another mutex, you could end up with a deadlock. Second, it is a good idea to lock mutexes for as short a time as possible (remember, locking a mutex prevents another thread from "eating"—that is, executing—concurrently). Calling `printf`, though, isn't likely to cause a deadlock in your code, because you don't lock any ANSI C library mutexes, and the ANSI C library doesn't lock any of your mutexes. If the call is into your own code, or if you call a library that may call back into your code, be careful.

If you need to lock more than one mutex at a time, avoid deadlocks by using a strict hierarchy or a backoff algorithm. The main disadvantage of mutex backoff is that the backoff loop can run a long time if there are lots of other threads locking the mutexes, even if they do so without any possibility of a deadlock. The backoff algorithm assumes that other threads may lock the first mutex after having locked one or more of the other mutexes. If all threads always lock mutexes in the order they're locked by the backoff loop, then you've got a fixed locking hierarchy and you don't need the backoff algorithm.

When a program has hung because of a deadlock, you require two important capabilities of your threaded debugger. First, it allows you to run your program in a mode where mutex ownership is recorded, and may be displayed using debugger commands. Finding a thread that is blocked on some mutex while it owns other mutexes is a good indication that you may have a deadlock. Second, you would like to be able to examine the call stack of threads that own mutexes to determine why the mutexes have remained locked.

The call stack may not always be sufficient, though. One common cause of a deadlock is that some thread has returned from a function without unlocking a mutex. In this case, you may need a more sophisticated tool to trace the synchronization behavior of the program. Such a tool would allow you to examine the data and determine, for example, that function `bad_lock` locked a mutex and failed to unlock that mutex.

8.1.4 Beware of priority inversion

"Priority inversion" is a problem unique to applications (or libraries) that rely on realtime priority scheduling. Priority inversion involves at least three threads of differing priority. The differing priorities are important—priority inversion is a conflict between synchronization and scheduling requirements. Priority inversion allows a low-priority thread to indefinitely prevent a higher-priority thread from running. The result usually is not a deadlock (though it can be), but it is always a severe problem. See Section 5.5.4 for more about priority inversion.

Most commonly, a priority inversion results from three threads of differing priority sharing resources. One example of a priority inversion is when a low-priority thread locks a mutex, and is preempted by a high-priority thread, which then blocks on the mutex currently locked by the low-priority thread. Normally, the low-priority thread would resume, allowing it to unlock the mutex, which would unblock the high-priority thread to continue. However, if a medium-priority thread was awakened (possibly by some action of the high-priority thread), it might prevent the lower-priority thread from running. The medium-priority thread (or other threads it awakens) may indefinitely prevent the low-priority thread from releasing the mutex, so a high-priority thread is blocked by the action of a lower-priority thread.

If the medium-priority thread blocks, the low-priority thread will be allowed to resume and release the mutex, at which point operation resumes. Because of this, many priority inversion deadlocks resolve themselves after a short time. If all priority inversion problems in a program reliably resolve themselves within a short time, the priority inversion may become a performance issue rather than a correctness issue. In either case, priority inversion can be a severe problem.

Here are a few ideas to avoid priority inversion:

- Avoid realtime scheduling entirely. That clearly is not practical in many realtime applications, however.

- Design your threads so that threads of differing priority do not need to use the same mutexes. This may be impractical, too; many ANSI C functions, for example, use mutexes.
- Use priority ceiling mutexes (Section 5.5.5.1) or priority inheritance (Section 5.5.5.2). These are optional features of Pthreads and will not be available everywhere. Also, you cannot set the mutex priority protocol for mutexes you do not create, including those used by ANSI C functions.
- Avoid calling functions that may lock mutexes you didn't create in any thread with elevated priority.

8.1.5 Never share condition variables between predicates

Your code will usually be cleaner and more efficient if you avoid using a single condition variable to manage more than one predicate condition. You should not, for example, define a single "queue" condition variable that is used to awaken threads waiting for the queue to become empty and also threads waiting for an element to be added to the queue.

But this isn't just a performance issue (or it would be in another section). If you use pthread_cond_signal to wake threads waiting on these shared condition variables, the program may hang with threads waiting on the condition variable and nobody left to wake them up.

Why? Because you can only *signal* a condition variable when you know that a single thread needs to be awakened, and that any thread waiting on the condition variable may be chosen. When multiple predicates share a condition variable, you can never be sure that the awakened thread was waiting for the predicate you set. If it was not, then it will see a *spurious wakeup* and wait again. Your signal has been lost, because no thread waiting for your predicate had a chance to see that it had changed.

It is not enough for a thread to resignal the condition variable when it gets a spurious wakeup, either. Threads may not wake up in the order they waited, especially when you use priority scheduling. "Resignaling" might result in an infinite loop with a few high-priority threads (all with the wrong predicate) alternately waking each other up.

The best solution, when you really want to share a condition variable between predicates, is always to use pthread_cond_broadcast. But when you broadcast, all waiting threads wake up to reevaluate their predicates. You always know that one set or the other cannot proceed—so why make them all wake up to find out? If 1 thread is waiting for write access, for example, and 100 are waiting for read access, all 101 threads must wake up when the broadcast means that it is now OK to write, but only the one writer can proceed—the other 100 threads must wait again. The result of this imprecision is a lot of wasted context switches, and there are more useful ways to keep your computer busy.

8.1.6 Sharing stacks and related memory corrupters

There's nothing wrong with sharing stack memory between threads. That is, it is legal and sometimes reasonable for a thread to allocate some variable on its own stack and communicate that address to one or more other threads. A correctly written program can share stack addresses with no risk at all; however (this may come as a surprise), not every program is written correctly, even when you want it to be correct. Sharing stack addresses can make small programming errors catastrophic, and these errors can be very difficult to isolate.

> Returning from the function that allocates shared stack memory, when other threads may still use that data, will result in undesirable behavior.

If you share stack memory, you must ensure that it is never possible for the thread that owns the stack to "pop" that shared memory from the stack until all other threads have forever ceased to make use of the shared data. Should the owning thread return from a stack frame containing the data, for example, the owning thread may call another function and thereby reallocate the space occupied by the shared variable. One or both of the following possible outcomes will eventually be observed:

1. Data written by another thread will be overwritten with saved register values, a return PC, or whatever. The shared data has been corrupted.
2. Saved register values, return PC, or whatever will be overwritten by another thread modifying the shared data. The owning thread's call frame has been corrupted.

Having carefully ensured that there is no possible way for the owning thread to pop the stack data while other threads are using the shared data, are you safe? Maybe not. We're stretching the point a little, but remember, we're talking about a programming error—maybe a silly thing like failing to initialize a pointer variable declared with `auto` storage class, for example. A pointer to the shared data must be stored somewhere to be useful—other threads have no other way to find the proper stack address. At some point, the pointer is likely to appear in various locations on the stack of every thread that uses the data. None of these pointers will necessarily be erased when the thread ceases to make use of the stack.

Writes through uninitialized pointers are a common programming error, regardless of threads, so to some extent this is nothing new or different. However, in the presence of threads and shared stack data, each thread has an opportunity to corrupt data used by some other thread asynchronously. The symptoms of that corruption may not appear until some time later, which can pose a particularly difficult debugging task.

If, in your program, sharing stack data seems convenient, then by all means take advantage of the capability. But if something unexpected happens during debugging, start by examining the code that shares stack data particularly carefully. If you routinely use an analysis tool that reports use of uninitialized variables (such as Third Degree on Digital UNIX), you may not need to worry about this class of problem—or many others.

8.2 Avoiding performance problems

"Well, in our country," said Alice, still panting a little, "you'd generally
get to somewhere else—if you ran very fast for a long time as we've
been doing."
"A slow sort of country!" said the Queen. "Now, here, you see, it takes all the
running you can do, to keep in the same place. If you want to get some-
where else, you must run at least twice as fast as that!"
—Lewis Carroll, Through the Looking-Glass

Sometimes, once a program works, it is "done." At least, until you want to
make it do something else. In many cases, though, "working" isn't good enough.
The program needs to meet performance goals. Sometimes the performance goals
are clear: "must perform so many transactions in this period of time." Other
times, the goals are looser: "must be very fast."

This section gives pointers on determining how fast you're going, what's slowing you up, and how to tell (maybe) when you're going as fast as you can go.
There are some very good tools to help you, and there will be a lot more as the
industry adjusts to supporting eager and outspoken thread programmers. But
there are no portable standards for threaded analysis tools. If your vendor supports threads, you'll probably find at least a thread-safe version of prof, which is
a nearly universal UNIX tool. Each system will probably require different switches
and environments to use it safely for threads, and the output will differ.

Performance tuning requires more than just answering the traditional question, "How much time does the application spend in each function?" You have to
analyze contention on mutexes, for example. Mutexes with high contention may
need to be split into several mutexes controlling more specialized data (finer-
grain concurrency), which can improve performance by increasing concurrency.
If finer grain mutexes have low contention, combining them may improve performance by reducing locking overhead.

8.2.1 Beware of concurrent serialization

The ideal parallel code is a set of tasks that is completely compute-bound.
They never synchronize, they never block—they just "think." If you start with a
program that calls three compute-bound functions in series, and change it to
create three threads each running one of those functions, the program will run
(nearly) three times faster. At least, it should do so if you're running on a multiprocessor with at least three CPUs that are, at that moment, allocated for your
use.

The ideal concurrent code is a set of tasks that is completely I/O-bound. They
never synchronize, and do little computation—they just issue I/O requests and
wait for them. If you start with a program that writes chunks of data to three

separate files (ideally, on three separate disks, with separate controllers), and change it to create three threads, each writing one of those chunks of data, all three I/O operations can progress simultaneously.

But what if you've gone to all that trouble to write a set of compute-bound parallel or I/O-bound concurrent threads and it turns out that you've just converted a straight-line serialized program into a multithreaded serialized program? The result will be a slower program that accomplishes the same result with substantially more overhead. Most likely, that is not what you intended. How could that have happened?

Let's say that your compute-bound operations call `malloc` and `free` in their work. Those functions modify the static process state, so they need to perform some type of synchronization. Most likely, they lock a mutex. If your threads run in a loop calling `malloc` and `free`, such that a substantial amount of their total time may be spent within those functions, you may find that there's very little real parallelism. The threads will spend a lot of time blocked on the mutex while one thread or another allocates or frees memory.

Similarly, the concurrent I/O threads may be using serialized resources. If the threads perform "concurrent" I/O using the same *stdio* `FILE` stream, for example, they will be locking mutexes to update the stream's shared buffer. Even if the threads are using separate files, if they are on the same disk there will be locking within the file system to synchronize the file cache and so forth. Even when using separate disks, true concurrency may be subject to limitations in the I/O bus or disk controller subsystems.

The point of all this is that writing a program that uses threads doesn't magically grant parallelism or even concurrency to your application. When you're analyzing performance, be aware that your program can be affected by factors that aren't within your control. You may not even be able to see what's happening in the file system, but what you can't see *can* hurt you.

8.2.2 Use the right number of mutexes

The first step in making a library thread-safe may be to create a "big mutex" that protects all entries into the library. If only one thread can execute within the library at a time, then most functions will be thread-safe. At least, no static data will be corrupted. If the library has no persistent state that needs to remain consistent across a series of calls, the big mutex may seem to be enough. Many libraries are left in this state. The standard X11 client library (Xlib) provides limited support for this big mutex approach to thread-safety, and has for years.

But thread-safety isn't enough anymore—now you want the library to perform well with threads. In most cases, that will require redesigning the library so that multiple threads can use it at the same time. The big mutex serializes all operations in the library, so you are getting no concurrency or parallelization within the library. If use of that library is the primary function of your threads, the program would run faster with a single thread and no synchronization. That big mutex in Xlib, remember, keeps all other threads from using any Xlib function until the first thread has received its response from the server, and that might take quite a while.

Map out your library functions, and determine what operations can reasonably run in parallel. A common strategy is to create a separate mutex for each data structure, and use those mutexes to serialize access to the shared data, rather than using the "big mutex" to serialize access to the library.

With a profiler that supports threads, you can determine that you have too much mutex activity, by looking for hot spots within calls to `pthread_mutex_lock`, `pthread_mutex_unlock`, and `pthread_mutex_trylock`. However, this data will not be conclusive, and it may be very difficult to determine whether the high activity is due to too much mutex contention or too much locking without contention. You need more specific information on mutex contention and that requires special tools. Some thread development systems provide detailed visual tracing information that shows synchronization costs. Others provide "metering" information on individual mutexes to tell how many times the mutex was locked, and how often threads found the mutex already locked.

8.2.2.1 Too many mutexes will not help

Beware, too, of exchanging a "big" mutex for lots of "tiny" mutexes. You may make matters worse. Remember, it takes time to lock a mutex, and more time to unlock that mutex. Even if you increase parallelism by designing a locking hierarchy that has very little contention, your threads may spend so much time locking and unlocking all those mutexes that they get less real work done.

Locking a mutex also affects the memory subsystem. In addition to the time you spend locking and unlocking, you may decrease the efficiency of the memory system by excessive locking. Locking a mutex, for example, might invalidate a block of cache on all processors. It might stall all bus activity within some range of physical addresses.

So find out where you really need mutexes. For example, in the previous section I suggested creating a separate mutex for each data structure. Yet, if two data structures are usually used together, or if one thread will hardly ever need to use one data structure while another thread is using the second data structure, the extra mutex may decrease your overall performance.

8.2.3 Never fight over cache lines

No modern computer reads data directly from main memory. Memory that is fast enough to keep up with the computer is too expensive for that to be practical. Instead, data is fetched by the memory management unit into a fast local cache array. When the computer writes data, that, too, goes into the local cache array. The modified data may also be written to main memory immediately or may be "flushed" to memory only when needed.

So if one processor in a multiprocessor system needs to read a value that another processor has in its cache, there must be some "cache coherency" mechanism to ensure that it can find the correct data. More importantly, when one processor writes data to some location, all other processors that have older copies of that location in cache need to copy the new data, or record that the old data is invalid.

Computer systems commonly cache data in relatively large blocks of 64 or 128 bytes. That can improve efficiency by optimizing the references to slow main memory. It also means that, when the same 64- or 128-byte block is cached by multiple processors, and one processor writes to any part of that block, all processors caching the block must throw away the entire block.

This has serious implications for high-performance parallel computation. If two threads access different data within the same cache block, no thread will be able to take advantage of the (fast) cached copy on the processor it is using. Each read will require a new cache fill from main memory, slowing down the program.

Cache behavior may vary widely even on different computer systems using the same microprocessor chip. It is not possible to write code that is guaranteed to be optimal on all possible systems. You can substantially improve your chances, however, by being very careful to align and separate any performance-critical data used by multiple threads.

You can optimize your code for a particular computer system by determining the cache characteristics of that system, and designing your code so that no two threads will ever need to write to the same cache block within performance-critical parallel loops. About the best you can hope to do without optimizing for a particular system would be to ensure that each thread has a private, page-aligned, segment of data. It is highly unlikely that any system would use a cache block as large as a page, because a page includes far too much varied data to provide any performance advantage in the memory management unit.

9 POSIX threads mini-reference

This chapter is a compact reference to the POSIX.1c standard.

9.1 POSIX 1003.1c–1995 options

Pthreads is intended to address a wide variety of audiences. High-performance computational programs can use it to support parallel decomposition of loops. Realtime programs can use it to support concurrent realtime I/O. Database and network servers can use it to easily support concurrent clients. Business or software development programs can use it to take advantage of parallel and concurrent operations on time-sharing systems.

The Pthreads standard allows you to determine which optional capabilities are provided by the system, by defining a set of feature-test macros, which are shown in Table 9.1. Any implementation of Pthreads must inform you whether each option is supported, by three means:

- By making a formal statement of support in the POSIX Conformance Document. You can use this information to help design your application to work on specific systems.
- By defining compile-time symbolic constants in the <unistd.h> header file. You can test for these symbolic constants using #ifdef or #ifndef preprocessor conditionals to support a variety of Pthreads systems.

- By returning a positive nonzero value when the sysconf function is called with the associated sysconf symbol. (This is not usually useful for the "feature-test" macros that specify whether options are present—if they are not, the associated interfaces usually are not supplied, and your code will not link, and may not even compile.)

You might, for example, choose to avoid relying on priority scheduling because after reading the conformance documents you discovered that three out of the four systems you wish to support do not provide the feature. Or you might prefer to use priority inheritance for your mutexes on systems that provide the feature, but write the code so that it will not try to access the mutex *protocol* attribute on systems that do not provide that option.

Symbolic constant, sysconf symbol name	Description
_POSIX_THREADS _SC_THREADS	You can use threads (if your system doesn't define this, you're out of luck).
_POSIX_THREAD_ATTR_STACKSIZE _SC_THREAD_ATTR_STACKSIZE	You can control the size of a thread's stack.
_POSIX_THREAD_ATTR_STACKADDR _SC_THREAD_ATTR_STACKADDR	You can allocate and control a thread's stack.
_POSIX_THREAD_PRIORITY_SCHEDULING _SC_THREAD_PRIORITY_SCHEDULING	You can use realtime scheduling.
_POSIX_THREAD_PRIO_INHERIT _SC_THREAD_PRIO_INHERIT	You can create priority inheritance mutexes.
_POSIX_THREAD_PRIO_PROTECT _SC_THREAD_PRIO_PROTECT	You can create priority ceiling mutexes.
_POSIX_THREAD_PROCESS_SHARED _SC_THREAD_PROCESS_SHARED	You can create mutexes and condition variables that can be shared with another process.
_POSIX_THREAD_SAFE_FUNCTIONS _SC_THREAD_SAFE_FUNCTIONS	You can use the special "_r" library functions that provide thread-safe behavior.

TABLE 9.1   *POSIX 1003.1c–1995 options*

9.2 POSIX 1003.1c–1995 limits

The Pthreads standard allows you to determine the run-time limits of the system that may affect your application, for example, how many threads you can create, by defining a set of macros, which are shown in Table 9.2. Any implementation of Pthreads must inform you of its limits, by three means:

- By making a formal statement in the POSIX Conformance Document. You can use this information to help design your application to work on specific systems.
- By defining compile-time symbolic constants in the <limits.h> header file. The symbolic constant may be omitted from <limits.h> when the limit is at least as large as the required minimum, but cannot be determined at compile time, for example, if it depends on available memory space. You can test for these symbolic constants using #ifdef or #ifndef preprocessor conditionals.
- By returning a positive nonzero value when the sysconf function is called with the associated sysconf symbol.

You might, for example, design your application to rely on no more than 64 threads, if the conformance documents showed that three out of the four systems

Run-time invariant values, sysconf symbol name	Description
PTHREAD_DESTRUCTOR_ITERATIONS _SC_THREAD_DESTRUCTOR_ITERATIONS	Maximum number of attempts to destroy a thread's thread-specific data on termination (must be at least 4).
PTHREAD_KEYS_MAX _SC_THREAD_KEYS_MAX	Maximum number of thread-specific data keys available per process (must be at least 128).
PTHREAD_STACK_MIN _SC_THREAD_STACK_MIN	Minimum supported stack size for a thread.
PTHREAD_THREADS_MAX _SC_THREAD_THREADS_MAX	Maximum number of threads support-ed per process (must be at least 64).

TABLE 9.2 *POSIX 1003.1c–1995 limits*

you wish to support do not support additional threads. Or you might prefer to write conditional code that relies on the value of the PTHREAD_THREADS_MAX symbolic constant (if defined) or call sysconf to determine the limit at run time.

9.3 POSIX 1003.1c–1995 interfaces

The interfaces are sorted by functional categories: threads, mutexes, and so forth. Within each category, the interfaces are listed in alphabetical order. Figure 9.1 describes the format of the entries.

First, the *header* entry (1) shows the name of the interface. If the interface is an optional feature of Pthreads, then the name of the feature-test macro for that

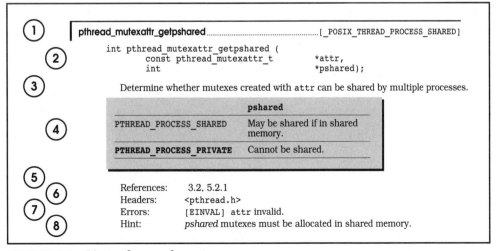

FIGURE 9.1 *Mini-reference format*

option is shown at the end of the line, in brackets. The interface `pthread_mutexattr_getpshared`, for example, is an option under the `_POSIX_THREAD_PROCESS_SHARED` feature.

The *prototype* entry (2) shows the full C language prototype for the interface, describing how to call the function, with all argument types.

The *description* entry (3) gives a brief synopsis of the interface. In this case, the purpose of the interface is to specify whether mutexes created using the attributes object can be shared between multiple processes.

Functions with arguments that have symbolic values, like `pshared` in this example, will include a table (4) that describes each possible value. The default value of the argument (the state of a new thread, or the default value of an attribute in a new attributes object, in this case `PTHREAD_PROCESS_PRIVATE`) is indicated by showing the name in bold.

The *references* entry (5) gives cross-references to the primary sections of this book that discuss the interface, or other closely related interfaces.

The *headers* entry (6) shows the header files needed to compile code using the function. If more than one header is shown, you need all of them.

The *errors* entry (7) describes each of the possible error numbers returned by the interface; Because Pthreads distinguishes between mandatory error detection ("if occurs" in POSIX terms) and optional error detection ("if detected" in POSIX terms), the errors that an interface must report (if they occur) are shown in bold (see Section 9.3.1 for details on Pthreads errors).

The *hint* entry (8) gives a single, and inevitably oversimplified, philosophical comment regarding the interface. Some hints point out common errors in using the interface; others describe something about the designers' intended use of the interface, or some fundamental restriction of the interface. In `pthread_mutexattr_getpshared`, for example, the hint points out that a mutex created to be "process shared" must be allocated in shared memory that's accessible by all participating processes.

9.3.1 Error detection and reporting

The POSIX standard distinguishes carefully between two categories of error:

1. Mandatory ("if occurs") errors involve circumstances beyond the control of the programmer. These errors must always be detected and reported by the system using a particular error code. If you cannot create a new thread because your process lacks sufficient virtual memory, then the implementation must always tell you. You can't possibly be expected to check whether there's enough memory before creating the thread—for one thing, you have no way to know how much memory would be required.
2. Optional ("if detected") errors are problems that are usually your mistake. You might try to lock a mutex that hadn't been initialized, for example, or try to unlock a mutex that's locked by another thread. Some systems may

not detect these errors, but they're still errors in your code, and you ought to be able to avoid them without help from the system.

While it would be "nice" for the system to detect optional errors and return the appropriate error number, sometimes it takes a lot of time to check or is difficult to check reliably. It may be expensive, for example, for the system to determine the identity of the current thread. Systems may therefore not remember which thread locked a mutex, and would be unable to detect that the unlock was erroneous. It may not make sense to slow down the basic synchronization operations for correct programs just to make it a little easier to debug incorrect programs.

Systems may provide debugging modes where some or all of the optional errors are detected. Digital UNIX, for example, provides "error check" mutexes and a "metered" execution mode, where the ownership of mutexes is always tracked and optional errors in locking and unlocking mutexes are reported. The UNIX98 specification includes "error check" mutexes (Section 10.1.2), so they will soon be available on most UNIX systems.

9.3.2 Use of `void*` type

ANSI C requires that you be allowed to convert any pointer type to `void*` and back, with the result being identical to the original value. However, ANSI C does not require that all pointer types have the same binary representation. Thus, a `long*` that you convert to `void*` in order to pass into a thread's start routine must always be used as a `long*`, not as, for example, a `char*`. In addition, the result of converting between pointer and integer types is "implementation defined." Most systems supporting UNIX will allow you to cast an integer value to `void*` and back, and to mix pointer types—but be aware that the code may not work on all systems.

Some other standards, notably the POSIX.1b realtime standard, have solved the same problem (the need for an argument or structure member that can take any type value) in different ways. The `sigevent` structure in POSIX.1b, for example, includes a member that contains a value to be passed into a signal-catching function, called `sigev_value`. Instead of defining `sigev_value` as a `void*`, however, and relying on the programmer to provide proper type casting, the `sigev_value` member is a `union sigval`, containing overlayed `int` and `void*` members. This mechanism avoids the problem of converting between integer and pointer types, eliminating one of the conflicts with ANSI C guarantees.

9.3.3 Threads

Threads provide *concurrency*, the ability to have more than one "stream of execution" within a process at the same time. Each thread has its own hardware registers and stack. All threads in a process share the full virtual address space, plus all file descriptors, signal actions, and other process resources.

pthread_attr_destroy

```
int pthread_attr_destroy (
        pthread_attr_t   *attr);
```

Destroy a thread attributes object. The object can no longer be used.

References: 2, 5.2.3
Headers: <pthread.h>
Errors: [EINVAL] attr is invalid.
Hint: Does not affect threads created using attr.

pthread_attr_getdetachstate

```
int pthread_attr_getdetachstate (
        const pthread_attr_t    *attr,
        int                     *detachstate);
```

Determine whether threads created with attr will run detached.

	detachstate
PTHREAD_CREATE_JOINABLE	Thread ID is valid, must be joined.
PTHREAD_CREATE_DETACHED	Thread ID is invalid, cannot be joined, canceled, or modified.

References: 2, 5.2.3
Headers: <pthread.h>
Errors: [EINVAL] attr is invalid.
Hint: You can't join or cancel detached threads.

pthread_attr_getstackaddr .... [_POSIX_THREAD_ATTR_STACKADDR]

```
int pthread_attr_getstackaddr (
        const pthread_attr_t    *attr,
        void                    **stackaddr);
```

Determine the address of the stack on which threads created with attr will run.

References: 2, 5.2.3
Headers: <pthread.h>
Errors: [EINVAL] attr is invalid.
               [ENOSYS] stacksize not supported.
Hint: Create only one thread for each stack address!

pthread_attr_getstacksize ....[_POSIX_THREAD_ATTR_STACKSIZE]

```
int pthread_attr_getstacksize (
        const pthread_attr_t    *attr,
        size_t                  *stacksize);
```

Determine the size of the stack on which threads created with attr will run.

References: 2, 5.2.3
Headers: <pthread.h>
Errors: [EINVAL] attr invalid.
               [ENOSYS] stacksize not supported.
Hint: Use on newly created attributes object to find the default stack size.

pthread_attr_init

```
int pthread_attr_init (
        pthread_attr_t    *attr);
```

Initialize a thread attributes object with default attributes.

References: 2, 5.2.3
Headers: <pthread.h>
Errors: **[ENOMEM]** insufficient memory for attr.
Hint: Use to define thread types.

pthread_attr_setdetachstate

```
int pthread_attr_setdetachstate (
        pthread_attr_t    *attr,
        int               detachstate);
```

Specify whether threads created with attr will run *detached*.

	detachstate
PTHREAD_CREATE_JOINABLE	Thread ID is valid, must be joined.
PTHREAD_CREATE_DETACHED	Thread ID is invalid, cannot be joined, canceled, or modified.

References: 2, 5.2.3
Headers: <pthread.h>
Errors: [EINVAL] attr invalid.
               [EINVAL] detachstate invalid.
Hint: You can't join or cancel detached threads.

pthread_attr_setstackaddr .... [_POSIX_THREAD_ATTR_STACKADDR]

```
int pthread_attr_setstackaddr (
        pthread_attr_t  *attr,
        void            *stackaddr);
```

Threads created with `attr` will run on the stack starting at `stackaddr`. Must be at least `PTHREAD_STACK_MIN` bytes.

References: 2, 5.2.3
Headers: <pthread.h>
Errors: [EINVAL] attr invalid.
               [ENOSYS] stackaddr not supported.
Hint: Create only one thread for each stack address, and be careful of stack alignment.

pthread_attr_setstacksize .... [_POSIX_THREAD_ATTR_STACKSIZE]

```
int pthread_attr_setstacksize (
        pthread_attr_t  *attr,
        size_t          stacksize);
```

Threads created with `attr` will run on a stack of at least `stacksize` bytes. Must be at least `PTHREAD_STACK_MIN` bytes.

References: 2, 5.2.3
Headers: <pthread.h>
Errors: [EINVAL] attr or stacksize invalid.
               [EINVAL] stacksize too small or too big.
               [ENOSYS] stacksize not supported.
Hint: Find the default first (pthread_attr_getstacksize), then increase by multiplying. Use only if a thread needs more than the default.

pthread_create

```
int pthread_create (
        pthread_t              *tid,
        const pthread_attr_t   *attr,
        void                   *(*start) (void *),
        void                   *arg);
```

Create a thread running the start function, essentially an asynchronous call to the function start with argument value `arg`. The `attr` argument specifies optional creation attributes, and the identification of the new thread is returned in `tid`.

References: 2, 5.2.3
Headers: <pthread.h>
Errors: **[EINVAL]** attr invalid.
               [EAGAIN] insufficient resources.
Hint: All resources needed by thread must already be initialized.

pthread_detach

```
int pthread_detach (
        pthread_t               thread);
```

Detach the `thread`. Use this to detach the main thread or to "change your mind" after creating a joinable thread in which you are no longer interested.

References: 2, 5.2.3
Headers: <pthread.h>
Errors: [EINVAL] thread is not a joinable thread.
             [ESRCH] no thread could be found for ID thread.
Hint: Detached threads cannot be joined or canceled; storage is freed immediately on termination.

pthread_equal

```
int pthread_equal (
        pthread_t               t1,
        pthread_t               t2);
```

Return value 0 if `t1` and `t2` are equal, otherwise return nonzero.

References: 2, 5.2.3
Headers: <pthread.h>
Hint: Compare pthread_self against stored thread identifier.

pthread_exit

```
int pthread_exit (
        void                    *value_ptr);
```

Terminate the calling `thread`, returning the value `value_ptr` to any joining thread.

References: 2, 5.2.3
Headers: <pthread.h>
Hint: value_ptr is treated as a value, not the address of a value.

pthread_join

```
int pthread_join (
        pthread_t               thread,
        void                    **value_ptr);
```

Wait for `thread` to terminate, and return thread's exit value if `value_ptr` is not NULL. This also detaches `thread` on successful completion.

References: 2, 5.2.3
Headers: <pthread.h>
Errors: [EINVAL] thread is not a joinable thread.
             [ESRCH] no thread could be found for ID thread.
             [EDEADLK] attempt to join with self.
Hint: Detached threads cannot be joined or canceled.

pthread_self

```
pthread_t pthread_self (void);
```

Return the calling thread's ID.

References: 2, 5.2.3
Headers: <pthread.h>
Hint: Use to set thread's scheduling parameters.

sched_yield

```
int sched_yield (void);
```

Make the calling thread *ready*, after other *ready* threads of the same priority, and select a new thread to run. This can allow cooperating threads of the same priority to share processor resources more equitably, especially on a uniprocessor. This function is from POSIX.1b (realtime extensions), and is declared in <sched.h>. It reports errors by setting the return value to –1 and storing an error code in errno.

References: 2, 5.2.3
Headers: <sched.h>
Errors: **[ENOSYS]** sched_yield not supported.
Hint: Use before locking mutex to reduce chances of a timeslice while mutex is locked.

9.3.4 Mutexes

Mutexes provide *synchronization,* the ability to control how threads share resources. You use mutexes to prevent multiple threads from modifying shared data at the same time, and to ensure that a thread can read consistent values for a set of resources (for example, memory) that may be modified by other threads.

pthread_mutexattr_destroy

```
int pthread_mutexattr_destroy (
        pthread_mutexattr_t     *attr);
```

Destroy a mutex attributes object. The object can no longer be used.

References: 3.2, 5.2.1
Headers: <pthread.h>
Errors: [EINVAL] attr invalid.
Hint: Does not affect mutexes created using attr.

pthread_mutexattr_getpshared..[_POSIX_THREAD_PROCESS_SHARED]

```
int pthread_mutexattr_getpshared (
        const pthread_mutexattr_t      *attr,
        int                            *pshared);
```

Determine whether mutexes created with `attr` can be shared by multiple processes.

	pshared
PTHREAD_PROCESS_SHARED	May be shared if in shared memory.
PTHREAD_PROCESS_PRIVATE	Cannot be shared.

References: 3.2, 5.2.1
Headers: <pthread.h>
Errors: [EINVAL] attr invalid.
Hint: *pshared* mutexes must be allocated in shared memory.

pthread_mutexattr_init

```
int pthread_mutexattr_init (
        pthread_mutexattr_t    *attr);
```

Initialize a mutex attributes object with default attributes.

References: 3.2, 5.2.1
Headers: <pthread.h>
Errors: **[ENOMEM]** insufficient memory for `attr`.
Hint: Use to define mutex types.

pthread_mutexattr_setpshared..[_POSIX_THREAD_PROCESS_SHARED]

```
int pthread_mutexattr_setpshared (
        pthread_mutexattr_t    *attr,
        int                    pshared);
```

Mutexes created with `attr` can be shared between processes if the `pthread_mutex_t` variable is allocated in memory shared by the processes.

	pshared
PTHREAD_PROCESS_SHARED	May be shared if in shared memory.
PTHREAD_PROCESS_PRIVATE	Cannot be shared.

References: 3.2, 5.2.1
Headers: <pthread.h>
Errors: [EINVAL] attr or detachstate invalid.
Hint: *pshared* mutexes must be allocated in shared memory.

pthread_mutex_destroy

```
int pthread_mutex_destroy (
        pthread_mutex_t                        *mutex);
```

Destroy a mutex that you no longer need.

References: 3.2, 5.2.1
Headers: <pthread.h>
Errors: [EBUSY] mutex is in use.
                [EINVAL] mutex is invalid.
Hint: Safest after unlocking mutex, when no other threads will lock.

pthread_mutex_init

```
int pthread_mutex_init (
        pthread_mutex_t                        *mutex,
        const pthread_mutexattr_t              *attr);
```

Initialize a mutex. The attr argument specifies optional creation attributes.

References: 3.2, 5.2.1
Headers: <pthread.h>
Errors: **[EAGAIN]** insufficient resources (other than memory).
                [ENOMEM] insufficient memory.
                [EPERM] no privilege to perform operation.
                [EBUSY] mutex is already initialized.
                [EINVAL] attr is invalid.
Hint: Use static initialization instead, if possible.

pthread_mutex_lock

```
int pthread_mutex_lock (
        pthread_mutex_t                        *mutex);
```

Lock a mutex. If the mutex is currently locked, the calling thread is blocked until mutex is unlocked. On return, the thread owns the mutex until it calls pthread_mutex_unlock.

References: 3.2, 5.2.1
Headers: <pthread.h>
Errors: **[EINVAL]** thread priority exceeds mutex priority ceiling.
                [EINVAL] mutex is invalid.
                [EDEADLK] calling thread already owns mutex.
Hint: Always unlock within the same thread.

pthread_mutex_trylock

```
int pthread_mutex_trylock (
        pthread_mutex_t                      *mutex);
```

Lock a `mutex`. If the `mutex` is currently locked, returns immediately with `EBUSY`. Otherwise, calling thread becomes owner until it unlocks.

References: 3.2, 5.2.1
Headers: `<pthread.h>`
Errors: **[EINVAL]** thread priority exceeds mutex priority ceiling.
    [EBUSY] mutex is already locked.
    [EINVAL] mutex is invalid.
    [EDEADLK] calling thread already owns `mutex`.
Hint: Always unlock within the same thread.

pthread_mutex_unlock

```
int pthread_mutex_unlock (
        pthread_mutex_t                      *mutex);
```

Unlock a `mutex`. The mutex becomes unowned. If any threads are waiting for the mutex, one is awakened (scheduling policy `SCHED_FIFO` and `SCHED_RR` policy waiters are chosen in priority order, then any others are chosen in unspecified order).

References: 3.2, 5.2.1
Headers: `<pthread.h>`
Errors: [EINVAL] mutex is invalid.
    [EPERM] calling thread does not own `mutex`.
Hint: Always unlock within the same thread.

9.3.5 Condition variables

Condition variables provide *communication,* the ability to wait for some shared resource to reach some desired state, or to signal that it has reached some state in which another thread may be interested. Each condition variable is closely associated with a mutex that protects the state of the resource.

pthread_condattr_destroy

```
int pthread_condattr_destroy (
        pthread_condattr_t      *attr);
```

Destroy a condition variable attributes object. The object can no longer be used.

References: 3.3, 5.2.2
Headers: `<pthread.h>`
Errors: [EINVAL] attr invalid.
Hint: Does not affect condition variables created using `attr`.

pthread_condattr_getpshared...[_POSIX_THREAD_PROCESS_SHARED]

```
int pthread_condattr_getpshared (
        const pthread_condattr_t        *attr,
        int                             *pshared);
```

Determine whether condition variables created with `attr` can be shared by multiple processes.

	pshared
PTHREAD_PROCESS_SHARED	May be shared if in shared memory.
PTHREAD_PROCESS_PRIVATE	Cannot be shared.

References: 3.3, 5.2.2
Headers: <pthread.h>
Errors: [EINVAL] attr invalid.
Hint: *pshared* condition variables must be allocated in shared memory and used with *pshared* mutexes.

pthread_condattr_init

```
int pthread_condattr_init (
        pthread_condattr_t       *attr);
```

Initialize a condition variable attributes object with default attributes.

References: 3.3, 5.2.2
Headers: <pthread.h>
Errors: **[ENOMEM]** insufficient memory for `attr`.
Hint: Use to define condition variable types.

pthread_condattr_setpshared...[_POSIX_THREAD_PROCESS_SHARED]

```
int pthread_condattr_setpshared (
        pthread_condattr_t       *attr,
        int                      pshared);
```

Condition variables created with `attr` can be shared between processes if the `pthread_cond_t` variable is allocated in memory shared by the processes.

	pshared
PTHREAD_PROCESS_SHARED	May be shared if in shared memory.
PTHREAD_PROCESS_PRIVATE	Cannot be shared.

References: 3.3, 5.2.2
Headers: <pthread.h>
Errors: [EINVAL] attr or detachstate invalid.
Hint: *pshared* condition variables must be allocated in shared memory
               and used with *pshared* mutexes.

pthread_cond_destroy

```
int pthread_cond_destroy (
        pthread_cond_t                  *cond);
```

Destroy condition variable cond that you no longer need.

References: 3.3, 5.2.2
Headers: <pthread.h>
Errors: [EBUSY] cond is in use.
               [EINVAL] cond is invalid.
Hint: Safest after wakeup from cond, when no other threads will wait.

pthread_cond_init

```
int pthread_cond_init (
        pthread_cond_t                  *cond,
        const pthread_condattr_t        *attr);
```

Initialize a condition variable cond. The attr argument specifies optional creation
attributes.

References: 3.3, 5.2.2
Headers: <pthread.h>
Errors: **[EAGAIN]** insufficient resources (other than memory).
               [ENOMEM] insufficient memory.
               [EBUSY] cond is already initialized.
               [EINVAL] attr is invalid.
Hint: Use static initialization instead, if possible.

pthread_cond_broadcast

```
int pthread_cond_broadcast (
        pthread_cond_t                  *cond);
```

Broadcast condition variable cond, waking all current waiters.

References: 3.3, 5.2.2
Headers: <pthread.h>
Errors: [EINVAL] cond is invalid.
Hint: Use when more than one waiter may respond to predicate change
               or if any waiting thread may not be able to respond.

pthread_cond_signal

```
int pthread_cond_signal (
        pthread_cond_t                  *cond);
```

Signal condition variable cond, waking one waiting thread. If SCHED_FIFO or SCHED_RR policy threads are waiting, the highest-priority waiter is awakened. Otherwise, an unspecified waiter is awakened.

References: 3.3, 5.2.2
Headers: <pthread.h>
Errors: [EINVAL] cond is invalid.
Hint: Use when any waiter can respond, and only one need respond. (All waiters are equal.)

pthread_cond_timedwait

```
int pthread_cond_timedwait (
        pthread_cond_t                  *cond,
        pthread_mutex_t                 *mutex,
        const struct timespec           *abstime);
```

Wait on condition variable cond, until awakened by a signal or broadcast, or until the absolute time abstime is reached.

References: 3.3, 5.2.2
Headers: <pthread.h>
Errors: **[ETIMEDOUT]** time specified by abstime has passed.
               [EINVAL] cond, mutex, or abstime is invalid.
               [EINVAL] different mutexes for concurrent waits.
               [EINVAL] mutex is not owned by calling thread.
Hint: Mutex is always unlocked (before wait) and relocked (after wait) inside pthread_cond_timedwait, even if the wait fails, times out, or is canceled.

pthread_cond_wait

```
int pthread_cond_wait (
        pthread_cond_t                  *cond,
        pthread_mutex_t                 *mutex);
```

Wait on condition variable cond, until awakened by a signal or broadcast.

References: 3.3, 5.2.2
Headers: <pthread.h>
Errors: [EINVAL] cond or mutex is invalid.
               [EINVAL] different mutexes for concurrent waits.
               [EINVAL] mutex is not owned by calling thread.
Hint: Mutex is always unlocked (before wait) and relocked (after wait) inside pthread_cond_wait, even if the wait fails or is canceled.

9.3.6 Cancellation

Cancellation provides a way to request that a thread terminate "gracefully" when you no longer need it to complete its normal execution. Each thread can control how and whether cancellation affects it, and can repair the shared state as it terminates due to cancellation.

---

pthread_cancel

```
int pthread_cancel (
        pthread_t        thread);
```

Requests that `thread` be canceled.

References: 5.3
Headers: `<pthread.h>`
Errors: `[ESRCH]` no `thread` found corresponding to `thread`.
Hint: Cancellation is asynchronous. Use `pthread_join` to wait for termination of `thread` if necessary.

---

pthread_cleanup_pop

```
void pthread_cleanup_pop (int execute);
```

Pop the most recently pushed cleanup handler. Invoke the cleanup handler if execute is nonzero.

References: 5.3
Headers: `<pthread.h>`
Hint: Specify `execute` as nonzero to avoid duplication of common cleanup code.

---

pthread_cleanup_push

```
void pthread_cleanup_push (
        void             (*routine)(void *),
        void             *arg);
```

Push a new cleanup handler onto the thread's stack of cleanup handlers. Invoke the cleanup handler if execute is nonzero. Each cleanup handler pushed onto the stack is popped and invoked with the argument `arg` when the thread exits by calling `pthread_exit`, when the thread acts on a cancellation request, or when the thread calls `pthread_cleanup_pop` with a nonzero execute argument.

References: 5.3
Headers: `<pthread.h>`
Hint: `pthread_cleanup_push` and `pthread_cleanup_pop` must be paired in the same lexical scope.

pthread_setcancelstate

```
int pthread_setcancelstate (
        int             state,
        int             *oldstate);
```

Atomically set the calling thread's cancelability state to `state` and return the previous cancelability state at the location referenced by `oldstate`.

	state, oldstate
PTHREAD_CANCEL_ENABLE	Cancellation is enabled.
PTHREAD_CANCEL_DISABLE	Cancellation is disabled.

References: 5.3
Headers: <pthread.h>
Errors: [EINVAL] state is invalid.
Hint: Use to disable cancellation around "atomic" code that includes cancellation points.

pthread_setcanceltype

```
int pthread_setcanceltype (
        int             type,
        int             *oldtype);
```

Atomically set the calling thread's cancelability type to `type` and return the previous cancelability type at the location referenced by `oldtype`.

	type, oldtype
PTHREAD_CANCEL_DEFERRED	Only deferred cancellation is allowed.
PTHREAD_CANCEL_ASYNCHRONOUS	Asynchronous cancellation is allowed.

References: 5.3
Headers: <pthread.h>
Errors: [EINVAL] type is invalid.
Hint: Use with caution—most code is not safe for use with asynchronous cancelability type.

pthread_testcancel

```
void pthread_testcancel (void);
```

Creates a deferred cancellation point in the calling thread. The call has no effect if the current cancelability state is PTHREAD_CANCEL_DISABLE.

References:	5.3
Headers:	<pthread.h>
Hint:	Cancellation is asynchronous. Use pthread_join to wait for termination of thread if necessary.

9.3.7 Thread-specific data

Thread-specific data provides a way to declare variables that have a common "name" in all threads, but a unique value in each thread. You should consider using thread-specific data in a threaded program in many cases where a non-threaded program would use "static" data. When the static data maintains context across a series of calls to some function, for example, the context should generally be thread-specific. (If not, the static data must be protected by a mutex.)

pthread_getspecific

```
void *pthread_getspecific (
        pthread_key_t    key);
```

Return the current value of key in the calling thread. If no value has been set for key in the thread, NULL is returned.

References:	5.4, 7.2, 7.3.1
Headers:	<pthread.h>
Errors:	The effect of calling pthread_getspecific with an invalid key is undefined. No errors are detected.
Hint:	Calling pthread_getspecific in a destructor function will return NULL. Use destructor's argument instead.

pthread_key_create

```
int pthread_key_create (
        pthread_key_t    *key,
        void             (*destructor)(void *));
```

Create a thread-specific data key visible to all threads. All existing and new threads have value NULL for key until set using pthread_setspecific. When any thread with a non-NULL value for key terminates, destructor is called with key's current value for that thread.

References: 5.4, 7.2, 7.3.1
Headers: <pthread.h>
Errors: **[EAGAIN]** insufficient resources or `PTHREAD_KEYS_MAX` exceeded.
                 [ENOMEM] insufficient memory to create the key.
Hint: Each key (`pthread_key_t` variable) must be created only once; use
                 a mutex or `pthread_once`.

pthread_key_delete

```
int pthread_key_delete (
        pthread_key_t    key);
```

Delete a thread-specific data key. This does not change the value of the thread-specific data key for any thread and does not run the key's destructor in any thread, so it should be used with great caution.

References: 5.4
Headers: <pthread.h>
Errors: [EINVAL] key is invalid.
Hint: Use only when you know all threads have NULL value.

pthread_setspecific

```
int pthread_setspecific (
        pthread_key_t    key,
        const void       *value);
```

Associate a thread-specific `value` within the calling thread for the specified key.

References: 5.4, 7.2, 7.3.1
Headers: <pthread.h>
Errors: **[ENOMEM]** insufficient memory.
                 [EINVAL] key is invalid.
Hint: If you set a `value` of NULL, the key's destructor will not be called at
                 thread termination.

9.3.8 Realtime scheduling

Realtime scheduling provides a predictable response time to important events within the process. Note that "predictable" does not always mean "fast," and in many cases realtime scheduling may impose overhead that results in slower execution. Realtime scheduling is also subject to synchronization problems such as priority inversion (Sections 5.5.4 and 8.1.4), although Pthreads provides optional facilities to address some of these problems.

pthread_attr_getinheritsched................................... [_POSIX_THREAD_PRIORITY_SCHEDULING]

```
int pthread_attr_getinheritsched (
        const pthread_attr_t    *attr,
        int                     *inheritsched);
```

Determine whether threads created with `attr` will run using the scheduling policy and parameters of the creator or those specified in the attributes object. The default `inheritsched` is implementation-defined.

	inheritsched
PTHREAD_INHERIT_SCHED	Use creator's scheduling policy and parameters.
PTHREAD_EXPLICIT_SCHED	Use scheduling policy and parameters in attributes object.

References: 5.2.3, 5.5
Headers: <pthread.h>
Errors: **[ENOSYS]** priority scheduling is not supported.
[EINVAL] attr invalid.

pthread_attr_getschedparam...................................... [_POSIX_THREAD_PRIORITY_SCHEDULING]

```
int pthread_attr_getschedparam (
        const pthread_attr_t    *attr,
        struct sched_param      *param);
```

Determine the scheduling parameters used by threads created with `attr`. The default `param` is implementation defined.

References: 5.2.3, 5.5
Headers: <pthread.h>
Errors: **[ENOSYS]** priority scheduling is not supported.
[EINVAL] attr invalid.

pthread_attr_getschedpolicy...................................... [_POSIX_THREAD_PRIORITY_SCHEDULING]

```
int pthread_attr_getschedpolicy (
        const pthread_attr_t    *attr,
        int                     *policy);
```

Determine the scheduling policy used by threads created with `attr`. The default `policy` is implementation defined.

	policy
SCHED_FIFO	Run thread until it blocks; preempt lower-priority threads when ready.
SCHED_RR	Like SCHED_FIFO, but subject to periodic timeslicing.
SCHED_OTHER	Implementation defined (may be SCHED_FIFO, SCHED_RR, or something else).

References: 5.2.3, 5.5
Headers: <pthread.h>
Errors: **[ENOSYS]** priority scheduling is not supported.
              [EINVAL] attr invalid.

---

pthread_attr_getscope .... [_POSIX_THREAD_PRIORITY_SCHEDULING]

```
int pthread_attr_getscope (
        const pthread_attr_t        *attr,
        int                         *contentionscope);
```

Determine the contention scope used by threads created with attr. The default is implementation defined.

	contentionscope
PTHREAD_SCOPE_PROCESS	Thread contends with other threads in the process for processor resources.
PTHREAD_SCOPE_SYSTEM	Thread contends with threads in all processes for processor resources.

References: 5.2.3, 5.5
Headers: <pthread.h>
Errors: **[ENOSYS]** priority scheduling is not supported.
              [EINVAL] attr invalid.
Hint: Implementation must support one or both of these, but need not support both.

pthread_attr_setinheritsched .... [_POSIX_THREAD_PRIORITY_SCHEDULING]

```
int pthread_attr_setinheritsched (
        pthread_attr_t    *attr,
        int               inheritsched);
```

Specify whether threads created with `attr` will run using the scheduling policy and parameters of the creator or those specified in the attributes object. When you change the scheduling policy or parameters in a thread attributes object, you must change the *inheritsched* attribute from `PTHREAD_INHERIT_SCHED` to `PTHREAD_EXPLICIT_SCHED`. The default is implementation-defined.

	inheritsched
`PTHREAD_INHERIT_SCHED`	Use creator's scheduling policy and parameters.
`PTHREAD_EXPLICIT_SCHED`	Use scheduling policy and parameters in attributes object.

References:	5.2.3, 5.5
Headers:	<pthread.h>
Errors:	**[ENOSYS]** priority scheduling is not supported.
	[EINVAL] attr or inheritsched invalid.

pthread_attr_setschedparam .... [_POSIX_THREAD_PRIORITY_SCHEDULING]

```
int pthread_attr_setschedparam (
        pthread_attr_t              *attr,
        const struct sched_param    *param);
```

Specify the scheduling parameters used by threads created with `attr`. The default `param` is implementation defined.

References:	5.2.3, 5.5
Headers:	<pthread.h>
Errors:	**[ENOSYS]** priority scheduling is not supported.
	[EINVAL] attr or param invalid.
	[ENOTSUP] param set to supported value.

pthread_attr_setschedpolicy .... [_POSIX_THREAD_PRIORITY_SCHEDULING]

```
int pthread_attr_setschedpolicy (
        pthread_attr_t    *attr,
        int               policy);
```

Specify the scheduling policy used by threads created with `attr`. The default `policy` is implementation defined.

	policy
SCHED_FIFO	Run thread until it blocks; preempt lower-priority threads when ready.
SCHED_RR	Like SCHED_FIFO, but subject to periodic timeslicing.
SCHED_OTHER	Implementation defined (may be SCHED_FIFO, SCHED_RR, or something else).

References: 5.2.3, 5.5
Headers: <pthread.h>
Errors: **[ENOSYS]** priority scheduling is not supported.
               [EINVAL] attr or policy invalid.
               [ENOTSUP] param set to supported value.

---

pthread_attr_setscope .... [_POSIX_THREAD_PRIORITY_SCHEDULING]

```
int pthread_attr_setscope (
        pthread_attr_t  *attr,
        int             contentionscope);
```

Specify the contention scope used by threads created with attr. The default is implementation defined.

	contentionscope
PTHREAD_SCOPE_PROCESS	Thread contends with other threads in the process for processor resources.
PTHREAD_SCOPE_SYSTEM	Thread contends with threads in all processes for processor resources.

References: 5.2.3, 5.5
Headers: <pthread.h>
Errors: **[ENOSYS]** priority scheduling is not supported.
               [EINVAL] attr or contentionscope invalid.
               [ENOTSUP] contentionscope set to supported value.
Hint: Implementation must support one or both of these, but need not support both.

pthread_getschedparam .... [_POSIX_THREAD_PRIORITY_SCHEDULING]

```
int pthread_getschedparam (
        pthread_t                    thread,
        int                          *policy
        struct sched_param           *param);
```

Determine the scheduling policy and parameters (param) currently used by thread.

	policy
SCHED_FIFO	Run thread until it blocks; preempt lower-priority threads when ready.
SCHED_RR	Like SCHED_FIFO, but subject to periodic timeslicing.
SCHED_OTHER	Implementation defined (may be SCHED_FIFO, SCHED_RR, or something else).

References: 5.2.3, 5.5
Headers: <pthread.h>
Errors: **[ENOSYS]** priority scheduling is not supported.
              [ESRCH] thread does not refer to an existing thread.
Hint: Try to avoid dynamically modifying thread scheduling policy and
              parameters, if possible.

pthread_mutex_getprioceiling .... [_POSIX_THREAD_PRIO_PROTECT]

```
int pthread_mutex_getprioceiling (
        const pthread_mutex_t    *mutex,
        int                      *prioceiling);
```

Determine the priority ceiling at which threads will run while owning mutex.

References: 3.2, 5.2.1, 5.5.5
Headers: <pthread.h>
Errors: **[ENOSYS]** priority scheduling is not supported.
              [EINVAL] mutex invalid.
Hint: *Protect* protocol is inappropriate unless the creator of the mutex
              also creates and controls all threads that might lock the mutex.

pthread_mutex_setprioceiling.. [_POSIX_THREAD_PRIO_PROTECT]

```
int pthread_mutex_getprioceiling (
       pthread_mutex_t  *mutex,
       int              prioceiling,
       int              *old_ceiling);
```

Specify the priority ceiling at which threads will run while owning `mutex`. Returns previous priority ceiling for mutex.

References:	3.2, 5.2.1, 5.5.5
Headers:	<pthread.h>
Errors:	**[ENOSYS]** priority scheduling is not supported.
	[EINVAL] mutex invalid, or `prioceiling` out of range.
	[EPERM] no privilege to set `prioceiling`.
Hint:	*Protect* protocol is inappropriate unless the creator of the mutex also creates and controls all threads that might lock the mutex.

pthread_mutexattr_getprioceiling... [_POSIX_THREAD_PRIO_PROTECT]

```
int pthread_mutexattr_getprioceiling (
       const pthread_mutexattr_t    *attr,
       int                          *prioceiling);
```

Determine the priority ceiling at which threads will run while owning a mutex created with `attr`.

References:	3.2, 5.2.1, 5.5.5
Headers:	<pthread.h>
Errors:	**[ENOSYS]** priority scheduling is not supported.
	[EINVAL] attr invalid.
Hint:	*Protect* protocol is inappropriate unless the creator of the mutex also creates and controls all threads that might lock the mutex.

pthread_mutexattr_getprotocol...[_POSIX_THREAD_PRIO_INHERIT_POSIX_THREAD_PRIO_PROTECT]

```
int pthread_mutexattr_getprotocol (
       const pthread_mutexattr_t    *attr,
       int                          *protocol);
```

Determine whether mutexes created with `attr` have priority ceiling protocol (*protect*), priority inheritance protocol (*inherit*), or no priority protocol (*none*).

	protocol
PTHREAD_PRIO_NONE	No priority inheritance protocol.
PTHREAD_PRIO_INHERIT	While owning mutex, thread inherits highest priority of any thread waiting for the mutex.
PTHREAD_PRIO_PROTECT	While owning mutex, thread inherits mutex priority ceiling.

References: 3.2, 5.2.1, 5.5.5
Headers: <pthread.h>
Errors: **[ENOSYS]** priority scheduling is not supported.
             [EINVAL] attr invalid.
Hint: *Inherit* protocol is expensive, and *protect* protocol is inappropriate unless the creator of the mutex also creates and controls all threads that might lock the mutex.

---

pthread_mutexattr_setprioceiling..[_POSIX_THREAD_PRIO_PROTECT]

```
int pthread_mutexattr_setprioceiling (
        pthread_mutexattr_t       *attr,
        int                       prioceiling);
```

Specify the priority ceiling at which threads will run while owning a mutex created with `attr`. The value of `prioceiling` must be a valid priority parameter for the `SCHED_FIFO` policy.

References: 3.2, 5.2.1, 5.5.5
Headers: <pthread.h>
Errors: **[ENOSYS]** priority scheduling is not supported.
             [EINVAL] attr or prioceiling invalid.
             [EPERM] no permission to set prioceiling.
Hint: *Protect* protocol is inappropriate unless the creator of the mutex also creates and controls all threads that might lock the mutex.

---

pthread_mutexattr_setprotocol ....(_POSIX_THREAD_PRIO_INHERIT_POSIX_THREAD_PRIO_PROTECT]

```
int pthread_mutexattr_setprotocol (
        pthread_mutexattr_t       *attr,
        int                       protocol);
```

Specify whether mutexes created with `attr` have priority ceiling protocol (*protect*), priority inheritance protocol (*inherit*), or no priority protocol (*none*).

	protocol
PTHREAD_PRIO_NONE	No priority inheritance protocol.
PTHREAD_PRIO_INHERIT	While owning mutex, thread inherits highest priority of any thread waiting for the mutex.
PTHREAD_PRIO_PROTECT	While owning mutex, thread inherits mutex priority ceiling.

References: 3.2, 5.2.1, 5.5.5
Headers: <pthread.h>
Errors: **[ENOSYS]** priority scheduling is not supported.
                [EINVAL] attr or protocol invalid.
                [ENOTSUP] protocol value is not supported.
Hint: *Inherit* protocol is expensive, and *protect* protocol is inappropriate unless the creator of the mutex also creates and controls all threads that might lock the mutex.

---

pthread_setschedparam .... [_POSIX_THREAD_PRIORITY_SCHEDULING]

```
int pthread_setschedparam (
        pthread_t                          thread,
        int                                policy
        const struct sched_param           *param);
```

Specify the scheduling policy and parameters (param) to be used by thread.

	policy
SCHED_FIFO	Run thread until it blocks; preempt lower-priority threads when ready.
SCHED_RR	Like SCHED_FIFO, but subject to periodic timeslicing.
SCHED_OTHER	Implementation defined (may be SCHED_FIFO, SCHED_RR, or something else).

References: 5.5
Headers: <pthread.h>
Errors: **[ENOSYS]** priority scheduling is not supported.
                [ESRCH] thread does not refer to an existing thread.
                [EINVAL] policy or param is invalid.
                [ENOTSUP] policy or param is unsupported value.
                [EPERM] no permission to set policy or param.
Hint: Try to avoid dynamically modifying thread scheduling policy and parameters, if possible.

sched_get_priority_max .... [_POSIX_PRIORITY_SCHEDULING]

```
int sched_get_priority_max (
        int              policy);
```

Return the maximum integer priority allowed for the specified scheduling policy.

	policy
SCHED_FIFO	Run thread until it blocks; preempt lower-priority threads when ready.
SCHED_RR	Like SCHED_FIFO, but subject to periodic timeslicing.
SCHED_OTHER	Implementation defined (may be SCHED_FIFO, SCHED_RR, or something else).

References:	5.5.2
Headers:	<sched.h>
Errors:	**[ENOSYS]** priority scheduling is not supported.
	[EINVAL] policy is invalid.
Hint:	Priority min and max are integer values—you can compute relative values, for example, half and quarter points in range.

sched_get_priority_min .... [_POSIX_PRIORITY_SCHEDULING]

```
int sched_get_priority_min (
        int              policy);
```

Return the minimum integer priority allowed for the specified scheduling policy.

	policy
SCHED_FIFO	Run thread until it blocks; preempt lower-priority threads when ready.
SCHED_RR	Like SCHED_FIFO, but subject to periodic timeslicing.
SCHED_OTHER	Implementation defined (may be SCHED_FIFO, SCHED_RR, or something else).

References:	5.5.2
Headers:	<sched.h>
Errors:	**[ENOSYS]** priority scheduling is not supported.
	[EINVAL] policy is invalid.
Hint:	Priority min and max are integer values—you can compute relative values, for example, half and quarter points in range.

9.3.9   Fork handlers

Pthreads provides some new functions to help the new threaded environment to coexist with the traditional process-based UNIX environment. Creation of a child process by copying the full address space, for example, causes problems for threaded applications because the `fork` call is asynchronous with respect to other threads in the process.

---

pthread_atfork

```
int pthread_atfork (
        void            (*prepare)(void),
        void            (*parent)(void),
        void            (*child)(void));
```

Define "fork handlers" that are run when the process creates a child process. Allows protection of synchronization objects and shared data in the child process (which is otherwise difficult to control).

References:	6.1.1
Headers:	`<unistd.h>`[*]
Errors:	[**ENOMEM**] insufficient space to record the handlers.
Hint:	All resources needed by child must be protected.

9.3.10   *Stdio*

Pthreads provides some new functions, and new versions of old functions, to access ANSI C *stdio* features safely from a threaded process. For safety reasons, the old forms of single-character access to *stdio* buffers have been altered to lock the file stream, which can decrease performance. You can change old code to instead lock the file stream manually and, within that locked region, use new character access operations that do not lock the file stream.

---

flockfile

```
void flockfile (
        FILE            *file);
```

Increase the lock count for a *stdio* file stream to gain exclusive access to the file stream. If the file stream is currently locked by another thread, the calling thread is blocked until the lock count for the file stream becomes zero. If the calling thread already owns the file stream lock, the lock count is incremented—an identical number of calls to `funlockfile` is required to release the file stream lock.

---

[*] Digital UNIX and Solaris both (incorrectly) place the definition in `<pthread.h>`. The UNIX 98 brand will require that they be fixed.

Although most *stdio* functions, such as `printf` and `fgets`, are thread-safe, you may sometimes find that it is important that a sequence of `printf` calls, for example, from one thread cannot be separated by calls made from another thread. Also, a few *stdio* functions are not thread-safe and can only be used while the file stream is locked by the caller.

References: 6.4.1
Headers: `<stdio.h>`
Hint: Use to protect a sequence of *stdio* operations.

---

ftrylockfile

```
int ftrylockfile (
        FILE            *file);
```

If the file stream is currently locked by another thread, return a nonzero value. Otherwise, increase the lock count for the file stream, and return the value zero.

References: 6.4.1
Headers: `<stdio.h>`
Hint: Use to protect a sequence of *stdio* operations.

---

funlockfile

```
void funlockfile (
        FILE            *file);
```

Decrease the lock count for a *stdio* file stream that was previously locked by a corresponding call to `funlockfile`. If the lock count becomes 0, release the lock so that another thread can lock it.

References: 6.4.1
Headers: `<stdio.h>`
Hint: Use to protect a sequence of *stdio* operations.

---

getc_unlocked

```
int getc_unlocked (
        FILE            *file);
```

Return a single character from the *stdio* stream file, without locking the file stream. This operation must only be used while the file stream has been locked by calling `flockfile`, or when you know that no other thread may access the file stream concurrently. Returns `EOF` for read errors or end-of-file condition.

References: 6.4.2
Headers: `<stdio.h>`
Hint: Replace old calls to `getc` to retain fastest access.

getchar_unlocked

```
int getc_unlocked (void);
```

Return a single character from the *stdio* stream stdin without locking the file stream. This operation must only be used while the file stream has been locked by calling flockfile, or when you know that no other thread may access the file stream concurrently. Returns EOF for read errors or end-of-file condition.

References: 6.4.2
Headers: <stdio.h>
Hint: Replace old calls to getchar to retain fastest access.

putc_unlocked

```
int putc_unlocked (
        int             c,
        FILE            *file);
```

Write a single character c (interpreted as an unsigned char) to the *stdio* stream file without locking the file stream. This operation must only be used while the file stream has been locked by calling flockfile, or when you know that no other thread may access the file stream concurrently. Returns the character or the value EOF if an error occurred.

References: 6.4.2
Headers: <stdio.h>
Hint: Replace old calls to putc to retain fastest access.

putchar_unlocked

```
int putchar_unlocked (
        int             c);
```

Write a single character c (interpreted as an unsigned char) to the *stdio* stream stdout without locking the file stream. This operation must only be used while the file stream has been locked by calling flockfile, or when you know that no other thread may access the file stream concurrently. Returns the character or the value EOF if an error occurred.

References: 6.4.2
Headers: <stdio.h>
Hint: Replace old calls to putchar to retain fastest access.

9.3.11 Thread-safe functions

Thread-safe functions provide improved access to traditional features of ANSI C and POSIX that cannot be effectively made thread-safe without interface changes. These routines are designated by the "_r" suffix added to the traditional function name they replace, for example, getlogin_r for getlogin.

getlogin_r

```
int getlogin_r (
        char            *name,
        size_t          namesize);
```

Write the user name associated with the current process into the buffer pointed to by name. The buffer is namesize bytes long, and should have space for the name and a terminating null character. The maximum size of the login name is LOGIN_NAME_MAX.

References: 6.5.1
Headers: <unistd.h>

readdir_r

```
int readdir_r (
        DIR             *dirp,
        struct dirent   *entry,
        struct dirent   **result);
```

Return a pointer (result) to the directory entry at the current position in the directory stream to which dirp refers. Whereas readdir retains the current position using a static variable, readdir_r uses the entry parameter, supplied by the caller.

References: 6.5.2
Headers: <sys/types.h>, <dirent.h>
Errors: **[EBADF]** dirp is not an open directory stream.

strtok_r

```
char *strtok_r (
        char            *s,
        const char      *sep,
        char            **lasts);
```

Return a pointer to the next token in the string s. Whereas strtok retains the current position within a string using a static variable, strtok_r uses the lasts parameter, supplied by the caller.

References: 6.5.3
Headers: <string.h>

asctime_r

```
char *asctime_r (
        const struct tm*tm,
        char            *buf);
```

Convert the "broken-down" time in the structure pointed to by tm into a string, which is stored in the buffer pointed to by buf. The buffer pointed to by buf must contain at least 26 bytes. The function returns a pointer to the buffer on success, or NULL on failure.

References: 6.5.4
Headers: <time.h>

---

ctime_r

```
char *ctime_r (
        const time_t      *clock,
        char              *buf);
```

Convert the calendar time pointed to by clock into a string representing the local time, which is stored in the buffer pointed to by buf. The buffer pointed to by buf must contain at least 26 bytes. The function returns a pointer to the buffer on success, or NULL on failure.

References: 6.5.4
Headers: <time.h>

---

gmtime_r

```
struct tm *gmtime_r (
        const time_t      *clock,
        struct tm         *result);
```

Convert the calendar time pointed to by clock into a "broken-down time" expressed as Coordinated Universal Time (UTC), which is stored in the structure pointed to by result. The function returns a pointer to the structure on success, or NULL on failure.

References: 6.5.4
Headers: <time.h>

---

localtime_r

```
struct tm *localtime_r (
        const time_t      *clock,
        struct tm         *result);
```

Convert the calendar time pointed to by clock into a "broken-down time" expressed as local time, which is stored in the structure pointed to by result. The function returns a pointer to the structure on success, or NULL on failure.

References: 6.5.4
Headers: <time.h>

rand_r

```
int rand_r (
        unsigned int    *seed);
```

Return the next value in a sequence of pseudorandom integers in the range of 0 to RAND_MAX. Whereas rand uses a static variable to maintain the context between a series of calls, rand_r uses the value pointed to by seed, which is supplied by the caller.

References: 6.5.5
Headers: <stdlib.h>

getgrgid_r

```
int getgrgid_r (
        gid_t               gid,
        struct group        *group,
        char                *buffer,
        size_t              bufsize,
        struct group        **result);
```

Locate an entry from the group database with a group id matching the gid argument. The group entry is stored in the memory pointed to by buffer, which contains bufsize bytes, and a pointer to the entry is stored at the address pointed to by result. The maximum buffer size required can be determined by calling sysconf with the _SC_GETGR_R_SIZE_MAX parameter.

References: 6.5.6
Headers: <sys/types.h>, <grp.h>
Errors: [ERANGE] the specified buffer is too small.

getgrnam_r

```
int getgrnam_r (
        const char          *name,
        struct group        *group,
        char                *buffer,
        size_t              bufsize,
        struct group        **result);
```

Locate an entry from the group database with a group name matching the name argument. The group entry is stored in the memory pointed to by buffer, which contains bufsize bytes, and a pointer to the entry is stored at the address pointed to by result. The maximum buffer size required can be determined by calling sysconf with the _SC_GETGR_R_SIZE_MAX parameter.

References: 6.5.6
Headers: <sys/types.h>, <grp.h>
Errors: [ERANGE] the specified buffer is too small.

getpwuid_r

```
int getpwuid_r (
        uid_t              uid,
        struct passwd      *pwd,
        char               *buffer,
        size_t             bufsize,
        struct passwd      **result);
```

Locate an entry from the user database with a user id matching the uid argument. The user entry is stored in the memory pointed to by buffer, which contains bufsize bytes, and a pointer to the entry is stored at the address pointed to by result. The maximum buffer size required can be determined by calling sysconf with the _SC_GETPW_R_SIZE_MAX parameter.

References: 6.5.6
Headers: <sys/types.h>, <pwd.h>
Errors: [ERANGE] the specified buffer is too small.

getpwnam_r

```
int getpwnam_r (
        const char         *name,
        struct passwd      *pwd,
        char               *buffer,
        size_t             bufsize,
        struct passwd      **result);
```

Locate an entry from the user database with a user name matching the name argument. The user entry is stored in the memory pointed to by buffer, which contains bufsize bytes, and a pointer to the entry is stored at the address pointed to by result. The maximum buffer size required can be determined by calling sysconf with the _SC_GETPW_R_SIZE_MAX parameter.

References: 6.5.6
Headers: <sys/types.h>, <pwd.h>
Errors: [ERANGE] the specified buffer is too small.

9.3.12 Signals

Pthreads provides functions that extend the POSIX signal model to support multithreaded processes. All threads in a process share the same signal actions. Each thread has its own pending and blocked signal masks. The process also has a pending signal mask so that asynchronous signals can pend against the process when all threads have the signal blocked. In a multithreaded process, the behavior of sigprocmask is undefined.

pthread_kill

```
int pthread_kill (
        pthread_t       thread,
        int             sig);
```

Request that the signal `sig` be delivered to thread. If `sig` is 0, no signal is sent, but error checking is performed. If the action of the signal is to terminate, stop, or continue, then the entire process is affected.

References: 6.6.3
Headers: <signal.h>
Errors: **[ESRCH]** no thread corresponding to thread.
               [EINVAL] `sig` is an invalid signal number.
Hint: To terminate a thread, use cancellation.

pthread_sigmask

```
int pthread_sigmask (
        int             how,
        const sigset_t *set,
        sigset_t        *oset);
```

Control the masking of signals within the calling thread.

	how
`SIG_BLOCK`	Resulting set is the union of the current set and the argument set.
`SIG_UNBLOCK`	Resulting set is the intersection of the current set and the argument set.
`SIG_SETMASK`	Resulting set is the set pointed to by the argument set.

References: 6.6.2
Headers: <signal.h>
Errors: **[EINVAL]** how is not one of the defined values.
Hint: You cannot prevent delivery of asynchronous signals to the process
               unless the signal is blocked in all threads.

sigtimedwait

```
int sigtimedwait (
        const sigset_t      *set,
        siginfo_t           *info,
        const struct timespec *timeout);
```

If a signal in `set` is pending, atomically clear it from the set of pending signals and return the signal number in the `si_signo` member of *info*. The cause of the signal shall be stored in the `si_code` member. If any value is queued to the selected signal, return the first queued value in the `si_value` member. If no signal in `set` is pending, suspend the calling thread until one or more become pending. If the time interval specified by `timeout` passes, `sigtimedwait` will return with the error `EAGAIN`. This function returns the signal number—on error, it returns –1 and sets `errno` to the appropriate error code.

References:	6.6.4
Headers:	`<signal.h>`
Errors:	[`EINVAL`] set contains an invalid signal number.
	[**`EAGAIN`**] the timeout interval passed.
	[**`ENOSYS`**] realtime signals are not supported.
Hint:	Use only for asynchronous signal delivery. All signals in `set` must be masked in the calling thread, and should usually be masked in all threads.

---

sigwait

```
int sigwait (
        const sigset_t  *set,
        int             *sig);
```

If a signal in `set` is pending, atomically clear it from the set of pending signals and return the signal number in the location referenced by `sig`. If no signal in `set` is pending, suspend the calling thread until one or more become pending.

References:	6.6.4
Headers:	`<signal.h>`
Errors:	[`EINVAL`] set contains an invalid signal number.
Hint:	Use only for asynchronous signal delivery. All signals in `set` must be masked in the calling thread, and should usually be masked in all threads.

---

sigwaitinfo

```
int sigwaitinfo (
        const sigset_t  *set,
        siginfo_t       *info);
```

If a signal in `set` is pending, atomically clear it from the set of pending signals and return the signal number in the `si_signo` member of *info*. The cause of the signal shall be stored in the `si_code` member. If any value is queued to the selected signal, return the first queued value in the `si_value` member. If no signal in `set` is pending, suspend the calling thread until one or more become pending. This function returns the signal number—on error, it returns –1 and sets `errno` to the appropriate error code.

References: 6.6.4
Headers: <signal.h>
Errors: [EINVAL] set contains an invalid signal number.
                 [ENOSYS] realtime signals are not supported.
Hint: Use only for asynchronous signal delivery. All signals in set must
                 be masked in the calling thread, and should usually be masked in
                 all threads.

9.3.13 Semaphores

Semaphores come from POSIX.1b (POSIX 1003.1b–1993) rather than from
Pthreads. They follow the older UNIX convention for reporting errors. That is, on
failure they return a value of –1 and store the appropriate error number into
errno. All of the semaphore functions require the header file <semaphore.h>.

sem_destroy .... [_POSIX_SEMAPHORES]

```
int sem_destroy (
        sem_t           *sem);
```

Destroy an unnamed semaphore.

References: 6.6.6
Headers: <semaphore.h>
Errors: **[EINVAL]** value exceeds SEM_VALUE_MAX.
                 [ENOSYS] semaphores are not supported.
                 [EBUSY] threads (or processes) are currently blocked on sem.

sem_init .... [_POSIX_SEMAPHORES]

```
int sem_init (
        sem_t           *sem,
        int             pshared,
        unsigned int    value);
```

Initialize an unnamed semaphore. The initial value of the semaphore counter is
value. If the pshared argument has a nonzero value, the semaphore can be shared
between processes. With a zero value, it can be shared only between threads in the
same process.

References: 6.6.6
Headers: <semaphore.h>
Errors: **[EINVAL]** sem is not a valid semaphore.
                 [ENOSPC] a required resource has been exhausted.
                 [ENOSYS] semaphores are not supported.
                 [EPERM] the process lacks appropriate privilege.
Hint: Use a value of 1 for a lock, a value of 0 for waiting.

sem_trywait ....[_POSIX_SEMAPHORES]

```
int sem_trywait (
        sem_t           *sem);
```

Try to wait on a semaphore (or "try to lock" the semaphore). If the semaphore value is greater than zero, decrease the value by one. If the semaphore value is 0, then return immediately with the error EAGAIN.

References:	6.6.6
Headers:	<semaphore.h>
Errors:	**[EAGAIN]** the semaphore was already locked.
	[EINVAL] sem is not a valid semaphore.
	[EINTR] the function was interrupted by a signal.
	[ENOSYS] semaphores are not supported.
	[EDEADLK] a deadlock condition was detected.
Hint:	When the semaphore's initial value was 1, this is a lock operation; when the initial value was 0, this is a wait operation.

sem_post..[_POSIX_SEMAPHORES]

```
int sem_post (
        sem_t           *sem);
```

Post a wakeup to a semaphore. If there are waiting threads (or processes), one is awakened. Otherwise the semaphore value is incremented by one.

References:	6.6.6
Headers:	<semaphore.h>
Errors:	**[EINVAL]** sem is not a valid semaphore.
	[ENOSYS] semaphores are not supported.
Hint:	May be used from within a signal-handling function.

sem_wait..[_POSIX_SEMAPHORES]

```
int sem_wait (
        sem_t           *sem);
```

Wait on a semaphore (or lock the semaphore). If the semaphore value is greater than zero, decrease the value by one. If the semaphore value is 0, then the calling thread (or process) is blocked until it can successfully decrease the value or until interrupted by a signal.

References:	6.6.6
Headers:	<semaphore.h>
Errors:	**[EINVAL]** sem is not a valid semaphore.
	[EINTR] the function was interrupted by a signal.
	[ENOSYS] semaphores are not supported.
	[EDEADLK] a deadlock condition was detected.
Hint:	When the semaphore's initial value was 1, this is a lock operation; when the initial value was 0, this is a wait operation.

10 Future standardization

Three primary standardization efforts affect Pthreads programmers. X/Open's XSH5 is a new interface specification that includes POSIX.1b, Pthreads, and a set of additional thread functions (part of the Aspen fast-track submission). The POSIX.1j draft standard proposes to add barriers, read/write locks, spinlocks, and improved support for "relative time" waits on condition variables. The POSIX.14 draft standard (a "POSIX Standard Profile") gives direction for managing the various options of Pthreads in a multiprocessor environment.

10.1 X/Open XSH5 (UNIX98)

Mutex type attribute:

```
int pthread_mutexattr_gettype (
    const pthread_mutexattr_t *attr, int *type);
int pthread_mutexattr_settype (
    pthread_mutexattr_t *attr, int type);
```

Read/write locks:

```
int pthread_rwlock_init (pthread_rwlock_t *rwlock,
    const pthread_rwlockattr_t *attr);
int pthread_rwlock_destroy (pthread_rwlock_t *rwlock);
pthread_rwlock_t rwlock = PTHREAD_RWLOCK_INITIALIZER;
int pthread_rwlock_rdlock (pthread_rwlock_t *rwlock);
int pthread_rwlock_tryrdlock (
    pthread_rwlock_t *rwlock);
int pthread_rwlock_unlock (pthread_rwlock_t *rwlock);
int pthread_rwlock_wrlock (pthread_rwlock_t *rwlock);
int pthread_rwlock_trywrlock (
    pthread_rwlock_t *rwlock);
int pthread_rwlockattr_init (
    pthread_rwlockattr_t *attr);
int pthread_rwlockattr_destroy (
    pthread_rwlockattr_t *attr);
int pthread_rwlockattr_getpshared (
    const pthread_rwlockattr_t *attr, int *pshared);
int pthread_rwlockattr_setpshared (
    pthread_rwlockattr_t *attr, int pshared);
```

Parallel I/O:

```
size_t pread (int fildes,
    void *buf, size_t nbyte, off_t offset);
size_t pwrite (int fildes,
    const void *buf, size_t nbyte, off_t offset);
```

Miscellaneous:

```
int pthread_attr_getguardsize (
    const pthread_attr_t *attr, size_t *guardsize);
int pthread_attr_setguardsize (
    pthread_attr_t *attr, size_t guardsize);
int pthread_getconcurrency ();
int pthread_setconcurrency (int new_level);
```

X/Open, which is part of The Open Group, owns the UNIX trademark and develops UNIX industry portability specifications and brands. The X/Open brands include XPG3, XPG4, UNIX93, and UNIX95. UNIX95 is also known as "SPEC1170" or the "Single UNIX Specification."

X/Open recently published the *X/Open CAE Specification, System Interfaces and Headers, Issue 5* (also known as XSH5), which is part of the new UNIX98 brand. XSH5 requires conformance to the POSIX.1–1996 standard, which includes the POSIX.1b and POSIX.1c amendments. The XSH5 specification also adds a set of extensions to POSIX. This section discusses the XSH5 extensions that specifically affect threaded programs. You can recognize a system conforming to XSH5 by a definition for the _XOPEN_VERSION symbol, in <unistd.h>, to the value 500 or higher.

The most valuable contribution of UNIX98 to the threaded programming industry, however, is possibly the development of a standardized, portable testing system. A number of complicated issues arise when developing an implementation of Pthreads, and some subtle aspects of the standard are ambiguous. Such an industry-wide testing system will require all vendors implementing UNIX98 branded systems to agree on interpretations of Pthreads.

10.1.1   POSIX options for XSH5

Some of the features that are options in the Pthreads standard are required by XSH5. If your code relies on these Pthreads options, it will work on any system conforming to XSH5:

- _POSIX_THREADS: Threads are supported.
- _POSIX_THREAD_ATTR_STACKADDR: The *stackaddr* attribute is supported.
- _POSIX_THREAD_ATTR_STACKSIZE: The *stacksize* attribute is supported.
- _POSIX_THREAD_PROCESS_SHARED: Mutexes, condition variables, and XSH5 read/write locks can be shared between processes.

- `_POSIX_THREAD_SAFE_FUNCTIONS`: The Pthreads thread-safe functions are supported.

Several additional Pthreads options are "bundled" into the XSH5 realtime threads option group. If your system conforms to XSH5 and supports the `_XOPEN_REALTIME_THREADS` option, then these Pthreads options are also supported:

- `_POSIX_THREAD_PRIORITY_SCHEDULING`: Realtime priority scheduling is supported.
- `_POSIX_THREAD_PRIO_PROTECT`: Priority ceiling mutexes are supported.
- `_POSIX_THREAD_PRIO_INHERIT`: Priority inheritance mutexes are supported.

10.1.2 Mutex type

The DCE threads package provided an extension that allowed the programmer to specify the "kind" of mutex to be created. DCE threads supplied *fast, recursive,* and *nonrecursive* mutex kinds. The XSH5 specification changes the attribute name from "kind" to "type," renames *fast* to *default,* renames *nonrecursive* to *errorcheck,* and adds a new type, *normal* (Table 10.1).

A *normal* mutex is not allowed to detect deadlock errors—that is, a thread will hang if it tries to lock a *normal* mutex that it already owns. The *default* mutex type, like the DCE *fast* mutex,[*] provides implementation-defined error checking. That is, *default* may be mapped to one of the other standard types or may be something entirely different.

Mutex type	Definition
PTHREAD_MUTEX_NORMAL	Basic mutex with no specific error checking built in. Does not report a deadlock error.
PTHREAD_MUTEX_RECURSIVE	Allows any thread to lock the mutex "recursively" —it must unlock an equal number of times to release the mutex.
PTHREAD_MUTEX_ERRORCHECK	Detects and reports simple usage errors—an attempt to unlock a mutex that's not locked by the calling thread (or that isn't locked at all), or an attempt to relock a mutex the thread already owns.
PTHREAD_MUTEX_DEFAULT	The default mutex type, with very loose semantics to allow unfettered innovation and experimentation. May be mapped to any of the other three defined types, or may be something else entirely.

TABLE 10.1 *XSH5 mutex types*

---

[*] DCE threads implemented *fast* mutexes much like the definition of XSH5 *normal* mutexes, with no error checking. This was not, however, specification of intent.

As an application developer, you can use any of the mutex types almost interchangeably as long as your code does not depend on the implementation to detect (or fail to detect) any particular errors. Never write code that counts on an implementation *failing* to detect any error. Do not lock a mutex in one thread and unlock it in another thread, for example, even if you are sure that the error won't be reported—use a semaphore instead, which has no "ownership" semantics.

All mutexes, regardless of type, are created using `pthread_mutex_init`, destroyed using `pthread_mutex_destroy`, and manipulated using `pthread_mutex_lock`, `pthread_mutex_unlock`, and `pthread_mutex_trylock`.

Normal mutexes will usually be the fastest implementation possible for the machine, but will provide the least error checking.

Recursive mutexes are primarily useful for converting old code where it is difficult to establish clear boundaries of synchronization, for example, when you must call a function with a mutex locked and the function you call—or some function it calls—may need to lock the same mutex. I have never seen a situation where recursive mutexes were *required* to solve a problem, but I have seen many cases where the alternate (and usually "better") solutions were impractical. Such situations frequently lead developers to create recursive mutexes, and it makes more sense to have a single implementation available to everyone. (But your code will usually be easier to follow, and perform better, if you avoid recursive mutexes.)

Errorcheck mutexes were devised as a debugging tool, although less intrusive debugging tools (where available) can be more powerful. To use errorcheck mutexes you must recompile code to turn the debugging feature on and off. It is far more useful to have an external option to force all mutexes to record debugging data. You may want to use errorcheck mutexes in final "production" code, of course, to detect serious problems early, but be aware that errorcheck mutexes will almost always be much slower than normal mutexes due to the extra state and checking.

Default mutexes allow each implementation to provide the mutex semantics the vendor feels will be most useful to the target audience. It may be useful to make *errorcheck* mutexes the default, for example, to improve the threaded debugging environment of a system. Or the vendor may choose to make *normal* mutexes the default to give most programs the benefit of any extra speed.

---

pthread_mutexattr_gettype

```
int pthread_mutexattr_gettype (
        const pthread_mutexattr_t        *attr,
        int                              *type);
```

Specify the type of mutexes created with `attr`.

	type
PTHREAD_MUTEX_DEFAULT	Unspecified type.
PTHREAD_MUTEX_NORMAL	Basic mutex, with no error checking.
PTHREAD_MUTEX_RECURSIVE	Thread can relock a mutex it owns.
PTHREAD_MUTEX_ERRORCHECK	Checks for usage errors.

References: 3.2, 5.2.1, 10.1.2
Errors: **[EINVAL]** type invalid.
                   [EINVAL] attr invalid.
Hint: *Normal* mutexes will usually be fastest; *errorcheck* mutexes are useful for debugging; *recursive* mutexes can be useful for making old interfaces thread-safe.

pthread_mutexattr_settype

```
int pthread_mutexattr_settype (
        pthread_mutexattr_t             *attr,
        int                             type);
```

Determine the type of mutexes created with `attr`.

	type
PTHREAD_MUTEX_DEFAULT	Unspecified type.
PTHREAD_MUTEX_NORMAL	Basic mutex, with no error checking.
PTHREAD_MUTEX_RECURSIVE	Thread can relock a mutex it owns.
PTHREAD_MUTEX_ERRORCHECK	Checks for usage errors.

References: 3.2, 5.2.1, 10.1.2
Errors: **[EINVAL]** type invalid.
                   [EINVAL] attr invalid.
Hint: *Normal* mutexes will usually be fastest; *errorcheck* mutexes are useful for debugging; *recursive* mutexes can be useful for making old interfaces thread-safe.

10.1.3 Set concurrency level

When you use Pthreads implementations that schedule user threads onto some smaller set of kernel entities (see Section 5.6.3), it may be possible to have *ready* user threads while all kernel entities allocated to the process are busy.

Some implementations, for example, "lock" a kernel entity to a user thread that blocks in the kernel, until the blocking condition, for example an I/O request, is completed. The system will create some reasonable number of kernel execution entities for the process, but eventually the pool of kernel entities may become exhausted. The process may be left with threads capable of performing useful work for the application, but no way to schedule them.

The `pthread_setconcurrency` function addresses this limitation by allowing the application to ask for more kernel entities. If the application designer realizes that 10 out of 15 threads may at any time become blocked in the kernel, and it is important for those other 5 threads to be able to continue processing, then the application may request that the kernel supply 15 kernel entities. If it is important that at least 1 of those 5 continue, but not that all continue, then the application could request the more conservative number of 11 kernel entities. Or if it is OK for all threads to block once in a while, but not often, and you know that only rarely will more than 6 threads block at any time, the application could request 7 kernel entities.

The `pthread_setconcurrency` function is a hint, and implementations may ignore it or modify the advice. You may use it freely on any system that conforms to the UNIX98 brand, but many systems will do nothing more than set a value that is returned by `pthread_getconcurrency`. On Digital UNIX, for example, there is no need to set a fixed concurrency level, because the kernel mode and user mode schedulers cooperate to ensure that ready user threads cannot be prevented from running by other threads blocked in the kernel.

pthread_getconcurrency

```
int pthread_getconcurrency ();
```

Returns the value set by a previous `pthread_setconcurrency` call. If there have been no previous calls to `pthread_setconcurrency`, returns 0 to indicate that the implementation is maintaining the concurrency level automatically.

References:	5.6.3, 10.1.3
Errors:	none.
Hint:	Concurrency level is a hint. It may be ignored by any implementation, and *will* be ignored by an implementation that does not need it to ensure concurrency.

pthread_setconcurrency

```
int pthread_getconcurrency (int new_level);
```

Allows the application to inform the threads implementation of its desired minimum concurrency level. The actual level of concurrency resulting from this call is unspecified.

References: 5.6.3, 10.1.3
Errors: **[EINVAL]** new_level is negative.
                [EAGAIN] new_level exceeds a system resource.
Hint: Concurrency level is a hint. It may be ignored by any implementa-
                tion, and *will* be ignored by an implementation that does not need
                it to ensure concurrency.

10.1.4 Stack guard size

Guard size comes from DCE threads. Most thread implementations add to the
thread's stack a "guard" region, a page or more of protected memory. This protected page is a safety zone, to prevent a stack overflow in one thread from
corrupting another thread's stack. There are two good reasons for wanting to
control a thread's guard size:

1. It allows an application or library that allocates large data arrays on the
   stack to increase the default guard size. For example, if a thread allocates
   two pages at once, a single guard page provides little protection against
   stack overflows—the thread can corrupt adjoining memory without touch-
   ing the protected page.
2. When creating a large number of threads, it may be that the extra page for
   each stack can become a severe burden. In addition to the extra page, the
   kernel's memory manager has to keep track of the differing protection on
   adjoining pages, which may strain system resources. Therefore, you may
   sometimes need to ask the system to "trust you" and avoid allocating any
   guard pages at all for your threads. You can do this by requesting a guard
   size of 0 bytes.

---

pthread_attr_getguardsize

```
int pthread_attr_getguardsize (
        const pthread_attr_t    *attr,
        size_t                  *guardsize);
```

Determine the size of the guard region for the stack on which threads created with
attr will run.

References: 2, 5.2.3
Errors: **[EINVAL]** attr invalid.
Hint: Specify 0 to fit lots of stacks in an address space, or increase default
                guardsize for threads that allocate large buffers on the stack.

pthread_attr_setguardsize

```
int pthread_attr_setguardsize (
        pthread_attr_t            *attr,
        size_t                    guardsize);
```

Threads created with `attr` will run on a stack with `guardsize` bytes protected against stack overflow. The implementation may round `guardsize` up to the next multiple of `PAGESIZE`. Specifying a value of 0 for `guardsize` will cause threads created using the attributes object to run without stack overflow protection.

References: 2, 5.2.3
Errors: **[EINVAL]** `guardsize` or `attr` invalid.
Hint: Specify 0 to fit lots of stacks in an address space, or increase default `guardsize` for threads that allocate large buffers on the stack.

10.1.5   Parallel I/O

Many high-performance systems, such as database engines, use threads, at least in part, to gain performance through parallel I/O. Unfortunately, Pthreads doesn't directly support parallel I/O. That is, two threads can independently issue I/O operations for files, or even for the same file, but the POSIX file I/O model places some restrictions on the level of parallelism.

One bottleneck is that the current file position is an attribute of the file descriptor. To read or write data from or to a specific position within a file, a thread must call `lseek` to seek to the proper byte offset in the file, and then `read` or `write`. If more than one thread does this at the same time, the first thread might seek, and then the second thread seek to a different place before the first thread can issue the `read` or `write` operation.

The X/Open `pread` and `pwrite` functions offer a solution, by making the seek and read or write combination atomic. Threads can issue `pread` or `pwrite` operations in parallel, and, in principle, the system can process those I/O requests completely in parallel without locking the file descriptor.

pread

```
size_t pread (
        int                       fildes,
        void                      *buf,
        size_t                    nbyte,
        off_t                     offset);
```

Read `nbyte` bytes from offset `offset` in the file opened on file descriptor `fildes`, placing the result into `buf`. The file descriptor's current offset is not affected, allowing multiple `pread` and/or `pwrite` operations to proceed in parallel.

References: none
Errors: **[EINVAL]** offset is negative.
                [EOVERFLOW] attempt to read beyond maximum.
                [ENXIO] request outside capabilities of device.
                [ESPIPE] file is pipe.
Hint: Allows high-performance parallel I/O.

---

pwrite

```
size_t pwrite (
        int                     fildes,
        const void              *buf,
        size_t                  nbyte,
        off_t                   offset);
```

Write nbyte bytes to offset offset in the file opened on file descriptor fildes, from buf. The file descriptor's current offset is not affected, allowing multiple pread and/ or pwrite operations to proceed in parallel.

References: none
Errors: **[EINVAL]** offset is negative.
                [ESPIPE] file is pipe.
Hint: Allows high-performance parallel I/O.

10.1.6 Cancellation points

Most UNIX systems support a substantial number of interfaces that do not come from POSIX. The select and poll interfaces, for example, should be deferred cancellation points. Pthreads did not require these functions to be cancellation points, however, because they do not exist within POSIX.1.

The select and poll functions, however, along with many others, exist in X/Open. The XSH5 standard includes an expanded list of cancellation points covering X/Open interfaces.

Additional functions that must be cancellation points in XSH5:

getmsg	pread	sigpause
getpmsg	putmsg	usleep
lockf	putpmsg	wait3
msgrcv	pwrite	waitid
msgsnd	readv	writev
poll	select	

Additional functions that may be cancellation points in XSH5:

catclose	fsetpos	popen
catgets	ftello	pututxline
catopen	ftw	putw
closelog	fwprintf	putwc
dbm_close	fwscanf	putwchar
dbm_delete	getgrent	readdir_r
dbm_fetch	getpwent	seekdir
dbm_nextkey	getutxent	semop
dbm_open	getutxid	setgrent
dbm_store	getutxline	setpwent
dlclose	getw	setutxent
dlopen	getwc	syslog
endgrent	getwchar	ungetwc
endpwent	iconv_close	vfprintf
endutxent	iconv_open	vfwprintf
fgetwc	ioctl	vprintf
fgetws	mkstemp	vwprintf
fputwc	nftw	wprintf
fputws	openlog	wscanf
fseeko	pclose	

10.2 POSIX 1003.1j

Condition variable wait clock:

```
int pthread_condattr_getclock (
    const pthread_condattr_t *attr,
    clockid_t *clock_id);
int pthread_condattr_setclock (
    pthread_condattr_t *attr,
    clockid_t clock_id);
```

Barriers:

```
int barrier_attr_init (barrier_attr_t *attr);
int barrier_attr_destroy (barrier_attr_t *attr);
int barrier_attr_getpshared (
    const barrier_attr_t *attr, int *pshared);
int barrier_attr_setpshared (
    barrier_attr_t *attr, int pshared);
int barrier_init (barrier_t *barrier,
    const barrier_attr_t *attr, int count);
int barrier_destroy (barrier_t *barrier);
int barrier_wait (barrier_t *barrier);
```

Reader/writer locks:

```
int rwlock_attr_init (rwlock_attr_t *attr);
int rwlock_attr_destroy (rwlock_attr_t *attr);
int rwlock_attr_getpshared (
    const rwlock_attr_t *attr, int *pshared);
int rwlock_attr_setpshared (
    rwlock_attr_t *attr, int pshared);
int rwlock_init (
    rwlock_t *lock, const rwlock_attr_t *attr);
int rwlock_destroy (rwlock_t *lock);
int rwlock_rlock (rwlock_t *lock);
int rwlock_timedrlock (rwlock_t *lock,
    const struct timespec *timeout);
int rwlock_tryrlock (rwlock_t *lock);
int rwlock_wlock (rwlock_t *lock);
int rwlock_timedwlock (rwlock_t *lock,
    const struct timespec *timeout);
int rwlock_trywlock (rwlock_t *lock);
int rwlock_unlock (rwlock_t *lock);
```

Spinlocks:

```
int spin_init (spinlock_t *lock);
int spin_destroy (spinlock_t *lock);
int spin_lock (spinlock_t *lock);
int spin_trylock (spinlock_t *lock);
int spin_unlock (spinlock_t *lock);
int pthread_spin_init (pthread_spinlock_t *lock);
int pthread_spin_destroy (pthread_spinlock_t *lock);
int pthread_spin_lock (pthread_spinlock_t *lock);
int pthread_spin_trylock (pthread_spinlock_t *lock);
int pthread_spin_unlock (pthread_spinlock_t *lock);
```

Thread abort:

```
int pthread_abort (pthread_t thread);
```

The same POSIX working group that developed POSIX.1b and Pthreads has developed a new set of extensions for realtime and threaded programming. Most of the extensions relevant to threads (and to this book) are the result of proposals developed by the POSIX 1003.14 profile group, which specialized in "tuning" the existing POSIX standards for multiprocessor systems.

POSIX.1j adds some thread synchronization mechanisms that have been common in a wide range of multiprocessor and thread programming, but that had been omitted from the original Pthreads standard. Barriers and spinlocks are primarily useful for fine-grained parallelism, for example, in systems that automatically generate parallel code from program loops. Read/write locks are useful in shared data algorithms where many threads are allowed to read simultaneously, but only one thread can be allowed to update data.

10.2.1 Barriers

"Barriers" are a form of synchronization most commonly used in parallel decomposition of loops. They're almost never used except in code designed to run only on multiprocessor systems. A barrier is a "meeting place" for a group of associated threads, where each will wait until all have reached the barrier. When the last one waits on the barrier, all the participating threads are released.

See Section 7.1.1 for details of barrier behavior and for an example showing how to implement a barrier using standard Pthreads synchronization. (Note that the behavior of this example is not precisely the same as that proposed by POSIX.1j.)

10.2.2 Read/write locks

A read/write lock (also sometimes known as "reader/writer lock") allows one thread to exclusively lock some shared data to write or modify that data, but also allows multiple threads to simultaneously lock the data for read access. UNIX98 specifies "read/write locks" very similar to POSIX.1j reader/writer locks. Although X/Open intends that the two specifications will be functionally identical, the names are different to avoid conflict should the POSIX standard change before approval.[*]

If your code relies on a data structure that is frequently referenced, but only occasionally updated, you should consider using a read/write lock rather than a mutex to access that data. Most threads will be able to read the data without waiting; they'll need to block only when some thread is in the process of modifying the data. (Similarly, a thread that desires to write the data will be blocked if any threads are reading the data.)

See Section 7.1.2 for details of read/write lock behavior and for an example showing how to implement a read/write lock using standard Pthreads synchronization. (Note that the behavior of this example is not precisely the same as that proposed by POSIX.1j.)

---

[*] The POSIX working group is considering the possibility of adapting the XSH5 read/write lock definition and abandoning the original POSIX.1j names, but the decision hasn't yet been made.

10.2.3 Spinlocks

Spinlocks are much like mutexes. There's been a lot of discussion about whether it even makes sense to standardize on a spinlock interface—since POSIX specifies only a source level API, there's very little POSIX.1j says about them that distinguishes them from mutexes. The essential idea is that a spinlock is the most primitive and fastest synchronization mechanism available on a given hardware architecture. On some systems, that may be a single "test and set" instruction—on others, it may be a substantial sequence of "load locked, test, store conditional, memory barrier" instructions.

The critical distinction is that a thread trying to lock a spinlock does not *necessarily* block when the spinlock is already held by another thread. The intent is that the thread will "spin," retrying the lock rapidly until it succeeds in locking the spinlock. (This is one of the "iffy" spots—on a uniprocessor it had better block, or it'll do nothing but spin out the rest of its timeslice . . . or spin to eternity if it isn't timesliced.)

Spinlocks are great for fine-grained parallelism, when the code is intended to run only on a multiprocessor, carefully tuned to hold the spinlock for only a few instructions, and getting ultimate performance is more important than sharing the system resources cordially with other processes. To be effective, a spinlock must never be locked for as long as it takes to "context switch" from one thread to another. If it does take as long or longer, you'll get better overall performance by blocking and allowing some other thread to do useful work.

POSIX.1j contains two sets of spinlock functions: one set with a `spin_` prefix, which allows spinlock synchronization between processes; and the other set with a `pthread_` prefix, allowing spinlock synchronization between threads within a process. This, you will notice, is very different from the model used for mutexes, condition variables, and read/write locks, where the same functions were used and the *pshared* attribute specifies whether the resulting synchronization object can be shared between processes.

The rationale for this is that spinlocks are intended to be very fast, and should not be subject to any possible overhead as a result of needing to decide, at run time, how to behave. It is, in fact, unlikely that the implementation of `spin_lock` and `pthread_spin_lock` will differ on most systems, but the standard allows them to be different.

10.2.4 Condition variable wait clock

Pthreads condition variables support only "absolute time" timeouts. That is, the thread specifies that it is willing to wait until "Jan 1 00:00:00 GMT 2001," rather than being able to specify that it wants to wait for "1 hour, 10 minutes." The reason for this is that a condition variable wait is subject to wakeups for various reasons that are beyond your control or not easy to control. When you wake early from a "1 hour, 10 minute" wait it is difficult to determine how much of that time is left. But when you wake early from the absolute wait, your target time is still "Jan 1 00:00:00 GMT 2001." (The reasons for early wakeup are discussed in Section 3.3.2.)

Despite all this excellent reasoning, "relative time" waits are useful. One important advantage is that absolute system time is subject to external changes. It might be modified to correct for an inaccurate clock chip, or brought up-to-date with a network time server, or adjusted for any number of other reasons. Both relative time waits and absolute time waits remain correct across that adjustment, but a relative time wait expressed as if it were an absolute time wait cannot. That is, when you want to wait for "1 hour, 10 minutes," but the best you can do is add that interval to the current clock and wait *until* that clock time, the system can't adjust the absolute timeout for you when the system time is changed.

POSIX.1j addresses this issue as part of a substantial and pervasive "cleanup" of POSIX time services. The standard (building on top of POSIX.1b, which introduced the realtime clock functions, and the CLOCK_REALTIME clock) introduces a new system clock called CLOCK_MONOTONIC. This new clock isn't a "relative timer" in the traditional sense, but it is never decreased, and it is never modified by date or time changes on the system. It increases at a constant rate. A "relative time" wait is nothing more than taking the current absolute value of the CLOCK_MONOTONIC clock, adding some fixed offset (4200 seconds for a wait of 1 hour and 10 minutes), and waiting until that value of the clock is reached.

This is accomplished by adding the condition variable attribute *clock*. You set the *clock* attribute in a thread attributes object using pthread_condattr_setclock and request the current value by calling pthread_condattr_getclock. The default value is CLOCK_MONOTONIC, on the assumption that most condition waits are intervals.

While this assumption may be incorrect, and it may seem to be an incompatible change from Pthreads (and it is, in a way), this was swept under the rug due to the fact that the timed condition wait function suffered from a problem that POSIX.1j found to be extremely common through the existing body of POSIX standards. "Time" in general was only very loosely defined. A timed condition wait, for example, does not say precisely what the timeout argument means. Only that "an error is returned if the absolute time specified by *abstime* passes (that is, system time equals or exceeds *abstime*)." The intent is clear—but there are no specific implementation or usage directives. One might reasonably assume that one should acquire the current time using clock_gettime (CLOCK_REALTIME,&now), as suggested in the associated rationale. However, POSIX "rationale" is little more than historical commentary, and is not part of the formal standard. Furthermore, clock_gettime is a part of the optional _POSIX_TIMERS subset of POSIX.1b, and therefore may not exist on many systems supporting threads.

POSIX.1j is attempting to "rationalize" all of these loose ends, at least for systems that implement the eventual POSIX.1j standard. Of course, the CLOCK_MONOTONIC feature is under an option of its own, and additionally relies on the _POSIX_TIMERS option, so it isn't a cure-all. In the absence of these options, there is no *clock* attribute, and no way to be sure of relative timeout behavior—or even completely portable behavior.

10.2.5 Thread abort

The `pthread_abort` function is essentially fail-safe cancellation. It is used only when you want to be sure the thread will terminate immediately. The dangerous aspect of `pthread_abort` is that the thread does not run cleanup handlers or have any other opportunity to clean up after itself. That is, if the target thread has a mutex locked, the thread will terminate with the mutex still locked. Because you cannot unlock the mutex from another thread, the application must be prepared to abandon that mutex entirely. Further, it means that any other threads that might be waiting for the abandoned mutex will continue to wait for the mutex forever unless they are also terminated by calling `pthread_abort`.

In general, real applications cannot recover from aborting a thread, and you should never, ever, use `pthread_abort`. However, for a certain class of applications this capability is required. Imagine, for example, a realtime embedded control system that cannot shut down and must run reliably across any transient failure in some algorithm. Should a thread encounter a rare boundary condition bug, and hang, the application must recover.

In such a system, all wait operations use timeouts, because realtime response is critical. Should one thread detect that something hasn't happened in a reasonable time, for example, a navigational thread hasn't received sensor input, it will notify an "error manager." If the error manager cannot determine why the thread monitoring the sensor hasn't responded, it will try to recover. It may attempt to cancel the sensor thread to achieve a safe shutdown, but if the sensor thread fails to respond to the cancel in a reasonable time, the application must continue anyway. The error manager would then abort the sensor thread, analyze and correct any data structures it might have corrupted, create and advertise new mutexes if necessary, and create a new sensor thread.

10.3 POSIX 1003.14

POSIX.14 is a different sort of standard, a "POSIX Standard profile." Unlike Pthreads and POSIX.1j, POSIX.14 does not add any new capabilities to the POSIX family. Instead, it attempts to provide some order to the maze of options that faces implementors and users of POSIX.

The POSIX.14 specifies which POSIX optional behavior should be considered "required" for multiprocessor hardware systems. It also raises some of the minimum values defined for various POSIX limits. The POSIX.14 working group also devised recommendations for additional POSIX interfaces based on the substantial multiprocessing and threading experience of the members. Many of the interfaces developed by POSIX.14 have been included in the POSIX.1j draft standard.

Once POSIX.14 becomes a standard, in theory, producers of POSIX implementations will be able to claim conformance to POSIX.14. And those who wish to develop multithreaded applications may find it convenient to look for POSIX.14 conformance rather than simply Pthreads conformance. (It remains to be seen whether vendors or users will actually do this, since experience with POSIX Standard Profiles is currently slight.)

The POSIX.14 working group also tried to address important issues such as these:

- Providing a way for threaded code to determine the number of active processors.
- Providing a way for threads to be "bound" onto physical processors.
- Providing a "processor management" command to control which processors are used by the system.

Although these capabilities are universally available in all multiprocessor systems of which the working group was aware, they were dropped from the standard because of many unresolved issues, including these:

- What good does it do to know how many processors there are, if you cannot tell how many your code may use at any time? Remember, the information can change while you are asking for it. What is really needed is a function asking the question "Would the current process benefit from creation of another thread?" We don't know how to answer that question, or how to provide enough information on all reasonable architectures that the application can answer it.
- How can we bind a thread to a processor across a wide range of multiprocessor architecture? On a nonuniform memory access system, for example, representing the processors as a uniform array of integer identifiers would be misleading and useless—binding one thread to processor 0 and another closely cooperative thread to processor 1 might put them across a relatively slow communications port rather than on two processors sharing a bank of memory.

Eventually, some standards organization (possibly POSIX) will need to address these issues and develop portable interfaces. The folks who attempt this feat may find that they need to limit the scope of the standard to a field narrower than "systems on which people may wish to use threads."

Bibliography

[Anderson, 1991] Thomas E. Anderson, Brian N. Bershad, Edward D. Lazowska, and Henry M. Levy, "Scheduler Activations: Effective Kernel Support for the User-Level Management of Parallelism," *Proceedings of the Thirteenth ACM Symposium on Operating Systems Principles*, October 1991.

Research paper describing the addition of an efficient "two-level scheduler" mechanism for operating systems. This is where all modern two-level scheduler systems started—everyone's read it, everyone references it, and everyone's been inspired by it.

[Birrell, 1989] Andrew D. Birrell, *An Introduction to Programming with Threads*, SRC Research Report 35, Digital Systems Research Center, 130 Lytton Ave., Palo Alto, CA 94301, January 1989. Available on Internet from http://www.research.digital.com/SRC/publications/src-rr.html

An introduction to the concepts of threaded programming. Although specifically oriented toward Modula-2+ and SRC's Taos multithreaded operating system, many essential concepts remain easily recognizable in Pthreads.

[Boykin, 1993] Joseph Boykin, David Kirschen, Alan Langerman, and Susan LoVerso, *Programming under Mach*, Addison-Wesley, Reading, MA, ISBN 0-201-52739-1, 1993.

[Custer, 1993] Helen Custer, *Inside Windows NT*, Microsoft Press, ISBN 1-55615-481-X, 1993.

[Digital, 1996] Digital Equipment Corporation, *Guide to DECthreads*, Digital Equipment Corporation, part number AA-Q2DPC-TK, 1996.

Reference manual for Digital's DECthreads implementation of the Pthreads standard. An appendix (which will be removed after the Digital UNIX 4.0 and OpenVMS 7.0 versions) provides reference information on the obsolete cma and DCE threads (POSIX 1003.4a draft 4) interfaces.

[Dijkstra, 1965] E. W. Dijkstra, "Solution of a Problem in Concurrent Programming Control," *Communications of the ACM*, Vol. 8 (9), September 1965, pp. 569–570.

[Dijkstra, 1968a] E. W. Dijkstra, "Cooperating Sequential Processes," *Programming Languages*, edited by F. Genuys, Academic Press, New York, 1968, pp. 43–112.

[Dijkstra, 1968b] E. W. Dijkstra, "The Structure of the 'THE'—Multiprogramming System," *Communications of the ACM*, Vol. 11 (5), 1968, pp. 341–346.

[Gallmeister, 1995] Bill O. Gallmeister, *POSIX.4: Programming for the Real World*, O'Reilly, Sebastopol, CA, ISBN 1-56592-074-0, 1995.

POSIX 1003.1b-1993 realtime programming (based on a near-final draft of the standard).

[Hoare, 1974] C.A.R. Hoare, "Monitors: An Operating System Structuring Concept," *Communications of the ACM*, Vol. 17 (10), 1974, pp. 549–557.

[IEEE, 1996] *9945–1:1996 (ISO/IEC) [IEEE/ANSI Std 1003.1 1996 Edition] Information Technology—Portable Operating System Interface (POSIX)—Part 1: System Application: Program Interface (API) [C Language] (ANSI)*, IEEE Standards Press, ISBN 1-55937-573-6, 1996.

The POSIX C Language interfaces, including realtime and threads.

[Jones, 1991] Michael B. Jones, "Bringing the C Libraries With Us into a Multi-Threaded Future," *Winter 1991 Usenix Conference Proceedings*, Dallas, TX, January 1991, pp. 81–91.

[Kleiman, 1996] Steve Kleiman, Devang Shah, and Bart Smaalders, *Programming with Threads*, Prentice Hall, Englewood Cliffs, NJ, ISBN 0-13-172389-8, 1996.

This book shares some characteristics with the book you are holding. Both, for example, involve authors who were directly involved in the POSIX standard working group, and were also principal architects of their respective companies' thread implementations.

[Lea, 1997] Doug Lea, *Concurrent Programming in Java*™, Addison-Wesley, Reading, MA, ISBN 0-201-69581-2, 1997.

A different view of threads, from the perspective of the Java™ language, which provides unique constructs for thread synchronization within the language.

[Lewis, 1995] Bil Lewis and Daniel J. Berg, *Threads Primer*, SunSoft Press, ISBN 0-13-443698-9, 1995.

A good introduction to threaded programming for the novice. The first edition primarily deals with Solaris "UI threads," with some information on POSIX threads.

[Lockhart, 1994] Harold W. Lockhart, Jr., *OSF DCE, Guide to Developing Distributed Applications*, McGraw-Hill, New York, ISBN 0-07-911481-4, 1994.

A chapter on DCE threads describes how to use threads in building DCE applications.

[McJones, 1989] Paul F. McJones and Garret F. Swart, "Evolving the UNIX System Interface to Support Multithreaded Programs," SRC Research Report 21, Digital Systems Research Center, 130 Lytton Ave., Palo Alto, CA 94301, September 1989. Available on Internet from http://www.research.digital.com/SRC/publications/src-rr.html

Report on adaptation of UNIX system for multithreaded programming.

[Schimmel, 1994] Curt Schimmel, *UNIX Systems for Modern Architectures*, Addison-Wesley, Reading, MA, ISBN 0-201-63338-8, 1994.

Substantial detail on the implementation of multiprocessors and shared memory systems. If Section 3.4 in the book you're holding doesn't satisfy your thirst for knowledge, this is where you should go.

Thread resources on the Internet

In the midst of the word he was trying to say,
In the midst of his laughter and glee,
He had softly and suddenly vanished away—
For the Snark was a Boojum, you see.
THE END

  —Lewis Carroll, The Hunting of the Snark

This list provides a few starting points for information. Of course, the web changes all the time, so no list committed to paper will ever be completely correct. That's life in the information age.

Newsgroups

comp.programming.threads

General, unmoderated discussion of anything related to threads. This group is frequented by a number of people highly knowledgeable about threads in general, and about various specific implementations of Pthreads. It's a nice, friendly place to ask about problems you're having, or things you would like to do. Please, don't ask about screensavers! And, if you want to ask about a problem, always remember to tell us what type of hardware and operating system you're using and include the version.

comp.unix.osf.osf1

The primary discussion group for the Digital UNIX operating system. There are, of course, historical reasons for the nonintuitive name. This is a reasonable place to ask questions about using threads on Digital UNIX. If the question (or problem) doesn't seem to be specific to Digital UNIX, comp.programming.threads may be more appropriate, because it presents your question to a larger audience of thread experts, and makes the answer available to a larger audience of thread users.

comp.unix.solaris

The primary discussion group for the Solaris operating system. This is a reasonable place to ask questions about using threads on Solaris. If the question (or problem) doesn't seem to be specific to Solaris, comp.programming.threads may be more appropriate, because it presents your question to a larger audience of thread experts, and makes the answer available to a larger audience of thread users.

Web sites

`http://altavista.digital.com/`

Altavista is a multithreaded web search engine developed by Digital Equipment Corporation. It is also an excellent search engine that you can use to find out about nearly anything. Always a good place to start.

`http://www.aw.com/cp/butenhof/posix.html`

The Addison-Wesley web page containing information about this book, including the source for all the example programs.

`http://www.best.com/~bos/threads-faq/`

This page is a list of frequently asked questions (FAQ) from the comp.programming.threads newsgroup. Please read this before you read comp.programming.threads, in order to avoid asking a wide range of questions that have been asked a million times before. The information in this page is also posted to the newsgroup at regular intervals.

`http://liinwww.ira.uka.de/bibliography/Os/threads.html`

A searchable bibliography of terms related to threading, maintained by the University of Oslo in Norway.

`http://www.digital.com/`

Digital Equipment Corporation web site. This site includes a lot of information on the Digital UNIX and OpenVMS operating systems, including information on threads and multiprocessor systems.

`http://www.sun.com/`

Sun Microsystems, Inc., web site. This site includes, as you might guess, a lot of information on the Solaris operating system. You can also find information about the Java language, which provides an interesting variant of thread support by making thread synchronization an explicit attribute of a class method.

`http://www.sgi.com/`

Silicon Graphics, Inc., web site. Information on SGI systems and the IRIX operating system.

`http://www.netcom.com/~brownell/pthreads++.html`

Information on an attempt to "define a standardized approach to the use of threading in the C++ language."

Index